The Cambridge Companion to Dostoevskii

Key dimensions of Dostoevskii's writing and life are explored in this collection of specially commissioned essays. While remaining accessible to an undergraduate and non-specialist readership, the essays as a whole seek to renegotiate the terms in which Dostoevskii and his works are to be approached. This is achieved by replacing the conventional 'life and works' format by one that seeks instead to foreground key aspects of the cultural context in which those works were produced. Contributors trace the often complex relationship between those aspects and the processes accompanying the creation of Dostoevskii's art. They examine topics such as Dostoevskii's relation to folk literature, money, religion, the family and science. The essays are well supported by supplementary material including a chronology of the period and detailed guides to further reading. Altogether the volume provides an invaluable resource for scholars and students.

WILLIAM J. LEATHERBARROW is Professor of Russian at the University of Sheffield. He is the author of many books and articles on Dostoevskii.

D1545844

CAMBRIDGE COMPANIONS TO LITERATURE

The Cambridge Companion to Spenser
edited by Andrew Hadfield

The Cambridge Companion to Ben Jonson
edited by Richard Harp and Stanley Stewart

The Cambridge Companion to Milton
edited by Dennis Danielson

The Cambridge Companion to Samuel
Johnson
edited by Greg Clingham

The Cambridge Companion to Mary
Wollstonecraft
edited by Claudia L. Johnson

The Cambridge Companion to Coleridge
edited by Lucy Newlyn

The Cambridge Companion to Keats
edited by Susan J. Wolfson

The Cambridge Companion to Jane Austen
edited by Edward Copeland and
Juliet McMaster

The Cambridge Companion to Charles
Dickens
edited by John O. Jordan

The Cambridge Companion to George Eliot
edited by George Levine

The Cambridge Companion to Thomas
Hardy
edited by Dale Kramer

The Cambridge Companion to Oscar Wilde
edited by Peter Raby

The Cambridge Companion to George
Bernard Shaw
edited by Christopher Innes

The Cambridge Companion to Joseph
Conrad
edited by J. H. Stape

The Cambridge Companion to D. H.
Lawrence
edited by Anne Fernihough

The Cambridge Companion to Virginia
Woolf
edited by Sue Roe and Susan Sellers

The Cambridge Companion to James Joyce
edited by Derek Attridge

The Cambridge Companion to T. S. Eliot
edited by A. David Moody

The Cambridge Companion to Ezra Pound
edited by Ira B. Nadel

The Cambridge Companion to Beckett
edited by John Pilling

The Cambridge Companion to Harold Pinter
edited by Peter Raby

The Cambridge Companion to Tom Stoppard
edited by Katherine E. Kelly

The Cambridge Companion to Herman
Melville
edited by Robert S. Levine

The Cambridge Companion to Edith
Wharton
edited by Millicent Bell

The Cambridge Companion to Henry James
edited by Jonathan Freedman

The Cambridge Companion to Walt
Whitman
edited by Ezra Greenspan

The Cambridge Companion to Henry David
Thoreau
edited by Joel Myerson

The Cambridge Companion to Mark Twain
edited by Forrest G. Robinson

The Cambridge Companion to Edgar Allan
Poe
edited by Kevin J. Hayes

The Cambridge Companion to Emily
Dickinson
edited by Wendy Martin

The Cambridge Companion to William
Faulkner
edited by Philip M. Weinstein

The Cambridge Companion to Ernest
Hemingway
edited by Scott Donaldson

The Cambridge Companion to F. Scott
Fitzgerald
edited by Ruth Prigozy

The Cambridge Companion to Robert Frost
edited by Robert Faggen

The Cambridge Companion to Eugene
O'Neill
edited by Michael Manheim

The Cambridge Companion to Tennessee
Williams
edited by Matthew C. Roudané

The Cambridge Companion to Arthur Miller
edited by Christopher Bigsby

CAMBRIDGE COMPANIONS TO CULTURE

The Cambridge Companion to Modern
German Culture
edited by Eva Kolinsky and
Wilfried van der Will

The Cambridge Companion to Modern
Russian Culture
edited by Nicholas Rzhevsky

The Cambridge Companion to Modern
Spanish Culture
edited by David T. Gies

The Cambridge Companion to Modern
Italian Culture
edited by Zygmunt G. Baranski and
Rebecca J. West

THE CAMBRIDGE
COMPANION TO
DOSTOEVSKII

EDITED BY
W. J. LEATHERBARROW

CAMBRIDGE
UNIVERSITY PRESS

PUBLISHED BY THE PRESS SYNDICATE OF THE UNIVERSITY OF CAMBRIDGE
The Pitt Building, Trumpington Street, Cambridge, United Kingdom

CAMBRIDGE UNIVERSITY PRESS
The Edinburgh Building, Cambridge CB2 2RU, UK
40 West 20th Street, New York, NY 10011-4211, USA
477 Williamstown Road, Port Melbourne, VIC 3207, Australia
Ruiz de Alarcón 13, 28014 Madrid, Spain
Dock House, The Waterfront, Cape Town 8001, South Africa

http://www.cambridge.org

First published 2002

Printed in the United Kingdom at the University Press, Cambridge

Typeface Sabon 10/13 pt   *System* LaTeX 2$_\varepsilon$ [TB]

A catalogue record for this book is available from the British Library

ISBN 0 521 65253 7 hardback
ISBN 0 521 65473 4 paperback

CONTENTS

DISCARDED

CONTENTS

ROBERT L. BELKNAP has been teaching Russian literature at Columbia University since the 1950s and has written two books about *The Brothers Karamazov*. He has been a member of a seminar on applied psychoanalysis for over twenty years, has been active in Columbia's core curriculum, and co-authored a book on General Education. More recently, he has been studying the nature and uses of literary plots.

BORIS CHRISTA was for twenty-five years Professor and Head of the Department of Russian at the University of Queensland. He is the author of a study of Andrei Belyi's lyric poetry and of several articles on the technique of symbolist verse. Recently he has published extensively on aspects of pragmatic semiotics.

SUSANNE FUSSO is Associate Professor of Russian Language and Literature at Wesleyan University, Connecticut, USA. She is the author of *Designing 'Dead Souls': An Anatomy of Disorder in Gogol*, and co-editor with Priscilla Meyer of *Essays on Gogol: Logos and the Russian Word*. She is at present working on a study of Dostoevskii's *A Raw Youth*.

MALCOLM V. JONES is Emeritus Professor of Russian at the University of Nottingham, and a former President of the International Dostoevsky Society. He has written many articles and books on Dostoevskii, and his *Dostoyevsky after Bakhtin* (Cambridge University Press, 1990) has also appeared in a Russian translation. He is also co-editor with Robin Feuer Miller of *The Cambridge Companion to the Classic Russian Novel* (Cambridge University Press, 1998).

WILLIAM LEATHERBARROW is Professor of Russian at the University of Sheffield. He is the author of many books and articles on Dostoevskii and co-editor with Derek C. Offord of *A Documentary History of Russian Thought: From the Enlightenment to Marxism* (1987). His recent works include *Dostoevskii and Britain* (1995) and *'The Devils': A Critical*

Companion (1999). He is currently completing a monograph on the demonic in Dostoevskii.

GARY SAUL MORSON is Frances Hooper Professor of the Arts and Humanities at Northwestern University and a Member of the American Academy of Arts and Sciences. His books include *The Boundaries of Genre: Dostoevsky's 'Diary of a Writer'* (1981), *Hidden in Plain View: Narrative and Creative Potentials in 'War and Peace'* (1987), and *Narrative and Freedom* (1994). He has recently published (under the pseudonym Alicia Chudo) a collection of parodies on Russian culture, *And Quiet Flows the Vodka* (2000).

DEREK OFFORD is Professor of Russian Intellectual History and Head of the Department of Russian Studies at the University of Bristol. His publications include books on nineteenth-century Russian liberal thinkers and on revolutionary Populism and, most recently, *Nineteenth-Century Russia: Opposition to Autocracy* (1999), for the Longman Seminar Studies in History series.

DIANE OENNING THOMPSON is an Affiliated Lecturer in the Department of Slavonic Studies at the University of Cambridge. She is the author of *'The Brothers Karamazov' and the Poetics of Memory* (Cambridge University Press, 1991) and several articles on Dostoevskii. She is co-editor of *Dostoevsky and the Christian Tradition* (Cambridge University Press, 2001).

WILLIAM MILLS TODD, III is Professor of Russian at Harvard University. He is the author of many books and articles on Russian literature, including *The Familiar Letter as a Literary Genre in the Age of Pushkin* (1976) and *Fiction and Society in the Age of Pushkin: Ideology, Institutions, and Narrative* (1986).

FAITH WIGZELL is Reader in Russian at the School of Slavonic and East European Studies, University College, London. She is the author of many articles on Russian folklore and literature, as well as of the monographs *Reading Russian Fortunes* (1998) and (under the name Faith C. M. Kitch) *The Literary Style of Epifanij Premudryj* (1976). She is also editor of *Russian Writers on Russian Writers* (1994) and *Nikolay Gogol: Text and Context* (1989).

EDITOR'S NOTE

References to Dostoevskii's works throughout this book are incorporated in the text and are by volume and page number (e.g. xiv, 255) to F. M. Dostoevskii, *Polnoe sobranie sochinenii v tridtsati tomakh* (Leningrad: Nauka, 1972–90). Where the publishers have divided a volume into two separately bound parts, an additional number appears after the volume number (e.g. xxix/1, 375). Unless otherwise stated all translations from the Russian are by the authors of individual essays. For the benefit of those reading Dostoevskii's works in English translation references to his fictional works are also given by Part (Pt), Book (Bk), Chapter (Ch.) or Section (Sec.), as appropriate.

The transliteration of Russian words and names is based upon the standard Library of Congress system without diacritics. The only exceptions are names of Russian tsars, where the more familiar anglicised forms have been used (e.g. Peter I, not Petr I), and usages that have become so familiar that to alter them would create uncertainty (e.g. Tchaikovskii, not Chaikovskii).

My thanks are due primarily to the contributors, whose insights have made my task as editor a great pleasure; but I am also indebted to the patience and careful editorial interventions of Linda Bree and Rachel De Wachter at Cambridge University Press.

CHRONOLOGY

	Dostoevskii's life and works	Major literary and historical events
1821	Born in Moscow at the Mariinskii hospital for the poor, where his father worked as a doctor.	
1823–31		Pushkin: *Eugene Onegin*.
1825		Decembrist Revolt and accession of Nicholas I.
1828		Birth of Tolstoi.
1830		Stendhal: *Le Rouge et le Noir*.
1831	Sees production of Schiller's *The Robbers* which affects him deeply.	
1833–7	At school in Moscow.	
1834		Pushkin: *The Queen of Spades*.
1835		Balzac: *Le Père Goriot*.
1836		Gogol: *The Government Inspector*.
1837	Death of mother.	Death of Pushkin. Dickens: *Pickwick Papers*.
1838	Enters St Petersburg Academy of Military Engineering.	
1839	Death of father in mysterious circumstances.	Stendhal: *The Charterhouse of Parma*.
1840		Lermontov: *A Hero of Our Time*.

1841	Attempts to write plays.	Death of Lermontov.
1842		Gogol: *Dead Souls* and 'The Overcoat'.
1843	Graduates from Military Academy.	
1844	Resigns commission in order to devote himself to literature. First published work: a translation of Balzac's *Eugénie Grandet*.	
1845	Finishes *Poor Folk*. Meets Belinskii.	
1846	*Poor Folk* published to widespread acclaim. A more subdued reception given to *The Double*. Epilepsy diagnosed.	
1847	*The Landlady*. Starts to attend meetings of the Petrashevskii circle.	Emigration of Herzen.
1848	'A Faint Heart' and 'White Nights'.	Revolutions in Europe. Death of Belinskii. Thackeray: *Vanity Fair*.
1849	*Netochka Nezvanova*. Becomes involved with more radical section of the Petrashevskii circle. 23 April: arrested and imprisoned in the Peter and Paul Fortress, where he writes *A Little Hero*. November: Commission of Enquiry reports and sentences Dostoevskii to death. December: mock execution. Death sentence commuted to Siberian hard labour and exile.	Russia invades Hungary.
1850	Arrives at Omsk prison settlement.	Dickens: *David Copperfield*.

1851		World Exhibition at Crystal Palace, London.
1852		Death of Gogol. Tolstoi: *Childhood*. Turgenev: *A Sportsman's Sketches*.
1853–6		Crimean War.
1854	Hard labour ends. Posted to Semipalatinsk as a common soldier.	
1855		Chernyshevskii joins *The Contemporary*. Death of Nicholas I and accession of Alexander II amidst hopes of social and political reform.
1856		Turgenev: *Rudin*.
1857	Marries Maria Dmitrevna Isaeva.	Flaubert: *Madame Bovary*. Baudelaire: *Les Fleurs du Mal*.
1859	*The Village of Stepanchikovo* and 'Uncle's Dream'. December: returns to St Petersburg.	Turgenev: *A Nest of Gentlefolk*. Goncharov: *Oblomov*. Tolstoi: *Family Happiness*. Darwin: *The Origin of Species*.
1860	Starts publication of *Notes from the House of the Dead*.	Turgenev: *On the Eve*. Birth of Chekhov. George Eliot: *The Mill on the Floss*.
1861	Starts publication of moderate periodical *Time*. *The Insulted and Injured*.	Emancipation of the serfs. Formation of revolutionary organisation *Land and Liberty*.
1862	Travels in Europe. Affair with Polina Suslova.	Turgenev: *Fathers and Sons*. Tense revolutionary mood in St Petersburg. *The Contemporary* suspended and Chernyshevskii arrested. Hugo: *Les Miserables*.
1863	*Winter Notes on Summer Impressions*. Closure of *Time*. Further travels in Europe with Suslova.	Polish uprising. Tolstoi: *The Cossacks*. Chernyshevskii: *What Is to Be Done?*

1864	Launches *Epoch. Notes from Underground*. Deaths of wife and brother Mikhail.	The First International. Student unrest in Kazan. Legal reforms in Russia, including introduction of trial by jury. Dickens: *Our Mutual Friend*.
1865	Financial collapse of *Epoch*. Severe financial difficulties. Starts work on *Crime and Punishment*.	
1865–9		Tolstoi: *War and Peace*.
1866	Publishes *Crime and Punishment*. Writes *The Gambler* in twenty-six days with help of stenographer Anna Grigorevna Snitkina.	Attempted assassination of Alexander II by Dmitri Karakozov.
1867	Marries Anna Grigorevna. Flees abroad to escape creditors. Meets Turgenev in Baden. Visits Dresden and Geneva.	Turgenev: *Smoke*.
1868	Still abroad. Death of infant daughter. *The Idiot*.	
1869	Returns to Dresden and plans 'The Life of a Great Sinner'.	Murder of student Ivanov in Moscow by Nechaev's political circle.
1870	*The Eternal Husband*.	Defeat of France in Franco-Prussian War. Death of Herzen. Birth of V. I. Ulianov (Lenin).
1871	Returns to St Petersburg.	Defeat of Paris Commune.
1871–2	*The Devils*.	
1872	Becomes editor of *The Citizen*.	Trial of Nechaev. Leskov: *Cathedral Folk*. Marx's *Das Kapital* published in Russia.
1873	Begins *The Diary of a Writer*.	
1874	Resigns from *The Citizen*. Visits Bad Ems for treatment for emphysema.	Attempts by thousands of Russian students to provoke revolutionary unrest amongst peasantry.

1875	*A Raw Youth.*	Political strikes in Odessa.
1875–8		Tolstoi: *Anna Karenina.*
1877		Russia declares war on Turkey. Turgenev: *Virgin Soil.*
1878	Death of son Alexei. Visit to Optina Monastery with Solovev.	Death of Nekrasov. Arrest and trial of Vera Zasulich.
1879–80	*The Brothers Karamazov* (completed November 1880).	Tolstoi's religious crisis, during which he writes *A Confession.*
1880	Delivers the Pushkin Speech.	
1880–1	Final issues of *The Diary of a Writer.*	
1881	January 28: dies in St Petersburg. February 1: funeral in Alexander Nevskii Monastery attended by over thirty thousand people.	Assassination of Alexander II.
1883		Death of Turgenev. Nietzsche: *Thus Spake Zarathustra.*
1889		Death of Chernyshevskii.
1904		Death of Chekhov.
1910		Death of Tolstoi.
1912		Constance Garnett's English translation of *The Brothers Karamazov.*

I

W. J. LEATHERBARROW

Introduction

When the idea for a *Cambridge Companion to Dostoevskii* was first mooted it was recognised, first, that Dostoevskii had been extremely well served over many years by his critical commentators, in the West as well as in Russia, and, secondly, that the need for a further volume designed to introduce this author to yet another generation of students and more general readers was not self-evident and perhaps required some justification. To acknowledge this latter point is not at all the same as to imply that Dostoevskii's star is somehow on the wane or that the immense popularity his work has enjoyed is in decline. At the start of the twenty-first century his work is as widely admired as it has ever been, and its impact continues to resonate in cultural activity throughout the world more than a century after his death. Moreover, this resonance has been felt not just in the 'higher' or 'élite' manifestations of literary activity, but is also discernible in more popular forms of fiction such as the detective novel. Put simply, Dostoevskii seems unwilling to settle into the role of venerable classic, that of an author admired for the way his work once spoke loudly to his contemporaries, but whose impact in the present is more akin to that of a whisper. To employ an over-used term, Dostoevskii's novels still seem pressingly 'relevant' to the most immediate concerns of the present age in a way that those of his contemporaries perhaps do not. The world depicted in, say, *Crime and Punishment* or *The Devils*, despite its chronological and social remoteness, looks so much more like the world we live in than any described by Tolstoi or Turgenev. George Steiner's challenging assertion that 'Dostoevsky has penetrated more deeply than Tolstoy into the fabric of contemporary thought', having done more than any other writer of the nineteenth century to set the agenda and determine the 'shape and psychology' of modern fiction, does not seem over-extravagant.[1] Nor does Alex de Jonge's claim that, along with Proust, Dostoevskii was the artist 'supremely representative' not only of his own age, but also of ours,[2] a nineteenth-century novelist who has continued to provoke strong reactions in his subsequent readership. One minute acclaimed by Albert Camus as a sort of prophet of twentieth-century Existentialism,[3] the next he is dismissed and ridiculed by Vladimir Nabokov as the poor relation of Russian literature, unworthy of admission to the pantheon of the great because of his uncouth literary manners and taste for the cheaply melodramatic.[4] Welcomed by John Middleton Murry for a revelatory art form that transcended the novel and dripped 'metaphysical obscenity',[5] he was scorned by George Moore as a mere exponent of shilling-shockers and penny-dreadfuls.[6] For Albert Einstein, the father of the modern scientific world-view, he provided an inspirational glimpse into the relativism and instability of reality and gave him 'more than any other thinker, more even than Gauss';[7] for D. H. Lawrence, though, he was a 'false artist' with a false vision, a 'big stinker' sliding along in the dark like a rat, and 'not nice'.[8]

The ubiquitous presence of Dostoevskii's ghost in the machine of twentieth-century culture is as straightforward to illustrate as it is complex to explain. Why do we still read him? And why should we continue to do so? As Russia continues to languish in post-communist social and economic collapse and to watch what is left of its superpower status decay, it cannot be because Dostoevskii somehow symbolises, and helps us to understand, the virility and force of a strategically important imperial power, as British novelists perhaps did in the nineteenth century. (Although, as we shall soon see, it might be because he offers acute insights into the causes and processes of that cultural collapse.) One possible explanation for Dostoevskii's enduring popularity lies in the unusual ability of his fiction to flatter our willingness to entertain and engage with 'high' serious intellectual and emotional issues while simultaneously rewarding any taste we may have for immediately compelling narrative energy and 'low' popular fictional devices. Nabokov was right (if not the first) to recognise that Dostoevskii drew some of the building blocks of his art from the literary slums of boulevard fiction, melodrama and cheap Romanticism, and George Moore was perceptive in recognising that the narrative hooks Dostoevskii employed to ensnare his readers' attention were indeed those used most frequently in the popular novel. The outraged condescension shown by both, however, is characteristic of an earlier age than ours, an age which had not seen to anywhere near the same extent the democratisation and mass commercialisation of culture, and in which 'élite' fiction was not supposed to slum it by appropriating the dynamic or fantastic plots, over-egged melodrama, cliff-hanger situations, larger-than-life characters and abnormal psychology of the penny-dreadful. Today we are surrounded by, and sensitised to, cultural products designed for mass rather than élite consumption, and we are consequently far more ready to accept the adoption of the aesthetics and discourses of such products in the name of 'high' art. Although still a literary 'toff', Dostoevskii seems much more like 'one of us' than Tolstoi or Turgenev.

Another feature of Dostoevskii's fiction that helps to account for its enduring popularity is its amenability to interpretation in terms of the changing concerns that have dominated literary criticism and cultural theory over the last century or so. Initially welcomed in Russia and the West as examples of critical and social realism, his novels rewarded such responses in their pre-occupation with social concerns like poverty, crime, alienation and money, as well as with the issues at stake in the dominant intellectual debates of the mid-to-late nineteenth century, such as the erosion of traditional spiritual values by the burgeoning capitalism and heroic materialism that went with industrialisation. Later, as realism gave ground to decadence, modernism and aestheticism in the European fin-de-siècle, the same novels were acclaimed for their ability to yield metaphysical rather than social insights, for their anti-materialism, and for the doubts they cast upon objectivity. We have already glimpsed how they were then subsequently pressed into the service of philosophical Existentialism and called upon to validate the perceptual revolutions accomplished by the new physics, not only of Einstein but also of Heisenberg and others. The rise to dominance of fascism in inter-war Europe also saw Dostoevskii and his works mobilised in the service of both sides. In Soviet Russia enduring doubts about his ideological acceptability were laid aside as official critics set about the task of mining his works for those nuggets of anti-German sentiment and national messianism that so neatly accorded with war aims, while in Germany Nazi critics laid claim to Dostoevskii for his nationalism, anti-semitism and cultural imperialism.[9] There is no room here to develop much further this attempt to illustrate Dostoevskii's adaptability to critical fashion, but we must at least recognise that such adaptability is not limited just to the social and ideological content of his art. The formal characteristics not only of his fiction, but also of such 'journalistic' writings as his *Diary of a Writer*, continue to attract much critical attention, and the notes and references accompanying the essays in the present volume acknowledge the frequency with which his works have been cited in demonstration of so many developments in literary theory, from the Russian Formalist school through Bakhtinian narrative theory to post-modernism.[10] The novelist called upon in the 1840s by the Russian critic Vissarion Belinskii to fly the flag of social realism has subsequently been enlisted in the service of most of the aesthetic manifestoes of the late nineteenth and twentieth centuries.

But, as Steiner's remark suggests, it is in Dostoevskii's enduring ability to keep his finger on the pulse of modernity that we find the most compelling explanation of the on-going popularity of his art. His novels and tales appear to capture, in both their thematic content and their narrative forms, the fluidity and instability of existence as experienced by most in an age when confidence in enduring political, social, spiritual, scientific and intellectual certainties has retreated in the face of relativism and a craving for immediacy and short-term intensity. The hero of *Notes from Underground* may have puzzled his contemporary readership with his defiant and perverse rejection of the 'benefits' of heroic materialism and scientific progress, but today's reader is much more likely to share that character's distrust of science, of rationality and of schemes that sacrifice the individual to objective and immutable forces. The chaotic and unstable narrative voice of *The Double*, confusing experience and hallucination and contaminating the narrative discourse with that of the hero, may have strained beyond endurance the patience of Belinskii, but it is unlikely to alienate a readership schooled in James Joyce or contemporary critical theory. Interestingly, Dostoevskii himself sensed that his artistic vision was more likely to be validated by the future. In the following passage from his notebooks for *A Raw Youth* he appears to acknowledge the instability of contemporary life as a condition largely unrecognised by fellow writers, as well as the prophetic qualities of his own art and the nature of its enduring relevance for future generations:

> Facts. They pass before us. No one notices them [...] I cannot tear myself away, and all the cries of the critics to the effect that I do not depict real life have not disenchanted me. There are no bases to our society [...] One colossal quake and the whole lot will come to an end, collapse and be negated as though it had never existed. And this is not just outwardly true, as in the West, but inwardly, morally so. Our talented writers, people like Tolstoi and Goncharov,[11] who with great artistry depict family life in upper-middle-class circles, think that they are depicting the life of the majority. In my view they have depicted only the life of the exceptions, but the life which I portray is the life that is the general rule. Future generations, more objective in their view, will see that this is so. The truth is on my side, I am convinced of that.
>
> (XVI, 329)

The views expressed in this passage to the effect that his own 'realism' is somehow superior to that of his contemporaries in its ability to suggest the essential nature of an unstable and disintegrating 'reality' are views voiced regularly by Dostoevskii in the last decade or so of his life. Most famously, in an undated notebook entry toward the end of his life he claimed to be 'a realist in a higher sense; that is, I depict all the depths of the human soul' (XXVII, 65). This is a suggestive, but tantalisingly cryptic claim. What is 'realism in a higher sense'? If realism in the novel resides in verisimilitude, truthfulness to life, the accurate depiction of experience (as Dostoevskii's contemporaries might well have claimed with a lack of that conscious provisionality that attends any discussion of the condition, or use of the term 'realism', today), then how is it possible to have 'higher' or 'lower' forms of it? In *The Idiot* Dostoevskii's narrator had dwelt on the problem of the nature of artistic realism and had concluded that novelists should try 'to select social types and present them in artistic form: types remarkably rarely encountered as such in real life, but which are almost more real than reality itself' (VIII, 383; Pt 4, Sec. 1). Implicit in such references to 'higher realism' and the creation of an artistic world that is 'almost more real than reality itself' is the suggestion that for Dostoevskii conventional realism, as practised by the other great Russian (and, for that matter, European) novelists of his age, was somehow inadequate and incapable of accomplishing what was surely the primary objective of realist art: the illusion that contemporary reality had been effectively and accurately replicated. In a letter of 26 February 1869 to his friend Nikolai Strakhov Dostoevskii made the following statement: 'I have my own view of reality (in art), and what most people regard as fantastic and exceptional is sometimes for me the very essence of reality. Everyday trivialities and a conventional view of them, in my opinion, not only fall short of realism but are even contrary to it' (XXIX/1, 19). Shortly before, in a letter of 11 December 1868, he had expressed much the same view to another friend, A. N. Maikov: 'I have entirely different notions of reality and realism from those of our realists and critics [...] With their kind of realism you cannot explain so much as a hundredth part of the real facts which have actually occurred. But with our idealism we have even prophesied facts' (XXVIII/2, 329).

Such comments all share the implication that the aim of achieving in novelistic form a robust illusion of reality is not adequately or appropriately served by the conventional realist practices of a Tolstoi or Goncharov. The letters to Strakhov and Maikov cited above suggest that Dostoevskii did not regard the naturalistic depiction of the norms and surface appearances of day-to-day reality as the sole, or even primary, objective of realism. Instead, references to his own 'idealism' which 'prophesies facts' suggest that such an objective should consist instead in the 'explanation' of 'the very essence of reality', its underlying structures and innermost nature. If this required rejection or amendment of the traditional devices and practices of naturalism, so be it. In a letter of January 1854 to N. D. Fonvizina Dostoevskii had described himself as 'a child of the age, a child of uncertainty and doubt' (XXVIII/1, 176). This view of the contemporary age as one of uncertainty was to be repeated many times, by characters in his later novels as well as in his own journalistic writings. For example, Lebedev in *The Idiot* complains that the modern age lacks a binding idea capable of uniting men and nations and preventing the disintegration and discord so characteristic of European political, social and personal life in the nineteenth century (VIII, 315; Pt 3, Sec. 4). While acknowledging here what Gary Saul Morson has called 'the irony of origins', in that these views are articulated by a character not otherwise identifiable with Dostoevskii, it would be perverse in the light of all the evidence not to sense the author's own values underpinning Lebedev's outburst.[12] For Dostoevskii Europe, including Russia, was at a transitional stage when the old social, moral and psychological structures were decaying and new ones had not yet fully emerged to take their place. In his *Diary of a Writer* for January 1877 he describes how in Russia the old landowning order is undergoing 'some new, still unknown, but radical change [...] some enormous regeneration into novel, still latent, almost utterly unknown forms' (XXV, 35). The same forces of uncertainty, dissolution, re-creation and unpredictability were at work also in most other areas of Russian and European life, in Dostoevskii's view. They manifested themselves in such political, social and cultural phenomena as the on-going processes of revolution, the rapidly changing social and economic order prompted by the industrial revolution and the rise of capitalism, the collapse or erosion of traditional unifying social structures such as church and family, and the growth of individualism in both society and, following the Romantic movement, the artistic and cultural products of that society.

The contemporary age was for Dostoevskii a 'thunderous epoch permeated with so many colossal, astounding and rapidly shifting actual events' (XXV, 193). The present was a process rather than a firmly defined condition, and surely it demanded a new 'realism' to capture its essential provisionality and uncertainty. Yet many novelists wrote as though nothing was changing. In the conclusion to *A Raw Youth* the hero's former mentor, to whom he has sent a copy of his disordered memoir, remarks that in the current age a writer who wishes to depict a stable and orderly pattern of life has no choice but to write historical novels about a vanished reality, for there is no such order and stability in the present. He goes on to say:

> Oh, and in the historical form you can depict a multitude of details that are still extraordinarily pleasant and comforting! You can even so enthral the reader that he will mistake a historical picture for one still possible nowadays. Such a work, in the hands of a great talent, would belong not so much to Russian literature as to Russian history. It would be an artistically finished picture of a Russian mirage, but one that actually existed as long as no one guessed it was a mirage. (XIII, 454)

The 'great talent' offering mirages of Russian life is a thinly veiled reference to Tolstoi whose work, like that of other contemporary realists, was for

Dostoevskii misleading and ultimately unrealistic in the way it suggested stability and permanence where there was in fact only discord and dissolution. While the majority of readers would probably not wish to join Dostoevskii in dismissing Tolstoi as a historical novelist even in works set ostensibly in his present – and, indeed, might even point, as Morson does in this volume, to the ways in which Dostoevskii's art represents a development rather than a rejection of Tolstoian narrative with its emphasis on presenting life as process – there is something in what he says. At the centre of Tolstoi's moral and artistic universe there does appear to remain a profound confidence in the enduring power of normality. This reveals itself in characters such as the Oblonskiis in *Anna Karenina* or the Rostovs in *War and Peace*, who stand as a touchstone of that normality and whose values ultimately endure in the face of the individual tragedy of others or cataclysmic historical events. Stability is the keynote of Tolstoi's novelistic world; life recomposes itself in the end; the ripples that have momentarily disturbed the surface eventually fade to reveal again the underlying permanencies.

For Dostoevskii, though, the ripples had now become the underlying permanency, and in his own art he struggled from the start to devise new artistic forms that would not finalise or stabilise the shifting uncertainties of the age they purported to depict: forms in which deep probing of the innermost and darkest recesses of the human soul took the place of portraiture and *paysage*; where coincidence, symbolism and mythography threatened to overwhelm the limits of verisimilitude; where the narrative point of view refused to locate itself in a secure vantage point and instead lured the reader into perceptual and ontological doubt; and where the clash of ideas took place not in the polite and limited confines of the conversation and the drawing room, but in the infinite spaces of the souls of his possessed characters. In his highly evocative meditation on the experience of reading Dostoevskii, which serves as a conclusion to this volume, Gary Saul Morson shows how Dostoevskii sought to find an alternative to traditional narrative, an alternative that would offer genuine uncertainty of outcome instead of the foreclosed possibilities and compromised immediacy of a structured and foreshadowed dénouement. Among the characteristics of this anti-determinist narrative, a form that bestows real freedom upon fiction and upon those who lead their lives within it, Morson identifies the following: *suspense*, or the intensification of moments when a character is confronted by a choice of possibilities, so that the reader experiences the reality of that choice; the technique of *sideshadowing*, which presents time 'not as a line of single points but as a *field of possibilities*' with no single structured outcome; and an approach to psychology based on the view that intentions are not fixed but an evolving process, so that actions too are part of a process, not the result or outcome of it. These characteristics contribute to a novel form in which 'at every moment the author would know what he was doing, but not what he was going to do. He would be guided not by a single design but by an evolving set of possibilities.'

Broadly speaking, the immense critical literature that has arisen in response to the challenge of explicating the nature of Dostoevskii's art is, like that devoted to most great writers, conventionally divisible into, on the one hand, specialised works explicitly directed at an academic readership comprised of 'experienced' Dostoevskii scholars (and therefore implicitly inaccessible to the general reader and those approaching the writer for the first time), and, on the other, 'introductory' works explicitly directed at that general readership (and therefore implicitly of little interest to the specialist). This conventional division has gone unchallenged for so long that it has acquired the status of a clear and immutable truth; yet it begs a lot of questions and makes a lot of assumptions. First of all it seems to contain the implication that the 'advanced' reader is somehow a more sophisticated, and therefore 'better', reader of Dostoevskii. This is not self-evidently true, and those who remember the impact of their first reading of the works of this most immediately challenging novelist will be loath to dismiss that reading as somehow inferior. Secondly, the division also contains the implication that the discourse required for critical mediation between Dostoevskii and his 'advanced' reader is necessarily different from that appropriate to a general readership, and that the former therefore necessarily excludes the latter. It is arguable, though, that whoever writes about this most accessible, and in a very real sense 'popular', author in a discourse that is exclusive and inaccessible has, at best, perpetrated a failure of judgement and, at worst, is guilty of that dry scholasticism which the Russian writer Alexander Herzen dismissed so adroitly in his description of 'the guild of scholars': 'This jealous caste wants to keep the light to itself, and it surrounds knowledge with a forest of scholasticism, barbarous terminology and ponderous, discouraging language. In the same way the farmer sows a thorny bush around his plot, so that those who impudently try to crawl through will prick themselves a dozen times and tear their clothing all to shreds. All in vain! The time of the aristocracy of knowledge has passed...'[13]

   The present volume, therefore, starts from the assumption that a critical work capable of offering fresh insights to the Dostoevskii specialist need not be inaccessible to the new reader, and indeed may be explicitly *directed* at the latter as well as the former. In order to achieve this dual objective the present *Companion* approaches its task in a way different from that adopted by other volumes in this series that are focussed on a single author, and indeed from that characteristic of most 'accessible' critical studies of Dostoevskii. These have tended to be of the 'life and works' variety and have offered a linear, evaluative account of the writer's biography, of his social/historical/cultural/intellectual 'context', and of his 'major' writings. To produce another account of that sort is clearly unnecessary, and to do so would also, arguably, be a disservice to Dostoevskii himself, in that it would serve to reconfirm the implications and assumptions that go along with a familiar and long-established approach to his art. This is not to say that there is necessarily anything wrong with such an approach. Quite the contrary: works such as Konstantin Mochulsky's *Dostoevsky: His Life and Work* (1967), Edward Wasiolek's *Dostoevsky: The Major Fiction* (1964) and, most recently, Joseph Frank's multi-volume critical biography (1976–2000) are outstanding contributions to Dostoevskii studies and will remain indispensable for future readers. But the approach they adopt is not the only one appropriate to an 'introductory' study, and in this volume we shall be seeking to establish parameters additional to those of 'life and works', 'text and context', onto which to map the characteristics of Dostoevskii's art.

We must start by asking ourselves what traditional 'life and works' studies in fact achieve. In particular, do they produce what might be termed 'collateral' effects in their readership, in the sense of effects additional to and aside from those explicitly intended by their authors? It seems to me first that, consciously or unconsciously, they promote in the reader a receptiveness to an exclusively linear account of progression from youth to experience and from artistic immaturity to genius. Such progression may indeed be a reality but it is often too neat and comforting an assumption, and one that discourages other, complementary ways of looking at Dostoevskii and the artistic works he has created. Secondly, such accounts establish, as a by-product of their concept of progression, a canonical description of Dostoevskii's 'major' and 'minor' works which is rarely, if ever, challenged. There may well be very sound reasons for the existence of such a canon and for the lack of challenge to the assumption that, say, *Crime and Punishment* is superior to Dostoevskii's unfinished early novel *Netochka Nezvanova*, and it is certainly not the intention here to encourage the sort of extreme cultural relativism and downright failures of judgement sometimes discernible in the more extreme manifestations of 'cultural studies'. Let us rather subject the traditional canon to fresh, implicit interrogation by other approaches to Dostoevskii, and let us not be too surprised if its hierarchies survive such interrogation more or less intact: *Crime and Punishment* does indeed receive more attention than *Netochka Nezvanova* in the present volume, but the important thing is that it does so as the result of an approach which, by not starting from the rehearsal of familiar canonical hierarchies among

Dostoevskii's texts, frees up the reader to approach those texts in different ways. Thirdly, all but the best of the traditional introductions to Dostoevskii, as they migrate between 'life' and 'works', are vulnerable to the tendency to suggest perhaps too simplistic an account of the relationship between 'text' and 'context', between Dostoevskii's artistic products and the environment in which they were created, usually in terms of the 'influence' of the latter upon the former. Moreover, in establishing contexts and sources of such 'influence', traditional accounts have tended in general to prioritise what is now familiarly termed 'high culture' over 'low culture'. These are terms that should not be allowed to go unscrutinised, and we shall return to them shortly.

The present volume seeks to occupy a different niche in the market by adopting an approach designed to persuade the student to think about Dostoevskii and his art in a way different from that encouraged by the implicit assumptions of the 'life and works' approach discussed above. Most obviously, it adopts a different approach to authorship by virtue of being an edited volume bringing together the insights of some of the finest contemporary Western Dostoevskii scholars in a way that militates against singularity of critical perception whilst hopefully not dissolving into lack of coherence. The multi-authored critical volume is already a familiar form in Dostoevskii studies, and there have been several very successful examples in both recent and not so recent times.[14] These have, though, tended to follow, in part if not in whole, the structures and embedded assumptions of the traditional approach, with essays devoted sequentially to separate 'major' works (sometimes with a more general preliminary essay on 'minor' or early works). The present volume seeks to avoid the assumptions that emerge as by-products of the linear, progressive view of Dostoevskii's career by adopting an approach structured upon what might be termed 'horizontal' (i.e. broadly speaking, 'thematic') sections through the author's life, works and cultural context, rather than the more familiar 'vertical' sections produced by linear accounts of Dostoevskii's life and works on a year-by-year or text-by-text basis. (Although for the sake of readers in need of some initial orientation in the chronology of Dostoevskii's career this Introduction does attempt to justify the selection of topics addressed by seeking to show how they emerge from the author's biographical, social and cultural experience, while the Chronology of major events and works offers a quick point of reference.) In selecting the topics that make up these horizontal sections the editor and contributors have sought to foreground the fact that Dostoevskii's writings were produced amidst a variety of cultural stimuli and assumptions, and to encourage awareness of the extent to which the nature of his texts was subject to manipulation – sometimes in ways acknowledged explicitly, on other occasions implicitly – by the effects of those cultural stimuli and of the societal structures and relationships in which the process of production was embedded. Some of these stimuli, assumptions, structures and relationships were highly public and visible, deriving from 'high' culture such as the Russian literary tradition or contemporary political, social or scientific debate; others arose in less overtly public circumstances and from 'low' cultural forms and relationships which, although perhaps less immediately visible to the reader of Dostoevskii's texts, impinged just as decisively on the day-to-day circumstances of their production. Examples of the latter might include Dostoevskii's economic status as a professional writer at the mercy of deadlines; the demands of serial publication; his sensitivity to the literary and moral tastes of his readership; his awareness of popular lore and tradition; and the requirements of censorship, whether explicitly stated or 'second-guessed' by the author himself as a form of self-censorship.

We need to be careful here, for this sort of easy assumption that the effects of 'high' culture may be clearly separated out from those of 'low' culture turns out to be highly problematical. For a start the reader might reasonably ask for an explanation of what these terms mean. Attempts to theorise categorical definitions have been made elsewhere and are beyond the remit of this volume, where the terms are used rather more casually in order to suggest the following distinctions. First of all, the effects of high culture manifest themselves primarily in what is now commonly termed a 'top-down' way, in that they emerge from the activities of those élite parts of society, individuals or social groups that enjoy the most authority, whether that authority be political, economic or cultural. The effects of low culture, a term which here is used to embrace commercial as well as popular culture, may be perceived as operating in a 'bottom-up' way through the conditions affecting the artist at work and through his experience of mass culture. In reality, of course, there is a complex interference among cultural forms: the effects of popular culture are as likely to find their way into the work of a writer like Dostoevskii through the way that culture has been mediated in *belles-lettres* as they are directly; and censorship – whether in its official form or through the ideological inclinations of particular journals and their editors – is just as likely to operate in a bottom-up way, since an author will inevitably write, consciously or unconsciously, to a pattern of what he thinks he can get away with.

It is hoped that discussion of the topics selected for the essays in this volume will disclose some of this complexity. In making that selection the overall principle has been to identify areas that had an enduring impact upon, and resonance in, Dostoevskii's art and which, in some cases if not all, have not been addressed in an appropriately persistent or sophisticated way in previous critical introductions. The period of Dostoevskii's youth and the circumstances surrounding his early career as a writer help us to identify at once several key areas that were to impinge upon the production of all his subsequent work in one way or another. The first of these is the way in which his own experience of family life in his youth and adolescence helped to shape his views both on the reality of family structures in mid-nineteenth-century Russia and on the ideal form he came to envisage that such relationships should take, views which were to contribute significantly to the conception and ideological shape of his writings. The young Dostoevskii's experience of family life was mixed. On the one hand, he did experience the intimacy of the nuclear family in the years before he was sent away to boarding school, albeit under the gaze of a strict and austere father who appears from the young man's correspondence to have evoked respect and fear, rather than warm devotion. Moreover, his subsequent relationship with his brother Mikhail – a relationship in which each served the other as best friend, confidant and literary ally – was extraordinarily intense and lasted until Mikhail's death in 1864. On the other hand, Dostoevskii's mother died in 1837, he found life difficult and lonely at school, and his father died in 1839 in circumstances that remain unclear but which suggest the possibility that he was murdered by his serfs – all indicating that Dostoevskii was not unaware of family disorder. Susanne Fusso's essay demonstrates how he subsequently developed a vision of the nineteenth-century Russian family that was the polar opposite of the idylls presented by Tolstoi and Turgenev, and how he came to see the depiction of the dissolution of the family as a civic duty. Indeed, that dissolution was to become for him a metaphor for the wider collapse of Russia's political, social, moral and spiritual fabric as traditional values were swept aside in the intelligentsia's rush to embrace foreign ideologies that were alien to the Russian way of life. Dostoevskii's belief that organic family relations, based upon a core of shared moral values, unconditional love and mutual reliance, were at the heart of an ideal social order explains the persistence with which the idea of family disorder recurs in his works as a means to explore the cognate themes of guilt and responsibility.

After his time in boarding school, in January 1838 Dostoevskii entered the St Petersburg Academy of Military Engineering, where with his dreamy and romantic nature he made an unlikely military trainee. He did, however, form an intense friendship with Ivan Shidlovskii, a Romantic poet who did much to shape the young man's aesthetic tastes, which during the years at the Academy embraced Pushkin and Gogol; the great European classics, Shakespeare, Goethe, Corneille and Racine; the adventure fiction of Walter Scott; the fantasies of E. T. A. Hoffmann; the works of Schiller; and the social melodramas of Balzac, George Sand, Victor Hugo and Eugène Sue. In August 1843 Dostoevskii completed his studies at the Academy and soon after entered the Engineering Corps, but his years of study had done little to attract him to a military career. He turned instead to literature, firstly with a translation of Balzac's *Eugénie Grandet* in 1844 and then with his debut as a novelist in his own right in 1846 when both *Poor Folk* and *The Double* appeared, the first to great critical acclaim, the second to critical disparagement. These were difficult years financially, and Dostoevskii's correspondence with his brother discloses a constant twin preoccupation with literature and money, to the extent that from this point onwards the act of writing was rarely free – both in his mind and in reality – from commercial and financial contamination. The significance of literature and money as components of the cultural environment in which Dostoevskii worked is addressed by several essays in the present volume. My own treatment of metafictional strategies in the early works sets out to suggest the extent to which the experience of literature was incorporated into the way the young Dostoevskii saw, and wrote, his world and to demonstrate how the acts of writing and reading are thematised in those works. The essay first shows how in *Poor Folk* the manipulation of the epistolary narrative form, with its creation of a hero who is also a reader and writer, permits a rich and subversive narrative irony, and secondly illustrates the complex way Dostoevskii uses 'source' texts to signpost routes through his other works of the period. Boris Christa's contribution sets out, with a clarity that has not been approached in previous treatments of the subject, the unusual level of significance that money possesses in Dostoevskii's works, a significance that derives not only from its thematic importance as a source of either great power or great suffering, but also from the use of named sums of money as semiotic markers that allow more precise navigation of Dostoevskii's texts. As Christa eloquently shows, 'money talks' in Dostoevskii, serving as a profoundly expressive means of literary communication. It is effective as a major element in the construction or deconstruction of plot or character identity, in that the way money is acquired (e.g. through crime) or used (e.g. in gambling) makes precise, if oblique, statements about its owner and his/her actions or intentions. It can also allow the sub-textual expression and apprehension of literary and social taboos, the direct confrontation of which was not permitted by the conventions of the time. Perhaps the clearest example of this in Dostoevskii's novels is the use of money to infer erotic subtexts of sexual subjugation and exploitation: financial transactions and relationships are readily deconstructible into sexual ones.

In the spring of 1846 Dostoevskii met Mikhail Petrashevskii, an eccentric intellectual with socialist leanings who ran a Friday-evening discussion group at his home. Within a year he was a regular at these gatherings, where the political thought of Fourier, Blanc, Saint-Simon, Leroux, Proudhon and others was discussed in the context of a Russia benighted by the reactionary policies of Tsar Nicholas I. Although hardly a political animal – despite later claims in his *Diary of a Writer* that he had dangerously revolutionary tendencies – Dostoevskii was drawn into a political conspiracy that resulted in the arrest of the Petrashevskii circle in April 1849. The ringleaders, including Dostoevskii, were imprisoned, tried, sentenced to death and subjected to a horrifying mock execution, before finally being sent into imprisonment and hard labour in Siberia, followed by a further period of exile. He did not return to European Russia, or resume his interrupted literary career, until the end of 1859. All biographies rightly emphasise the importance of this period for Dostoevskii, a period when he was forced to mingle with ordinary criminals (political prisoners were not segregated); when he discovered the inner strength and spiritual depths of the ordinary Russian, as well as the extent to which the intellectual classes had lost touch with that strength and those depths; when he was forced to rethink his deepest convictions, and when he rediscovered the meaning of the Orthodox faith that had been instilled in him by a zealous father in his childhood. In her essay on Dostoevskii and the Russian folk heritage Faith Wigzell shows how the writer's interest in folklore was also stimulated and changed by his Siberian experiences, and how the profound knowledge of the people and their beliefs which he gained in prison provided him with a means to articulate his evolving moral and intellectual stance, to the extent that he came to see the values of ordinary Russians, as embodied in their oral and religious culture, as the key to Russia's salvation from the diseases of Western European intellectualism that had infected the educated classes. Wigzell shows that the novels that best express these views, especially *The Devils* and *The Brothers Karamazov*, are profoundly folklorised in the sense that their philosophical, religious and narrative cores are contaminated with, and enlarged by, folk discourses and references. Her attempt to unravel the extent and nature of this contamination for a readership unversed in Russian folk tradition profoundly enriches appreciation of the works. Malcolm Jones's essay complements Wigzell's by showing how the Siberian experience and direct encounter with the unspoilt Russian folk revitalised Dostoevskii's religious faith to the extent that he returned from exile not only a Christian, but also a Christian novelist. However, although Christianity was central to Dostoevskii's subsequent art, its centrality was problematical. The great novels are not vehicles for the straightforward, finalised affirmation of a Christian world-view, but rather arenas in which faith is 'engaged in pitched battle with the most desolate atheism'. Jones analyses the post-Siberian work in the light of Dostoevskii's ability to identify himself imaginatively with both faith and the extremes of unbelief and to dramatise the process of rethinking Christianity in dialogue with disbelief and the various challenges posed by a Godless 'scientific' age. The great achievement of that work is the way it leaves the impression that the outcome of this dialogue is uncertain, and Dostoevskii's treatment of religion perfectly accords with Morson's description of an artist who 'knew what he was doing, but not what he was going to do'. As Jones concludes, whatever the 'real author' may have believed or desired, the 'implied author' of the texts confronts us with a world in which questions remain unresolved and unresolvable.

It was not only Dostoevskii who underwent a process of radical transformation during the years of his Siberian imprisonment and exile. The Russia to which he returned at the start of the 1860s was unrecognisable from that he had left a decade earlier. Nicholas I had died in 1855, after thirty years of stultifying rule that had led to political and economic stagnation and Russia's catastrophic defeat at the hands of Western powers in the Crimean War. The new tsar Alexander II came to the throne pledged to a process of fundamental reform that culminated in 1861 with the emancipation of the serfs. In the new, more tolerant climate intellectual life was also reinvigorated, and debate on major issues exploded in the pages of newspapers and periodicals. However, the revitalisation of intellectual activity also led to factionalism as conservatives, liberals and radicals disagreed over the nature and extent of the reforms. This period saw the emergence of a younger generation of radical thinkers intolerant of tradition, implacably opposed to a reforming government that had not gone far enough, and dismissive of the previous generation that had tolerated the stagnation of Nicholaevan Russia. The mood of this moment is beautifully caught in Turgenev's novel of 1862, *Fathers and Sons*. Dostoevskii threw himself into the polemical fray, and between 1861 and 1865 he edited, along with his brother Mikhail, the periodicals *Time* (1861–3) and *Epoch* (1864–5). Initially he used the pages of these publications to urge a process of national reconciliation, but he became progressively more intolerant of the extremism, materialism, utilitarianism and a-historic indifference to national identity espoused by the radical camp led by the journalists N. G. Chernyshevskii and N. A. Dobroliubov, and *Time* and *Epoch* became mouthpieces for an increasingly conservative nationalism. Derek Offord's essay seeks to locate Dostoevskii in the polemical exchanges of his time and to evaluate his role as an *intelligent*, that is a member of the socially engaged Russian intelligentsia. It demonstrates his explicit assumption of that role through his willingness to pursue a career in journalism, or 'publicism' (*publitsistika*), alongside that of author of imaginative fiction, and through the way he used his own journalism as a test-bed for the world-view that informs the novels for which he is better remembered. Dostoevskii's journalistic contributions to intellectual debate continued to the end of his life through his editorship of the journal *The Citizen* in the 1870s and through his *Diary of a Writer*, which was still on-going at the time of his death in 1881; but Offord's essay concentrates on case studies offered by his journalism of the early 1860s and his travel memoir of 1863, *Winter Notes on Summer Impressions*. As well as this sort of overt identification through publicistic activity, it is clear that Dostoevskii also assumed the role of member of the intelligentsia *implicitly*. In the 1840s, as I point out, his sense of being in a literary tradition had contributed to his self-image and helped to shape his verbal persona. It is clear from Offord's essay that Dostoevskii was similarly aware of the 'job-description' of an *intelligent*, and evidence of his willingness to assume such a persona emerges from the way his journalistic writings appropriate verbal or structural characteristics (Offord calls them 'flaws') typical of the genre as it was currently practised, from the way *Winter Notes on Summer Impressions* appears self-consciously to flaunt its own indebtedness to travel writing of the past, and from the way Dostoevskii uses verbal and stylistic parody to summon up the ghosts of his ideological opponents and thereby dialogise his assertions.

Offord makes it clear that at the heart of Dostoevskii's hostility to the radicalism of the 1860s was the latter's exclusive reliance on the findings of human reason and its elevation of the natural sciences to the summit of human knowledge at the expense of spiritual insight, instinct or faith. Such foregrounding of scientific enquiry and the scientific method was, of course, characteristic of an age which was witnessing the technological progress generated by industrialisation, and the retreat of metaphysical explanations in the face of the triumphal entry of scientific rationality into areas where it had previously been deemed inappropriate: Darwin's *Origin of Species* was challenging traditional assumptions about creation; Marx was offering explanations of society and history in terms of objective and immutable 'scientific' laws. Diane Thompson shows that, despite the heroic march of science in the nineteenth century, the truths it offered were finite truths constrained and frozen within the reductive formulae of inflexible physical laws. For Dostoevskii, however, truth was infinite, commensurate with the wisdom of God's creation, and the search for it was an unfinalisable spiritual – not merely intellectual – quest. The nineteenth-century worship of science was a modern form of idolatry, and the idols had come from Western Europe as Russia caught on late to the scientific revolution. Dostoevskii's attitude to science therefore plays out in another key his trepidation at the sacrifice of traditional Russian cultural principles and values on the altar of Westernisation. Thompson's essay, however, resists the temptation to explore science solely as a barometer of Dostoevskii's intellectual condition, and focusses instead on the poetics of scientific allusions in the post-Siberian fiction, where references to scientific facts are absorbed into the utterances of a particular character and are thus charged with that character's 'idea', in the sense of what he stands for. The pretensions of science to the assertion of absolute, unchallenged and therefore 'monologic' truth are thus relativised and 'dialogised' in Dostoevskii's fiction, and truth is shown to reside not in concepts but in the person, Christ serving as what Thompson calls the 'model of personhood'.

The scientific method embraced so enthusiastically by the radicals was also applied by them to psychology, and the result was a reductive 'science' of human nature and behaviour that emphasised self-interest and utilitarianism and stripped man of free moral choice. The hero of *Notes from Underground* (1864) was Dostoevskii's first sustained attempt to put such reductive theoretical psychology to the test of a morally complex individual who dodges and weaves through the challenges posed by contingency, rationality and physical necessity in order to secure the goal of independence and free moral choice. As a champion of these values he is hardly exemplary, as Thompson shows, and he subsides into inertia; but he does embody Dostoevskii's acute awareness of the complexity of human psychology, a complexity strikingly embodied in the major characters of all the great novels to come: *Crime and Punishment* (1866), *The Idiot* (1868), *The Devils* (1872), *A Raw Youth* (1875) and *The Brothers Karamazov* (1880). Robert Belknap's essay shows how in creating such a psychology for his fictional characters Dostoevskii revealed his awareness of existing psychological systems and theories and how these entered his fiction either directly or as something to be reacted against. Belknap's analysis confirms that of Thompson by describing Dostoevskii's rejection of the materialist neurological psychology that formed part of the deterministic scientific outlook of the radicals of the 1860s. But the existence of such a psychological system and his own strong reactions against it were instrumental in helping shape his own approach to and use of psychology, an approach structured upon the revelation of the psyche outside the realm of causation and reaction, by means of the gratuitous act. This led Dostoevskii to a preoccupation in his major novels with the psychology of crime, the psychology of violence and the psychology of guilt. Belknap discusses how Dostoevskii also took issue with the stance of the radicals in his elaboration of a psychology of artistic creation that emphasised the inspirational process and unconscious creation in the face of those like Chernyshevskii and Dobroliubov who would reduce art, along with the rest of human activity, to the predictable outcome of self-interest and utility.

It is generally acknowledged by Dostoevskii's critics and biographers that the appearance of *Notes from Underground* signalled the end of his literary apprenticeship and ushered in the period of the great novels, to which it stands as a preface in its philosophical toughness, psychological depth and narrative complexity (an apparent monologue that dissolves into a plurality of conflicting voices). But it was the great popularity enjoyed by *Crime and Punishment* that secured the author his position at the heart of Russian literary and intellectual activity and a literary reputation matched only by that of Tolstoi, whose *War and Peace* was serialised alongside *Crime and Punishment* in the same periodical, the *Russian Herald*. But Dostoevskii was dependent upon that activity not only for his reputation, but also for his livelihood, a situation that remained essentially unaltered until his death in 1881. By the end of his life his financial affairs were more or less in order, but the period between the collapse of his journal *Epoch* in 1865 (a year which also saw him assume financial responsibility for the family of his late brother Mikhail) and the completion of *The Devils* in 1872 were years of acute financial hardship, not helped by his pathological addiction to roulette. The period is marked by constant indebtedness, advances from editors against impossible deadlines, and writing against the clock. In Dostoevskii's own mind commercial pressures 'competed' with 'pure' artistic judgement in a way his rivals had never experienced. In 1866 he had to hire the stenographer Anna Snitkina, later his wife, in order to write *The Gambler* within a month, whilst simultaneously working on *Crime and Punishment*, and thus discharge his obligation to the unscrupulous publisher Stellovskii. During his work on *The Idiot* he felt that financial pressure had forced him to use an idea that was not yet ready; and while working on *The Devils* he wrote to his niece Sonia on 17 August 1870 complaining: 'If only you knew how hard it is to be a writer, and to carry such a burden! I know for certain that if I had two or three stable years for this novel, as Turgenev, Goncharov and Tolstoi have, I would write a work they would still be talking about in a hundred years!' (XXIX/1, 136). As we have seen, Christa's essay demonstrates how in Dostoevskii's novels due acknowledgement is given to the power of money and to the way commercial transactions and relationships may be transmuted into the psychological and existential. William Mills Todd's essay complements this approach perfectly by concentrating on money and the commercial transaction not just as an ingredient of the artistic product, but also as an accompaniment to the creative process, giving due recognition to the fact that Dostoevskii was not only a writer – he was also a professional writer. Todd's essay gives the lie to the sort of notion expressed by Dostoevskii to his niece that there can be any state of 'pure' aesthetic creation independent of 'competing' commercial pressures, as well as to the idea that the dependence of the text on such external pressures must necessarily produce aesthetically adverse consequences. He pays particular attention to the fact that Dostoevskii's major novels were serialised and indicates how the pressures of deadlines were reflected in the form of those novels, leading to the creation of a specific poetics of serial publication. This is a theme that Morson also takes up when he suggests that Dostoevskii exploited the commercial reality of serial publication of his works in order to create his 'processual' novel form, a form that intensified the sense of presentness and kept open character destinies and plot options.

The above paragraphs have sought to justify the selection of what has been included in this volume. A word, finally, about what has been omitted. There is no doubt that a different editor relying on different contributors would have come up with a different selection of topics and would have argued just as emphatically in justification of that selection. I am aware of several themes that would have enhanced the approach adopted here, but which have had to be omitted for reasons of space or because their inclusion would have encroached significantly on the areas treated by existing contributors. I have also tried to avoid the inclusion of topics that have been thoroughly treated elsewhere in the critical literature. There is therefore nothing specifically on illness, despite the fact that Dostoevskii was himself an epileptic who exploited the pathology of that disease for his own artistic purposes, for the subject has been comprehensively investigated by James L. Rice.[15] The same is true of the theme of suicide, equally prominent in the novels as an artistic device and equally well studied by Irina Paperno and N. N. Shneidman.[16] The city is a major component of Dostoevskii's fiction right from the works of the 1840s, serving to ground the neuroses of his characters and to bind his novels to the 'St Petersburg tradition' evident in Russian literature from Alexander Pushkin's *Bronze Horseman* (1833) to Andrei Bitov's *Pushkin House* (1978) and beyond; but this too has been comprehensively covered in the critical literature. Issues of sexuality and gender are touched upon in several essays in this volume, but they have received fuller treatment elsewhere.[17]

Notwithstanding such omissions, the issues that are addressed in the present collection do serve to map out the most significant areas of the cultural territory in which the production of Dostoevskii's texts was located, and this surely should be a major aim of any critical companion to that writer.

Notes

1 George Steiner, *Tolstoy or Dostoevsky* (London: Faber, 1959), pp. 346–7.
2 Alex de Jonge, *Dostoevsky and the Age of Intensity* (London: Secker & Warburg, 1975), p. 1.
3 See, for example, *Le mythe de Sisyphe* (Paris: Gallimard, 1942), pp. 140–50.
4 Vladimir Nabokov, 'Fyodor Dostoevski' in *Lectures on Russian Literature* (London: Weidenfeld & Nicolson, 1982), pp. 97–135.

5 John Middleton Murry, *Fyodor Dostoevsky: A Critical Study* (London: Martin Secker, 1916).

6 George Moore, 'Preface' to F. Dostoevsky, *Poor Folk*, trans. Lena Milman (London: Elkin Mathews and John Lane, 1894), pp. vii–xx.

7 See B. Kuznetsov, *Einstein and Dostoevsky* (London: Hutchinson, 1972), p. 7.

8 For a summary of Lawrence's views on Dostoevskii see W. J. Leatherbarrow (ed.), *Dostoevskii and Britain* (Oxford and Providence: Berg, 1995), pp. 31–3.

9 Richard Kappen's *Die Idee des Volkes bei Dostojewski* (Würzburg: Triltsch, 1936) is an example of such an approach. It is now of historical interest only.

10 For an over-view of Dostoevskii's critical reception see W. J. Leatherbarrow, *Fedor Dostoevsky: A Reference Guide* (Boston: G. K. Hall, 1990), pp. xv–xxxi.

11 Ivan Alexandrovich Goncharov (1812–91). Russian novelist, best known for *Oblomov* (1859).

12 Gary Saul Morson, *The Boundaries of Genre: Dostoevsky's 'Diary of a Writer' and the Traditions of Literary Utopia* (Austin: University of Texas Press, 1981), p. 77.

13 A. I. Herzen, 'Dilettantism in Science' (1843). Quoted from W. J. Leatherbarrow and D. C. Offord (eds.), *A Documentary History of Russian Thought from the Enlightenment to Marxism* (Ann Arbor: Ardis, 1987), p. 136.

14 See, for example, Rene Wellek (ed.), *Dostoevsky: A Collection of Critical Essays* (Englewood Cliffs: Prentice Hall, 1962); and Malcolm V. Jones and Garth M. Terry (eds.), *New Essays on Dostoyevsky* (Cambridge University Press, 1983).

15 James L. Rice, *Dostoevsky and the Healing Art: An Essay in Literary and Medical History* (Ann Arbor: Ardis, 1985).

16 Irina Paperno, *Suicide as a Cultural Institution in Dostoevsky's Russia* (Ithaca, N.Y. and London: Cornell University Press, 1997), and N. N. Shneidman, *Dostoevsky and Suicide* (Oakville, N.Y. and London: Mosaic Press, 1984).

17 See, for example, Nina Pelikan Strauss, *Dostoevsky and the Woman Question: Rereadings at the End of a Century* (New York: St Martin's Press, 1994), and Barbara Heldt, *Terrible Perfection: Women and Russian Literature* (Bloomington and Indianapolis: Indiana University Press, 1987).

2

FAITH WIGZELL

Dostoevskii and the Russian folk heritage

Outside Russia it is the philosophical, moral, psychological and political problems in Dostoevskii's work that have fascinated readers, not its possible folkloric connections. Even in Russia for several decades the question of the writer's relationship to the folk heritage was barely posed – somewhat surprisingly, since Dostoevskii was writing when the mainly illiterate peasantry, numerically by far the largest social group, depended on an oral culture that shaped and expressed their world-view. Furthermore, the writer himself came to see the religious and moral ideals of ordinary Russians, which were embodied in their oral culture, as the key to Russia's salvation. That oral culture was also appearing in print in great quantities in the 1860s and 1870s when the major novels were being written: not only the standard collection of folktales (1855–63) and proverbs (1862), but also Christian legends (1859) and all kinds of sung poetry, especially the epic (*bylina*) and songs about Russian history (1861–7 and 1873), as well as folk-poetic laments (1872), and spiritual songs (*dukhovnye stikhi*) (1860 and 1861–4). These were accompanied by the continuing publication of accounts of peasant rituals, beliefs and superstitions. The reason for this lack of interest is not so much the undeniable importance of the larger philosophical issues in the novels as Dostoevskii's creative method. Whereas most Russian writers who draw on folklore make their source clear, whether through quotation, imitation or parallels, Dostoevskii tended to rework folkloric material, to integrate it into an image, a character, an incident or even his method of narration along with material from other sources, all subjected to his controlling vision. In particular, he was fond of interweaving motifs drawn from the Bible or official Orthodoxy with those from folk Christianity, though other combinations with philosophical concepts, literature, discussion of contemporary social and political issues and so on are common. Despite the opaqueness of many of these references, even harder for a modern reader who is not Russian to appreciate, it is no over-statement to suggest that Dostoevskii's work, especially *The Devils* and *The Brothers Karamazov*, is profoundly folklorised. In this case the word 'profoundly' indicates not merely frequency but also the manner in which such references are embedded in the work. Decoding them enriches the reader's understanding of the writer, as well as, for those unfamiliar with Russian popular life in the second half of the nineteenth century, helping to elucidate characters and episodes in the great novels. Although the evolution of Dostoevskii's artistic use of the Russian folk heritage needs surveying, if only by means of selective examples, in the limited space of this chapter the main focus must be on the later, more profoundly folklorised novels. Here I shall concentrate on major conceptual references as well as a few of the many telling details which gain resonance when the folk subtext is appreciated.

Just as with other aspects of his work, Dostoevskii's interest in folklore was stimulated and changed by imprisonment and exile in Siberia. As his views about the state of Russia developed, he drew on the profound knowledge of the people and their beliefs acquired during his years in labour camp. As he makes clear in his *Notes from the House of the Dead* (1860–2), he had been startled to discover the deep hostility of ordinary convicts towards the upper classes, and with time came to believe that it was for the privileged classes to merge with ordinary Russians by adopting their values.[1] These years afforded him a unique opportunity to deepen his childhood acquaintance with the roots of Russian life and the riches of the popular language.[2] Given his growing concern with ethics, he was also fascinated by the values and ideals of convict society, however depraved some of his fellow inmates might be. Amidst violence, malice and depravity, he was struck by the innate feeling for truth and justice among his fellow inmates, and by the refusal of the common people to upbraid criminals or sinners. What Dostoevskii wrote once he had returned from his grim experiences as a convict differs radically from his earlier work in its philosophical depth, moral searchings, grasp of human psychology and innovative approach to narrative. As his views about the nature of Russia and her destiny developed, he wove an intricate web of allusions to Russian folk belief and folklore into the texture of his later work. Often acting as symbols, these allusions play a major role in developing that sense of other worlds existing beyond the Russian provincial here and now in which the novels are located.

Nonetheless, the folk heritage was not something Dostoevskii discovered in Siberia. His upbringing had differed from that of aristocratic writers like Tolstoi or Turgenev. In nineteenth-century Russia the upper classes, even if sometimes educated by foreign tutors ignorant of Russian culture, did observe traditional Yuletide customs and enjoyed Shrovetide carnival festivities. The children had nannies who sang folk songs, knew Russian proverbs and told them about the Baba Iaga, the firebird and the wood goblin. Folk culture was presented as fun and part of the childhood experience. However, once adult, they were expected to view it as an essential part of their Russian identity, but not to believe in it. Where Dostoevskii's family background makes a difference is not in the perception of folklore as fun, colour and heritage, but in the greater familiarity it afforded him with the world of the Russian peasant and with Orthodoxy. It is always a matter of surprise to learn how superficial was the practice of Russian Orthodoxy in many aristocratic families in the nineteenth century. Certainly, like his wealthier counterparts, Dostoevskii had a nanny, Alena Frolovna, who told Fedor and his brothers folktales and terrifying *bylichki* (tales of supernatural encounters), as did the children's former wet nurses on their visits to the house.[3] At Easter their uncle took them to see the puppet theatre, dancing bears and other popular entertainments (Frank, *Seeds of Revolt*, p. 11). Crucially, though, as Dostoevskii remarked, he came 'from a pious Russian family' (here the word 'Russian' implies 'not highly Westernised').[4] With devout Orthodox parents who taught him to read from a religious primer, a nanny who told him tales from the lives of popular Orthodox saints, participation in the daily practice of Orthodoxy with its fasts, feasts and pilgrimages, young Fedor was much closer to ordinary Russians than were children of the gentry. Furthermore, contact with ordinary people was not discouraged; when Dostoevskii's father acquired a country property, the young Dostoevskiis played with the peasant children and even helped the adults in the fields (Frank, *Seeds of Revolt*, pp. 29–30). This association with those for whom Russian folklore formed an integral part of their world-view influenced Fedor throughout his life. The hostility he faced in the prison camp notwithstanding, his Orthodox background and early encounters with peasants provided an invaluable stepping stone towards an appreciation of the ethical values and world-view of ordinary Russians.

He also took his childhood experiences forward into his earliest works. For example, his favourite place on the small estate was the wood, through which ran various ravines he was forbidden to visit. Woods were held to be the dwelling place of the wood goblin (the *leshii*), who enjoyed frightening people and leading them into the darkest, most impenetrable parts, perhaps to the very edge of, or into, a precipitous ravine, where the demonic unclean force was known to lurk. Once, while in the forest, the young Dostoevskii, thinking he heard a cry that a wolf was approaching, fled in terror to a peasant working in the fields nearby. Soothingly making the sign of the cross over the boy, the peasant sent him home. Although this episode may, and has been, understood as an auditory hallucination and the only early sign of nervous disorder (Frank, *Seeds of Revolt*, p. 50), placed in the context of folk belief it equally demonstrates how the fears of an imaginative child may take traditional folkloric form.

Dostoevskii adapted this incident in the original version of *Poor Folk*, where the heroine Varenka recollects her visits to the forest. After poetically describing the wild natural beauty and calm of the forest edges, she is drawn, despite her own anxieties, towards the densest areas: 'it was as though someone was summoning me, beckoning me towards the place where [...] the forest becomes darker, and the ravines begin' (I, 443). In accordance with the conviction that naming the *leshii* risked attracting his unwelcome attentions, her summoner is unnamed. Though the youthful Varenka's fears are comprehensible to a modern reader, the manner of their presentation owes to folk belief the location and the taboo on naming, as well as the behaviour of the 'someone'. More heavily folklorised than the account of the incident in Dostoevskii's own childhood which was recorded many years afterwards, it serves to poeticise Varenka's image, especially as it foreshadows her loveless marriage to the dreadful Bykov, who after the wedding takes her away to his country lair. The passage continues (and these details are retained in the final version) with her recollection of the 'terrible tales' of sorcerers and corpses her nanny had told her, supernatural (yet enjoyable) horror ironically contrasting with the drab but all too real horrors of her life now.

The passages mentioned above reveal how a work set in the most westernised city in Russia draws on folklore. This is not the paradox it might seem. Varenka has grown up in the country, like the majority of the inhabitants of St Petersburg at the time. In Petersburg in 1864, for example, half the population were peasants, many of whom returned to their villages in summer. Thus ordinary people in towns also shared to some degree the predominantly oral culture of the peasants. Reflecting this situation, the prime use of folkloric material in *Poor Folk* is nonetheless not so much folk-poetic as ethnographic. Only when the two main characters, Varenka and Devushkin, feel constricted by the straitjacket of conventional letter discourse do they express themselves in folk-poetic images and expressions. Take, for example, Makar Devushkin's fondness for bird metaphors: 'golubushka moia', 'ptenchik vy moi', 'ptashka vesennaia' ('my little dove', 'you are my fledgling', 'my little spring bird' etc.). Although these fit his modest background and hence may be considered ethnographic in character, in this instance it is the folk-poetic resonances that are artistically significant. The folk lyric song often features a sad heroine who, mourning the loss of youth and love in an unhappy marriage, is compared to a bird. Later, in Devushkin's final letter to Varenka, just before she leaves for life with Bykov, he expresses such depths of incoherent pain that the letter breaks with the etiquette of both the epistolary novel and ordinary social letter-writing, shifting to agonised exclamation and barely concealed sobs: 'to whom shall I write now, little mother [...] Who am I going to call little mother now; who shall I call by such a lovely name now? Where shall I find you from now on, my little angel? I shall die, Varenka, I shall surely die; my heart will not endure such unhappiness' (1, 107). The rhetorical questions and tragic cries, just like his reproaches, have their roots in the poetics of the Russian folk funeral lament, something carried forward into the later work as well, especially Sonia's lamentation in *Crime and Punishment*.

Elsewhere in *Poor Folk*, Dostoevskii utilised contemporary urban lore as a way of locating his characters in their social environment. In this respect he was reflecting literary trends: in the 1830s and 1840s a popular genre was the so-called physiological sketch which featured ethnographically accurate portraits of city dwellers. For example, in a typically careful choice of names he calls the hero of *Poor Folk* Makar. The writer was undoubtedly aware that in a whole range of folk genres, from proverbs to popular theatre, humorous songs and *lubok* prints (the Russian equivalent of broadsheets), Makar is a joke, a poor unfortunate mocked for his inadequacies. Makar's language reflects his social position so precisely that one contemporary critic placed it in the everyday conversational style of specific Petersburg regions, Peski and the Peterburgskaia storona. He peppers his speech with popular sayings, such as 'ne radost' starost'' – 'old age is no fun' – and folkloric expressions, such as the rhyming noun combination describing himself elegantly proceeding to his office 'gogolem-shchegolem' – 'like a strutting dandy' (1, 19; letter of 8 April).

In his next work, *The Double*, Dostoevskii moved away from the life of the poor to depict the psychological breakdown of Iakov Goliadkin, a civil servant with limited inner resources (as his name and clichéd language suggest, he is spiritually naked, *golyi*). Here, as elsewhere, folkoric influence is deeply embedded in the work. Without denying the influence of Romantic plots about doubles, the treatment in Dostoevskii's story seems to depend partly also on other discourses – first, on *bylichki* in its reflection of folk belief about doubles. Linked to popular conceptions about doubles is the idea of the mirror as a boundary with the world beyond, hence possessing demonic associations. Indeed, the first thing Goliadkin does on waking up is to look in the mirror, where he naturally sees a double of his own face (1, 109–10; Ch. 1). All too soon the double takes on three-dimensional form and Goliadkin's life descends into nightmare. In accordance with popular belief, Goliadkin Senior interprets Goliadkin Junior as the product of sorcery and witchcraft (1, 173, 174; Ch. 9) or as the interference of the devil (1, 153; Ch. 7); as will be seen below, his double does behave like a folk devil at times. Poor Goliadkin is also informed by the garrulous Anton Antonovich that doubles come 'from the other world' ('ne iz zdeshnikh') and foreshadow death, entirely in accordance with folk belief (1, 149; Ch. 6).

Apart from reference to folk beliefs and tales about the supernatural, *The Double* also draws on the discourse of the wonder tale (*volshebnaia skazka*, or fairy tale as it is usually known in English), albeit with parody and inversion. For Goliadkin events offer a cruel awakening from the fairy-tale dream from which he is emerging on the first page. From his regret that he is no longer in the magic realm of what Russians call 'the thrice-tenth kingdom' ('tridesiatoe gosudarstvo'), it may be deduced that in his dream he is the hero of the tale, rescuing his bride from the clutches of an otherworld monster. It soon emerges that Goliadkin is indeed seeking a wife, Klara Olsufevna, whose remote image reflects, apart from Goliadkin's own unreal view of women and romance, the distant beauty who is the object of the wonder-tale hero's quest. Characteristic also of the structure of many wonder tales is the false hero (often the hero's brother) who takes his place and steals his bride. He is usually unmasked by the hero who comes in disguise to rescue his bride at the wedding feast. In *The Double*, however, Goliadkin Junior steals everything from Goliadkin *except* the bride, and, furthermore, implies through his worldly, confident behaviour that it is Goliadkin Senior who is the false hero. All the same, in Goliadkin's view, the bride has certainly been 'stolen', but by Vladimir Semenovich. Goliadkin does attend the feast – here the betrothal ceremony – cowering behind the woodpile in the yard. Eventually, cold and bedraggled, he is recognised by the jeering guests standing at the windows and brought inside (I, 218–25; Ch. 13). This episode may be seen as a hideous inversion of the motif of 'hero recognised', for Goliadkin is indeed now finally recognised, but only as a madman. And so the story ends with a journey (Goliadkin is borne away), an inversion of the wonder-tale ending in which the hero's journey is always satisfactorily concluded.[5]

Of all the early works the most heavily folklorised is undoubtedly *The Landlady* (1847), but this statement needs qualification since its folkloric elements largely come via literary Romanticism (particularly Gogol's *A Terrible Vengeance*, Pushkin's *The Undertaker* and to a lesser extent stories such as Marlinskii's *A Terrible Prophecy*, which owe much to writers such as Hoffmann).[6] In essence the plot of this highly coloured story has parallels with the wonder tale: the hero is a young seeker (Ordynov at the beginning of the story has devoted himself to a major academic project). Like the folktale hero he sets out on a quest (for new lodgings but also to discover life), encountering a beautiful girl, Katerina, whom he yearns to rescue from the clutches of the evil sorcerer, Murin. As on the wonder-tale hero, an interdiction is placed upon Ordynov (Katerina bids him see her only as a sister) but he ignores it (declares his love), and as a consequence loses her. Whereas at this point in the wonder tale the hero finds magic helpers or objects with whose help he defeats the monster and rescues the object of his quest, Ordynov, who is physically and psychologically weak and isolated, is unable to break Murin's grip on Katerina who is taken away from him. The tragic ending fits the Romantic mould rather than the happy ending of the wonder tale, but it also has reminiscences of *bylichki* which often end tragically. In Murin Dostoevskii combined the image of the devil with that of the village sorcerer, who was deemed to have acquired his power from the unclean force/devil. References to the unclean force, devilry, death and the colour black surround Murin's image: he reads black books (1, 307; Pt 2, Sec. 2), calls himself a sorcerer (1, 308; Pt 2, Sec. 2), is termed 'enemy' (*vrag*) by Ordynov (1, 294; Pt 2, Sec. 1) and 'master' (*khoziain*) by Katerina (1, 275, 303; Pt 1, Sec. 2, Pt 2, Sec. 2). These last two are both common popular euphemisms for the devil. His name, which means 'Moor', hence 'black', possesses traditional literary connotations: in early Russian literature *murin* could mean 'devil'. Furthermore, the stark contrasts in the story between good and evil, darkness and light, Murin's black books and Ordynov's project for a book with a system for life, all reflect the traditional folkloric attachment to opposites, as well as the sense of omnipresent danger from demonic forces (Vetlovskaia, 'Poeticheskaia deklaratsiia', pp. 95–100). Folklorisation is extended to the speech of the characters, Katerina in particular, for whom Dostoevskii created his own folk-poetic stylistic mélange from folk epic, lyric song and proverbs (Gibian, 'Dostoevsky's use', p. 247). His aim may have been to lend a story with the everyday setting of Petersburg a mythic level about the battle between good and evil, power and subservience (both involuntary and voluntary). The inspiration for this folkloric stylistic jumble was largely literary, but Dostoevskii made a clear attempt to give *The Landlady* a Russian flavouring, not simply choosing material which had come via Western European Romanticism.

It may be concluded that Dostoevskii's childhood gave him some familiarity with popular superstition, festivities, folktales and the world-view of ordinary Russians, together with a much more profound knowledge of popular Orthodoxy. On top of these he possessed a natural ear for colloquial language and an eye for everyday detail, and made good use of most of these in his early writing career. It was not, however, until folklore entered Dostoevskii's system of ideas about Christianity and Russian messianism that it was integrated fully into his work, with increasing density in the last two great novels, *The Devils* and *The Brothers Karamazov*. In these he made a shift away from the folktale towards the folklore of popular Orthodoxy. In using these facets of traditional culture and belief, Dostoevskii sought to bring the world of the educated together with that of the ordinary Russian, since it was only this 'that could lead to the redemption of the whole'.[7] The peasants were interesting for their moral ideals and spiritual beliefs which were, in his view, connected with true national values. As he said of his own beliefs, they were 'not so much Slavophile as Orthodox, that is, close to the beliefs of the Russian peasant – Christian belief, that is'.[8] Whatever the accuracy of this statement, and without doubt it is a highly partial conception of the peasant world-view, it conveys his intellectual alignment with moral, spiritual and national folk values. Given the focus of his interests, Dostoevskii was led to interpret some aspects of folk belief idiosyncratically. For example, he perceived belief in the supernatural to be a representation of the peasants' desire for an ideal, an escape from the misery of their lives, rather than conventionally as charming colour or rural backwardness (although he was far from idealising or approving of all aspects of the peasant belief system). Where feasible, he also inclined to place a Christian interpretation on popular belief, as will be seen in the discussion below on the concept of Mother Moist Earth. As a result of the emphasis on values many facets of the great novels bear symbolic significance, whose decoding involves reference not only to Russian folklore, but also to biblical/Christian symbolism. The two are frequently combined in a manner that reaches beyond the syncretism found in popular Orthodoxy in Russia to acquire a rich and uniquely Dostoevskian range of meanings. Rather than disembowelling works in turn, I propose to concentrate on a few of the folklorised concepts underpinning Dostoevskii's mature writing.

Of these one of the most significant is the cult of Mother Moist Earth (*mat' syra-zemlia*). For centuries, as far as can be judged, peasants revered the soil for its unfailing capacity each spring to renew nature, thus sustaining man and beast. Equating this nurturing role with motherhood, the earth was deemed not merely grammatically feminine, but, as in many other cultures, a mother. Since in an agricultural society fertility and growth were crucial for survival in the face of harsh weather or sickness, villagers performed traditional calendar rituals with the aim of ensuring the continuing protection of the earth. After the conversion to Christianity in 988, elements of the pre-Christian belief system were, as in other European countries, integrated into the official religion, although this process took until the fifteenth century in the countryside. As elsewhere, the new religion syncretistically blended Christian and pre-Christian elements. Indeed, the Orthodox emphasis on Mary as Mother of God (*Bogoroditsa*), rather than as Virgin as in Catholic Europe, may well stem from a strong pre-existing cult of a maternal earth among the Slavs.[9] In popular Orthodoxy (that practised by peasants in particular), thanks perhaps to the late arrival of Christianity together with economic backwardness, pre-Christian elements are particularly striking. In religious folklore a clear connection is made between Mary Mother of God and Mother Earth, despite the church's refusal to accept such an obviously heretical belief.[10]

It was in the spiritual songs of Russia (*dukhovnye pesni* or *dukhovnye stikhi*) that Dostoevskii found a Christianised version of the cult of the earth, as well as the folk slant on Orthodoxy emphasising earthly sorrow and suffering. The songs were performed by the religious sects of Old Believers or a special category of itinerant blind beggars known as *kaleki perekhozhie*. Market-places, monastery gates, church doorways, even the courtyards of city apartment blocks might harbour a singer or a group of singers, moved to tears by their own song while onlookers wept as they listened.[11] One of the major themes in the songs of the religious beggars illustrates Christ's words that 'it is easier for a camel to pass through the eye of a needle than for a rich man to enter the kingdom of God'. The familiar song 'The Two Lazarus Brothers', which Dostoevskii may also have had in mind in *Crime and Punishment* when depicting Sonia reading to Raskolnikov the gospel story of the raising of Lazarus, follows exactly these lines. It is the humble beggar Lazarus whose soul is raised to heaven, while the soul of the rich but arrogant and heartless brother roasts in hell. The values epitomised by Sonia, suffering, humility and love, are extolled in this and other spiritual songs. Raskolnikov showed himself aware of the image, if only negatively, when he earlier suggested 'singing Lazarus' (vi, 189; Pt 3, Sec. 4), an expression meaning to pretend to be a false beggar or complain of one's lot. His spiritual journey in the novel involves him learning not just to 'sing Lazarus' but, in being raised like the biblical Lazarus, to model himself on the long-suffering beggar Lazarus of the song.

Amidst the images of sorrow and suffering in the spiritual songs the dominant one is that of the grieving mother, in particular Mary, Mother of God. In the 'Lament of the Mother of God' Mary, who has learnt of her Son's crucifixion, begs Mother Moist Earth to take her to her bosom. Tears not only of sorrow but also of repentance define attitudes to the earth, which is seen as the repository of moral purity. In the 'Lament of the Earth', the burden of bearing so many sinful people causes Mother Earth to cry out to the Lord. One variant specifically refers to the wicked who fail to honour their father or mother (note the parallels with the Karamazov family), another asserts that only tears of repentance will save them (parallels in Dostoevskii's works too numerous to mention). In yet another the earth cannot forgive someone who has killed his sworn brother, reminding us of the brotherhood pact between Rogozhin and Prince Myshkin in *The Idiot*, to which the Prince agrees, hoping that Rogozhin, who has become detached from the moral values of the people, will be saved from wickedness. In fact, only Myshkin's epileptic fit saves him from being stabbed. In Dostoevskii's outlook, where personal resurrection and national salvation came to be closely connected, it is the Russian earth that often plays a greater role than the Mother of God.

The motif appears in the autobiographical reminiscence from 1876, 'The Peasant Marei', recounting the incident that appears in fictionalised form in *Poor Folk*, but, whereas there he had emphasised the folk supernatural, here the stress is laid on the figure of the peasant who calms the young Dostoevskii, touching his cheek with a thick earth-encrusted finger. With the words 'earth-encrusted' the natural kindness of Marei is connected to the soil and hence the protection of Mother Earth. Marei's tender smile and protective movement, as he makes the sign of the cross over the boy, reinforce this link. Not surprisingly, this key concept is woven into many of Dostoevskii's later works. In *Crime and Punishment* Sonia exhorts Raskolnikov to go to the crossroads, ask forgiveness of the people and accept tears and humility by kissing the earth. When he finds it in himself to accept her guidance, he takes his first step towards spiritual regeneration (VI, 405; Pt 6, Sec. 8). The acceptance of sinfulness and need for repentance accompany the traditional values assigned to Mother Moist Earth in spiritual songs. The interweaving of official and folk Orthodoxy is characteristic of Dostoevskii and, in the case of the Mother Earth motif, is reflected in the epigraph from John 12:24 used in *The Brothers Karamazov*: 'I tell you, most solemnly, unless a grain of wheat falls upon the ground and dies, it remains a single grain; but if it dies, it yields a rich harvest.' Acceptance of the Russian land and its people signals humility and hence the possibility of resurrection in Christ, as when at the end of *The Devils* Stepan Verkhovenskii goes wandering in the countryside, meeting peasants and hearing the gospel (X, 480–99; Pt 3, Ch. 7). In so doing he turns away from the proud and godless Western ideas to which he has devoted his life.

The true significance of Mother Moist Earth is expressed most forcibly by Maria Lebiadkina (*The Devils*), whose attachment to the earth is a direct echo of spiritual songs and hence folk piety as a whole. She recounts a conversation with a lay sister at the convent where she was living who had told her: 'Yes, she [the Mother of God] is the great Mother Moist Earth [...] and when you have given the earth to drink of your tears to the depth of a foot, you will rejoice at everything straightaway. And none of your sorrows will exist any longer' (X, 116; Pt 1, Ch. 4). Whether or not Dostoevskii himself would have agreed with this extreme view, Maria nonetheless represents Russian folk Christianity in the novel, and, though she is obviously half-demented, her thoughts are far more than mere babblings.[12]

In *Dream of a Ridiculous Man* (1877) the hero, who has essentially lost his humanity, feels only indifference to everything and everybody. He has a dream in which he is first taken up into space and then brought back, whereupon he discovers a love for the earth, declaring 'I yearn and thirst here and now to kiss the one and only earth with tears streaming down my face' (xxv, 112; Sec. 3). A similar idea underlies Zosima's teaching in *The Brothers Karamazov* where he preaches that falling to the earth and kissing it, watering it with tears, will help those in despair and loneliness. The final action of his life is to kneel, kiss the earth and pray (xiv, 291; Bk 6, Sec. 3). It is some time before Alesha can accept the full implications of the elder's teaching. His brother Dmitrii, on the other hand, shows he accepts the worship of the earth when he declaims Schiller's 'The Feast of Eleusis' (xiv, 99; Bk 3, Sec. 3), but without the folk-religious values of repentance, humility and tears found in the spiritual songs. Only at the end, recognising the need for forgiveness and repentance, does he discover his love for Russia and its God (xv, 186; Epilogue, Sec. 2).

Motifs from spiritual songs also mould the image of Alesha Karamazov. The choice of name directly reflects that of perhaps the most popular saint in Russia, Alexis Man of God, whose *Life*, as well as the song containing the popular reworking of the *Life*, were well known to Dostoevskii.[13] As a pointer to the link between Alesha and his namesake the saint is mentioned several times in the novel, as when Zosima expresses his admiration for him during a conversation with a woman whose son had been called Aleksei (xiv, 47; Bk 2, Sec. 3). St Alexis was the only child of wealthy parents living in Rome, who fled his wife and family to devote himself to a life of prayer and poverty. After a vision of the Mother of God ordering his return to his parents, he reappeared as a beggar, and his grieving parents failed to recognise him. He told his father that in building him a modest shelter he would discover his son. In fact the family discovered his real identity only after his death. In the folk song, unlike in the *Life*, his mother's lament does not inveigh against Aleksei for concealing his identity, but acquires notes of repentance in lamenting that his parents did not treat their beggar son better. The message in the song, as opposed to the *Life*, lauds love in the name of the Lord encompassing all, however humble, over and beyond narrow family ties. Christian love of all, regardless of status, is of course a key element of Dostoevskii's message in this novel. The link between Alesha and Alexis is made clearer with the repetition in the novel of the motif (found in both *Life* and song) of being forced to return to the world and one's family to save oneself and others. Though in the novel it is Zosima rather than the Mother of God who sends Alesha back into the world to look after his family, Dostoevskii makes a point of noting that pride of place in his cell goes to a huge icon of the Mother of God (xiv, 37; Bk 2, Sec. 2). Furthermore, Zosima's own emphasis on love and suffering for humanity corresponds to the image of the Mother of God in spiritual songs.

In Dostoevskii's folk-inspired system of Christian ethics, therefore, some accept or learn to accept Mother Moist Earth. For those who cannot, their rejection of the earth is akin to death, since they belong nowhere. Consequently, such figures in Dostoevskii often commit suicide (or drive others to do so). Though suicide in Dostoevskii and in the Russia of his day is a complex cultural phenomenon reaching far beyond its traditional meaning,[14] folk belief offers a significant extra insight into suicide in Dostoevskii's works and in particular into that of Svidrigailov, the evil presence of *Crime and Punishment*. According to traditional Russian views, taking one's own life constituted the gravest of sins. Most importantly (and here folk belief concurs with Orthodox prescription), suicides should be buried not in cemeteries but outside the community. Indeed folk belief held that they should be left in liminal places such as crossroads, ravines, beside roads or at the edge of fields; the earth, it was thought, would not accept them, forcing them to live on as unclean dead (*zalozhnye pokoiniki*) haunting the living. By the nineteenth century, church insistence on interment meant that they were usually buried or at least covered with stones (Paperno, *Suicide*, p. 54). One may note as an aside that such attitudes explain the landlady's rejection of the idea that little Iliusha in *The Brothers Karamazov* should be buried by a stone at the edge of a field; such places were for the unclean dead only (xv, 191; Epilogue, Sec. 3).[15] In the case of Svidrigailov, given the Dostoevskian concept of the earth as the repository of good, his suicide represents his complete refusal or inability to accept the values represented by Mother Earth, for he ultimately commits suicide himself after seeing visions/dreams of those he has driven to take their own lives. While Dostoevskii's Christian views and background would surely not have supported the idea that, after his death, Svidrigailov exists in a liminal space between the world of the living and that of the dead, the view of suicide as a demonically incited sin that casts the perpetrator out of a Christian community in harmony with Mother Earth gives added resonance to the episode as well as linking it with the positive ideology of the novel.[16]

In connection with the above, it is notable that Svidrigailov is associated with one particular liminal place, the threshold. In general, Dostoevskian characters are frequently to be found pausing at a physical or psychological threshold, stepping over it or existing on the threshold of major change. Without denying the universality of the symbol of a threshold as transitional space between two places, stages in life, or states of being, it seems that the significance and persistence of this motif in Dostoevskii also depend upon the magical significance of the threshold specific to Russian folk belief. For the peasant the threshold was a physical representation of liminality, a key concept in his world-view. The term, which derives from the Latin word for threshold, *limen*, indicates a transitional space between this world and the next/other. In Russian folk belief, certain places or times were designated as liminal. It was here that the unclean force in its various manifestations (including that of the devil) might be encountered; such times and locations, therefore, presented particular danger. Liminal places included cemeteries, crossroads and thresholds; times included Yuletide, midsummer and midnight. In folk belief pausing on a threshold brought dire consequences, except for those such as sorcerers, who could tap the unclean force. To this day Russians believe it unlucky to greet a visitor over a threshold, to stand on it, or go back over it after setting out on a journey.[17] The threshold symbolically represents a space in which it is dangerous to linger for fear of attracting evil, as well as the more widely held sense of a barrier between one stage or state and another.

Svidrigailov, a man who, having killed himself morally, is akin to a suicide even before he takes his own life, first appears standing motionless in the doorway of Raskolnikov's cubby-hole before stepping over it (VI, 213–14; Pt 4, Sec. 6). And indeed Raskolnikov, emerging from a nightmare, is not sure he is seeing a real person (Ivanits, 'Suicide', pp. 138–9). Svidrigailov then departs this world by shooting himself. He had intended going to Petrovskii but, as a building with a high watch tower looms up, he changes his mind. The gates are locked, implying that the heavenly realm, with its watch tower looking over the city, is forever closed to Svidrigailov (VI, 394; Pt 6, Sec. 6). It may also be noted that the only other inhabitant of this liminal space, the gateway to the next world, is not a Russian but a drunk with a heavy accent, who sees this as his space. He is Jewish, and in the anti-semitic lore of the time Jews were excluded from heaven for their crucifixion of Christ.

Threshold motifs also surround the figure of Nikolai Stavrogin in *The Devils*. The reader first glimpses him pausing on the threshold of a room in his mother's house (X, 145; Pt 1, Ch. 5). Later, in his confession, he describes the suicide of the little girl, Matresha, whom he had dishonoured. As he explains, he is haunted by the image of her standing on the threshold, threatening him with the shake of her small fist. With his depraved attempt to compromise her innocence he had drawn her from her world into his amoral one, from which she had no escape except into death (XI, 16–19; 'At Tikhon's', Sec. 2). Just as he had invaded the world of little Matresha and caused her destruction, so he invades the privacy of his wife, the simple Maria Lebiadkina, entering her room while she sleeps. He stops by the door, looking around but not moving even after she wakes up (X, 214–19; Pt 2, Ch. 2). After a moment of terror at his stern gaze and unnatural, death-like (perhaps unclean death-like) immobility, she relaxes, but a few minutes later, orders Stavrogin to go out of the room and then to cross the threshold again. For five years she has been waiting for 'him' to come. When Stavrogin refuses, she calls him an impostor, no longer her prince or her 'bright falcon' (*iasnyi sokol*, a folk epithet for a young hero), but an owl (*sova* and *filin*, eagle owl) (x, 217–19; Pt 2, Ch. 2). Since owls were believed unlucky, and hearing the cry of the eagle owl signified death (Ryan, *Bathhouse*, p. 125), Maria is correctly predicting her own imminent murder at the hands of the convict Fedka, who believes he is fulfilling Stavrogin's wishes. Here, initially, we find Stavrogin in the dangerous liminal place he inhabits, the threshold (which in the scene he is evidently unwilling to leave). Maria makes clear she has been awaiting her prince, but Stavrogin is unable to cross the threshold into the land of the living and the Russian Orthodox community. The far-sighted Maria understands this. And to further emphasise Stavrogin's connection with evil forces, Fedka, the criminal desecrator of holy icons, looms up out of the literal and symbolic darkness on the threshold of the room where Verkhovenskii and Stavrogin are discussing the murders of Lebiadkin and his sister (x, 321; Pt 2, Ch. 8). It is no surprise, then, that Maria is discovered with multiple stab wounds, lying across the threshold of her house which has been consumed by fire (x, 396; Pt 3, Ch. 2). Fire here may symbolise the fires of hell. Maria's place across the threshold may represent her position half-way between the godliness of the holy fool (see below) and the damnation of her marriage to the chief devil of the novel.

Stavrogin, the indirect instigator of Maria's murder, stands outside the community of Christian love, and it turns out that in Dostoevskii all those who do not belong to this community are outside, essentially in hell. The dichotomy corresponds to a peasant world-view structured in paired opposites: us/them, good/evil, light/darkness, etc. The 'us/them' pair might encompass village community versus a threatening external world, or the human world versus hostile nature, or good as opposed to evil/the devil. Whereas the opposition 'village community versus the outside (human and natural)' could be seen in spatial terms, the division into good and evil infiltrated the village community itself. Although peasants believed in a range of spirits, these generally remained in their habitats (forest, pond, fields etc). The folk devil, by contrast, was omnipresent and ubiquitous; it was necessary to ward off his, or more likely their, attacks at every juncture. Folk belief swarms with small malevolent devils. So acute was the peasants' sense that danger lurked everywhere that as a rule they referred to the devil far more frequently than to God and the saints, if only via common exclamations such as 'the devil take it' (*chert poberi*) or by crossing themselves for protection.[18]

The demonic motifs in *The Devils* and *The Brothers Karamazov* are so numerous that it is only possible within the confines of this essay to deal with some typical examples of folkloric-style devilish manifestation.[19] Just like Gogol before him, Dostoevskii marks the presence of the devil by intensifying the use of demonic invocations and casual references, as in the scene preceding Svidrigailov's suicide; the motif builds on the common taboo on naming the devil. Beyond this, the revolutionaries as a group refer to the devil casually but constantly.[20] In particular, not only does Petr Verkhovenskii call his activities demonic (x, 478; Pt 3, Ch. 6), but little devils pop up in his thoughts and words with remarkable frequency. But then the whole of *The Devils* is permeated by demonic references, in which the folk context plays no small part (Leatherbarrow, 'Devils' vaudeville', pp. 281–5). Some of the revolutionaries, who are demonically possessed, even have the facial features of the folk devil which is based on depictions in icons, in particular icons of the Last Judgement. Of Petr Verkhovenskii it is said: 'his head was elongated at the back and as though flattened at the sides, so that his face seemed pointed. His forehead was high and narrow, but his facial features were small. His eyes were sharp, his nose small and pointed, his lips long and thin' (x, 143–4; Pt 1, Ch. 5). Or take Shigalev, who has unnaturally large ears, broad, thick and protruding, just like the small demons that push sinners down to hell (x, 110; Pt 1, Ch. 4).

Despite a shift after *The Devils* from an inherently demonic theme (given Dostoevskii's views on political radicals), the diabolical presence still lurks in *The Brothers Karamazov*. For example, Ferapont exorcises them (xiv, 153–4; Bk 4, Sec. 1); old Karamazov fears their hooks will drag him down to hell, a motif probably taken from the spiritual song 'The Two Lazarus Brothers' (xiv, 23–4; Bk 1, Sec. 5); Lise and Alesha dream of them (xv, 23; Bk 11, Sec. 3; Ivanits, 'Folk beliefs', p. 137). Such devils belong as much to ecclesiastical as to folk tradition. The demonic is, however, most closely associated with Ivan, and here popular elements emerge distinctly. As Ivan descends into mental illness, he sees (or believes he sees) the devil. But a devil in human form, Smerdiakov (folk devils could appear as ordinary people), has been dogging him much earlier, taking the role of the enactor of Ivan's evil intentions and amoral ideas. When Smerdiakov hints that Ivan should go to Chermashnia (which will function as an invitation to Smerdiakov to kill old Karamazov), Ivan calls him a devil (xiv, 249; Bk 5, Sec. 6). Subsequently, when Smerdiakov finally confesses the murder to Ivan, he takes the stolen money from his left foot (the left having popular demonic connotations) and Ivan says, 'the devil himself must have helped you' (xv, 60, 66; Bk 11, Sec. 8). As Smerdiakov has insisted and Ivan comes to recognise, it is he and his own parricidal desires and amoral theories that are demonic and have inspired Smerdiakov's act. Thus Ivan has become possessed, and, as we learn in the following chapter, has already had hallucinations/visitations from the devil. In describing Ivan's devil, Dostoevskii adopts the folk euphemisms for the devil, 'guest' and 'gentleman', but lends them realistic form, so that he manifests himself as a shabby gent and Ivan's visitor. Like a folk devil he is both fond of malicious teasing and evidently lame (he has rheumatism). The lameness typical of the folk devil spreads to Ivan, reinforcing the suggestion of demonic possession. At the end of the conversation in which Ivan has in devilish fashion tempted Alesha into demanding justice for the suffering of innocent children, thereby denying the teaching of Zosima, Alesha observes his brother's awkward gait, apparently the result of a deformity: 'For some reason he suddenly noticed that his brother Ivan walked with a sort of swaying motion, and that his right shoulder, viewed from behind, seemed lower than the left. He had never noticed this before' (xiv, 241; Bk 5, Sec. 5).

Apart from Ivan, lameness affects various characters in *The Brothers Karamazov* and *The Devils*. Not only may those associated with the devil be lame (Lise and the schoolmaster member of the Verkhovenskii circle, for example), but also others: Grigorii limps because of his lumbago (but only after the murder), Zosima has weak legs, Madame Khokhlakova has a swollen foot, Maria Lebiadkina as well as Iliusha's mother and sister are lame, Lizaveta Nikolaevna dreams of being crippled by a fall from a horse (Leatherbarrow, 'Devils' vaudeville', p. 289). Beyond these lie numerous casual references to cripples in the cast of characters of both novels, implying that the 'motif serves to fuse the representation of human suffering with the suggestion of the presence of the devil, and its extensiveness suggests the pervasiveness of both' (Ivanits, 'Folk beliefs', p. 137).

Though devils were ubiquitous, the chances of encountering one were increased in liminal places such as the bathhouse, an 'unclean' place, where the sorcerer went (not to bathe) while good folk were at church (Ryan, *Bathhouse*, pp. 50–4). Because it was customary to remove one's cross in the bathhouse, visitors were highly vulnerable to attacks from demonic powers. In Dostoevskian poetics, the bathhouse apparently symbolises hell. Little wonder that Svidrigailov dreams of a smoky bathhouse, the smoke suggesting the fires of hell (vi, 221; Pt 4, Sec. 1), and Ivan tells Alesha that his devil goes to the bathhouse (xv, 86; Bk 11, Sec. 10). Smerdiakov's birth is linked to the bathhouse, although in the description by the narrator of the circumstances surrounding his birth, the actual place is only implied (xiv, 92; Bk 3, Sec. 2). The reason for this is probably that, since custom dictated that babies be born in the bathhouse, it was too ordinary a location to possess the demonic associations Dostoevskii wished to attach to Smerdiakov. Instead the potential demonic implications of his birth are brought out later when Grigorii remarks to Smerdiakov not only that he is the son of a devil, but adds: 'You're not human, you came from the damp of the bathhouse' (xiv, 114; Bk 3, Sec. 6). Behind this comment lies a set of folk perceptions about the relationship between birth and personality. A folk reading of Smerdiakov's life would interpret his childhood pastime of torturing cats to death and then blasphemously reading mock funeral rites over them as implying, firstly, that the precautions against demonic attack during his birth were self-evidently inadequate, and, secondly, that the substitution of Grigorii's dead son by the little Smerdiakov was an instance of the well-known belief in demonic changelings who take the place of a human child (XIV, 92–3; Bk 3, Sec. 2; Ivanits, 'Folk beliefs', pp. 140–1).

Another facet of the folk demonic is its connection with mirthless, cruel or destructive laughter. Folk *bylichki* and folktales often depict the devil as prankster, playing nasty tricks on men, especially the pious. As the devil led a man astray he was believed to laugh mockingly. Indeed the ecclesiastical culture of old Russia and, following from it, religious folklore explicitly opposed saintliness to laughter, which therefore was demonically tainted.[21] Hence the common euphemism *shut* (joker) for the devil. This link between the devil and laughter and/or practical jokes was picked up by Dostoevskii and attached to those who are unable or unwilling to take noble aspirations or goodness seriously. Horrible laughter is a feature of his negative characters, beginning with the smirking Goliadkin Junior in *The Double* and moving on to Svidrigailov, who during his first meeting with Raskolnikov (VI, 214–24; Pt 4, Sec. 1) laughs unexpectedly several times. In *The Devils* Stepan Trofimovich complains of his son's endless laughter (X, 171; Pt 2, Ch. 1). The impulse to play unpleasant tricks is characteristic of Goliadkin Junior, but applies most of all to the revolutionaries and those they have affected in *The Devils*. Petr himself suggests he is a joker (X, 408; Pt 3, Ch. 3), and, under his influence, an atmosphere of irresponsible anti-social merriment spreads into Iulia Mikhailovna's circle (X, 249; Pt 2, Ch. 5), leading to mindless acts such as the planting of obscene photographs in the bag of a poor woman who sells bibles (X, 251; Pt 2, Ch. 5). Indeed destructive and hysterical laughter regularly punctuates the course of the novel. In *The Brothers Karamazov* it is Ivan (the demonically possessed), not the devil, who laughs frequently during their conversation (XV, 71–84; Bk 11, Sec. 9), though it is the devil who is termed *shut* by Ivan. The diabolical delight in pranks that mock and undermine is transferred in this novel into the figure of Fedor Pavlovich Karamazov, whose grotesque and irreverent buffoonery in the monastery at the beginning of Book 2, just like his behaviour generally, mocks all that is good and loving in fatherhood (whether God the Father, Alesha's spiritual father Zosima, or Fedor's own relations with his children) and 'desecrates the divine and human image in himself and others' (Murav, *Holy Foolishness*, p. 137). Not for nothing is the chapter about his antics entitled 'Staryi shut' (usually rendered as 'The Old Buffoon'). Although Fedor

Pavlovich depicts himself as a seeker after truth – and, were he genuinely so, his behaviour might be deemed to conform to the holy fool paradigm – in fact he gets pleasure from his destructive behaviour, which renders him demonic rather than someone whose goodness is concealed behind a mask of buffoonery.

In Russian folk life a figure that was traditionally the butt of cruel laughter and contempt was that of the holy fool (*iurodivyi*). The phenomenon of voluntary folly in the name of Christ is attested from the eleventh century in Russian culture, but also exists in Byzantium and Western Christianity. In Russia, for reasons that remain obscure, huge numbers of holy fools emerged in the sixteenth and seventeenth centuries, attracting widespread devotion, though few were ever canonised by the church.[22] In the history of Russian Orthodoxy the phenomenon is interpreted as the voluntary adoption of madness or folly, an ascetic feat involving self-humiliation by exposure to laughter and contempt. However, among ordinary folk in Russia, the concept was extended to include a wide range of mentally deficient or ill people (involuntary fools). Both voluntary and involuntary holy fools were distinguished by outrageous, even obscene, behaviour, which challenged the norms of society. They rejected decent clothing (or, at an earlier period, clothes of any kind), paid no attention to personal hygiene and were frequently incoherent. The treatment they received was part of a severe asceticism that denied the body in favour of the spirit. Some mortified the flesh through the wearing of heavy chains. All saints are deemed to imitate Christ in some form or other; holy fools, it was believed, modelled themselves on the homeless self-abnegating Christ, who was reviled and unrecognised by all but the few. As saintly figures they were sometimes believed to possess powers of healing, but in the nineteenth century generally it was prophetic gifts that led to their widespread veneration. Unlike the fool or jester figure of the medieval period, 'the holy fool mocked the world out of love, the fool out of hatred and a desire for revenge' (Murav, *Holy Foolishness*, p. 138). It was for the pious to make the transition past the fool's appearance and behaviour to the supreme example of Christian meekness and love. Among pious ordinary folk, acceptance of the fool's blessed nature dictated that holy fools should be offered charity and their excesses be tolerated. In this context, the probable rape of Elizaveta Smerdiashchaia by Fedor Karamazov in *The Brothers Karamazov* is not only repellent because it takes advantage of an unfortunate simpleton, but also sacrilegious and symbolic of the demonic and destructive sensuality of old Karamazov.

The idea of a hidden inner saintliness masked by a deranged exterior challenged the hegemony of science and reason in the nineteenth century because the saintliness could not be demonstrated (ibid., pp. 49–50). It required a leap of faith to see through the repellent exterior and grotesque behaviour of the fool. What lay within could not be explained in physiological terms or quantified. It is easy to see why holy foolishness should attract Dostoevskii, with his emphasis on reading inner meaning and motivation rather than the mask of external behaviour. Over and above this, holy foolishness was regarded as an essentially Russian phenomenon. Indeed, it could be said to symbolise the widely held messianic view of Russia as poor, wretched and economically backward, but with hidden spiritual resources which would ultimately be revealed. Dostoevskii utilises the holy-foolish code of behaviour in the creation of a whole range of characters. At the same time, he also portrays actual recognised fools in his novels, but not favourably. However highly he esteemed the institution of holy foolishness, he was far from approving some aspects of the veneration of contemporary holy fools, as the negative portraits of Ferapont in *The Brothers Karamazov* and Semen Iakovlevich in *The Devils* demonstrate. Ferapont lives an ascetic life, fasting, going barefoot and wearing penitential chains beneath his robes. The holy foolishness that many ascribe to him is reflected in his visions of devils, his incoherent comments and his refusal to accept normal monastic discipline. These characteristic features are marred by his arrogant assumption of his own holiness and his malice and envy in attacking Zosima. The love the true holy fool is supposed to feel for his fellow man is obviously absent.

In Semen Iakovlevich, by contrast, Dostoevskii condemns the fashionable adulation of holy fools, in particular the famous demented, ill-mannered Ivan Koreisha. Crowds of women from the merchant and upper classes flocked to see Koreisha in his Moscow asylum between 1822 and 1865, hanging on his every word, however incomprehensible, because they believed him to be clairvoyant (Thompson, *Understanding Russia*, pp. 36–40). In the novel a number of the characters go on a fun visit to their local holy fool, Semen Iakovlevich, but neither their frivolous attitude nor Semen Iakovlevich's eccentric pronouncements do anyone any credit, or indeed any good (x, 256–60; Pt 2, Ch. 5).

If, on the one hand, Dostoevskii attacks recognised holy fools for exploiting their position and their fashionable supporters for their interest in sensational miracle rather than spiritual succour, on the other hand he presents unrecognised holy fools like Maria Lebiadkina in *The Devils* much more positively. Despite her feeblemindedness, her appearance and behaviour both reflect and conceal some facets of Russian piety and holy foolishness in particular. Her appearance is grotesque: she is crippled and her face crudely daubed with make-up. In typical holy-foolish fashion she shuns the world, living in filthy conditions, eating only charitable offerings, and though she does not wear chains she is beaten daily (a version of the asceticism of the holy fool). And yet her eyes, the mirror of the soul, reflect sincerity and a serene joy, and she appears to possess some powers of prescience (x, 113–14; Pt 1, Ch. 4). Amidst the frenzy and demonic buffoonery of the novel she presents the starkest of contrasts.

Apart from actual holy fools, recognised or unrecognised, Dostoevskii's later novels draw on the holy fool paradigm in the creation of positive characters, most obviously Prince Myshkin and Alesha Karamazov, and to a lesser extent Sonia Marmeladova and Zosima. Dostoevskii himself planned for Myshkin to have Christ-like features, and since, as already noted, saints' lives demonstrated different ways of imitating Christ, the use of the holy fool model may be said in the Russian context to be no less appropriate than any other. It is well known that Dostoevskii struggled with the creation of his positively beautiful hero; given his view that Christ was the only truly positively beautiful person, creating a good character presented huge problems. In moulding his image after the holy fool, Dostoevskii made Myshkin an epileptic, a condition many holy fools suffered, and which in the nineteenth century was regarded by many as a form of idiocy, just as holy fools were deemed idiots by those who failed to recognise their worth. Meekness, genuine compassion, a childlike innocence, unworldliness and simplicity are all features that can be seen as holy-foolish. Many of these are shared by Alesha Karamazov, although neither character can be reduced simply to a version of the holy fool paradigm. In other characters the connection may be less obvious. The figure of Sonia Marmeladova obviously depends to a certain extent on the clichéd literary figure of the prostitute with a heart of gold, but the degradation of her profession contrasts in the novel not just with conventional good-heartedness and moral purity, but with a Christian meekness typical of holy-foolish behaviour. Furthermore, her demand that Raskolnikov humiliate himself by publicly kissing the earth is strongly reminiscent of the odd commands sometimes issued by holy fools to those who sought guidance from them.

There is a sense in which the whole of Dostoevskii's writing is folklorised. In many and varied ways, as the famous scholar Bakhtin argued in his hugely influential book *Problems of Dostoevsky's Poetics*,[23] Dostoevskii's work is carnivalised, that is, inspired by the anarchic spirit of carnival, the popular Shrovetide festival of Europe with its pre-Christian antecedents in a festival celebrating the end of winter. Characteristic of this festival is a release of tensions in laughter and derision. This could take the form of mockery of authority and mummery in which role reversal (male/female, high/low) took place. Bakhtin argued that the roots of the ancient Greek genre of Menippean satire reached back directly into carnivalistic folklore, which over time spread its subversive influence into different literary forms, especially satire and parody.

In Dostoevskii Bakhtin saw this influence as a literary one, remarking that its origins were most likely not evident to Dostoevskii himself, but that its spirit came to him through a variety of literary works. This aspect of Dostoevskii's literary carnivalisation is so far from Russian folklore that it need not be discussed here. Nevertheless, elements of carnivalisation are characteristic of facets of Russian folk culture. It is true that the features of carnival ritual known in medieval Europe, in particular the crowning of a joke king who is then stripped of his powers, extensive role reversal and cross-dressing, are less manifest in the Russian folk tradition. However, some of the underlying concepts of carnival were present in the folk festivals of Russia, not just at Lent but also at other times of year and more widely in folklore. The year was divided into ordinary work days (*budnye dni*) and festivals, when it was sinful to work, as witnessed in the word for festival, *prazdnik*, meaning a day without work. Every festival was therefore in some sense a reversal of normal procedures and life, when conventionally prohibited behaviour, such as sexual licence and excessive eating and drinking, was sanctioned, and work was banned (ill luck would befall anyone who tried working on a *prazdnik*). In fact the idea of the reversal of accepted situations and structures is characteristic of other aspects of folklore as well, in particular certain types of folktale. Furthermore, motifs of non-recognition and subsequent discovery are also a feature of some folktales, as well as of ballads, Christian legends, spiritual songs and the phenomenon of holy foolishness. Not all of these involve life-affirming carnivalistic humour, although the type of folktale that involves reversal of hierarchies, thereby mocking the rich and powerful, is intended to be comic. The laughter certainly does offer a release from everyday tensions for the audience as in the Bakhtinian carnival, but it is cruel laughter and so not positively life-affirming. Indeed this type of tale, which operates on the principle of wish fulfilment, may arguably be said to be not anarchic but supportive of the status quo, since it allows the poor and deprived to fantasise before reverting to drab reality. It is right, I think, to question the life-affirming nature of carnivalistic elements in Dostoevskii, especially in *The Devils*, and to see the buffoonery and cruel pranks in that novel as more closely linked to Russian folk culture where laughter can be diabolical. The suggestion that the grotesque and disgusting actions of the holy fool are 'performed in order to confound the world, to damn those who are already damned and to see only the saint's outward appearance' (Murav, *Holy Foolishness*, p. 10) fits better with Dostoevskii's novels as a whole, his polyphonic narrative manner included. Within the text the author effaces himself by giving his characters independent voices. His narrative approach, combining authorial effacement and literary provocation (readers' expectations are confounded and boundaries shifted), reflects the paradoxical aspects of the holy fool, who also effaces his true self while provoking and challenging the world through his appearance and behaviour (ibid., pp. 13–14). This is not to suggest that Dostoevskii consciously transposed the holy fool model into his manner of narration, but rather that holy foolishness was a product of the folk heritage forming his cultural context, one to which he was closely attuned and which most clearly embodied some of his most cherished ideas about Russian Christianity and the essence of Russianness.

This survey has certainly not covered every instance of the facets of folk culture discussed above. Space constraints have dictated the total omission of, or briefest of reference to, others. One that should be mentioned without fail is the folk subtext to the relationship between Prince Myshkin and Rogozhin in *The Idiot*. Although the sacred quality of friendship sealed with a brotherhood pact is, as already noted, recorded in a variant of the spiritual song 'Lament of the Earth', in fact much closer links exist with oral and written versions of a Christian legend, 'The Sworn Brother of Christ', about an encounter between a man, in one version a rich merchant like Rogozhin, and Christ (who is unrecognised).[24] The motif of the exchange of crosses (VIII, 184–5; Pt 2, Sec. 4), for example, derives from the legend, and, along with holy-foolish elements in the character of Myshkin, underscores his presentation as a Christ-like figure. Equally, in the depiction of Maria Lebiadkina, perhaps the most folklorised character in the whole of Dostoevskii's work, we find multiple references to folklore in the realisation of her image: not just to the holy fool tradition and connections with Mary, Mother of God, through her name and attachment to Mother Earth, but also to wedding ritual and the folklore about childbirth and baptism, as a way of lending her symbolic meaning as a representative of folk Russia, downtrodden, with her true essence disguised. Her surname, Lebiadkina, connects her with swans, a traditional image for the maiden in folk lyrics and wedding laments, while her use of the term 'prince' is partly taken from the folk wedding ritual, in which the groom was termed 'prince' (although it also carries overtones of 'the prince of darkness'). In the week-long ceremony the bride was kept secluded in a kind of limbo awaiting the groom during which she ritually lamented the loss of her carefree unmarried existence and expressed dread of the future. Maria too is a bride, in an unconsummated marriage, and so exists in a kind of limbo. Many details in her depiction suggest that she symbolises folk Russia, in particular her connection with fortune-telling, which in the village context was seen as tapping into the unclean force, and hence potentially dangerous. For example, a girl divining with a mirror at midnight, in the hope of glimpsing her intended in the glass, risked seeing not him but the devil.[25] Maria's marriage to Stavrogin is thus a union with the devil (revealed in her recognition that Stavrogin is not her prince), but may be said to represent Russia's doomed marriage to Western political ideas. Maria can only wait and mourn the loss of her child, whose very existence can be doubted and who she says she carried unbaptised through the forest to a pond. Unbaptised children were thought unacceptable to Mother Earth and at risk from attack by the unclean spirits who dwelt in forests and pools. This hypothetical child may represent the vain desire for fruit from this union of traditional Russia and Western political ideas – vain because it is damned.

As a final illustration of a folk subtext furnishing an extra layer of meaning, one may note that in folk belief the mouse was a creature who emerged from a dark place and so was thought to bring catastrophe. A mouse inside someone's clothing meant misfortune, but seeing a mouse foreshadowed death (Ryan, *Bathhouse*, p. 54). In *Crime and Punishment* Svidrigailov holes up in a miserable hotel room smelling of mice on the night before he commits suicide. As he is dozing off, a mouse scurries over his body inside his shirt (VI, 389–90; Pt 6, Sec. 6). The detail is unpleasant enough, but the meaning of the folk omen underscores the significance of the suicide of a man who is spiritually dead and who in the previous few lines has thrice invoked the devil. Folk belief may well also add resonance to the choice of the name Myshkin (from *mysh'* meaning 'a mouse') for the hero of *The Idiot*. His surname starkly contrasts with his Christian name, Lev (lion), but, thanks to the folk connotations, may express less the contrasting aspects of his character (a certain boldness combined with meekness) than his fate and that of other characters who come in contact with him (the death, unhappiness, illness and destruction which dominate the end of the novel).

In conclusion, it may be said that in his work of the pre-Siberian period, Dostoevskii was already beginning to move away from the simple ethnographic references of *Poor Folk* and the stylised literary usage of *The Landlady* towards multiple parallel references to a range of discourses in a single image, episode or character (as illustrated by the examples from *The Double*). Later this method was considerably refined and developed. In the figure of Petr Verkhovenskii in *The Devils*, for example, we have references not only to biblical and folk devils, but also to the revolutionary Nechaev and Petr's namesake Petrushka, the Punch figure of the Russian puppet theatre. Petr Verkhovenskii's swaggering boastfulness and aggressive attitude to others, together with the potential for anarchy and violence that spreads out into the whole revolutionary circle, link him to the figure of Petrushka, who, despite his Italian origins, had acquired local features in Russia, notably a greater predilection for violence.[26] Dostoevskii certainly thought of Petrushka as completely Russianised. Even Petr's hunchbacked appearance underlines the connection, although, as we have seen, his facial features, though not dissimilar to Petrushka's, are clearly demonic. Through the reference to the puppet theatre Dostoevskii further underlines the destructive quality of the 'comic' pranks of Petr and his circle (Leatherbarrow, 'Devils' vaudeville', pp. 290–3).

Consider also the choice of three brothers as the heroes of *The Brothers Karamazov*. Although the number three has obvious Christian resonances, the fact that Alesha, the true hero, is the youngest immediately suggests a parallel with the type of wonder tale in which the youngest son of three is an apparent fool. Despite his unpromising exterior, the fool ultimately turns out wiser than his brothers, and is the one who gets the 'prize'. As has already been noted, Alesha's unworldliness also links him both to the holy fool and (in other respects) to St Alexis. The final portrait, here as elsewhere, is a complex web of allusions and symbols, based on the motif of a poor or ugly exterior concealing inner qualities.

Without question Dostoevskii's selection of material from folklore reflects his own interests, primarily in the positive Christian values he saw embodied within it, even to the point of integrating into the text actual folk legends, such as Grushenka's tale of the onion in *The Brothers Karamazov*. At other times he might also employ direct quotation from various sung genres, such as laments and folk or popular urban songs, mostly in order to add depth to characterisation. Above all, however, his personal view of religious virtue coincided with the values of the spiritual songs, while his interest in the inner essence or motivation of his characters drew him increasingly to characters and situations depicting unrecognised virtue (hence the attraction of the holy fool). In *The Devils* in particular he also presents the reverse situation, instances of imposture (Stavrogin, for example), drawing on the historical and folkloric view of royal impostors as allied with demonic forces (Leatherbarrow, 'Devil's vaudeville', pp. 293–8), as well as the common motif of the devil disguised found in tales of various kinds. Dostoevskii's selection is highly distinctive, for there is much in Russian folklore that lauds aspirations and values he could never have approved of: one thinks of the huge number of tales, songs and *bylichki* in which the acquisition of riches makes up the happy ending, or of historical songs in which the hero does not reject the possibility of a reward of property and money in order to embrace a life of poverty and humility, preferring to get the wherewithal to drink himself stupid whenever he wants. Dostoevskii's choice of sources is, however, entirely consistent with his literary aims, which dictated both the focus on religious themes and his interest in representations and concepts of evil and wrongdoing in Russian folklore. Interwoven with other folk, biblical, literary, political and social discourses, Russian folk-cultural references contribute to the process whereby Dostoevskii's works transcend the description of apparently finite events in finite places and assume great metaphysical significance. They add another dimension to a reading of this profoundly Russian writer.

Notes

1 Leonid Grossman, *Dostoevsky: A Biography*, trans. Mary Mackler (London: Allen Lane, 1974), p. 180.
2 See his collection of sayings in the 'Siberian Notebook' (IV, 235–48).
3 Joseph Frank, *Dostoevsky: The Seeds of Revolt, 1821–1849* (Princeton University Press, 1977), pp. 48–9; G. Gibian, 'Dostoevsky's use of Russian folklore', *Journal of American Folklore* 69 (1956), p. 239.
4 *Diary of a Writer* for 1873 (XXI, 134).
5 On the links with the wonder tale see V. E. Vetlovskaia, 'F. M. Dostoevskii' in A. A. Gorelov (ed.), *Russkaia literatura i fol'klor. (Vtoraia polovina XIX veka)* (Russian Literature and Folklore) (Leningrad: Nauka, 1982), pp. 12–75.
6 On the folkloric and pseudofolkloric elements in this story: see V. E. Vetlovskaia, 'Poeticheskaia deklaratsiia rannego Dostoevskogo (Simvolika povesti *Khoziaika*)' (Poetic declaration in the early Dostoevskii), *Zbornik za slavistiku* 28 (1985), pp. 91–104.
7 Harriet Murav, *Holy Foolishness: Dostoevsky's Novels and the Poetics of Cultural Critique* (Stanford University Press, 1992), p. 6.
8 Carl R. Proffer (ed.), *The Unpublished Dostoevsky: Diaries and Notebooks, 1860–81*, 3 vols. (Ann Arbor: Ardis, 1973–6), vol. 2, p. 98.
9 On Mother Earth and the relationship with the Mother of God, see Joanna Hubbs, *Mother Russia: The Feminine Myth in Russian Culture* (Bloomington and Indianapolis: Indiana University Press, 1988), pp. 52–86, 99–101, 114–16.
10 L. A. Zander, *Dostoevsky*, trans. Natalie Duddington (London: SCM Press, 1948), pp. 53–4, cites examples of the equation between Mary and earth/nature from the Orthodox liturgy.
11 See the chapter 'Klin' in Aleksandr Radishchev's *Journey from Petersburg to Moscow* (1790).
12 On Maria and the cult of the earth, see Linda J. Ivanits, 'Dostoevskij's Mar'ja Lebjadkina', *Slavic and East European Journal* 22 (1978), pp. 130–1.
13 See V. E. Vetlovskaia, 'Literaturnye i fol'klornye istochniki "Brat'ev Karamazovykh"' (Literary and folkloric sources of *The Brothers Karamazov*) in V. Kirpotin (ed.), *Dostoevskii i russkie pisateli. Traditsii, novatorstvo, masterstvo* (Dostoevskii and Russian Writers) (Moscow: Sovetskii pisatel', 1971), pp. 325–54, on the respective roles played by hagiographical and folk sources in the image of Alesha.
14 See Irina Paperno, *Suicide as a Cultural Institution in Dostoevsky's Russia* (Ithaca, N.Y. and London: Cornell University Press, 1997).
15 Linda J. Ivanits, 'Folk beliefs about the unclean force in *The Brothers Karamazov*' in George L. Gutsche and Lauren G. Leighton (eds.), *New Perspectives on Nineteenth-Century Russian Prose* (Columbus, Ohio: Slavica, 1982), p. 142.
16 Linda Ivanits, 'Suicide and folk beliefs in Dostoevsky's *Crime and Punishment*' in D. Offord (ed.), *The Golden Age of Russian Literature and Thought* (New York:

St Martins Press, 1992), pp. 139–40; Paperno, *Suicide*, pp. 52–5. Curiously, Paperno does not accept that the idea of demonic incitement to suicide was a common folk belief, though she admits it existed.

17 W. F. Ryan, *The Bathhouse at Midnight: An Historical Survey of Magic and Divination in Russia*, Magic in History Series (Stroud: Sutton, 1999), pp. 127–8.

18 On the attributes of the folk devil, see Faith Wigzell, 'The Russian folk devil and his literary reflections' in Pamela Davidson (ed.), *Russian Literature and its Demons* (Oxford: Berghahn, 2000), pp. 59–86.

19 For more details see W. J. Leatherbarrow, 'The devils' vaudeville: "decoding" the demonic in Dostoevsky's *The Devils*' in Davidson (ed.), *Russian Literature and its Demons*, pp. 279–306; Ivanits, 'Folk beliefs'.

20 Unfortunately these references are variously rendered in English translations of Dostoevskii, thereby losing any sense of the demonic infiltration of certain characters' language.

21 J. M. Lotman and B. A. Uspenskij, 'New aspects in the study of early Russian culture' in A. Shukman (ed.), *The Semiotics of Russian Culture*, Michigan Slavic Contributions, 11 (Ann Arbor: Dept. of Slavic Languages and Literatures, University of Michigan, 1984), p. 40.

22 On the history of the phenomenon in Russia see Ewa M. Thompson, *Understanding Russia: The Holy Fool in Russian Culture* (Lanham, Md: University Press of America, 1987); Murav, *Holy Foolishness*, pp. 17–31.

23 For an English version see M. M. Bakhtin, *Problems of Dostoevsky's Poetics*, ed. and trans. Caryl Emerson (Manchester University Press, 1984).

24 L. M. Lotman, 'Romany Dostoevskogo i russkaia legenda' (Dostoevskii's novels and Russian legend), *Russkaia Literatura* 15 (1972), no. 2, pp. 132–5.

25 Faith Wigzell, *Reading Russian Fortunes: Print Culture, Gender and Divination in Russia from 1765* (Cambridge University Press, 1998), pp. 47–8.

26 Catriona Kelly, *Petrushka, the Russian Carnival Puppet Theatre* (Cambridge University Press, 1990), pp. 84–91.

3

W. J. LEATHERBARROW

Dostoevskii and literature: works of the 1840s

Dostoevskii's correspondence of the 1840s, and in particular the letters sent to his brother Mikhail, to whom he was especially close both emotionally and intellectually, disclose an individual acutely sensitive to his role as a budding author. On the most immediate level the letters reveal Dostoevskii's keen awareness of the economic realities of the profession he has decided to adopt. References to money, indebtedness and publishers' advances are everywhere, alongside the occasional and not entirely convincing assertion that he writes primarily for money: 'What's the point of fame here, when I'm writing to earn a crust?' (XXVIII/1, 106; letter of 24 March 1845). He describes the writer's relationship to the publisher as that of a slave to his master (XXVIII/1, 128; 7 October 1846) and even draws attention to the alarming number of German poets who have died of hunger and cold or have ended up in asylums (XXVIII/1, 108; 24 March 1845). Behind these details we can discern Dostoevskii's emerging awareness of himself as a figure in an established literary tradition. He constantly refers to and compares himself to other writers, both European and Russian: he relates his financial hardship to that experienced by Pushkin and Gogol before their fame was secure (XXVIII/1, 107; 24 March 1845); in revising for the umpteenth time his drafts of *Poor Folk*, he justifies himself by reference to the writing and rewriting practices of Chateaubriand, Pushkin, Gogol and Laurence Sterne (XXVIII/1, 108; 4 May 1845); he draws comfort from the fact that the hostility aroused in some quarters by his novel is no worse than that experienced by Pushkin and Gogol; and he is sensitive to the fact that he is in competition with several other new writers such as Goncharov and Herzen (XXVIII/1, 120; 1 April 1846). With the success of *Poor Folk* he also becomes extravagantly aware of his own fame and pre-eminence in contemporary Russian literature.

A particularly interesting development from this is the fact that Dostoevskii derives from this sense of being in a literary tradition not only his self-image, but also on occasion his voice and verbal persona. We sense in his letters from as early as 1838 the discontinuity between the dry narrative style in which

47

he recounts his school experiences and the assumption of a romantically elevated linguistic register in order to discuss literary matters. For example, in referring to a poem by his brother, he comments that 'inspiration, like a heavenly mystery, sanctifies the pages over which you have wept and posterity will continue to weep' (XXVIII/1, 55; 31 October 1838). Elsewhere, he describes the sufferings of his friend Ivan Shidlovskii in terms of those experienced by literary characters such as Pushkin's Onegin (XXVIII/1, 68; 1 January 1840). These examples are perhaps a mark of the young Dostoevskii's naivety and a measure of the extent to which he has withdrawn from reality, but they also suggest the degree to which the experience of literature was incorporated into the way he saw his world.

This chapter attempts to explore the related theme of how literature and Dostoevskii's willingness to appropriate it inform the way he approached the writing of his own fictional texts in the 1840s. By this I do not mean to offer a study of how other writers might have 'influenced' Dostoevskii, for this has been attempted many times before, and in any case it is debatable whether so general a concept as 'influence' can be reduced to anything genuinely meaningful in attempting to understand how Dostoevskii went about his writing. Instead, what follows takes the form of two case studies of specific ways in which the discussion of literature and writing forms part of the author's strategies in the creation of his early works. The first of these looks at the ways in which Dostoevskii's first novel exploits the opportunities offered by the epistolary narrative form for setting up a tension between the contributions made to the text by the letter-writers, on the one hand, and by the author-figure on the other. The second examines the use made of 'source' texts by Pushkin and Gogol throughout Dostoevskii's work of this period.

Poor Folk

The figure of the little government clerk, crushed by poverty and his own insignificance in the bureaucratic and social hierarchy in which he worked and lived, had become a cliché of the so-called Natural School of Russian literature by the 1840s. Championed by the great social and literary critic Vissarion Belinskii, the 'School' was characterised by works structured upon the naturalistic description of the lower reaches of Russian social life, often combined with a sentimental account of the depredations inflicted by that society on its lowly victims. Today, the reader who adopts Belinskii's reading of Poor Folk and interprets the figures of Makar Devushkin and Varvara Dobroselova just as social lessons, incarnations of the downtrodden heroes of sentimental naturalism and material for those who would champion social equality, will surely quickly tire of the drab self-righteousness of these characters. That is not to say that we should not acknowledge their origins in the portrait gallery of the Natural School. However, the reader who goes on to recognise both them and their correspondence as products of, and ingredients in, Dostoevskii's playful engagement with his own reading and his reflection on literary traditions and forms will sense above all the striking modernity (if not 'post-modernity') of his first novel. To read *Poor Folk* simply as a critically engaged, naturalistic work is to consign it to the past as a not particularly inspired example of the European social novel. To read it as a meditation on literature is to set free its rich, sophisticated and enduring irony.

Both explicitly and implicitly, the discussion of literature is everywhere in *Poor Folk*. On the one hand, and despite Dostoevskii's protestation in a letter of 1 February 1846 that he does not allow his own 'mug' to show in the novel (XXVIII/1, 117), we sense the presence of the young author knocking at the door of literary fame and affirming his credentials for admission through a display of his own reading. Literary allusions are scattered like calling cards as Dostoevskii seeks to locate his novel against a background of literary tradition and history. Thus the very form chosen for the novel invites us to consider its relationship to the traditional practice of the epistolary novel. Is Dostoevskii betraying his inexperience by the adoption of an outmoded form, or is he seeking to renegotiate the terms of its practice? There are many other references to individual authors and works of literature. The servants in the house are referred to as Teresa and Faldoni, after the heroes of a sentimental epistolary novel by the French writer N. G. Léonard, translated into Russian in 1804. The inserted narrative of Varenka's early life owes much to the plot of *Katenka, or the Child of Misfortune*, the translation of a novel by F. G. Ducray-Duminil which appeared in Russia in 1820. (In the original the heroine's name is Emma.) The works of Ducray-Duminil were very popular in Russia, and Makar Devushkin makes reference to another of them, *The Little Bell-Ringer* (1, 59; 1 July). Devushkin is ironically referred to by his fellow-lodger Rataziaev as Lovelace, the hero of Samuel Richardson's novel *Clarissa* (1, 79; 11 August). Rataziaev himself is a *littérateur*, much admired by Devushkin but recognisable to the reader, through the texts that Devushkin quotes verbatim and at length, as a parody of the over-blown Romanticism of A. A. Bestuzhev-Marlinskii and other writers of the time (1, 52–3; 26 June). At one point, oblique reference is made to the current Russian taste for the literary 'physiological sketch': 'books with little pictures and various descriptions' (1, 60; 1 July), and Devushkin's letter of 5 September contains an implied engagement with Grigorovich's work in that mode, *The Organ-Grinders of St Petersburg* (1, 86). Most evident of all, of course, among the metafictional elements of *Poor Folk* is the polemic it sustains with Pushkin and Gogol, as Devushkin confronts in their works what he sees as conflicting images of himself. Other literary allusions to which we could refer have already been treated at length in the existing critical literature.[1]

Of course, the epistolary form of *Poor Folk* means that such references to Dostoevskii's reading emerge initially as evidence of Devushkin's. This alerts us to the fact that this is a text in which, as Vinogradov has pointed out,[2] the hero himself becomes a man of letters and sometimes wittingly, but more often than not unwittingly, defines and refines his self-image through the medium of literature. By making Devushkin a writer and allowing direct access to his correspondence with Varvara, Dostoevskii enriches *Poor Folk* with the ambiguities offered by an apparently unmediated narrative form. For example, from the outset he exploits the epistolary novel's pretence at the condition of 'framelessness', i.e. the apparent absence of an overall organising authorial presence. We are almost, but not quite, plunged directly into the correspondence, and the novel ends with us reading Devushkin's final despairing letter. The words on the page are those of the participants in the fiction: no conclusions are drawn, nor any comments made, in the absence of an authoritative narrative voice. As Dostoevskii wrote to his brother Mikhail in February 1846, 'people don't understand how it is possible to write in such a style. They are accustomed to seeing the author's mug in everything, and I have not shown mine. It never occurred to them that it is Devushkin speaking, not me, and that Devushkin cannot speak in any other way' (XXVIII/1, 117).

But, as John Jones has pointed out,[3] this is a tease on Dostoevskii's part, and the pretence at framelessness is a device used by the author to enlarge the concerns of his novel beyond those accessible to its protagonists. The clearest evidence of the fallacy of authorlessness is the presence of an epigraph. Who put it there? And for what purpose? Given its content and its impatient dismissal of storytellers who write about unsavoury matters, we can be certain that it does not come from either Devushkin or Varvara, unless in their metaliterary guise they have assumed a hitherto unsuspected sense of irony. Moreover, the epigraph is not a neutral quotation from Prince V. F. Odoevskii's tale *A Living Corpse* (1838): it has been altered. The infinitive form *zapretit'* (to forbid), which in Odoevskii's original yields the impersonal final sentence: 'They should be forbidden from writing; they should simply be forbidden altogether', is replaced in the text of *Poor Folk* by a masculine past tense, which changes the emphasis to the much more personal: 'I would forbid them from writing; I would simply forbid them altogether.' Is this an insignificant and unintentional event, a mere mistranscription on Dostoevskii's part, one more likely in the old Russian orthography of the time? Or is it a conscious attempt to conjure up a narrative persona out of a deliberate misquotation? If so, who is this 'I'? Is it Dostoevskii 'showing his mug' after all? Or, more intriguingly, is it the malevolent Rataziaev, the author who not only threatens to put Devushkin and Varvara in a novel, but who is also in a position to lay hands on their correspondence? Devushkin's final letter implies that he is ill and that his days are numbered, and we can be certain that he has kept all Varvara's letters to him for his nosy neighbour to find after his death. Moreover, before her departure Varvara writes that she has left all Devushkin's letters to her in the top drawer of a chest of drawers in Fedora's room, a clear trail that Rataziaev might have followed!

Definitive answers to the questions identified above are elusive, but in any case they are less important than the fact that such questions are raised in a way that invites us to focus on the nature of the text of *Poor Folk*. The same is true of the gaps in the correspondence that have been noted by John Jones. He supplies convincing textual evidence that some letters are missing from the correspondence as it is presented.[4] Compare this with Varvara's insistence, cited above, that she has returned *all* Devushkin's letters! Such missing letters also eat away at the illusion of framelessness, for *someone* has decided to omit them from the exchange while simultaneously leaving evidence pointing to the fact that they once existed. Through such tactics *Poor Folk* is transformed from straightforward naturalistic novel into one that invites meditation on its own status and condition.

The narrative of *Poor Folk* creates gaps not only in the sequence of the correspondence, but also in the perceptions supported by that correspondence. The fact that we witness events as the protagonists see and understand them means that we are party to their perceptual failures and to their emotional and intellectual limitations. Varvara's account of her friendship with the student Pokrovskii, for example, contains (but does not actively *present*) evidence suggesting that he is the illegitimate son of Bykov. We draw this conclusion easily from facts that Varvara reports without appearing to understand their import:

> But fate smiled upon the young Pokrovskii. The landowner Bykov, who knew the clerk Pokrovskii and had once been his benefactor, took the boy under his wing and placed him in some school or other. He took an interest in him because he had known his late mother, who while still a girl had received the good favours of Anna Fedorovna and had been married off by her to the clerk Pokrovskii [. . .] They say that his mother was very good looking, and it seems strange to me that she should have made such an unsuccessful match to such an insignificant man . . .   (1, 33; 1 June)

The narrative irony is thick here. Is Varvara so stupid that she does not see the implications of what she writes? Or is she fully aware and unwilling to say more to Devushkin because of the similarity of the mother's fate to her own seduction by Bykov? In either case we will recall this episode later when Devushkin recounts how he has been on the receiving end of the good favours of his superior:

> It is not only me he has been good to: he is known to everyone for the goodness of his heart. From many quarters people sing his praises and shed tears of gratitude. He brought up an orphan girl in his house. He made all the arrangements for her: he married her off to a certain man, a clerk who lived in His Excellency's home in order to carry out special commissions for him. He set up the son of a certain widow in a government office, and has done many other good deeds like that. (I, 95; 11 September)

Critics of Dostoevskii's novel have on the whole taken this episode at face value, seeing in His Excellency's generosity a humane reversal of Akakii Akakievich's treatment by his superior in Gogol's *The Overcoat*. Devushkin's outrage at the lack of humanity in Gogol's story, of course, encourages such a reading. But the spectre of Bykov's similar 'good deeds' hangs over and ironises His Excellency's behaviour here, poisoning any admiration we may be tempted to feel, and leading us to believe that Devushkin in his naivety has entirely missed the point, both about his superior and about *The Overcoat*.

We also see Varvara through Devushkin's eyes, as well as through her own words. Is she what she seems – a downtrodden and sexually abused innocent – or is this a misreading conjured out of a combination of Devushkin's naive and slavish devotion, Varvara's desire to present herself in the best possible light, and our own expectations as readers of what we take, initially at least, to be a sentimental epistolary novel? Varvara's wholesome image becomes increasingly threadbare as the novel progresses and our expectations are revised. Her surname, which like most names in Dostoevskii is significant, initially suggests *dobro* ('good'). However, in view of her enthusiasm for the good things in life shortly before her marriage to Bykov, and her gross insensitivity in urging the spurned Devushkin to do her pre-nuptial shopping for her, there may be an ironic reference here to the other meaning of *dobro* – 'property' – and to the verb *selit'sia* ('to take up residence'). We have already seen how her 'love' for Devushkin does not extend to keeping his letters, which she discards before leaving (I, 106; 30 September), and when Devushkin visits her room after her departure, he finds that she has used one of his 'miserable little letters' to wind her wool (I, 105; 29 September). On other occasions she incites him to borrow money at exorbitant interest so she can move to a new flat (I, 73; 4 August). She deflates his delight at the thought that her raised curtain might be a lover's signal – 'I never gave it a thought; it must have got caught up when I moved the flower pot' (1, 18; 8 April) – and discourages any view he might have of himself as a romantic suitor by telling him not to worry about what the neighbours might think: 'You're a friend, and that's all there is to it!' (1, 22; 9 April).

We also wonder about her status as an innocent victim of sexual abuse who is otherwise pure. The words in which she describes her early life with Anna Fedorovna are evasive and softened by the conceits of the sentimental tale in which they are embedded (for Varvara writes more than letters!), but their meaning emerges – for us, if not for Devushkin:

> Anna Fedorovna lived very well, much better than one might have supposed; but the source of her wealth was unclear, as were her affairs [. . .] She had a large and varied circle of acquaintances. She had a constant stream of visitors, and Lord knows what kind of people they were, always dropping in on some kind of business and never staying very long. Mother always took me off to our room as soon as the front door-bell rang. Anna Fedorovna was terribly angry at mother for this and constantly insisted that we were too proud [. . .] To this day it's a mystery to me precisely why she [Anna] invited us to stay with her.
> (1, 30; June 1)

Despite the coy final protestation of ignorance, it is clear that Anna's business is prostitution; she is a procuress and Varvara is one of her victims. The latter implicitly acknowledges the sexual nature of her past relationship with Bykov in terms hesitant enough to pass over Devushkin's head, but clear enough to the reader: 'She [Anna] says that Mr Bykov is completely in the right and that a man does not simply go and marry every girl who . . . but why write about that!' (1, 25; 25 April). What is not clear is her present moral status: officers still importune her, and she lets slip the intriguing detail that, before finally offering to marry her, Bykov has made extensive and detailed enquiries about her '*present* behaviour' (1, 100; 23 September – my italics)! Such details, allowed to float free and unmediated in the epistolary novel's convention of authorlessness, invest with great irony the moment when Devushkin reports what he takes to be the outrage of the neighbours over his pursuit of the much younger Varvara: 'The landlady told me people are saying that the devil has taken up with the infant, and then she called you by an indecent name' (1, 70; 1 August). We wonder who is the devil and who is the infant, particularly given the virginal implications of Devushkin's name (*devushka* – 'maiden').

Such inversions of the conventions of the sentimental epistolary novel are the essence of *Poor Folk*. Joseph Frank has pointed out that the very fact of handing the correspondence over to a middle-aged copying clerk and a dishonoured girl violates the conventions of a form used traditionally to express the 'lofty feelings and noble thoughts' of 'models of virtue and sensibility', 'exemplary figures from the point of view of education and breeding'.[5] Not that such conventions had always been slavishly followed in the past: Choderlos de Laclos's *Dangerous Liaisons* (1782) had offered a correspondence about seduction and the corruption of virtue that avoided sentiment in favour of a sophisticated amoralism. There is no direct evidence that Dostoevskii ever read Laclos's novel: there is no reference to it in his writings and we have no indication that it was in his library. The reader of *Poor Folk* may nonetheless feel that the work nods in the direction of *Dangerous Liaisons* by offering an account of seduction and manipulation, written on this occasion from the point of view of the victims.

'What a fine thing literature is!' Devushkin's words after his induction into Rataziaev's literary evenings remind us that, thanks to the epistolary form of *Poor Folk*, it is not just Dostoevskii who is in a position to exploit the potential of the written word for making things seem what they are not. Devushkin may well possess execrable literary taste, admiring Rataziaev's prose and mentioning in the same breath Homer and the popular writer Baron Brambeus (1, 16; 8 April), but he understands instinctively the creative power of writing. In his position of social inferiority, helplessness and total dependence on the will of those above him, literature is something that allows him to assume a measure of control over his life. He uses words to *re-present* things as he would like them to be and to impose order and meaning on the contingency around him. This is evident from the very start of his correspondence with Varvara, where he uses words like sheepdogs to round up and close off the unpleasantness of his new surroundings:

> I live in the kitchen, or rather it would be much more accurate to put it this way: right next to the kitchen there's a room (and I must point out to you that our kitchen is clean, light, and a very nice one), a small room, a modest sort of corner [...] that is, or to put it even better, the kitchen has three windows, and I have a partition running along the side wall, so that you end up with what is practically another room, a supernumerary one; everything is spacious, convenient, and there's a window and everything – in a word, it is all most convenient. (1, 16; 8 April)

These apparent verbal tics (what does that final '*and everything*' mean?) are not fortuitous: they are the considered choices of a careful writer who, as we later learn almost by chance, writes *drafts* of his letters (1, 79; 11 August)! They are a part of Devushkin's constant preoccupation with *style*, something that is not a natural extension of his normal being, but a mode that he assumes, no doubt in recognition of the fact that the only control he possesses over his life is over how he *writes* it (see, for example, I, 88, 91; 5–9 September). This explains his desire to be a poet and to publish *The Poems of Makar Devushkin*. It explains also his verbal flights of fancy on the winged horse Pegasus in order to escape the smell of rotting rubbish under his window (I, 19; 8 April). But, above all, it explains the nature of his engagement with Pushkin's *The Stationmaster* and Gogol's *The Overcoat*, for he sees these works primarily as the attempts of others to write his life for him.

Devushkin's enthusiasm for *The Stationmaster* is based on his conviction that 'it is real! It is life!' (I, 59; I July). But, of course, it is not life: it is literature, a work of the imagination that has managed to write the life of the little man as Devushkin himself would like. 'I am dim-witted and stupid by nature,' he writes, 'and I cannot read works that are too weighty. But you read this one and it is as though I had written it myself; as though, so to speak, I had taken my own heart, just as it is, and turned it inside out for people to see and described it all in detail. And it's so simple, by God!' Devushkin's confusion of life with literature, and his belief that Pushkin's work is 'simple', betray his own lack of sophistication as a reader and his lack of alertness to the possibility of ambiguity. For *The Stationmaster* is part of a larger work, *The Tales of Belkin*, so that, like Devushkin's, the life of Samson Vyrin is *framed* by a narrative structure that exploits to the full the potential for irony. Similarly his outrage at Gogol's unsympathetic 'lampoon' of the little clerk in *The Overcoat* culminates in Devushkin setting out how he would *rewrite* the work: 'It would have been best of all not to leave him to die, poor devil, but to have his overcoat be found and have that general find out more about his virtues, transfer him to his own office, give him a promotion and a decent increase in salary, so that then, you see, evil would be punished and virtue rewarded [. . .] That's how I, for example, would have done it' (I, 63; 8 July). Devushkin would like Gogol to have created a work and a hero in the tradition of sentimental naturalism; he cannot see the purpose of *The Overcoat* as it stands: 'What is the point of writing such things? What use does it serve?' His own narrow view of literature as 'a picture and a mirror' that 'fortifies people's hearts and instructs them' (I, 51; 26 June) – a view matching that of Belinskii and the Natural School – prevents him from seeing that the figure of Akakii Akakievich is a convention, an ingredient in a complex and grotesque literary game being played by his creator. The real irony, of course, arises from the way this mirrors the conflict emerging between Devushkin's literary aspirations and those of *his* creator. For while Devushkin's letters allow him to 'turn his heart inside out' and write himself and his relationship with Varvara as he would like them to be seen, the implicit frame that encloses these letters, one that derives from and exploits the ambiguities of the epistolary form, transforms these characters, like Akakii, into ingredients in a literary game being played above their heads. To put it another way: while Devushkin attempts to write himself and Varvara into the portrait gallery of the Natural School, Dostoevskii is busy writing them out.

The final achievement of this game is to rob Devushkin of his role as unrequited lover and *Poor Folk* of the primary thematic ingredient of any pretensions it might have to being a novel of sentimental naturalism: its love story. The hero's final letter certainly reveals despair at the prospect of Varvara's departure, but it also makes clear that this despair derives largely from the loss of her as correspondent. In pleading with her to continue writing after her marriage, he says: 'Otherwise, my heavenly angel, this will be my last letter and, you see, there's no way this letter can be the last. I mean, how could it so suddenly be the last! No, I will write and you will write [. . .] Otherwise, the style I am now developing . . .' (I, 108). It is *writing to* Varvara, rather than Varvara herself, that has been the love of Devushkin's life for, as John Jones says, *Poor Folk* is not *that sort* of love story.[6] In fact, the writing ends and Devushkin disappears. We could read this naturalistically, take note of Devushkin's earlier references to his illness, and assume that he has died the touching death of a downtrodden hero of sentimental fiction. Or we could recognise that, just as *Poor Folk* is not that sort of love story, so Devushkin is not that sort of hero. What has come to an end is not his life, but his words: he has disappeared because he no longer *writes himself*.

Gogol and Pushkin

The discussion in *Poor Folk* of the relative merits of Gogol and Pushkin, at least as far as their depiction of the lowly individual is concerned, has attracted much critical attention from commentators who have seen it variously as evidence of Dostoevskii's indebtedness to Gogol, of his willingness to engage that writer polemically, or of his humanisation of Gogol's 'masks' using Pushkin's 'compassion' as a model. Most of this attention has focussed on Dostoevskii's literary relationship to Gogol, although Konstantin Mochulsky has argued that *Poor Folk* demonstrates how 'Dostoevskii was to learn the art of words from Gogol', but that he 'mastered the art of the psychological short story through the mentorship of Pushkin'.[7] Such views may well be correct in general terms, but in the particular instance of *Poor Folk* they overlook the fact that the preferences expressed in that novel's overt discussion of Gogol and Pushkin are Devushkin's, and there is no immediate reason to suppose that they necessarily coincide with those of Dostoevskii.

Notwithstanding such reservations, there is indeed evidence that the engagement with Gogol and Pushkin is not confined solely to Devushkin's discourse, but that it also inhabits the 'frame' of the novel and derives from the voice of an organising authorial presence. Such evidence might include our earlier argument that Devushkin and his creator are 'writing against each other', and that whereas Devushkin concentrates on characterisation in *The Overcoat* and *The Stationmaster*, the implicit authorial presence directs attention to the narrative frames of these works. A further example of the authorial presence operating in this way behind Devushkin's back is to be found in the latter's letter of 26 June. Devushkin's enthusiasm for Rataziaev's 'humorous' extract about Ivan Prokofevich Zheltopuz ('Yellowbelly') is not informed by awareness of that piece's parodistic relationship to the account of Anton Prokofevich Pupopuz ('Navel-Belly') in Gogol's *Tale of How Ivan Ivanovich Quarrelled with Ivan Nikiforovich*. The piece might well be Rataziaev's, but the use of Gogol to keep Devushkin in the dark, and to reveal his lack of literary awareness, is the responsibility of the framing authorial figure.

The implicit and explicit discussion of Gogol and Pushkin is extended into several of Dostoevskii's other works of the 1840s, and in these subsequent works there is further evidence of the responsibility for such discussion being assumed by the organising authorial voice. It would still be rash to talk uncritically in terms of such works disclosing 'Dostoevskii's views' on his two great precursors, and we must remain alert to the presence of narrative irony. But the continuing juxtaposition of the two writers is clearly suggestive of a metafictional purpose ascribable ultimately to Dostoevskii. For example, when at the start of *The Double* Goliadkin approaches his small round mirror in order to see whether a pimple or something similarly unpleasant has sprouted on his nose (1, 110; Ch. 1), it is not he who is steering the reader to recall the almost identical scene at the start of Gogol's *The Nose*. But somebody is. When the novel's narrator abandons imitation of Goliadkin's verbal characteristics in favour of a long, hyperbolically Gogolesque digression on the wonders of Klara Olsufevna's birthday party, bemoaning the fact that 'I am not a poet', we can be sure that this 'I' is not Goliadkin's but that of some organising parodistic presence (1, 128–31; Ch. 4). Similarly, when Goliadkin first confronts his double on a foul Petersburg night in November and is prompted by the sound of a cannon to wonder whether the Neva is about to flood (1, 140; Ch. 5), it is not he but the reader who recalls a similarly foul November night in Pushkin's *The Bronze Horseman*, when the hero Evgenii meets his nemesis – a statue of Peter the Great that chases him to madness through a flooded Petersburg landscape. Both *The Nose* and *The Bronze Horseman* are structured upon the presence of the uncanny, and their juxtaposition in the text of *The Double* serves to remind us that, whereas in *The Nose* the uncanny is rooted in the presence of the genuinely fantastic, in Dostoevskii's work, as in Pushkin's poem, it derives from the incipient madness of the hero. The juxtaposition thus serves the metaliterary function of suggesting to the reader how to read the uncanny experiences of Goliadkin. As in *Poor Folk*, this understanding between reader and authorial presence is struck behind the back of the character concerned, for Goliadkin is denied any such insight into the nature of what he is going through.

When *The Landlady* appeared in 1847 it provoked a confused and largely hostile response from Dostoevskii's contemporaries, and critical opinion has subsequently, with only a few exceptions, continued to dismiss it as a failure. The sticking point for many is the confusion produced by a point of view that never really secures itself, either in narrative objectivity or in the dramatisation of the hero's delirium as he falls beneath the spell of the beautiful Katerina and her forbidding companion Ilia Murin. As a result the work combines down-to-earth depiction of daily Petersburg life with soaringly exotic passages drawn from folk tradition. Belinskii saw it as a strange hybrid, an attempt 'to reconcile Marlinskii and Hoffmann, having stirred in a little humour of the latest kind and covering the whole thing in a lacquer of Russian folksiness', before dismissing it as 'terrible rubbish'. The first part of this judgement is not that far from the mark, for the key to *The Landlady* lies in the way source literary texts are reworked both on the fictional level, by the hero Ordynov, and on the metafictional level by the organising narrative voice. Malcolm Jones's comment about *The Double*, to the effect that collusion between reader and author generates the ghosts of other texts which serve to shed light on the text under consideration, is even more appropriate to *The Landlady*.[8] Such 'ghosts' help us to steer a course through the confusion of Ordynov's dream, when he falls ill shortly after moving in with Murin and Katerina. The apparently chaotic fantasy is domesticated and brought within the reader's experience by the gradual revelation that the dream is constructed from fragments of Ordynov's own reading. The attentive reader will discern images drawn from Lermontov's lyrics '1st January', 'Cossack Cradle Song' and 'The Angel', from Gogol's Ukrainian tales, especially *A Terrible Vengeance*, from Pushkin's *The Miserly Knight*, and from Russian folk literature – all of which we might reasonably expect to form part of the cultural 'baggage' of an educated Russian of the 1840s such as Ordynov. His almost complete estrangement from the mundane world means that for him literature comes to take the place of life, and the figures of Katerina and Murin are absorbed into an imaginative displacement of his experiences that is fed by source texts. The proximity of the narrative voice to Ordynov's subjective experience, and the absence of a clearly authoritative narrative voice to steer the reader, mean that the latter is drawn into the confusion of this displacement with only his ability to recognise those source texts as a means of self-orientation. The identification of such source texts has been widely treated in the critical literature on *The Landlady*, particular attention having been drawn to Ordynov's indebtedness to Gogol's *A Terrible Vengeance* in constructing the figures of Katerina and Murin for his delirium. Both Ordynov's tale and Gogol's story centre on a beautiful girl called Katerina and a malignant and possibly supernatural father-figure with whom, it is intimated, she conducts an incestuous relationship. In contrast, relatively little attention has been paid to the presence of works by Pushkin amongst the source texts of *The Landlady*, or to the fact that such source texts are not only used unwittingly by Ordynov to fuel his delirium, but are also manipulated quite consciously at authorial level for metafictional purposes, in particular to focus attention upon the status of the fantastic in this work.

In terms of overt acknowledgement Pushkin is much more evident in *The Landlady* than Gogol. In particular, Iaroslav Ilich, a police official and Ordynov's friend (insofar as we can tell through the confusion of the narrative), seems unable to resist mentioning him. When they first renew their acquaintance, Iaroslav remarks to Ordynov apropos of nothing that he has read a great deal since their last encounter: 'I have read all of Pushkin [. . .] He portrays human passion remarkably, sir' (1, 284; Pt 1, Sec. 3). Later, when discussing Murin's gifts as a fortune-teller, he counters Ordynov's scepticism by claiming: 'He is not a charlatan. Pushkin himself mentions something similar in his works' (1, 287; Pt 1, Sec. 3). At their final meeting Iaroslav again makes mention of his beloved Pushkin.

These surface allusions to Pushkin are supported by an undercurrent of covert gestures in the direction of his works. Iaroslav's comment on Murin's fortune-telling steers us towards *The Queen of Spades*; Ordynov's dream includes a vision of the dead rising from their graves, which brings to mind the lines from the Baron's monologue in scene 2 of *The Miserly Knight*: 'the moon grows dim and graves / Confounded send forth their dead'. Also, it is difficult not to see a resemblance between Katerina's tale of how the brigand Murin burned her father's barges on the Volga before running off with her and the following extract from Pushkin's drafts for the narrative poem *The Robber Brothers*: 'Near Astrakhan; they smash up the merchants' boat; he takes another woman – the other goes out of her mind.' In *The Landlady* Murin abandons Katerina's mother, who has been his mistress, in order to abscond with Katerina. The distraught mother then curses her daughter. The resemblance is striking, but inconclusive in the absence of evidence of Dostoevskii's familiarity with Pushkin's draft. More promising is the debt *The Landlady* seems to owe to Pushkin's folk tale *Ruslan and*

Liudmila. There are, of course, many folk motifs in Dostoevskii's tale: Murin
as a sorcerer with an apparently supernatural hold over Katerina; the suggestion that Katerina is his illegitimate daughter and that their relationship
is incestuous; Ordynov's assumption of the role of 'prince' pledged to her
liberation; the exotic speech of the characters, infused with the imagery and
inflections of folk literature. While acknowledging that these motifs are most
obviously traceable to Gogol's *A Terrible Vengeance*, we must not overlook
the ghosts of Pushkin's folk tale in Dostoevskii's text. Like *The Landlady*,
Ruslan and Liudmila describes the attempts of a young hero to rescue his
beloved from the clutches of a sorcerer. Like Murin, Pushkin's Chernomor
is 'an abductor of beautiful women' ('krasavits davnii pokhititel''), who has
ensnared the much younger heroine through mysterious means. Their names
also resonate: Chernomor implies 'black' (*chernyi*), as does Murin (a negro,
a Moor).

Given the unclear relationship of the narrative voice in *The Landlady* to
the consciousness of the hero, we must at least acknowledge the possibility
that such 'ghost' texts are brought into the overall narrative of the tale,
as similar ones are brought into his dream, by Ordynov himself from his
own reading. But to leave the matter there would be to overlook evidence
of the sort of collusion between author and reader mentioned by Jones,
a collusion that excludes the hero and frames his experiences. As in *The
Double*, the juxtaposition of works by Pushkin and Gogol here too serves
the more authoritative function of suggesting to the reader how to approach
the delirium of the hero and how to understand the part played by the
fantastic in the work. This function turns on the different attitudes to the
nature and role of the fantastic implicit in the works of Gogol and Pushkin.
In his early Ukrainian tales in particular Gogol shows a willingness to accept
the fantastic and incorporate it into his work on its own terms. In *A Terrible
Vengeance*, for example, there is no trace of irony in the account of sorcerers,
magic and ghosts. Indeed, this tale is one of the most humourless of Gogol's
works, and the incredible is presented without that ironic naivety which
gives the later Petersburg tales their peculiarly wry quality. In it the status
and nature of the supernatural go unchallenged. Pushkin's works, however,
rarely allow the reader the opportunity to accept the supernatural on its
own terms. It would be a particularly obtuse reader who took *Ruslan and
Liudmila* at face value, as a fairy tale pure and simple. As John Bayley has
indicated, the poem offers us not so much the fantastic as 'a sophisticated
sport with the fantastic'.[9] Its most striking feature, one that sets it apart
from *A Terrible Vengeance*, is the disbelief with which the author professes
his belief as he ironically transcends the limits of the genre by combining the
expected role of credulous narrator with a wholly unexpected one, that of

sceptical, worldly sophisticate. The result is a narrator who invites the reader to suspend his disbelief while at the same time encouraging that disbelief; who invites the reader into the world of the fantastic while simultaneously undermining the status and credibility of that world.

The Landlady is constructed on a similarly ironic manipulation of the fantastic, as the reader is invited to question its status in the light of Ordynov's psychological condition. Here too Dostoevskii's indebtedness to Pushkin, rather than Gogol, is clear, for Pushkin also had used fantasy as a key to his hero's psychological state in *The Queen of Spades*. The apparently supernatural events that befall Hermann may be seen merely as the subjective product of an imagination fed by guilt and irritated by drink, although to do so would be to rob the tale of the delicious ambiguity which Dostoevskii himself so admired:

> There is a limit and a rule for the fantastic in art. The fantastic must be so close to the real that you *almost* have to believe it. Pushkin, who has given us almost all forms of art, wrote *The Queen of Spades* – a masterpiece of fantastic art. And you believe that Hermann really had a vision, and one in precise agreement with his philosophy. However, at the end of the story, i.e. when you have read it through, you cannot make up your mind. Did this vision come out of Hermann's nature, or was he really one of those who are in contact with another world, one of the evil spirits hostile to mankind? [. . .] Now, that is art! (xxx/1, 192; letter of 15 June 1880)

It is therefore fitting that, in a stroke of authorial mischief towards the end of the tale, *The Landlady* should acknowledge its debt to Pushkin's treatment of the fantastic. The reader familiar with *The Queen of Spades* should have no difficulty recognising the resemblance between the scene where Hermann approaches the coffin of the dead Countess and the passage where Ordynov contemplates murdering the sleeping Murin:

> He looked at the old man . . .
>
> At that moment it seemed to him [*emu pokazalos'* – Pushkin expresses Hermann's uncertainty in the same words] that one of the old man's eyes slowly opened and looked at him laughingly. Their eyes met. For a few moments Ordynov looked at him without stirring [. . .] Suddenly it seemed to him that the old man's whole face broke into a laugh and that a diabolic, murderous and chilling burst of laughter at last resounded throughout the room.
>
> (1, 310; Pt 2, Sec. 2)

Dostoevskii's tale of 1846, *Mister Prokharchin*, also discusses themes to be found in works by Gogol and Pushkin – those of miserliness and insecurity – and like other works of the period it seeks to do so through a collusion between author and reader which emerges from the acknowledgement of ghost texts embedded in the narrative. In this work, however, unlike in *Poor Folk* and *The Landlady*, there is no possibility of confusion over whether these texts derive from the hero's reading or the author's. Responsibility for the generation of these source texts has now been assumed entirely by the author, in that the hero, a figure 'more like the shadow of a rational creature than the rational creature itself' (1, 245), is completely lacking in literary consciousness and unable to express himself either directly, through articulate speech, or indirectly through his reading. Indeed, there is no evidence that Prokharchin does any reading. His characteristics are drawn on the one hand from the figure of the Baron in Pushkin's dramatic sketch *The Miserly Knight* and, on the other, from a medley of Gogolian grotesques including Pliushkin (*Dead Souls*) and Akakii Akakievich (*The Overcoat*). He is another of Dostoevskii's lowly civil servants, typical of the works of the 1840s, but he has a novel trait, his pathological miserliness. He lives in the most squalid poverty, denying himself food and company, but on his death he is found to be in possession of a considerable amount of money, concealed in his mattress.

The wordy narrative manner of the work is entirely after Gogol. The characters possess eccentric names suggesting they could once have inhabited Gogol's imagination. There are at least two indirect references to *The Nose*: one where Prokharchin scolds a fellow lodger with the words 'You, you, you're stupid! They could bite off your nose and you would eat it up with your bread without noticing' (1, 255), and the other where Prokharchin's landlady is described as 'a most respectable and portly woman, who was particularly partial to meat dishes and coffee' (1, 240), which echoes in detail the comment on the barber's wife in Gogol's tale: 'quite a respectable woman, who was very fond of drinking coffee'. But such superficial and tangential allusions and narrative mannerisms would appear to be as far as the text of *Mister Prokharchin* is prepared to go in Gogol's direction. The latter's stylistic and comic virtuosity is thematically corrosive, often consuming all sense and potential social relevance in a cauldron of semantic nonsense. It would appear that Dostoevskii was not prepared to lose the implications of Prokharchin in such a way, for he saw his miser as a figure of enormous significance in the context of contemporary Russian society: 'Suddenly it seemed to me that my Solovev [the name of Prokharchin's real-life prototype] was a colossal figure. He had retreated from the world and withdrawn from all its temptations into a world of his own behind a screen. What did all this hollow splendour, all this magnificence of ours mean to him?' (XIX, 73). Dostoevskii recognised that the miserliness of Prokharchin and his kind represented a quest for security: money could offer the certainty, power and sense of individual identity which the low-grade clerk could not otherwise hope to attain. In investing his hero with such significance Dostoevskii draws his source text not from Gogol, but from Pushkin, from the Baron's monologue in *The Miserly Knight*. Like Prokharchin, the Baron sees his fortune as representing a sort of abstract existential possibility, rather than any reality of immediate wealth:

> I am above all desires; I am content,
> I know my power, and such consciousness
> Is enough for me . . . (*He looks at his gold*)

As for both Prokharchin and the Baron the whole meaning of life is concentrated in consciousness of their unrealised wealth, it follows that their lives too are mere abstractions. They both live meagrely, for the awareness of their potential wealth and power facilitates withdrawal and isolationism, but their contentment is that of physical stagnation and emotional atrophy. Pushkin contrasts the spectre-like Baron with the vivid physicality of his son, Albert, whose appetite for a life of jousting, socialising and drinking is limited only by his own poverty. He wants to lay hands on his father's money *in order to spend it* and thus release its possibilities.

'I felt that I was not going to the point of stealing from Pushkin,' wrote Dostoevskii in his article of 1861, 'Petersburg Dreams in Verse and Prose' (XIX, 74), and this alerts us to the fact that although *The Miserly Knight* is used as a ghost text in *Mister Prokharchin*, Dostoevskii's miser is a distinct variation on the figure of Pushkin's Baron. True, Pushkin's character had provided an insight into the complex psychology of acquisitiveness which Gogol's Pliushkin had not, but Prokharchin in turn possesses a specific cultural and chronological identity lacking in the Baron. In *Mister Prokharchin* Dostoevskii achieves what Pushkin, with his eye for the universal implications of particular situations, had not attempted: he locates Prokharchin's miserliness not as a generic feature of the human condition, but as a specific product of the age and society in which he lives. Pushkin's Baron is as universal a figure as Shylock, Lear or Hamlet. He is as loosely bound to sixteenth-century France (the apparent setting of the sketch) as Hamlet is to the Denmark of the dark ages. In order to promote the permanent features of his sketch at the expense of the particular, Pushkin withholds those specific historical or topographical details that would allow the reader to locate the action in a particular time or place. *Mister Prokharchin* is an altogether different proposition: it is inextricably linked into Russian social and literary realities of the 1840s, those of the Natural School. Its hero, with his inarticulateness, his pathological yet indefinite unease, his defiant individualism, and his lack of all social and spiritual foundations apart from those afforded by his money, exemplifies the acuity of Dostoevskii's insight into the alienation and anxiety experienced by the individual in an age characterised by increasing complexity, specialisation, division of labour and fragmentation of life. It is Prokharchin's *anxiety* that most clearly separates him from Pushkin's Baron, whose status in the end is dependent not on his wealth but on his class. Prokharchin's miserliness is not an amusing eccentricity, but grows from a basic animal terror at the fact that his very identity, unsupported by the privileges of rank and class, is indefinite and insecure. A tiny cog in a vast bureaucratic machine whose function he cannot begin to divine, Prokharchin senses in a primitive and inarticulate way that his position offers him no control over his life. His fears are fed by rumours that certain chancery offices are to be closed and that his own job might be under threat. Like Devushkin and Goliadkin before him, Prokharchin is vaguely aware that, unenviable as the lowly situation of government clerk might be, it does at least offer the security of self-definition through one's social identity.

Without this security the individual is isolated and left to his inner resources. He must ask himself again what he is. This is what happens to Prokharchin. He retreats into individualism, both physical and spiritual, by hiding in his little corner and shunning the company of his fellow lodgers. But in turning to his own resources he finds himself wanting. After all, what sort of self does he possess? He is a dislocated cipher lacking the class and confident self-sufficiency of Pushkin's Baron. Faced with the possibility of an existence without meaning or purpose, Prokharchin seeks self-identification through property. Lacking both social and spiritual bases, he becomes merely what he owns. Unlike the Baron, he contemplates his property not with pleasure, but with a fear that shows his consciousness of the fragility of his existence:

> He put his feet on his sacred trunk, cried out at the top of his voice, squatted back almost on his heels and, trembling and shaking all over, cleared as much space as he could with his arms and body on the bed, while gazing with a trembling yet strangely resolute look at those present, as if protesting that he would sooner die than yield to anyone even a hundredth part of his meagre belongings. (I, 248–9)

Conclusion

On 24 March 1845 Dostoevskii wrote to his brother: 'You perhaps would like to know how I occupy myself when I am not writing? I read. I read an awful lot, and reading has a strange effect on me. I will read through something I read a long time ago and it is as though I am wound up with new powers. I pay attention to everything, understand everything clearly, and draw from it the ability to create for myself' (XXVIII/I, 108). This comment would appear substantially to confirm the argument we have pursued in this essay: that the relationship of Dostoevskii's writing to his own reading was a complex one, rendering suspect any recourse critics might make to over-simple explanations of that relationship, such as that of 'influence'. It might seem trite to draw from Dostoevskii's comment above the conclusion that he brought to his reading as much as he took from it, but that very dialogical relationship permitted him to use his reading in a creative way, as an ingredient in the composition of his works that allowed him to mediate his own presence as author alongside that of his fictional characters. The presence of ghost texts and familiar, historically redundant narrative genres in Dostoevskii's texts of the 1840s was a measure not of his slavish indebtedness to what he had read, but of his willingness to strike out in wholly new directions.

Notes

1 See, for example, Victor Terras, *The Young Dostoevskij, 1846–1849: A Critical Study* (The Hague: Mouton, 1969), and Viktor Vinogradov, 'The School of Sentimental Naturalism' in Priscilla Meyer and Stephen Rudy (eds.), *Dostoevsky and Gogol* (Ann Arbor: Ardis, 1979), pp. 161–228.
2 Vinogradov, 'School', p. 192.
3 John Jones, *Dostoevsky* (Oxford: Clarendon Press, 1983), p. 10.
4 Ibid., p. 10.
5 Joseph Frank, *Dostoevsky. The Seeds of Revolt, 1821–1849* (Princeton University Press, 1976), p. 149.
6 Jones, *Dostoevsky*, p. 46.
7 Konstantin Mochulsky, *Dostoevsky. His Life and Work*, trans. Michael Minihan (Princeton University Press, 1967), pp. 29, 31.
8 Malcolm V. Jones, *Dostoyevsky after Bakhtin: Readings in Dostoyevsky's Fantastic Realism* (Cambridge University Press, 1990), pp. 56–7.
9 John Bayley, *Pushkin. A Comparative Commentary* (Cambridge University Press, 1971), p. 41.

4

WILLIAM MILLS TODD, III

Dostoevskii as a professional writer

Dostoevskii marks a turning point in his career as a fiction writer when he begins to endow his literary characters with sufficient funds to go about their daily lives, as he had not done in his first novel *Poor Folk*, and when he makes economic security a secondary concern for his heroes, as, for instance, in *The Double* and *Notes from Underground*. In the fictions for which he is best remembered, plots do not turn fundamentally on sudden financial reversals (e.g. the discovery of a will, a bankruptcy, a windfall profit); moral, ideological and psychological problems haunt the principal characters more than financial ones. The youthful Dostoevskii's concern with the crushing effects of environment yielded – but not entirely – in his mature work to penetrating investigations of free will and moral responsibility. The prominence of these issues in Dostoevskii's fictions earned him the authorial image of a philosophical novelist, a profound psychologist, even a religious prophet.

Only in recent decades have scholars begun to rediscover what Dostoevskii's contemporary readers and fellow writers knew well, that he was a thoroughly professional writer in all senses of the word 'professional', seriously engaged throughout his post-exile career with contemporary media, audiences, and institutional possibilities, rarely able (unlike many of his characters) to ignore financial problems and issues of professional status. He experienced all that Russian literary life offered, from imprisonment, censorship and heavy indebtedness to fame, influence and relative prosperity. His professional activities spanned fiction writing, criticism, journalism, editing, publishing and a responsible post in Russia's first association of writers.

The word 'professional' seems not to have been in Dostoevskii's vocabulary. Representatives of the liberal professions (doctors, lawyers, teachers) play at best secondary roles in his fiction. But, as will be seen, Dostoevskii became a consummate professional in the course of his writing career. In so doing, he not only participated in the transformation of Russian literary culture, but also took part in one of the salient phenomena in the modernisation of post-Emancipation Russian society, the rise of the professions. This chapter will explore the ways in which Dostoevskii, for all of the timelessness of his themes and the enduring fascination of his work, contributed to these gradually unfolding socio-cultural processes. It will also suggest that his concerns as a professional writer helped shape his major fiction and that his solutions to narrative challenges made virtues of the necessary material conditions under which he laboured.

'Professional' encompasses several related, but distinct notions. First, it may be used in the sense of *vocation*. Russians were called to literature for several generations before Dostoevskii took up his pen to translate Balzac's *Eugénie Grandet* and write *Poor Folk* in his early twenties. For Derzhavin, Karamzin, Zhukovskii, Batiushkov, Gogol, Pushkin and Lermontov – to name a few – imaginative literature was the activity they turned to first and most frequently at many periods of their lives. They filled letters, memoirs and conversations with their literary obsessions. They devoted hours of time to literary activity well beyond the amateur versifying that counted as a social grace in the polite educated society of late eighteenth- and early nineteenth-century Russia. They wrote memorable works subsequently inscribed in a Russian canon which has remained stable during Imperial, Soviet and post-Soviet regimes. But none of these writers – members of the nobility, landowners, recipients of state subsidies, civil servants and military officers in varying degrees – could be called 'professional' in a second sense of the word: pursuing this vocation as a principal means of livelihood. Among these writers Pushkin had the clearest vision of a profession of letters, one culled from his acute observation of English and continental practices and from his trenchant critique of Russian ones. He was the boldest of the group in challenging aristocratic prejudices against what he called the 'trade' of writing. But he could not build on the success of his early narrative poems to make an independent career and he died with catastrophic debts, scorned by many in his own time and later as an irrelevant 'aristocrat'.

During the decades before Dostoevskii's first publications, some participants in the world of letters did earn a living from their activity: booksellers, translators, editors of periodicals and writers of bestsellers (in verse or prose). Some of these won enduring fame: A. F. Smirdin (bookseller), F. V. Bulgarin (newspaper editor, novelist, police informant), O. I. Senkovskii (journal editor, fiction writer, critic) and N. I. Novikov (publisher, journalist, critic). Translators of fiction and writers of popular chapbooks and broadsides (*lubki*) remained faceless and nameless to their public. To be associated with this last group did not appeal to the gentlemen amateurs who aspired to translate their literary vocations into a profession, and Pushkin employed such association as a satiric device in his polemics with Bulgarin.

To turn a gift for writing and a willingness to practise it into a sustainable career required more than a vocation. It called for institutional possibilities which Russia was only beginning to acquire by the time Dostoevskii began to dream of a literary career in the 1830s. Candidates for authorship possessed of talent, imagination, learning and initial financial support were a necessity, of course, and these were available. Dostoevskii himself serves as an example. Although by no means of lofty lineage or great personal wealth, he had acquired a love of literature in his family surroundings and at school (the Bible, the best of Russian literature of the time, popular Western European literature in translation). At the Imperial Academy of Military Engineering he received instruction in Russian and French literature, German and history. This cultural capital and family funds sufficed when he came to launch his literary career in the 1840s.

But other institutional features of Russian literature raised serious barriers before the aspiring professional, barriers which would remain high throughout Dostoevskii's lifetime. The lack of a readership is a good place to start. Only in 1897 was mass literacy measured in the Russian Empire, at which time, after several decades of increased educational opportunities, the level of literacy reached only 21%, well below the level which facilitated profitable publishing in England and America. In Dostoevskii's youth the figure was probably between 5 and 10%, but this would have included many people with minimal functional literacy, unable to read imaginative literature even if they had been able to afford the relatively high prices of books and periodicals. This minuscule public for imaginative literature could support only a few periodicals, a few publishers and a few writers. The most popular journal of the 1830s and early 1840s, Senkovskii's *Library for Reading* (1834–64), topped out at approximately 7,000 subscribers in 1837, the same year in which the second edition of Pushkin's *Eugene Onegin* sold 5,000 copies. A numerical index of the professional possibilities of Russian literature is given by the fact that Smirdin paid Senkovskii 29,000 roubles for editing the journal that year; Pushkin's publisher gave the poet, the youthful Dostoevskii's idol, a mere 3,000 roubles for this profit-making edition of Russia's first great novel. Publishers and editors might hope for high returns on their efforts, but most writers could not. And all of them competed for the small public able to read the books and journals and either purchase them or afford the high annual subscriptions to a lending library.

The market for literature in Dostoevskii's youth, moreover, was not a free one. The Russian Empire was an autocracy, and the autocratic government was neither consistent nor encouraging in its treatment of the press. During the period 1780–1848, for example, private presses were permitted, banned, and then re-established; ambiguous passages in a text were held against the author, then disregarded and – de facto – held against him; the importation of foreign books was banned, permitted, then severely curtailed. And censorship agencies proliferated, often contradicting one another; by the end of this period there were no fewer than twelve. But this unsettled and rapidly changing legal process was not, in itself, the chief problem facing the would-be professional writer such as Dostoevskii. Laws, however rapidly they changed, could enable writers and publishers to predict the consequences of their actions. Some laws could be beneficial: the copyright law of 1828, for instance, gave the Russian author rights which made writing a financially sustainable occupation. The central problem for writers and publishers was surely the unpredictability, arbitrariness and vindictiveness of the government, from the Emperor to the officials in his agencies. Although the censorship examined works prior to publication, writers and publishers could be punished subsequent to publication, even when the laws ostensibly protected them, if the published work incurred the displeasure of someone in high places. The censor Nikitenko could justly complain in 1830 that 'there is no legality in Russia'.[1]

No less capricious than the autocracy was the fashion-driven taste of the reading public, which could drop writers as quickly as it had raised them and which was not guided by principled public criticism as Russian literature tentatively made its way from salons and student circles to the marketplace during the 1820s and 1830s. Even Pushkin, subsequently canonised as Russia's 'national poet', in part by Dostoevskii, experienced these vicissitudes in full measure, as the unexpected success of his narrative poems of the early 1820s was followed by the commercial and critical failures of his prose and poetry in the 1830s. Periodicals could be – and were – crippled by capricious censorship, and most were fortunate to survive a few years; but book publishers, dependent on the small public sufficiently wealthy to buy their editions, were also vulnerable to economic failure. The enterprising Smirdin, for instance, became financially over-extended as he tried to produce less expensive editions, and he fell a half million roubles into debt.

As Dostoevskii was beginning to immerse himself in Russian literature, two complex public controversies recorded its growing pains as an incipient profession. The first, which began as a debate over the enduring value of Karamzin's *History of the Russian State*, quickly became an argument over issues of authorial dignity between Bulgarin and his fellows on one side and Pushkin and the so-called 'aristocrats' on the other. As the debate degenerated into satires, crude personal attacks and denunciations to the tsarist secret police – the infamous Third Section – it revealed Russia's lack of public criticism and conventions for public debate. Here became painfully obvious a lack of 'professionals' in a third sense of the word: that of *conformity to the ethical standards of an élite occupational group.* It became clear to all participants that Russia had no such standards for writers and critics and, indeed, that literary people and journalists did not form any sort of self-recognising and self-monitoring group.

As this controversy quieted down in the early 1830s, a new one sprang up, precipitated by the success of Senkovskii's *Library for Reading* and other enterprises funded by Smirdin. This new controversy, over 'literature and commerce', not only showed that the former problems remained unresolved but introduced new ones that concerned no less vital aspects of modern literature and journalism: editing, publishing, readership and the commodification of the printed word. The combatants of the first one took part in this as well, but a new group assumed leadership: Senkovskii, S. P. Shevyrev (a cultural conservative), V. G. Belinskii (the critic who made Dostoevskii's reputation) and N. V. Gogol (the Russian prose writer who most engaged Dostoevskii's attention during the 1840s and 1850s). Smirdin's ownership of a virtual monopoly over the print media (including *The Library for Reading*) occasioned Belinskii's famous label for the 1830s: 'the age of Smirdin'. All Russian writers who aspired to any public career had to reckon with his editors and with his commercial network. Belinskii, who saluted Smirdin's honesty and reliability, nevertheless noted that books not published by Smirdin and not written or protected by his editors tended not to circulate very widely.[2]

Why did these successful enterprises, including a journal which appeared with unusual regularity, rewarded its contributors generously, and published brilliant works such as Pushkin's *Queen of Spades*, provoke such a storm of controversy? The answer shows how far Russia was from having, or even understanding, a profession of literature. Shevyrev's attack on *The Library for Reading* in his essay 'Literature and Commerce' (*The Moscow Observer*, 1835) is the most extreme example of resistance to a professionalised literature. Much of his essay borders on hysteria: accusations that payment by the signature (or printer's page) made writers long-winded; hyperbolic accounts of the fortunes to be made in Russian letters; fears that commerce would destroy all taste, thought, morality, learning and honest criticism; and the piously romantic assertion that poetry alone had not fallen into the clutches of commerce.

Gogol and Belinskii themselves embraced the professionalisation of literary life, so their objection to Senkovskii's efforts did not reject remuneration as a corruption of literary vocations. Their concerns addressed, rather, ethical requirements for a dignified literary profession, professionalism in the third sense of the word – in particular, respect for the author's text, responsible criticism addressed to the public, and critical awareness of the cultural needs of that public. By no means the least striking of Senkovskii's practices was his unashamed editorial free-handedness, which Gogol found unprecedented in Russian culture. He could only quote Senkovskii in amazement: 'we leave no story in its prior form, but redo every one; sometimes we work up one out of two, sometimes out of three, and the piece gains significantly from our alterations'.[3] Senkovskii probably never went this far, but he did add a happy conclusion to Balzac's *Père Goriot*, alter scholarly articles, and insert his own ideas into other critics' essays. Some of his alterations merely reflected the presence of an editorial policy, theretofore unknown in Russia, but many represented a blatant assault on the text and, by extension, on the name and unique mission of the poet, so celebrated in the age of Romanticism. To Belinskii, this was nothing less than a betrayal of the reader's trust. At a time when Belinskii, Shevyrev and a young generation of philosophically oriented writers and critics were calling for responsible criticism, *The Library for Reading* struck them as irresponsible, capricious and outright dishonest. It was, in Lidiia Ginzburg's deft phrase, 'in principle unprincipled'.[4]

Such was the uncertain state of Russian literature as Dostoevskii was pursuing his studies. Yet the success of Karamzin, Pushkin and Gogol could allow a young writer to dream of pursuing a literary vocation; Smirdin's policies, however devastating ultimately to his enterprises, proffered the possibility of significant remuneration, independent of court patronage and state service. Hopeful young Russians could look abroad to a range of authorial models and precedents: lofty images of the poet in German philosophical aesthetics; social responsibility in French fiction (George Sand, Eugène Sue); literary triumphs by French and English public figures (Constant, Chateaubriand, Hugo, Disraeli); and combinations of financial and critical success (Scott, Dickens, Balzac – to name but a few). Belinskii, the most influential critic of the 1840s, tried to articulate the dream of a literary profession for his generation. He looked beyond the commodification of literature to literature as a '*res publica*, great and important, a source of lofty moral enjoyment and live ecstasy'. The necessary public of this literature would be 'a single living personality, historically developed, with a certain direction, taste and view of things', and it would see literature as 'its *own*, flesh of its flesh, bone of its bone, and not something alien, accidentally filling a certain number of books and journals'. Only such a public could, argued Belinskii, make the titles 'writer' and 'critic' meaningful.[5]

Dostoevskii first encountered this fragile institution of Russian literature as he left the Academy of Military Engineering, filled with literary ambition and with blissfully little understanding of the practical difficulties this entailed in the Russia of the 1840s. Of the three senses of the word 'professional' discussed so far, the first, vocation, was so far the only one that could be applied to him. Years later he would reminisce about naive dreams of the 'sublime and beautiful' in his *Diary of a Writer* (January 1876), about his plans to write a novel on Venetian life, about his brother Mikhail's poetry. But the letters which have survived from the late 1830s and early 1840s show that these dreams of poetry, fiction, drama and philosophy were no exaggeration. Dostoevskii shows little interest in his engineering curriculum and in the officer's career which loomed before him, a career from which his father's death liberated him and from which he resigned as soon as it became feasible, in 1844.

While Dostoevskii was consumed by his authorial vocation and immersed himself in literary reading, he was otherwise blissfully ignorant of the more material aspects of a writing career. He would soon have to discover them. Unlike other great Russian novelists of his generation, Dostoevskii had few resources aside from those he earned with his pen. Tolstoi would inherit a large estate (approximately 800 taxable male serfs), Turgenev divided an estate of 4,000 serfs with his brother. These grand holdings considerably dwarfed the small, debt-ridden property of Dostoevskii's father. Both Ivan Goncharov and Mikhail Saltykov-Shchedrin came from families that enjoyed noble status and merchant wealth, and both made significant careers in state service, from which Dostoevskii had quickly resigned. Dostoevskii's family background was decidedly more modest: his mother was from the merchant estate and his father had worked his way into the lower nobility from the even less prosperous caste-estate of the parish clergy. Once Dostoevskii had surrendered his ensign's pay and exchanged his share of his father's insignificant estate for a thousand roubles, he had no other sources of support save small loans from friends and relations and income from his writing.

At first Dostoevskii responded to these pressures fecklessly, by living the life of a young officer about town, frequenting theatres and restaurants, accumulating debts, and generally revealing the 'low economic time horizon' characteristic of his age group, estate and time.[6] Soon he turned to an unrealistic fantasy characteristic of educated young people in the middle of the nineteenth century, that of generating income through translating; but here, at least, he achieved success, placing his translation of *Eugénie Grandet* almost immediately. This anonymous start to his career was followed by a piece of good timing of the sort the later Dostoevskii, a skilled journalist, would learn to court. His school fellow Dmitrii Grigorovich, himself drawn to French social romanticism, read and was taken by the manuscript of Dostoevskii's first novel *Poor Folk* and showed it to Nikolai Nekrasov, Dostoevskii's coeval, who had recently made a successful debut as a reviewer, poet and editor of physiological sketches. The two of them in turn rushed, in the middle of a Petersburg 'white night', to share it with Belinskii, a critic so influential by then that provincial booksellers were said to place their orders in accordance with his reviews. Belinskii greeted the novel ecstatically – as well he might, for the novel's critical, yet humane, view of contemporary social reality was congruent with the critic's own evolving views; moreover, the unknown Dostoevskii had become the first Russian writer to realise such a view of reality in a full-length narrative.

In the small literary world of 1840s St Petersburg word of the new novel spread quickly, well before it appeared in print, and Dostoevskii suddenly found himself the centre of considerable interest and attention. Despite the growth of commercial possibilities in Russian letters, this was still a milieu of salons and literary groups, frequented by people with greater social sophistication than the young Dostoevskii, who responded to the attention with the extravagant immaturity of his later 'raw youth' characters (or of Balzac's earlier ones). Contemporary memoirs and his own letters to his brother Mikhail record an extraordinary series of blunders: behaving rudely to a well-meaning salon host, fainting at the feet of a society beauty who had wished to meet him, dooming his circle's proposed humorous magazine to being banned by the censorship because of his impolitic advertisement for it. Belinskii, too senior to feel threatened by Dostoevskii's post-adolescent obstreperousness, did not react negatively to the young author, but the beginning writers of Dostoevskii's own age did. Nekrasov and Turgenev jointly characterised him in a satiric poem as a 'new pimple on the nose of literature'. The fact that copies of the poem were made by Aleksandr Herzen and Grigorovich shows how irritating Dostoevskii had become to the members of the Belinskii circle.

Belinskii, like Dostoevskii the son of an army doctor, was in no position to give the young author lessons in high society deportment, but he at least tried to beat some financial sense into Dostoevskii's spinning head: 'Two weeks ago Belinskii delivered a full exhortation to me on how one can make it in our literary life and in conclusion declared to me that I absolutely must, for the sake of my soul's salvation, demand no less than 200 roubles a signature. Thus my Goliadkin [*The Double*] will go for at least 1,500 roubles.' Dostoevskii's soul would have to seek its salvation elsewhere, as this would have been one of the highest honoraria of the time, not at all appropriate for a beginning writer, as Dostoevskii immediately discovered in dealing with his first novel's publisher, Nekrasov: 'Tormented by pangs of conscience, Nekrasov ran like a rabbit and promised me 100 silver roubles for *Poor Folk*, which he had bought from me. For he himself sincerely confessed that 150 silver roubles is not Christian payment. And thus he is adding 100 roubles for me out of repentance . . .' The repentant Nekrasov, who had accepted

Poor Folk for an almanac, was not yet the successful literary entrepreneur he would later become, and Dostoevskii reports further difficulties:

> All of that is fine for now, here's what's nasty: I've heard absolutely nothing from the censorship about *Poor Folk*. Such an innocent novel, but they drag on and on, and I don't know how it will end. What if they ban it? Cross out passages from top to bottom? It's awful, simply awful, and Nekrasov is saying that he won't be able to publish the almanac, that he has already wasted 4,000 roubles on it.   (XXVIII/1, 112–13; letter of 8 October 1845)[7]

Three months later, in January 1846, the novel did appear, but neither it nor *The Double* would make the profit he anticipated. The anxious novelist would soon encounter still another disappointment: reviews much more negative than he had been led to expect. Even Belinskii, while generally positive, expressed reservations when reviewing the novel for *Notes of the Fatherland*, a journal which he had led to prominence when he became its leading critic in 1839. When Belinskii left *Notes of the Fatherland* to join *The Contemporary*, his year-end review of *Poor Folk* was less enthusiastic, and he faulted it for prolixity and repetitiveness.

Even a less sensitive and insecure author than Dostoevskii might have been dismayed, and Dostoevskii was certainly far from the modern commercial belief that any review is a good review. He found himself in a precarious position: he had been faulted by many critics for being too close to the philanthropic aesthetics of Belinskii's 'Natural School', and now he found himself dropped by the very critic who had helped him break into print. Dostoevskii's evolving interests as a writer, moreover, carried him in directions more psychological (*The Double*) and fantastic (*The Landlady*) than Belinskii could welcome and thus further alienated him from the critic and his circle.

To add to his problems Dostoevskii, whose *Poor Folk* had broken a barrier for the prose of the Natural School, soon found his first novel overtaken by no less significant literary achievements: the stories which would make up Turgenev's *Notes of a Hunter* were beginning to appear; Herzen's *Who is to Blame?* (1847) offered a greater range of characters than *Poor Folk*; Ivan Goncharov's first novel, *A Common Story* (1847), won Belinskii's approval for its confrontation of naive romanticism with practical life; Grigorovich treated peasant life in unprecedented detail in two novellas, *The Village* (1846) and *Anton Goremyka* (1847); and A. V. Druzhinin broke new literary ground (at least in Russia) with his treatment of a liberated woman in *Polinka Saks* (1847). As Dostoevskii lost criticism's praise and fashion's favour, these other writers of his generation gained both, fulfilling more successfully a widely felt need for works which could raise significant social problems without directly confronting the censorship.

These events gave Dostoevskii's fragile self-esteem a jolt, but he was now a professional writer to the extent that this was possible in the mid-1840s. He received an advance from A. A. Kraevskii, the publisher of *Notes of the Fatherland*, for his projected novel *Netochka Nezvanova*, and although the advance bound him to this journal after Belinskii left it for *The Contemporary* and although Dostoevskii became something of a laughing stock in literary circles for his failure to deliver the novel on time, this large sum (4,000 roubles) helped sustain him, as did the income from the series of stories he published up to his arrest in 1849. His pre-exile works appeared regularly in *Notes of the Fatherland*, including three instalments of the never-to-be-finished *Netochka Nezvanova* (1849). That Dostoevskii could place the fiction he wrote during these years shows that he had won a solid place in Russian letters. Whatever his fellow writers thought of his personality or the stylistic quality of his writing, they included him in the leading journals of the time and reviewed his works. However bitterly Dostoevskii complained of his indebtedness to Kraevskii and worried that writing to pay it off compromised the quality of his work, these advances made it possible for him to make a living as a writer, one of few in his time to do so (XXVIII/1, 135–6; letter of 17 December 1846 to M. M. Dostoevskii). But the term Dostoevskii uses in these complaints, 'day labourer' (*podenshchik*), is a far cry from the more dignified 'professional'. (In fairness to Kraevskii, it should be noted that the rate he offered Dostoevskii for advances, fifty silver roubles a signature, was not far from the sixty silver roubles Dostoevskii claimed he was offered by *The Contemporary*.)

It should not be surprising that Dostoevskii did not publish any of these works as separate volumes. The economic conditions of the time militated against separate publication for all but the most successful and best-known writers. Dostoevskii achieved this status only after his return from exile, but even then his novels and stories inevitably appeared first in journals in serialised form. Separate editions yielded their authors approximately a tenth of the journals' honoraria.

In this early period, Dostoevskii began to explore a second form of professional writing: journalism. He had barely begun this line of work before arrest and exile interrupted it. Although most of his contemporaries also had recourse to this marginal literary work, Dostoevskii took no particular pride in it and did not reprint these early columns, or feuilletons, during his lifetime. Nevertheless, participation in the workings of the periodical press would suggest styles, themes, characterisations and even narrative techniques for his fictional work. The chatty tone of the feuilleton licensed the writer to leap from theme to theme, wax lyrical, create personas, discuss character types, engage in polemics, even issue confessions in a very personal voice.

Earlier writers, such as Batiushkov, Viazemskii and Belinskii, had adopted a conversational manner in their prose essays, especially the last two. But the feuilleton made this manner particularly fashionable and broadened its scope, and Dostoevskii would practise it until the end of his career, not only in his journalism, but in his highly original *Diary of a Writer* and in the narrators and fictive authors for a number of his fictions, such as *Notes from Underground* and *The Brothers Karamazov*. The four feuilletons that Dostoevskii wrote for *The St Petersburg News* under the title of 'Petersburg Chronicle' (1847), moreover, gave him the opportunity to comment on contemporary urban culture. His conclusions are largely negative, as he incisively depicts a Russia in which the lack of a free press makes it impossible to report the news, driving people home to their circles: 'Petersburg is nothing but a collection of a huge number of little circles, each of which has its regulations, its decorum, its laws, its logic and its oracle.' Only in those circles could one answer the question 'What's the news?' (XVIII, 12). And yet those circles sooner or later fall apart and deliver the same trivia as the public periodicals. In this, the first of the feuilletons, Dostoevskii sarcastically sums up his discoveries about the state of Russian intellectual life and the failure of Russians to develop, through the press, a public sphere.

In April 1849 Dostoevskii was to lose another illusion, about the security of familiar associations, as he was arrested, imprisoned, nearly executed, and sentenced to penal servitude for his participation in a set of circles. His four years in Omsk cut him off from literary life, even from his family; he received no letters and sent only two. But he cultivated his powers of observation and memory, gathering the impressions, insights and understanding which, when gathered in his *Notes from the House of the Dead* (1860–1), would make his reputation as a writer of the first rank. At first, however, as he left prison for compulsory service in the military, it must have seemed that he had to start all over again. His first literary plans in 1854–5 were throwbacks to earlier modes of work: a patriotic ode (a genre out of literary fashion already in the early nineteenth century, highly compromised for its venality) and possible translations. Promotion to officer's rank and permission to publish offered better prospects, but Dostoevskii enjoyed no windfall success, as he had with *Poor Folk*, and influential editors remembered his youthful obstreperousness of the previous decade. One of the first things that greeted him upon his release from prison was a nasty sketch of a vain young writer by I. I. Panaev, co-editor with Nekrasov of *The Contemporary*, a sketch in which Dostoevskii could easily recognise himself.[8]

Dostoevskii's first post-exile fictions, important for his own artistic development, were as poorly received by contemporary editors and critics as his last pre-exile ones. *Uncle's Dream* (1859) was rejected by *Notes of the*

Fatherland, as was *The Village of Stepanchikovo* by *The Russian Herald* (1859). To make matters even more discouraging, the publisher of the latter journal, M. N. Katkov, had sent Dostoevskii a badly needed advance, and the author now had to return it. Finally *Notes of the Fatherland* took *The Village of Stepanchikovo*, but for a mere 120 roubles a signature, that is, for a fraction of what Dostoevskii had earned before his exile (II, 499).

However grimly familiar the literary world must have looked from afar (the same editors and journals, the same police surveillance), Dostoevskii found that much had changed when he finally returned to St Petersburg in December 1859. The age of censorship terror had passed; the Great Reforms were about to change the institutions and social structure of the Russian Empire. Relaxed censorship practices and a new tolerance of political reporting in the press facilitated the growth of journalism: 150 new periodicals (newspapers and journals) appeared between 1855 and 1860, although the lack of a concomitant growth in literacy doomed many new enterprises to rapid failure, and the subscription lists of the leading journals of the time did not exceed that of *The Library for Reading* in the 1830s. Among the new periodicals licensed by the government was Mikhail Dostoevskii's proposed newspaper *Time*. Its censor was to be a fellow writer, Goncharov, who had already passed *The Village of Stepanchikovo* without demanding excisions.

This promising development was followed by a second: Dostoevskii was able to publish a two-volume collection of his early works in 1860. The sum he received was not a great one, 2,000 roubles, but it provided the minimal yearly income that one contemporary observer thought necessary for a writer with a family (S. Sashkov, 'Literary Endeavour in Russia,' *The Deed*, no. 8, 1876). The instructions for negotiation that Dostoevskii sent his brother Mikhail showed that he had mastered some basic principles of literary commerce: 'The contract should be as follows: (1) once the manuscript's in their hands, the money's in mine; (2) print 2,000 copies – by no means more (at most 2,400); (3) I have the right to reprint two years after this edition; (4) in the course of this time, if all copies sell out, the bookseller does not have the right to print a second edition; (5) the publishing should begin immediately' (XXVIII/1, 351; letter of 9 October 1859). In other words, Dostoevskii well understood the unscrupulous publishing practices of the time, and he guarded himself as best he could against them.

These developments concern professionalisation in the second, commercial, sense of the word. In St Petersburg Dostoevskii was soon to discover even sharper developments in the third, social and ethical, sense of being a professional. Two events stand out as landmarks in this process. The first involved Goncharov's misguided accusation that Turgenev had plagiarised his plans for *The Precipice* and used them to write his novels *A Nest of the Gentry*

(1859) and *On the Eve* (1860). In an earlier decade this sorry episode, universally considered a product of Goncharov's jealousy and paranoia, might have been resolved by a duel or, less likely, a civil procedure. Now Turgenev demanded that their fellow littérateurs adjudicate Goncharov's charge. In March 1860 Pavel Annenkov, Aleksandr Druzhinin, Stepan Dudyshkin and Aleksandr Nikitenko resolved the issue firmly in Turgenev's favour. Literature – at least in this instance – had become a professionalised occupation, one regulated by those educated in its practices. A quarter-century before only state censorship had imposed civility in the Grub Street warfare between Bulgarin and Pushkin.

The second significant event in the professionalisation of Russian writers soon involved Dostoevskii directly: the founding of the Literary Fund (Society for the Aid of Needy Writers and Scholars) in 1859 took place shortly before he returned to St Petersburg. Druzhinin, knowing that Turgenev attended the annual dinners of the Royal Literary Fund in England, asked Turgenev to describe this annual meeting, which he did for the January 1858 issue of *The Library for Reading*. A significant group of Russian writers decided to draft a proposal for a Russian equivalent, a society to support writers, scholars and their families through loans, grants and pensions. While the autocracy would remain hostile to the formation of autonomous, self-regulating professional associations, it did in 1859 begin to permit apolitical charitable organisations, banned since 1848. Turgenev cited the precedent of such societies in a proposal. The new society brought together most of the writers, critics and editors of the period from the 1840s to the 1860s that I have mentioned in this chapter. Its first meeting took place in November 1859, and almost immediately the Dostoevskii brothers were recommended for membership. They joined it in December of that year.

General excitement over the forthcoming Great Reforms, including the emancipation of the serfs, gripped the Petersburg intelligentsia, and representatives of previously and subsequently disparate groups could come together in a collegial and charitable undertaking. Radical thinkers of the younger generation, such as Chernyshevskii and Dobroliubov, could join older moderates, such as Turgenev, Annenkov, Grigorovich, and Kraevskii. E. P. Kovalevskii, the Minister of Popular Education, chaired the first executive committee, and the imperial family itself, reported Turgenev, contributed to the Literary Fund. Dostoevskii soon had the opportunity to witness the new society being pulled in radical directions, when Chernyshevskii, Dobroliubov and Nekrasov lobbied on behalf of arrested students and former political convicts, such as Dostoevskii's co-conspirator Sergei Durov. The records of the Literary Fund show that Dostoevskii consistently supported extending its aid to these intellectuals who had fallen foul of the state. Himself a former conspirator and political prisoner, he could well understand their hardships.

In February 1863 the Literary Fund elected Dostoevskii its secretary and a member of the executive committee, posts he held until his own need for loans created a conflict of interest and he stepped down in 1865. He drafted letters for the organisation and looked into requests for support which came to its attention, personally visiting candidates in hospitals and in their apartments. This responsible administrative activity runs counter to the popular image of Dostoevskii as an impractical outsider, but it is quite compatible with the communal traditions of the Russian Orthodox Church and with the practice, if not the theory, of the Russian intelligentsia. (In the 1860s some radicals, such as Chernyshevskii and Petr Tkachev, wrote against alms-giving because it did not lead to permanent social improvement. N. N. Strakhov defended it in *Time* as a practice which elevated and joined together both rich and poor.) Dostoevskii was a lifelong giver of alms, even when he had little to give, and charity figures significantly in his fiction, from *Poor Folk* to *The Brothers Karamazov* – in which Ivan Karamazov and Father Zosima take different approaches to it, distant and abstract in Ivan's case, immediate and personal in Zosima's. With his work for the Literary Fund, Dostoevskii played both parts, as did his contemporary and at times bitter rival, Turgenev, who, like Dostoevskii, personally helped writers whom the Literary Fund was not able to aid.

The Literary Fund gained its income from donations, from percentages of honoraria contributed by writers, and from the proceeds of public performances. Dostoevskii aided the society in this capacity as well, exercising his under-appreciated comic gift with a memorable performance of the postmaster in Gogol's *The Government Inspector* in April 1860. He would continue this support to the Literary Fund and to other charities (for the Sunday School movement, for women's higher education) throughout his career, becoming, at his best, an animated, dramatically arresting reader. Even in the last two years of his life, ill and over-worked, he maintained a heavy schedule of such performances. Dostoevskii was never at ease in large gatherings; his authorial vanity made it hard for him to bear the presence of rivals, such as the more polished Turgenev. That he could bring himself to take part in these affairs, often reading from works in progress, is a measure of his professionalism and of his commitment to the Literary Fund.

Dostoevskii soon settled into St Petersburg, found a circle of old and new friends, set to writing, and took an active part in planning the new periodical *Time*, now to be a 'thick journal', not a newspaper. The 'thick journal' – the epithet signifies its range of articles and its seriousness – had become the centre of literary and intellectual life. Its endless board meetings replaced the literary salons and bookshops of the previous generation as a gathering place for littérateurs. Aspiring writers could hope to contribute articles, feuilletons, translations and short stories (rarely verse) to fill the pages between the more substantial contributions – serialised novels, memoirs and scholarly works. The economics of publishing continued to make thick journals the first place of publication for new fiction, even for the best-known and most popular novelists. The thick journal would hope to lure subscribers by promising them a complete novel by a respected novelist within the course of the subscription year. Interest in the new novel would be fuelled by newspaper and journal reviews, which would begin to appear even as the novel was still being serialised.

Scarcely less important for a journal than its literary and intellectual quality was its 'tendency', and the possibilities ranged during the 1850s, 1860s and 1870s from *The Russian Word* (1859–66), *The Contemporary* (1836–66) and *The Deed* (1866–84) on the radical left, to the more moderate *Notes of the Fatherland* (1839–84) and *Herald of Europe* (1866–1918), to the right-of-centre *Russian Herald* (1856–1906) and *Library for Reading* (1834–64), to a succession of short-lived conservative nationalist journals, *The Day* (1861–5), *Moscow* (1867–8), *The Dawn* (1869–72) and *Russia* (1880–6). The tendencies could change as critics and editors migrated from journal to journal, and, at least until Chernyshevskii's arrest in 1862, they were not rigid. The date 1866 stands out in this list: it marks the first attempt to assassinate Alexander II, an attempt which deeply shocked patriarchal Russia and which resulted in censorship reprisals against journals associated with the radicals of the 1860s.

The Dostoevskii brothers and their most important collaborators, Strakhov and Grigorev, soon established the new journal's tendency, *pochvennichestvo*, a word derived from 'soil' which Robert Belknap has aptly translated as 'grassroots'.[9] It occupied an ideological middle ground between Slavophiles and Westernisers, and it focussed on cultural rather than economic politics as it advocated a 'Russian idea' which could synthesise the cultural achievements of the Russian people and the European Enlightenment. Such a programme could make *Time* attractive to open-minded people of all positions, and, indeed, it became the most successful new journal of the early 1860s, drawing an impressive 4,000 subscribers. Mikhail Dostoevskii was the publisher and, formally, the editor, but Fedor did much of the editorial work, and made substantial contributions as feuilletonist, critic, polemicist and fiction writer. He figured in over three-quarters of the journal's twenty-eight issues, publishing two full-length fictions, *The Insulted and Injured* (1861) and *Notes from the House of the Dead* (1861–2) as well as his *Winter Notes on Summer Impressions* (1863). However clumsy,

irascible and off-putting Dostoevskii could be in social situations, as a journalist he had a flair for capturing the attention of his readers, particularly
young ones, and his status as a former political prisoner earned him sympathy and heroic stature in the eyes of the intelligentsia, especially after
his *Notes from the House of the Dead* became the first work to come to
grips with Russia's harsh penal system. The journal's defence of mass education and women's education earned it further credibility, but Dostoevskii
was not merely catering to liberal fashion. He and other contributors also
wrote against the grain of regnant critical dogma, as, for instance, when he
deftly but incisively defended the value, freedom and inherent activism of
art against demands, primarily by Dobroliubov and Chernyshevskii, that art
serve immediate and determinate social ends ('Mr —bov and the Question
of Art', *Time*, February 1861). By and large, the journal held its position
against the criticism of both the 'nihilist' left and the jingoist right.

Dostoevskii estimated, perhaps with some exaggeration, that after returning to St Petersburg he earned a comfortable 8,000–10,000 roubles a year
(xxviii/2, 118; letter of 31 March–14 April 1865 to A. E. Vrangel). But just
as he seemed to have finally established himself as a professional writer, a
series of disasters struck, showing how fragile a literary career remained in
the 1860s. The first disaster was the banning of *Time* in May 1863. The Polish
Uprising of 1863 had galvanised public opinion against the insurgents. The
radicals by and large supported them, but only Herzen in exile could do so in
print. Moscow journalists, led by Katkov, seized the opportunity to lash out
at their Petersburg competitors, who reported the events of the insurrection
in a more neutral tone. In this volatile situation Strakhov, whose learned
and intricate arguments were more suited to academic than to journalistic
discourse, wrote an essay which could be taken to celebrate Polish culture at
the expense of Russian. *Time* immediately became a target for the inflamed
rhetoric of the Moscow press, and the government took advantage of the
situation to close the journal. That Dostoevskii, a Russian nationalist who
sprinkled unsympathetic Polish characters across his novels, should have suffered this fate indicates the capriciousness of the government, which, even
as it was banning *Time*, was allowing the publication of Chernyshevskii's
utopian novel, *What Is To Be Done?*, which would become gospel for radical
youth. The grounds for the ban, which was ordered by the Emperor at the
prompting of the Minister of the Interior, included not only Strakhov's con-
voluted article, but also the journal's 'harmful tendency'.[10] In the late 1870s
Dostoevskii would become a respected acquaintance of the imperial family,
but for now he remained a potentially dangerous political conspirator.

Strakhov displayed enough contrition for Katkov to intercede on his behalf with the authorities, but it was too late to resurrect *Time*. Mikhail

Dostoevskii's efforts did, however, result in permission for a new journal, *Epoch*, scheduled to appear in early 1864. Ensuing catastrophes – the deaths of Fedor Dostoevskii's niece (February 1864), wife (April 1864) and brother Mikhail (July 1864) – were of a personal nature, but they had a major impact on Dostoevskii's ability to conduct his professional life. *Epoch* got off to a slow start, each issue appearing two months late throughout the first year. It produced little income because subscribers to *Time* were given a reduced rate to compensate for the issues they had not received when that journal was banned. To make matters worse, with one notable exception, its fiction did not meet the standard that *Time* had set. The first issue, for instance, featured Turgenev's 'Phantoms', a lengthy prose poem that the Dostoevskii brothers had eagerly solicited from the popular novelist, but which was far not only from the taste of the times, but from Fedor Dostoevskii's own literary fixations; he later characterised it as 'garbage'. The one exception was Dostoevskii's own *Notes from Underground*, arguably his most challenging fiction. But here the circumstances of serialisation worked against the novella: over two months elapsed between the appearance of the first and second parts, giving the journal's readers little chance to see the intricate connections between the two parts. It received no critical reviews in the periodical press and only one short mention in M. E. Saltykov-Shchedrin's satire 'The Swallows' (*The Contemporary*, June 1864).

Meanwhile, Mikhail's family, a widow and young children, inherited an immense debt of 33,000 roubles, connected not only with the journal but with a project for a printing plant that he had initiated. In an effort to repair the damage and support himself, his stepson and his brother's family Fedor Dostoevskii made two very risky financial decisions. The first was to continue *Epoch*, instead of abandoning it (as an liquefiable asset) to his brother's creditors and supporting the family with the income from his fiction. Dostoevskii badly miscalculated his chances of success. Burdened with the management of the journal (editing, acquisition, finances, negotiations with the censors), he was unable to contribute more than a few pieces, none of them major. The last issue appeared in March 1865 with the beginning of his unfinished story 'Crocodile'. Attracting half the subscribers it needed to show a profit (1,300 instead of 2,500), *Epoch* joined the vast majority of nineteenth-century Russian journals – fuelled by bright hopes and serious purpose but understaffed, undercapitalised and undersubscribed. Dostoevskii's skills and energy as editor, critic and polemicist were superior to most, but they did not save him from a crushing indebtedness.

No less desperate were Dostoevskii's decisions about the publication of his writings. He considered reprinting his most popular work, *Notes from the House of the Dead*, in illustrated parts, as he knew that Dickens and others had done with their works in England. But to be economically feasible this risky mode of publication required the mass popularity of a Dickens as well as the high literacy rate and well-developed distribution networks that England could provide and Russia could not. Nobody had attempted this in Russia since Pushkin, at the very height of his popularity, had published *Eugene Onegin* in separate chapters. Dostoevskii dreamed, too, of becoming his own publisher, thereby avoiding middlemen, but this would not become possible for him until the 1870s. When word of *Epoch*'s failure spread, Dostoevskii became a bad credit risk, and Kraevskii, who had supported him with advances in the 1840s, refused to take the future *Crime and Punishment* on Dostoevskii's terms (an advance of 3,000 roubles and an honorarium of 150 roubles a signature, well below the 250 roubles a signature he had received from *Time*: XXVIII/2, 127, letter of 8 June 1865).

These circumstances drove Dostoevskii to take a second major risk, agreeing to finish two novels in 1866, a Trollope-like rate of production which he never before or afterwards met. For *Crime and Punishment* he secured a place in Katkov's *Russian Herald*, but at a rate similar to the one he had offered Kraevskii, 150 roubles a signature, a rate that he would continue to receive for his next two novels, *The Idiot* and *The Devils*. Katkov would regularly send Dostoevskii advances during these years, thereby providing a sort of salary, but at a cost. The rate Katkov paid him took him out of the first rank of Russian writers. Rates were well known in the literary world, and this drop in income would have brought with it a concomitant drop in prestige, a handicap in negotiating future honoraria. Dostoevskii regretted having to conclude this contract when he came to realise that Turgenev and Tolstoi were not writing for Katkov and that Katkov was, therefore, short of first-rate fiction (Tolstoi broke off serialisation of *War and Peace* in 1866; Turgenev did not publish *Smoke* until 1867). When *Crime and Punishment* brought the publisher an estimated 500 new subscribers, Dostoevskii would have had further reason to believe he was short-changed.

Publishing with *The Russian Herald* entailed artistic as well as ideological hazards. Dostoevskii suspected that Katkov was knocking down his rate to compel him to produce a longer work. 'A novel is a poetic matter,' he wrote to A. E. Vrangel, 'it demands spiritual calm and imagination' (XXVIII/2, 150–1). In the years to come, he would discover that Katkov's journal impinged not only on the 'poetry' of his novels, but on their concrete realisation, their 'art', as he called it. Katkov would insist that he change the scene of Sonia reading the gospels in *Crime and Punishment* and that he drop Stavrogin's confession to Tikhon from *The Devils*. Dostoevskii feared the worst in sending *The Russian Herald* Ivan's blasphemous attack on God and Christ in Part 5 of *The Brothers Karamazov*, but here, at least, he carried the day.

Meanwhile, he would find ways to make the frantic pressure under which he worked part and parcel of his 'poetry': narrator-chroniclers frantically trying to capture the multiplicity of events surrounding them (*The Devils*, *The Brothers Karamazov*); a narrator-journalist employing the devices of the time (e.g. characterisation by 'types') to come to grips, however ineptly, with extraordinary psyches (*The Idiot*); feverish all-night scenes in which characters hysterically play out extreme intellectual scenarios. The characters of Dostoevskii's mature fiction, unlike their author in his letters, are not obsessed with the financial struggles of everyday life, but they share his frantic pace and desperate attempts to pull stories and interpretations together.

Dostoevskii had not met Katkov personally when he concluded the agreement for *Crime and Punishment*, but he had good reason to remember that Katkov's newspaper, *The Moscow News*, had played a part in the banning of *Time*. Dostoevskii was certainly no socialist and no Westerniser by this time, and his politics were not incompatible with those of Katkov's journal and newspaper. But he had endured prison, exile and financial ruin at the hands of the government, and he never supported political oppression of the ideological opponents with whom he had polemicised resolutely in *Time* and *Epoch*. Katkov had developed no such professional solidarity with his fellow journalists and publishers and had no scruples about lobbying to have their periodicals banned. Tolstoi later described Katkov as a 'terrifying, omnipotent force in Russia', feared by provincial governors and powerful in his knowledge of Petersburg intrigues and his ability to be on the winning side.[11] It took some courage, therefore, for Dostoevskii to write to Katkov in defence of freedom of expression as Katkov was defending a reactionary response to the assassination attempt of 4 April 1866:

> 4 April mathematically proved the powerful, extraordinary, holy union of the Tsar with the people. In light of such a union certain government figures could show much more faith in the people and in educated society. People await with terror now the repression of speech and thought . . . How can one struggle with Nihilism without freedom of speech? If one gives even them, the Nihilists, freedom of speech, that can be even more advantageous: they will make all of Russia laugh with their positive explanations of their doctrine. But now they are given the appearance of sphinxes, riddles, wisdom and mysteriousness, and this lures the inexperienced.   (xxviii/2, 155; letter of 25 April 1866)

Readers of Dostoevskii will recognise in Dostoevskii's defence the tools of his own fictional and journalistic arguments against the radicals of his time: laughter and reduction to absurdity aimed against mysteriously seductive thinkers. These, not political intrigue, were the tools of a professional in the ethical sense of the word.

The contract for Dostoevskii's other novel of 1866, *The Gambler*, was even more threatening to his art and livelihood than the contract with Katkov. Six years earlier Dostoevskii had published a collected edition of his works. Tempted again by this possibility he agreed to a contract with F. T. Stellovskii that is legendary for its penalty clause:

> I was in such poor financial circumstances that I was compelled to sell the right to publish everything I had previously written to a speculator, Stellovskii, a rather bad person and a publisher who understands absolutely nothing. But in our contract there was a clause according to which I promised to prepare a novel of no fewer than twelve signatures for the edition, and if I do not deliver it to him by 1 November at the latest, then he, Stellovskii, will be free to publish for the next nine years, at no cost and however he chooses, everything that I write with no remuneration for me.

Unfortunately for Dostoevskii, Stellovskii understood very well with whom he was dealing, an author who had a well-established record of not meeting deadlines:

> 1 November is four months away. I thought of buying myself out with money, paid as a penalty, but he does not want it. I asked him for a three-month extension, but he does not want to give it to me and tells me directly that since he is convinced I have no time to write a novel of twelve signatures, all the more because I have written only half for *The Russian Herald*, that it is more profitable for him not to agree to an extension and a penalty, because then everything that I write will be his.
>
> (XXVIII/2, 159–60; letter of 17 June 1866 to A. V. Korvin-Krukovskaia)

This was as melodramatic a predicament as any 'Victorian' novelist, including Dostoevskii, ever created.

Fortunately for Dostoevskii the melodrama's opening acts of tragedy were followed by the obligatory comic ending, a rescue-in-the-nick-of-time. He honourably resisted the suggestion of an old friend, Aleksandr Miliukov, that a group of friends write *The Gambler*, but he did agree to another proposal: that he work with a pupil of Russia's first stenography professor. He would dictate passages to her, and she would transcribe them and promptly return them neatly copied for editing. With her help he met Stellovskii's deadline, although not without a further novelistic adventure: Dostoevskii was forced to register the manuscript with the police at 10 p.m. on 1 November 1866, because Stellovskii had absented himself in hope that this would make it impossible for Dostoevskii to fulfil the contract.

In a life remarkable for ill-health, poverty and misfortune (some of his own making), his engagement of the stenographer turned out to be the best thing that ever happened to Dostoevskii. The young woman, Anna

Grigorevna Snitkina (1846–1918), was broadly educated, fluent in German, and, like other literate young Russians of the time, devoted to literature. Half Dostoevskii's age, she became his wife in early 1867, shortly before the newlyweds were forced abroad by debts. No account of Dostoevskii as a professional writer can neglect the extraordinary contributions she made to his career and reputation. Not only did he dictate all of his remaining fiction to her, she managed his publishing affairs and a bookselling business after they returned from their four years of wandering in Europe. In her archive an 'Album of Confessions' from the late 1880s lists her goal in life as 'disseminating the works of my husband'.[12] Disseminating his works is only a part of what she did to secure his legacy. She kept a stenographic diary of their time abroad, she wrote valuable memoirs, and she prepared Dostoevskii's letters to her for publication. In different ways these are important sources for the biographer, but the letters are particularly valuable in showing the agony Dostoevskii experienced in dealing with journals, editors and publishers. She prepared bibliographical information and archival material for publication. Modern bibliographies, archives and literary museums build on her orderly and conscientious work. In her notebooks she kept lists of subscribers to his editions and lists of payments for his fiction; modern scholarship has yet to take full advantage of these resources.

This rich legacy was not yet something to anticipate, as the couple's immediate concern in 1867 was avoiding debtors' prison. Her diary and Dostoevskii's letters of the ensuing four years chronicle his financial desperation in excruciating detail. His frequent and painful attacks of epilepsy, his gambling, his quarrel with Turgenev, his disenchantment with Europe, and his longing for Russia are well-known aspects of his biography. Also during these years he managed to write two major novels, *The Idiot* and *The Devils*, and to ensure their serialisation in a relatively timely manner while writing a novella, *The Eternal Husband*, for a new journal, *Dawn*. Almost all of *The Idiot* appeared during 1868. *The Devils* did spill over into two issues of a second subscription year (1871–2) in *The Russian Herald*, but much of the delay was occasioned by Katkov's refusal to publish even a toned-down version of the controversial chapter 'At Tikhon's' and by the journal's delay in conveying this decision to the novelist.

Dostoevskii was not always saintly when it came to dealing with journals: he took a substantial advance (900 roubles) from *Dawn* for a long novel, but he had not delivered it by the time the journal folded, and he did not return the advance. But he was as much sinned against as sinning during these years: it took five years and threats of legal action before the infamous Stellovskii paid Dostoevskii the 3,000 roubles he owed the novelist for a second edition of *Crime and Punishment*. Nevertheless, Dostoevskii even in the worst of times was a model of professional regularity by comparison with many of his fellow novelists. Tolstoi did not complete the serialisation of *War and Peace* in *The Russian Herald*; the serialisation of *Anna Karenina* had spread out over two and a half years before Katkov refused to publish its final part in 1877. Two contemporary novels appeared at an even more dilatory pace: Melnikov's anthropological novel *In The Hills* was supported by *The Russian Herald* between 1875 and 1881, while Saltykov-Shchedrin's *The Golovlevs* evolved from a series of sketches to a novel between 1876 and 1881 in *Notes of the Fatherland*. Turgenev's novels, it is true, did not present such challenges to their readers' long-term memory, but they were much shorter, and sometimes appeared within a single issue of a thick journal (*Fathers and Sons*, *Smoke*). Dostoevskii's relative reliability is all the more striking because he generally had not completed a draft of a novel when serialisation commenced.

Dostoevskii returned to St Petersburg in 1871 to begin what would become, all things considered, the most professionally calm and prosperous decade of his life. Serialisation of two major novels (*A Raw Youth*, 1875, and *The Brothers Karamazov*, 1879–80), the editorship of a weekly newspaper (*The Citizen*, 1873–4), and the publication of his highly original one-person journal, *The Diary of a Writer* (1876–8, single issues in 1880 and 1881) ensured a steady income. Beginning with the first separate edition of *The Devils*, the intrepid Anna Grigorevna took over the republication of Dostoevskii's major fiction, contracting with printers and selling his books from their own apartment. The contrast between this successful cottage enterprise and the large-scale dissemination networks of British and American publishers provides a striking demonstration of Russia's circumscribed literary life.

The orderly sequence of Dostoevskii's activities conceals, however, his continuing struggles over honoraria and new challenges to his independence and integrity as a writer and journalist as he made his way between conservative and radical periodicals, between militant nationalism and Christian populism. Early in the decade the former political prisoner became friendly with K. P. Pobedonostsev, the arch-conservative tutor to the future Alexander III and Nicholas II, and through him became an acquaintance of the imperial family. He personally presented a copy of *The Brothers Karamazov* to Grand Prince Alexander in 1880. But Dostoevskii's return to Russia began with a search of his papers at the border (interrupted when his baby daughter started crying) and would include a brief incarceration in a St Petersburg jail for reporting news of an important person without obtaining official permission. The government lifted official surveillance of him in 1875, but he did not learn of this until 1880, if then. Had Dostoevskii known that the gendarmes also struck Pushkin (d. 1837) from the list of those under surveillance in 1875, he might have taken surveillance less seriously, although a series of repressions and executions through the decade created an atmosphere that made him highly anxious for the country he loved.

Dostoevskii entered this new circle of acquaintance through his editorship of *The Citizen*, which was published by a wealthy conservative publicist, Prince V. P. Meshcherskii. The regular salary (250 roubles a month, in addition to honoraria for pieces he published in the paper) was impossible to resist, but so also was the opportunity to address the public on matters of current concern. Dostoevskii had followed Russian developments carefully while abroad, taking pride in his fictions' uncanny anticipation of unfolding events. And he had been considering publishing his own periodical, a news-paper or almanac, for several years (e.g. xxviii/2, 224; letter of 29 September 1867 to S. A. Ivanova).

Dostoevskii used his time with the journal to write a series of sixteen columns, 'The Diary of a Writer'. Some of his very best essayistic work, they drew on his experience as a feuilletonist in the 1840s and a polemicist for *Time* and *Epoch*. Deftly conversational, playful, at times satirical, they challenged the unquestioned presuppositions of the Westernised intelligentsia, such as environmental determinism, and played them off against trenchantly observed current situations as well as against the columnist's reminiscences of three decades of literary life. Unexpected conclusions, crisp formulations and an engaging persona contributed to the success of the columns and gave Dostoevskii confidence to expand the column into a monthly periodical. But other aspects of Dostoevskii's work for the paper – the day-to-day negotiations, copy editing, correcting the inept prose of the proprietor – became onerous. He left the editorship in March 1874. It is not certain that he would have been comfortable remaining with it in any case. Although ideologically compatible with Meshcherskii's conservative, monarchist positions, Dostoevskii took the professional position that government subsidies compromise the press (xxviii/2, 153–4; letter of 15 April 1866 to M. N. Katkov), and *The Citizen* would become a notorious recipient of large sums from the government's 'reptile fund'.[13]

Dostoevskii's next turn must have struck some of his old friends as ideological betrayal. He agreed to serialise his new novel, *A Raw Youth*, in a left-leaning journal, *Notes of the Fatherland*, now edited by his old opponent Nekrasov. It helped that Nekrasov offered a generous advance and a first-rate honorarium, 250 roubles a signature, and Dostoevskii's authorial vanity had been wounded by the prior commitment of *The Russian Herald* to *Anna Karenina*, at a magnificent rate of 500 roubles. When Liubimov learned that Dostoevskii might publish with a rival journal, he clumsily proposed in a letter of 4 May 1874 a compromise that was hardly flattering to Dostoevskii:

> The editors can no doubt agree to add three thousand for an esteemed contributor. But to raise official, so to speak, honoraria could have consequences which would make publishing impossible. Nekrasov has already resorted to the device we have in mind ten times. We did this with Turgenev and Melnikov. If a significant increase in honorarium for your new novel became known, then demands could appear from all sides for increases in payment, and then publishing would be quite impossible, even if the number of subscribers were to rise greatly. If it were possible to preserve the previous nominal honoraria, but to add a considerable sum for you, so that what you received overall would correspond to your wishes, the matter would be settled without the general consequences of which I am speaking. It would only be necessary to keep this supplement a secret between us. In this way your conditions would be taken as a particular case and would not turn into a general rule.[14]

That Liubimov seemed in no particular hurry to see the novel would have reminded Dostoevskii that Tolstoi's work took precedence over his, and that too would have made it easier to accept Nekrasov's offer. But Dostoevskii's decision need not have been based only on financial considerations and hurt pride. He was no Rakitin, the disreputable figure in *The Brothers Karamazov* who could write simultaneously for radical and ecclesiastical journals. The ideological distance between Dostoevskii and *Notes of the Fatherland* had narrowed to the point of compatibility by 1874, as the radicals' Nihilist politics of the 1860s had yielded to the idealistic populism of the 1870s. Dostoevskii could find common ground with the younger generation as it turned its attention to thc values of the Russian countryside, since he himself had been arguing since the 1860s for such a turn.[15]

By now Dostoevskii's financial situation was stable, and he was able to return to *The Diary of a Writer*, this time as his own publication. In format each monthly issue was a brochure, usually a signature and a half in length, and the issues could be bound in yearly volumes; the enterprise was successful, and the first year's issues were already reprinted in book format by 1879. By now Dostoevskii had the authorial status to risk part publication, or at least a version of it. He (more accurately, Anna Grigorevna) printed two to three times as many copies each month as they had subscriptions; they were able to sell the rest on news stands and to booksellers. At its best the *Diary* included some of Dostoevskii's most memorable fictional, feuilletonistic and argumentative writing; at its worst – harsh ethnic, religious and national chauvinism. For many reasons, incisively recounted by Deborah Martinsen, the *Diary* was a timely enterprise: it capitalised on patriotic fervour aroused by the Russo-Turkish war, it appealed to both populists and conservatives, it polemicised with all positions.[16] Most of all, it did this with a conversational intimacy that engaged its readers. Of all of Dostoevskii's works, it is the one which most provoked his readers to write to him, and they did so on topics of immediate personal concern.

For two years Dostoevskii published the journal regularly. The compositor with whom he worked, M. A. Aleksandrov, has left a detailed memoir which testifies to Dostoevskii's professionalism. But Aleksandrov also noted that journalistic labour was not, as he put it, congenial to Dostoevskii's muse. Ill-health and a desire to devote himself to his last novel led Dostoevskii to break it off. He returned to the *Diary* in 1880 only to publish his Pushkin speech. Death frustrated his plan to resume regular publication in 1881.

Spring 1878 found Dostoevskii already hard at work on his new novel, and he planned to serialise it during 1879. Tolstoi had by now entirely broken off relations with Katkov, and Turgenev, in the twilight of his career, was publishing with *The Herald of Europe*. Consequently, Dostoevskii returned to *The Russian Herald* better able to dictate his terms than ever before. And while Katkov's face may have twisted in pain at Dostoevskii's terms – 300 roubles a signature and an advance – and while he may have threatened to cease publishing *The Russian Herald*, he did agree to these terms (XXX/1, 32; letter of 20–1 June 1878 to A. G. Dostoevskaia). And while Dostoevskii may have feared for the more controversial passages in the novel, remembering Katkov's excisions from *Crime and Punishment* and *The Devils*, he was treated with much more respect in publishing this novel. Judicious argumentation with Liubimov and Katkov as well as with the influential Pobedonostsev carried the day with the journal and censorship, and Dostoevskii could worry about how the daring 'Grand Inquisitor' section would be understood by his readers: in the overall context of the novel or separately, as a devastating argument against the novelist's own beliefs. His letters about the novel to these three potentially critical figures represent some his best writing about the art of fiction and, in particular, the art of serialisation.

Despite his hopes and plans, serialisation of *The Brothers Karamazov* did not end during the 1879 subscription year, but only with its sixteenth instalment, in November 1880. Unlike Tolstoi, who left it to the journal to apologise when *Anna Karenina* spilled over into a third subscription year, the more professional Dostoevskii himself apologised to the journal's subscribers, in a letter published in the December 1879 issue. His poor health played a role in the delays, as did his work on the Pushkin speech, but he also found that he had to conduct substantial research on monasticism and on police investigative procedures before publishing these parts of the novel. Taking his time, Dostoevskii was able to build on his thematic experiments in *The Diary of a Writer* and consciously to create a new type of serialised novel, one which relied not on tried-and-true plotting tricks of suspense and surprise, but rather on making each of the novel's twelve books a relatively complete thematic unit.[17]

Death found Dostoevskii a professional writer in all three senses of the word. True to his vocation he was planning to continue *The Diary of a Writer* and *The Brothers Karamazov*. Supported solely by income from his writing once he resigned from government service, he wrote his last letter to Liubimov, to enquire after the 4,000 roubles he was owed for his last novel. His commitment to the profession he had helped make élite through his principled journalism and fiction writing was recognised by his public and by the government. Many memoirs testify to the unprecedented outpouring of public grief as the late writer's body was carried from his apartment to the church and grave. Schoolchildren and students made up a large part of the throng and provided many of the wreaths. The government granted Dostoevskii's widow and children a pension of 2,000 roubles a year, making him the first writer not in government service to be honoured in this way – that is, he was honoured for his literary work alone. In death Dostoevskii the paradoxalist had revealed two final paradoxes: a frequent critic of the Russian intelligentsia for its automatised thought and excessive theorising, he became one of its foremost cultural heroes; no less critical of professionals (lawyers, doctors, professors) for their short-sighted and rational discourse, he became one of Russia's first true professionals in his own field, helping to establish its norms of collegial responsibility and ethical behaviour.

Notes

1 Aleksandr Nikitenko, *The Diary of a Russian Censor*, abridged, edited and translated by H. S. Jacobson (Amherst: University of Massachusetts Press, 1975), p. 30.

2 V. G. Belinskii, 'Neskol'ko slov o "Sovremennike"' (A few words about *The Contemporary*) in *Polnoe sobranie sochinenii v deviati tomakh* (Complete Works in nine volumes) (Moscow: Khudozhestvennaia literatura, 1976–82), vol. 1, p. 489.

3 N. V. Gogol', 'O dvizhenii zhurnal'noi literatury v 1834 i 1835 godu' (On the movement of journalistic literature in 1834 and 1835) in *Polnoe sobranie sochinenii* 14 vols. (Moscow: Nauka, 1937–52), vol. 8, p. 162.

4 V. E. Evgen'ev-Maksimov *et al.* (eds.), *Ocherki po istorii russkoi zhurnalistiki i kritiki* (Studies in the History of Russian Journalism and Criticism), vol. 1 (Leningrad: Izd. Leningradskogo Universiteta, 1950), p. 332.

5 V. G. Belinskii, 'Russkaia literatura v 1840 godu' (Russian literature in 1840) in *Polnoe sobranie sochinenii v deviati tomakh*, vol. 3, pp. 195–8.

6 Alexander Gerschenkron, 'Time horizon in Russian literature', *Slavic Review* 34:4 (December 1975), pp. 692–715.

7 In Dostoevsky's time one silver rouble was equal in value to 3.5 paper roubles. Unless otherwise stated all sums in this study are given in paper roubles. The 'signature' (*pechatnyi list*) remains the basis for literary honoraria to this day in Russia; it is the sheet of paper which the printer folds and binds. In the books and journals of Dostoevskii's time it typically yielded sixteen pages.

8 Joseph Frank, *Dostoevsky: The Years of Ordeal, 1850–1859* (Princeton University Press, 1983), pp. 236–40.

9 Robert Belknap, 'Survey of Russian journals, 1840–80' in Deborah A. Martinsen (ed.), *Literary Journals in Imperial Russia* (Cambridge University Press, 1997), p. 108.

10 V. S. Nechaeva, *Zhurnal M. M. i F. M. Dostoevskikh 'Vremia' 1861–63* (The Dostoevskii Brothers' Journal *Time* 1861–63) (Moscow: Nauka, 1972), pp. 306–8.

11 G. A. and A. G. Rusanov, *Vospominaniia o L.N. Tolstom, 1883–1901gg.* (Reminiscences, about Tolstoi, 1883–1901) (Voronezh: Tsentr-Chernozem. kn. izd., 1972), p. 53.

12 Archival reference details are: A. G. Dostoevskaia, 'Al'bom priznanii', OR GBL, Fond 93, razd. III, kart. 3, ed. khr. 2, page 3.

13 Charles A. Ruud, *Fighting Words: Imperial Censorship and the Russian Press, 1804–1906* (Toronto: University of Toronto Press, 1982), p. 198.

14 Archival reference: OR GBL, Fonds 93, razd. II, kart. 6, ed. khr. 33, page 14.

15 Joseph Frank, 'Dostoevsky and Russian Populism' in Alan Cheuse and Richard Koffler (eds.), *The Rarer Action: Essays in Honor of Francis Fergusson* (New Brunswick: Rutgers University Press, 1970), p. 302.

16 Deborah A. Martinsen, 'Dostoevsky's "Diary of a Writer": journal of the 1870s', in Martinsen (ed.), *Literary Journals in Imperial Russia*, pp. 150–68.

17 William Mills Todd, III, '*The Brothers Karamazov* and the poetics of serial publication', *Dostoevsky Studies* 7 (1986), pp. 87–97.

5

BORIS CHRISTA

Dostoevskii and money

Dostoevskii's fictional world is dominated by money. One critic has identified it, along with epilepsy, as 'the ruling power in Dostoyevsky's creative environment'.[1] It confronts his characters at every step and their awareness of it is often articulated. Dmitrii in *The Brothers Karamazov* reflects ruefully: 'without money you can't take a step in any direction' (XIV, 344; Bk 8, Sec. 3). Makar Ivanovich, the wise old peasant in *A Raw Youth*, says: 'Even if money is not God – it is at least a demi-god' (XIII, 311; Pt 3, Ch. 3). Aleksei puts it even more strongly in *The Gambler*, when he states categorically: 'Money is everything!' (V, 229; Ch. 5)

Painfully sensitive to the significance of money in human affairs, Dostoevskii was fully conscious of its ability to function as a medium in literary communication. But money as theme and message is also central to his writing. He recognises that money is power and its unequal distribution a cause of massive suffering and conflict. The close examination of social hardship is one of his primary concerns as a novelist. Rejecting the option of forcible redistribution of wealth through revolution and bloodshed, he nevertheless opposes strongly the frenzied pursuit of money by fair means or foul and the unprincipled use of money-based power. He presents money above all as a touchstone, a moral challenge, and his concern is how individuals obtain it, spend it and live with it. He lived and wrote at a time in Russian history when the old feudal society, which provided subsistence as a birthright, was superseded by a free-for-all capitalist society that demanded strenuous struggle to survive. His own highly dramatic career strongly confirmed him in his views on the central importance of money in life and human relationships. References to it abound in his correspondence and non-fictional prose, and as medium, theme and message, it forms one of the basic building blocks of his creative writing.

Although chronically incapable of handling his own financial affairs, Dostoevskii was very alert and well-informed about money. So often presented as a 'seer of the spirit', a visionary and mystic, he is, in his fictional writing, extremely street-wise. He knows exactly what a rouble will buy, mentions the various currencies of Europe in a casual and authoritative way and is even familiar with the rates of exchange. He knows the ways of rich merchant-tycoons, shopkeepers, pawnbrokers and lodging-house keepers. There is frequent mention of loans and interest rates, promissory notes, bonds and other securities and, above all, the major works are strewn with meaningful references to named sums of roubles and kopecks, demonstrating that money had for Dostoevskii a level of significance that seems unmatched by any other of the world's great writers. It is a hallmark of his technique to present much information in asides and subtextual indications that require the reader to be, as it were, 'interactive' with the author. This style gives depth and realistic texture to his literary discourse. He is a pioneer in bringing to the surface, and into the realm of literature, mundane facts of existence that are often hidden or falsified. He realised that in this context money was of singular significance. Named sums of cash are hard facts and they can serve to deconstruct any façade of pretensions, opinions or lies. 'Money talks', as the popular adage has it, and Dostoevskii is adept at making it speak expressively and frankly.

In the social world which Dostoevskii describes, genteel poverty is the norm and, in self-defence, his characters tend to spin around themselves a cocoon of deception and social pretence. To maintain authenticity, he faithfully describes these attempts at social camouflage, but his 'cruel talent' refuses to accept a taboo on intrusion. As a critical realist, it was axiomatic for him that no characterisation was complete without full information regarding the financial circumstances which influenced the development of a particular person and motivated his or her behaviour and outlook. The precise extent of personal income, for instance, is very significant in the case of individual major characters, since their life-style and view of the world are conditioned fundamentally by the money they have available to spend. For example, the hero in the seminal story *Notes from Underground* reveals in answer to an imaginary interrogator that he was a totally unmotivated public servant. He retired at once when he received an unexpected legacy of 6,000 roubles. He now lives on the income from this modest capital and this gives a key to his drab and oppressive 'underground' existence. He subsists, but can afford nothing. By retiring from work and society and becoming a solitary outsider, he has struck a blow for intellectual independence. But the only freedom he has is to muse and rant endlessly, and his meagre income inevitably conditions his attitudes and his bitter and subversive thoughts.

In the story *White Nights*, written in an uncharacteristic romantic vein, the references to cash signal the intrusion of reality and the approaching end of romance. In euphoric mood Nastenka, the heroine, exchanges confidences with her suitor. She reveals that she is living with her grandmother, who only has a small pension and takes in a lodger to make ends meet. She is clearly looking for security and can't afford to indulge in 'childish stuff'. Unguardedly, he confesses that he manages on a modest salary of 1,200 roubles yearly. From the intoxication of glamorous, 'white' summer nights in St Petersburg, we descend abruptly to the harsh world of economic reality and it heralds the end of a dream. In the morning comes her terminal letter severing the relationship.

The device of using such references to precise sums not only serves to reveal genteel poverty, but can equally well unmask unsuspected misers and hoarders. This happens in the case of several Dostoevskian characters who build their existence around the accumulation of hidden wealth, while their life-style is one of apparent indigence. A notable case is the eponymous, eccentric hero of the story of *Mister Prokharchin*, who, while living an outwardly beggarly life, stuffs every coin he can scrounge into a trunk under his bed. When he feels threatened he goes berserk, attacks his fellow lodgers and dies in a mysterious brawl. When his hoard is opened, it contains a treasure-trove of coins and the myth is born that he was a millionaire.

The narrational development of this quirky story depends entirely for its effect on the deployment of monetary semiotic markers. The final éclat here comes when Dostoevskii chooses to deconstruct the newly created image of Prokharchin as a closet millionaire and to highlight the futility of a life dedicated to hoarding. After careful counting, it turns out that after all the years of skimping and saving, he has accumulated precisely 2,497 roubles and 50 kopecks – 'an extremely significant sum', according to the tale's narrator, but not the millions some of his fellow lodgers had first estimated (1, 261).

In Dostoevskii's novels money is invariably a major element of characterisation. In the introduction of new characters, the information regarding financial status is sometimes withheld to maintain an element of mystery, to be resolved later, but generally it is given at once. It is usually expressed by the capital at their disposal, sometimes by the number of serfs on their estate and sometimes by yearly income. Women generally have their position in the social hierarchy defined by reference to the amount of their marriage dowry.

In the case of Fedor, the negative father-figure in *The Brothers Karamazov*, the initial description makes the money indication work very subtly. He is portrayed as a worthless, immoral, slow-witted misfit, who sponges on everybody and scrounges for meals; but the mental image which the reader is forming has to be radically reconstructed when Dostoevskii informs us that old man Karamazov has built up an unencumbered fortune of 100,000 roubles. The naming of the specific sum makes a big impact. It suddenly becomes apparent that the character that we are getting to know is not an insignificant drop-out, but a wily, secretive and tough man, utterly unprincipled in his relations with others and ruthlessly grasping in his pursuit of money.

Dostoevskii's sensitivity in matters of social and financial status is always acute and he does not find it necessary in all cases to spell out details of monetary worth in full to achieve definition. Often a brief reference, apparently just in passing, names a sum of cash or indicates a value which serves his purpose. For instance, a request by a character to borrow a small sum of cash with promises of repayment, a frequently recurring situation, can reveal a great deal. So do the references to prices of everyday items and personal reactions to these. In *Crime and Punishment*, for example, we learn much from Razumikhin's precise detailing of the clothing purchases he has made for Raskolnikov. Every item here is clearly described and exactly priced. Dostoevskii is acutely aware of the value of such status symbols, especially vestimentary markers – matters of clothing, hairstyle and adornment that make statements about the wearer. Living in a cold climate, Russians have traditionally been aware of the status-value of outer garments: winter coats and fur hats are semiotic markers that make a major statement. Living up to the statement so often attributed to him – 'we have all come from under Gogol's *Overcoat*' – Dostoevskii uses these garments purposefully to convey information. In *A Raw Youth*, for example, it gives insight into the dynamics of Arkadii Dolgorukii's upward social mobility when we read of his complaint that a new winter season is coming and his old coonskin coat is worth merely twenty-five roubles. Such references to values and prices are always totally authentic. Dostoevskii knows precisely the cost of a fur coat or the rent of an apartment. In fact, his knowledge of St Petersburg real estate seems almost professional. In describing the apartment of General Ivolgin in *The Idiot*, for example, he sees at a glance that it is beyond the reach of a civil servant on 2,000 roubles per annum, which in the subtext translates to immediate doubts regarding the integrity of this gentleman.

Dostoevskii's sharp and well-trained eye for the value of status-symbols is often in evidence. He notes the 'cheap and under-size' clock on the wall of Father Zosima's cell and the 'low-priced', large glass vase on the marble stand in old Karamazov's reception room. In the macabre story *Bobok*, there is even much talk of the prices of coffins and who can afford the various styles. The supply of such down-to-earth information brings clarity and precision and so plays a particularly significant role in Dostoevskii's idiosyncratic technique of narration. This tends to oscillate between mystification and lucidity. To heighten curiosity and increase tension, he sets false trails, allows characters to make misleading statements, makes puzzling allusions to events in the past, future or even outside the action of the novel, and withholds information which the reader is anxiously awaiting. This haziness and uncertainty – which he has created very deliberately, as evidenced by his notebooks – is dispelled effectively by the introduction of mundane matters such as money, prices and values. Money 'speaks' unequivocally, and especially the naming of precise sums brings the narrative sharply back into focus.

The technique is well illustrated by the treatment of Prince Myshkin's status in *The Idiot*. As Myshkin enters the novel, travelling in the railway compartment that takes the main characters of the novel to St Petersburg as chance acquaintances, there is much mystery about him. Apart from his ancient title, his only worldly assets are contained in a bundle which he drags around the salons and which seems to symbolise his nomadic and impoverished situation. Subsequently, we learn that his financial position has changed dramatically when he unexpectedly inherits a fortune from a distant, very rich relative. We now have various reports regarding his alleged new enormous wealth, but all is rumour and uncertainty and there is a baffling break in the action when he disappears to Moscow for many months to claim his inheritance. Prince Myshkin's courtship of Aglaia on his return to St Petersburg again is full of ambivalences and mystification. Finally, in Part 4 of the novel, comes the moment when the narrator tells us that all the misunderstandings are to be resolved. Aglaia publicly demands to know the extent of Myshkin's fortune. With typical candour he replies very precisely: his assets amount to exactly 135,000 roubles. No doubt Dostoevskii chose the sum very carefully. Aglaia's immediate response is disappointment. After the build-up of Myshkin as the heir to a vast fortune, the reality is sobering. But Myshkin, having earlier graduated from pauper to fairy-tale prince with untold riches, now becomes a realistic character: a well-off, but not extravagantly rich young man, who tells us that he intends to study to become a professional teacher. Aglaia and the reader now face a deconstructed fairy prince and her reactions and subsequent relations with him give a new slant on her character.

Money again is the medium which totally deconstructs the dream which Grushenka, in *The Brothers Karamazov*, has cherished for years – of the handsome officer who seduced her in her teens with his Polish charm. Having heard that she is now quite affluent, the ex-lover returns towards the end of the novel to renew his conquest. However, he betrays his real nature at every step. Desperately mean, he grabs every rouble he can, cheats at cards and sends letters begging for cash. The named sums of money he asks for get progressively smaller. Beginning with a long flowery letter asking for a loan of 2,000 roubles, eventually he asks just to borrow a single rouble. Grushenka recognises the real man behind the façade and sends him packing. Her expansive Russian nature is repelled by pettiness and greed and she turns towards the free-spending, wildly generous Dmitrii Karamazov.

The technique of using money as a medium to penetrate to the reality of a situation is also very effective in imparting to the reader information that, if stated explicitly, would have offended the literary canons of the time. For example, sums of money given by a man to a woman generally have covert sexual meaning, but Dostoevskii has to leave it to the reader to decipher the code. Sexual transactions which in his time were masked by conventional hypocrisy and taboos of speech are revealed through the language of money. In *Crime and Punishment*, we are told by the drunken Marmeladov about the hopeless situation faced by girls without means or education. 'Honest work' would bring them less than fifteen kopecks a day, but none is available. His own daughter, the frail but sensitive and attractive Sonia, cannot find employment and has to endure the constant reproaches of her stepmother that she eats and is kept warm while the younger siblings go hungry. Finally, she makes her decision, dresses as prettily as she can and goes out. Three hours later she returns and puts thirty roubles on the table in front of her stepmother and then covers her head and lies sobbing with her face to the wall. No aspect of the sexual act that has taken place is described explicitly, all is left to the imagination; but the adult reader has been informed, by the subtext created by the named sum of thirty roubles, what has happened. She has risked her health, surrendered her virginity, jeopardised her future and embarked on a life of prostitution.

Money supplies the semiotic markers for subtextual communication in all cases of consenting sexual relations that occur in the pages of Dostoevskii. Usually, the inferences are clear, but occasionally the verdict is left open. For instance, in *A Raw Youth*, when Versilov learns how much money the rich Prince Sergei is giving to his son Arkadii, he takes it as a sign that they are having a homosexual relationship. No additional information is supplied and the judgement is left to the reader.

Money does not, of course, merely serve Dostoevskii as a literary device to deconstruct the text and reveal realities hidden behind the smug façades of convention: in his development as a writer it evolves from being a medium into a message which proves a rich source of major themes and plots. This process can be observed already in the novel with which he made his literary début – money, from being the catalyst for revelations and psychological characterisation, leads to a thematic focussing on poverty as a social phenomenon. The opening of *Poor Folk* seems nostalgic for a romantic past. Devushkin, the timid hero, is painfully sensitive to convention and communicates with his beloved Varvara only by letters. In spite of his lack of means, he clings desperately to the last remnants of gentility. He makes believe that he has money to spare, and showers his sweetheart with gifts to maintain a façade of solvency. But gradually the mood changes. His increasingly critical shortage of cash, carefully documented in the text, inevitably brings out the bitter truth. Finally, he has precisely one rouble to his name, a loan has been refused, and he has ten days to go before his pitifully low pay is due.

The deconstructive functioning of the harsh and semiotically powerful references to money totally breaks down the earlier romantic element. In *Poor Folk*, Devushkin is gradually and painfully stripped of all dignity, status or even privacy. Dostoevskii exploits his new literary technique to the full, even allowing his hero to 'lay bare the device' by an analogy in one of his letters to Varvara: 'Forgive me, Varenka, for the indelicate expression, but the poor man experiences the same kind of shame as does a young, chaste girl like yourself. Do, please, forgive the indelicate expression, but you would not undress in front of everybody, would you? Well in exactly the same way a poor man doesn't like to have his intimate, personal life revealed' (I, 69; 1 August). At the tragic climax, Devushkin is shown totally defeated in his struggle against dire poverty and he loses Varvara forever. The thematic emphasis has shifted from the sentimental and psychological to the grimly realistic, and almost inadvertently the novel ends up making a forceful social statement.

Poor Folk firmly established the theme of poverty in Dostoevskii's literary repertoire.[2] It continues to be the most significant issue in works such as *The Insulted and Injured*, where again money is the powerful corroding force that eats through the surface of an otherwise sentimental novel, releasing energy, spawning conflict and bringing the action closer to reality. Poverty remains an indispensable background theme even in the great novels of the final two decades, where other concerns move to the centre of the stage. *Crime and Punishment* is unthinkable without the agonising, but intensely memorable, portrayal of the Marmeladov family, or *The Brothers Karamazov* without the Snegirevs.

Dostoevskii's novels mirror a changing world. Poverty and social disadvantage no longer appear as a God-given fate to be meekly accepted without complaint. Opportunities beckon in a new, free-enterprise society, leading to a rapid redistribution of wealth with the possession of money outweighing any advantages of social origin. As Arkadii says in *A Raw Youth*: 'In our era the main thing is the individual and then his money' (XIII, 363; Pt 3, Ch. 6). Writing in his own name in *Diary of a Writer* for October 1876, Dostoevskii puts it even more forcefully: 'The power of money was understood also in past times, but never in Russia, until now, was money considered to be the greatest thing in the world' (XXIII, 159). It was an insight as valid for the time as it was prophetic for the future.

The abuse of money-based power and the moral corruption which it engendered constantly engage Dostoevskii's attention. His novels abound with vivid and often repulsive episodes in which money plays the key role for evil. They range from the overtly criminal to the merely malicious. Maksim Ivanovich, the rich factory owner in *A Raw Youth*, for example, wilfully orders his men to flog a boy who has inadvertently bumped into him. When the boy turns out to be badly injured and lies critically ill, he simply sends the mother fifteen roubles in compensation. Trivial by comparison, but nevertheless telling, is an incident quoted in the same novel. We learn of a Moscow tavern that has a singing nightingale. A rich merchant comes in and asks: 'How much for the nightingale?' – 'A hundred roubles' – 'Right, roast it and serve it up!' When the dish is brought, he looks at it and says: 'All right, cut me off twenty kopecks' worth' (XIII, 222; Pt 2, Ch. 5). Although, probably, an apocryphal black humour anecdote of the time, Dostoevskii's citation of it draws attention to the wanton ruthlessness and caprice of some of the rich tycoons of the period.

Money and its potential for good and evil is the primary theme of Dostoevskii's greatest novels. He recognised money as equating with power and saw that in the Russia of his day there was virtually unrestricted scope for its exercise. Corruption was rife and ready cash could gain all ends. Fedka, in *The Devils*, offers to commit murders for 1,500 roubles each and is willing to bargain. References to bribery abound even when they indict the judicial system. Zametov, for instance, a senior court official, is described as a noted taker of bribes in *Crime and Punishment*, and Svidrigailov in the same novel boasts that with his money and connections, he can easily obtain a passport to allow Raskolnikov, the murderer, to flee the country. Similarly, in *The Brothers Karamazov*, Ivan organises a scheme to get his brother free: 10,000 roubles to get him out of prison, 20,000 for a passage to America.

Interestingly enough, in his very wide-ranging treatment of the theme of social abuse and injustice based on the power of money, Dostoevskii betrays relatively little indignation or reformist fervour. His treatment of rich aristocrats with 'old' money tends to be tolerant and forgiving, while highlighting their propensity to decadence and self-destruction. But even the people with the 'new' money – the successful entrepreneurs, merchants and money-lenders – come off lightly when they are using money unscrupulously to further their enterprises. Where Dostoevskii becomes strongly emotionally involved is when he takes up the theme of money and sexual power. In this area he was a pioneering publicist totally aware of the realities of sexual power and the deplorable economic position of women. Virtually the only legitimate careers available to females were those of the governess or teacher. While the 'feminist question' was beginning to achieve prominence on the intellectual agenda, the social reality was far behind. Young women could find economic security only in marriage and this entailed being able to attract prospective husbands by the possession of a suitable dowry. Although the process of courtship was veiled by an aura of romanticism, the underlying reality was often harsh and materialistic. In Dostoevskii's perception every woman has her price. This view not only finds expression in his novels as an element of the plot, but also frequently leads him to the creation of an erotic subtext which adds significantly to the tension of the narrative.[3]

Plots based on the sexual conquest of an unwilling, poor woman by a wealthy man occur throughout Dostoevskii's work. His attention was especially captured by the dilemma of the very young, virginal woman pursued by the rich, old profligate. The victimised heroines all share the same background. They come from 'good' families that have lost their money and status. However virtuous, intelligent, beautiful or proud they might be, the dice are loaded in favour of the wealthy predator. The description of the unequal contest with all its poignancy and sexual overtones provided Dostoevskii with a powerful source of tension, a stimulus to the erotic imagination and a theme with a strong personal emotional challenge.

In this context, Dostoevskii once again finds the citation of named sums of money a valuable vehicle of literary communication. In the initial stage when the characters are introduced and established, it informs the reader very precisely regarding the parameters of the contest. Subsequently, as the action proceeds, the medium becomes part of the message. While the conventions of the time and the ever watchful censor made any explicit depiction of physical conquest unthinkable, the reader's reception and interpretation of the financial transactions involved provide all the required leverage for the imagination. The named sums of cash allow the reader to deconstruct the overt text. Every act of acceptance of financial assistance by the victim, for instance, brings her closer to submission and we can visualise clearly the stages in the process of institutionalised enslavement and legal rape that follow.

In *Poor Folk* the numerous references to named sums of money document the abject poverty of the main characters and reveal the ruthlessness of Bykov's conquest of the pretty, young Varvara. On the surface, we have a perfectly proper courtship by an elderly widower of an unmarried spinster, but the fact that she is a slip of a girl, who finds him loathsome, puts a totally different slant on the situation. Bykov deploys his money to force her into submission. He clinches his suit by tricking her into accepting 500 roubles as a gift to buy little luxuries. Unable to resist, she embarks on a shopping spree, then realises that she has been trapped into surrender.

The tale of Olia, a virtually self-contained subplot woven into the complex fabric of *A Raw Youth*, is even more poignant. Here, too, named sums of cash carry the meaning and determine the outcome. Well-bred, intelligent and sensitive, Olia is the archetypal Dostoevskian victimised heroine. Harassed at every turn by rich men seeking to take advantage of her poverty, she finally despairs and hangs herself. Her story exemplifies a cycle of literary variations on the theme of money and sexual power, which culminates in the similarly tragic *A Timid Creature*, written during Dostoevskii's final creative period.

In his mature period, Dostoevskii changes the emphasis in his treatment of the theme of sexual power. The characterisation evolves and the female protagonists gain in stature. In *Crime and Punishment* we have two wealthy men pitting their resources against each other to secure the favours of the proud and 'phenomenally chaste' beauty Dunia, Raskolnikov's young sister. Impoverished and without dowry, she is at first inclined to accept the proposal of the insufferable Luzhin so that she can extend financial help to her beloved brother. Raskolnikov is, however, incensed when he gets the measure of Luzhin and realises that Dunia is selling herself to 'become a legal concubine'. His decisive actions put a stop to Luzhin's plans. Simultaneously, she is being pursued by the rich and perverse, middle-aged sensualist Svidrigailov, who on his own admission uses his money to procure himself young girls. Totally besotted with Dunia he offers her 30,000 roubles to 'run away' with him. Proudly, she refuses and, defending herself with a revolver, she escapes his attempt to rape her.

Twenty years separate *Poor Folk* from *Crime and Punishment*, and increased attention to women's education and growing awareness of social justice issues are beginning to show some results. Dunia is not hapless and fragile but a characterful and capable young woman. She can resist the temptations of money and is able to defend herself. The largeness of the sexual bribe offered – 30,000 roubles – enables Dostoevskii to demonstrate graphically that, from being an easy prey, the 'quarry' has graduated to being a kind of 'trophy woman'. Dunia, in her restrained way, is a new age heroine.

The financial stakes go even higher in *The Idiot*. Here, too, the price increases in ratio to the psychological evolution and maturation of the heroine. In this novel, the sexual conquest of the heroine through money-power actually occurs twice. Her initial seduction follows classic Dostoevskian lines. We learn from the monetary signals in the text that the old and rich roué Totskii has procured for himself his well-born, but orphaned, poor and totally defenceless ward, Nastasia Filippovna. Having paid for her private education and genteel upbringing, he begins abusing her sexually while she is still a young girl, boasting how little his 'conquest' has cost him. When eventually he tires of her he sets her up in a luxurious apartment in St Petersburg and puts her on the marriage market with a handsome dowry.

Nastasia Filippovna's past history suggests that her favours might be available for money and the competition for them develops into a frenzied auction at which Rogozhin and Gania make their bids. Rogozhin, working on the male chauvinistic hypothesis that every woman has her price, keeps adding to his offer. When his bid has reached 100,000 roubles, she agrees to be his. However, when he has handed her the money, she demonstrates dramatically that she is anything but a will-less chattel, flinging the packet with the bank notes into the open fire. Her days as a powerless victim of money-based, sexual conquest are behind her. She is an electrifying, dark-haired beauty, who has adroitly built up her resources and is now fully in control of her independent status. By burning the money she signals that he has not bought her, but that she has chosen to enter the relationship on her own terms.

A similar metamorphosis of vulnerable, defenceless teenager into mature and empowered woman occurs with the two main heroines of *The Brothers Karamazov*. The proud Katerina Ivanovna has run the gauntlet of money-based sexual power as a schoolgirl. Humiliating herself, she has gone to the apartment of Dmitrii Karamazov, at this time a rich and dashing officer, to borrow 4,500 roubles to save her father and family from imminent disgrace and ruin. Although nothing is stated explicitly, the semiotic monetary marker, combined with the 'improper' location, clearly conveys the message that he might accede only at the price of her sexual submission. She is prepared for this and her fate is in the balance, but after a considerable emotional struggle he gives her the money and lets her go unmolested. Dostoevskii then deliberately reverses the circumstances: she becomes rich through an unexpected legacy and he becomes impoverished. His loan is repaid and presently he is 3,000 roubles in her debt. Katerina Ivanovna grows into a self-possessed young woman with authority and status, who now exercises a commanding influence over Dmitrii's fate.

Notable also is the evolution of the characteristically Russian beauty, Grushenka, in the same novel. Victim in her teens of money-based sexual abuse, she has become the kept woman of the rich merchant Samsonov. Charismatic and proud, she does not allow her ambivalent social status to inhibit her personal development. As her lover grows old and decrepit, she becomes independent and confident. Realising that her vulnerability has been due to her lack of means, she takes every opportunity to increase her savings. Now street-wise and experienced, she proves herself an excellent manager and even increases her assets by lending out money at interest. Her new financial position endows her with freedom of action and she can afford to reject the propositions of the rich old philanderer Fedor Karamazov, who seeks to entice her by baiting his particular sex-trap with a packet containing 3,000 roubles.

In the main heroines of Dostoevskii's later novels a remarkable change has taken place. Although all have been helpless in the face of sexual aggression, they have drawn appropriate conclusions and are now themselves using the power of money to defend themselves. Dostoevskii, with characteristic far-sightedness, has charted for them a path leading to emancipation and equality.

The 'money-equals-power' theme extends forcefully into the storyline and proves a powerful motive also in the case of Dostoevskii's most memorable male heroes. They explore in turn possible ways of making money and getting rich that range from frenzied work through to gambling and crime. The variants in the quest for money supply the plot in their respective novels which, taken together, offer an almost encyclopaedic coverage of the role of money in the society of Dostoevskii's time.

The most extreme example of dedication to the goal of amassing a fortune by legitimate means is the hero of *A Raw Youth*. Possessed by the idea of becoming a Russian Rothschild, young Arkadii Dolgorukii begins training himself to become a consummate miser. To save money on food, he will ration himself for months to black bread and water. To reduce his living costs to a minimum, he will occupy only a corner in a communal doss-house and he will walk the streets searching for opportunities to buy some article at a bargain price, so that he can resell it at a hefty profit. In the long term, however, Arkadii's hopes of gaining money through relentless effort come to naught. It is an outcome which does not surprise. In Dostoevskii's very Russian fictional world, money is invariably associated with drama. His heroes are not industrious, persevering plodders and money is an unpredictable, elusive element. At best it comes through an unexpected reversal of fortune that turns the previous position upside down. Windfalls of massive sums of cash, in fact, occur quite frequently in the pages of the Dostoevskian novel. Although they stretch credibility to the limit, they also allow the text to function as a kind of sociological laboratory.

The device figures particularly prominently in *The Idiot*, where we encounter spectacular fluctuations of fortune: from living virtually from hand to mouth in provincial exile, Rogozhin returns home to St Petersburg as a newly baked multi-millionaire. At the end of the novel he will depart for Siberia as a penniless convict. The initially impoverished Myshkin also inherits great riches, while the dashing Radomskii suffers a sudden decline when it transpires that he is plagued by debt and that his rich uncle has been caught embezzling 350,000 roubles from the government and has shot himself. Such transformations in status occur again and again. They obviously enliven the narrative, but they also give Dostoevskii the chance to compare the before and after, leaving the reader to draw his own conclusions. From the moment that he becomes rich, Rogozhin, for instance, is surrounded by sycophantic hangers-on, ready to applaud and do his bidding. When Myshkin is suddenly presented as the heir to great wealth, the attitude towards him changes dramatically from condescension and contempt to total acceptance and respect.

While the chance of an unexpected windfall sustains the aristocrats in the novels, several of the more impetuous heroes choose to pursue a less passive method of trying to get rich, namely gambling. Although equally unpredictable and uncertain, this was an option with which his own experiences had made Dostoevskii painfully familiar, and it seems natural that he should seek to recreate these in his fiction.

Gambling as a possible way of making money fascinated and tantalised Dostoevskii. For years it was a totally irresistible passion which brought him untold misery. His letters bear witness to his aspirations which seemed to him totally realistic and realisable: if he could develop a sensible system that minimised the risks, and exercise firm judgement, there was no reason why he could not acquire great wealth. The reality was different. Piles of money would suddenly appear before him on the gaming table and disappear just as quickly. Win or lose, he would become highly excited, throw caution to the winds and follow irrational hunches, often with disastrous results. Back in his room, after a night of gambling, he perceived his losses as bitter personal failure and was determined to try his luck again at the earliest opportunity. Such too are the experiences of Arkadii recounted in *A Raw Youth*, which bear witness to the highs and lows in the life of a gambler. As yet they represent only one strand in a very polyphonic narrative, but the theme was important to Dostoevskii.

The Gambler is Dostoevskii's most autobiographical novel and it is totally dominated by money. All the characters have their secrets and these are related to financial transactions motivated by their passion for gambling, which is greater even than their interest in love. Apart from its compelling descriptions of the gambling fever, the novel has many sequences where Dostoevskii exploits the semiotic value of sums of cash to further his narrative. For example, we are told by the hero how his massively debt-ridden employer maintains an appearance of being wealthy:

> Everybody here takes the General for a very rich and important person. Before dinner he took the trouble to give me the job, among other things, of getting change for a couple of thousand-franc notes. I changed them at the desk in the hotel. Now, for at least a week, they will think we are millionaires.
>
> (v, 208; Ch. 1)

Very telling in *The Gambler* is Dostoevskii's use of named sums of cash to deconstruct financial façades and the prevalent, conventional myth that gambling was a recreational activity of ladies and gentlemen who did not care whether they won or lost. He describes in minute and vivid detail the play at the roulette table and the betting moves of his characters. These are suffused not only with high narrative tension but also with unexpected ideological interest as Dostoevskii manifests his Slavophile views by contrasting the betting style of the Russians with that of the Western Europeans. As the action unfolds, the extravagant stakes wagered by the Russians become a literary metaphor for the passion and maximalism of the Russian temperament, which is contrasted favourably with the calculating, cold prudence of the Western gamblers, where he sees a thin veneer of pseudo-culture masking egoism and greed. Aleksei even asserts that roulette might have been invented expressly for the Russians.

The Russian approach is exemplified by the gambling style of Tarasevicha, the visiting grand old lady from Moscow, who is presented as a typical Russian of the old school: simple and generous, unaffected and direct, intolerant of Western sophistication. Her final day at the tables is paradigmatic of Russian maximalism. To the heavy losses of the previous day she adds another 90,000 roubles, having converted into cash all the securities she has brought with her: five-percent bills, government loan bonds and all her other paper assets. Her gambling session has lasted nearly seven hours and at the end she has lost everything.

The gambling of Aleksei, the hero, is equally reckless. In the final sentences of *The Gambler* he asks us to believe that what motivates him to go on gambling is not so much the urge to make money as the existentialist sensation of draining the cup of experience to the dregs. Nothing, he assures us, can compare with the feeling of being alone in a strange country, not knowing where the next meal will come from, and then staking one's 'very, very last gulden' on the turn of a roulette-wheel (v, 318; Ch. 17). So even if gambling has been a total failure as a strategy for making money, it has not failed to provide some compensatory thrills. The final words of the novel, however, are extremely ominous: 'Tomorrow, tomorrow, all will be over!'

Evaluating the ability of the Russians to make money, Aleksei asserts that while they are not good at it, they still need it, and he suggests that in the history of civilisation it rates as probably the most important of all human activities. Dostoevskii himself clearly understands this view, and having demonstrated convincingly the failure of his heroes to make money within the law, he turns to examining the outcome of attempts by others to make money and achieve power through crime. The methods they adopt are nothing if not drastic. They range from murder with an axe, through fomenting general revolution, to parricide.

Writing in an era when the furthering of idealistic causes by terrorist activity was high on the reformist political agenda, Dostoevskii saw the acquisition of money through crime as a rational option for an impoverished intellectual. The key theme of *Crime and Punishment* is the attempt of Raskolnikov, a twenty-three-year-old student drop-out, to obtain wealth by murdering and robbing a rich pawnbroker. The laudable ends of using the ill-gotten riches to alleviate social injustice and suffering were to off-set the foul means of the deed. Raskolnikov finds further justification in his theory that humanity from time to time produces extraordinary personalities or supermen, who, because of their strength of will and high intelligence, stand above good and evil and can disregard man-made laws. He sees himself as belonging to this category and this impels him to set out on the deadly mission that ends with the slaying of the old pawnbroker and her totally innocent and God-fearing sister.

Even while Raskolnikov is still at the scene of his crime, it becomes apparent that his enterprise will be a fiasco. The semiotic monetary markers communicate his incompetence as a criminal. Although he has taken a purse stuffed with money and golden trinkets, he does not even count his money or assess the loot. In utter panic, he nearly throws it all into the river and finally hides it in a vacant yard under a stone. In the epilogue, we leave our deconstructed 'superman' in a convict prison in Siberia, regaining his capacity to trust emotions and intuition, and about to undergo a spiritual renaissance.

The theme of criminality and money-based power is also very prominent in *The Devils*, although this novel, with all its insights and intellectual brilliance, hardly takes very seriously the idealistic revolutionary impulse to redistribute wealth and eliminate social injustice. The unprincipled but charismatic hero Stavrogin, for example, sympathises with the conspirators not because of ideological conviction, but because it fits in with his image as an aristocratic eccentric. His self-willed behaviour is based on inherited wealth and the revolutionaries have cast him in the role of their future national leader. Their local commander, Verkhovenskii, also freely admits to his lack of any utopian goals and his aim is simply to grab power. He plans to harness the prevailing vogue for nihilistic thinking in order to overthrow the old order and create unlimited scope for murder and mayhem: 'How can we expect an educated man not to commit murder,' he asks, 'if he is in need of money?' (x, 324; Pt 2, Ch. 8).

In Dostoevskii's final monumental novel, *The Brothers Karamazov*, the theme of getting money by crime dominates the plot. At the heart is the tension between Fedor Karamazov and his sons, which is constantly exacerbated by his parsimony. Dmitrii, the eldest, considers he has a rightful claim to money brought into the family by his mother, who died young. The father rejects this outright, which leads to a bitter confrontation between the two men. When the old man is found murdered, Dmitrii is the obvious prime suspect, and indeed, at the end of the courtroom drama that concludes the novel, he is found guilty of the crime. The reader, however, has learnt in the interim that the real culprit is Smerdiakov, an illegitimate son, who works in the house as a servant. He also wants money to start a new life and is strongly influenced by the intellectual Ivan, who has introduced him to nihilistic ideas, rejecting traditional values of right and wrong, and teaching him that 'everything is permitted'. Ivan also hankers after his father's money so that, carrying out the deed, Smerdiakov is in many respects the agent of his will: 'I am the murderer!' Ivan cries at the trial. 'Is there anybody who doesn't want their father to be dead?' (xv, 117; Bk 12, Sec. 5).

Not only is *The Brothers Karamazov* centred on the theme of money, but the Dostoevskian technique of using named sums of cash for communication and semiotic impact rises to a crescendo. The dispute between the main protagonists, for example, focusses sharply on the struggle for 3,000 roubles for which Dmitrii is prepared to settle his claim against his father. This sum is mentioned in the novel literally hundreds of times and it acquires powerful symbolic meaning. It provides the pivot around which the characters gyrate, since 3,000 roubles is the sum which Katerina Ivanovna has entrusted to Dmitrii and which he has misappropriated. He now desperately needs 3,000 to avoid disgrace. He tries to borrow it from Samsonov, from Gorstin and even from Khokhlakova. Old man Karamazov has 3,000 gift-wrapped and ready as a bait to lure the beautiful Grushenka to his bed. Dmitrii finally tries to steal it and Smerdiakov kills for it. At the trial, the matter of the 3,000 roubles is dissected in minute detail. It is found to constitute the main evidence against Dmitrii and it sends him to Siberia.

It is a matter much to Dostoevskii's credit that, although he held strong views on many religious and philosophical issues, he rarely allowed these to obtrude into his literary narrative and destroy the integrity of the artistic text. So while recognising and foregrounding the elemental and universal significance of money throughout his fiction, he consistently refrains from moralising about its role in human affairs. The closest that he comes to being overtly judgemental is in the context of Ivan Karamazov's famous 'poem', 'The Grand Inquisitor', in which money is castigated as the pursuit of the common herd that prefers to live mindlessly under the tutelage of an authoritarian régime, rather than being encouraged by a charismatic, spiritual leader to develop their individual moral consciousness in freedom and to emancipate themselves from the narrow confines of purely materialistic values. In the text Dostoevskii frequently uses the word 'bread' rather than 'money', but the concepts clearly fuse into one. It is not by chance that in English slang 'bread' is a word for 'money'.

The Brothers Karamazov is a novel of immense intellectual scope and although the issues are presented in very concrete and specific terms, they have far-ranging philosophical implications. We are confronted not merely by conflict over 3,000 roubles between a wayward son and an obdurate father, but by a symbolic representation of the eternal struggle between good and evil, in which money plays a crucial and sinister role. The characters in the novel that particularly impress by their moral stature are those who have not as yet been corrupted by money, such as Alesha, the youngest of the Karamazov brothers, or those who have experienced its temptations and have freed themselves from subservience to it, like Father Zosima, the ex-officer, who has retreated from worldly life to his hermitage and extends guidance and spiritual help to all who seek them. The final message of *The Brothers Karamazov* is forceful and it is revealed by the reactions of the characters to the challenge of the materialistic and hedonistic values symbolised by money. Dostoevskii's personal world-view, as expressed directly in his journalistic and polemical writing, saw money, and the frenzied pursuit of it, in a very negative light. He regarded it as an aspect of decadent Western culture which was threatening the integrity of the Russian ethnic tradition of brotherhood and spirituality. As he puts it in his *Diary of a Writer* for October 1876: 'Let me say it again – the power of money was understood by everybody also in past times, but never until now was money considered in Russia to be the greatest thing in the world' (XXIII, 159). Money with its attendant materialism was the root of all evil, responsible for unleashing powerful destructive forces. Cash is power and power corrupts, so that almost by definition wealth was associated with moral degeneration and spiritual atrophy. Given this underlying antagonistic position, it becomes apparent how in Dostoevskii's fiction money functions on the moral plane as a touchstone – a stone that tests for the presence of precious metals by contact with its dark surface.

It is in their exposure and reaction to money that Dostoevskii's characters reveal their moral identity and spiritual worth. Without fail, all of them, from Arkadii to Zosima, are made to undergo 'trial by money'. Simple peasants show remarkable generosity, giving away their last kopecks to those poorer than themselves, while the affluent are often strikingly mean. The elect few that rise above the temptations of money and remain uncontaminated are the true heroines and heroes of his novels. Not only does their moral integrity identify them as free spirits that stand out above the common herd, but they incarnate the true Russian soul in which Dostoevskii believed so fervently.

Categoric statements regarding the relative significance of any single facet of Dostoevskii's work serve little critical purpose. He is neither a unilinear nor a monophonic writer and makes use of a wide range of literary approaches and narrative techniques. There is no question, however, that his skill in making money 'talk' is a characteristic and vital element of his artistic craft. Its language functions as a versatile medium for communication, with its deconstructive power contributing greatly to his impact as a critical realist. The medium also becomes the message and in this capacity exercises a heuristic role in the portrayal of the characters and in their moral evaluation. Its influence extends powerfully into the area of theme and plot and into the inmost philosophic substance of the novels. Dostoevskii's work is invariably intellectually challenging, and a critical appreciation of the significance of money in his writing can provide a valuable navigational aid in the exploration of his absorbing fictional world.

Notes

1 Jacques Catteau, *Dostoyevsky and the Process of Literary Creation*, trans. Audrey Littlewood (Cambridge University Press, 1989), p. 135.
2 S. K. Somerwil-Ayrton, *Poverty and Power in the Early Works of Dostoevskij* (Amsterdam: Rodopi, 1988), pp. 37–100.
3 See Barbara Heldt, *Terrible Perfection: Women and Russian Literature* (Bloomington and Indianapolis: Indiana University Press, 1987).

6

DEREK OFFORD

Dostoevskii and the intelligentsia

Satisfactory definitions of the Russian terms *intelligentsiia* and *intelligent* or *intelligentka* (as the individual male and female members of the group are respectively known) are elusive.[1] For one thing the terms are somewhat anachronistic. Although it now seems that the word *intelligentsiia* occurs at least as early as 1836, when it appears in a diary entry by the poet Zhukovskii,[2] it was evidently not used in the mid-nineteenth century by or about the group which is now commonly described as the intelligentsia. It therefore does not occur in Dostoevskii's works of the period 1861–2, which are examined here, although it does appear to have come into common use slightly later as Dostoevskii's novelistic career blossomed. A further difficulty lies in the fact that the term does not really denote a distinct social group but rather a collection of deracinated individuals from various social backgrounds who share certain attitudes, including an aspiration to create a new identity based on their cultural and political role in society rather than on their economic position. Nor, given the uncertainty about what precisely the term denotes, can there be complete agreement as to when the force which we now call the intelligentsia came into being.

The Russian term *intelligentsiia* itself is of Western origin, being derived, it seems, from the Latin *intelligentia*, 'intelligence'. This etymology suggests a group perceiving itself, perhaps generally perceived, as a product of Westernisation, a group for whose development the reforms of Peter the Great (sole ruler 1696–1725) created propitious conditions and which was brought properly into being by the flowering of Western culture in Russia under Catherine II (ruled 1762–96). And yet within little more than a century this alien growth was clearly felt to have become so peculiarly Russian in character that the Russian term denoting it began to be used as a neologism in Western languages, which had no resources of their own to describe it. The word 'intelligentsia' appears in both English and French in the early years of the twentieth century, first in relation to the Russian educated class itself and then also to denote certain groups in other societies. According to the

Oxford English Dictionary, its first recorded use in English seems to have been by Maurice Baring in 1907, while the same source suggests that it soon took on a rather pejorative sense in English usage: in a work by H. G. Wells, published in 1916, for example, a character defines the intelligentsia, with a combination of reverence for bourgeois decorum and disdain for intellectual life, as 'an irresponsible middle class with ideas'.[3]

Modern English lexicography tends to give the term 'intelligentsia' both the broad sense of 'part of a nation, orig. in pre-revolutionary Russia, that aspires to intellectual activity', and a narrower sense of 'the class of society regarded as possessing culture and political initiative'.[4] Similarly French lexicography describes the 'intelligentsia' as 'ensemble des intellectuels d'un pays', and (specifically in relation to nineteenth-century tsarist Russia), 'classe des intellectuels, réformateurs'.[5] The conjunction of 'culture' and 'political initiative', intellectual life and reform, which is contained in these English and French definitions of the term 'intelligentsia' (a conjunction that may seem rather curious to the English mind), is implicit in the definition of the term by the minor Russian writer of the late nineteenth and early twentieth centuries, Boborykin, who spuriously claimed to have coined it: 'the most educated, cultured and *progressive* stratum of the society of a given country'.[6] Soviet lexicography, on the other hand, identified only one of these meanings, the first, broader meaning, describing *intelligentsiia* as the collectivity of those who perform intellectual labour and have special training and knowledge in various branches of science, technology and culture. This Soviet definition deprived the concept of properties that were unacceptable to Soviet officialdom and yet inherent in the nineteenth-century and early twentieth-century Russian intelligentsia and its Soviet successors, namely the independence and – in the political conditions of tsarist Russia and the Soviet Union – the consequent subversiveness, potential or actual, of the grouping. For the intelligentsia was a group apart: since culture, as Herzen observed, put down a boundary in Russia which much that was abominable never crossed,[7] the intelligentsia staked a claim to more civilised territory than other elements in Russian society, but at the same time it could not become a part of power, observing it instead from outside, as the late Soviet dissident Siniavskii has put it.[8] It represented public opinion in a society in which educated, cultured, morally concerned, socially aware individuals, whatever their position on a notional political spectrum, were alienated from the government. Indeed the alienation of educated opinion from government and the formation of the intelligentsia are really the same process. Moreover, in a state that tolerated no heterodoxy, the activity of this 'critically thinking minority', to use an expression given currency in the late 1860s by Lavrov, was always liable to take on a political dimension and lead its members into conflict with the state, as a result of which many of them – like Dostoevskii himself in the late 1840s and 1850s – suffered more or less life-threatening persecution.

Let us turn from the independence and essential subversiveness of the role of the intelligentsia to the preoccupations of its members and the qualities of their thought. The intelligentsia is notable, from the age of Catherine, for its breadth of culture and the range of inter-related fields and questions covered in its writings. In addition to a rich imaginative literature it produced a large corpus of literary criticism, which examined among other things the nature of beauty and inspiration, the relation of art to reality, the function of art, and the mission of the writer and critic. In its excursions into literary history the intelligentsia dwelt particularly on the development in Russia of a secular literature of a Western sort and on the relationship of that literature to Russian society. It discussed social questions, often seen through the prism of imaginative literature, literary criticism and literary history, including the predicament and role of the intelligentsia itself, the nature of the common people or *narod* (though this entity is arguably a construct of the intelligentsia itself as much as a social reality), and the relationship between the intelligentsia and the *narod*. Examination of political questions tended to be less explicit but often, insofar as censorship allowed, touched upon serfdom and urban poverty and on the nature of autocracy and its perniciousness or suitability in Russian conditions. Essays in what might be best described as moral philosophy included evaluations of Russian and Western *mores* and enquiries into the themes of egoism and altruism, duty, service and self-sacrifice. There were discussions of a theological nature into the relationship between rational knowledge and faith and the differences between Orthodoxy and the Western forms of Christianity, and at the same time speculation on the extent of the jurisdiction of scientific method, its implications for religious faith, and the similarities and dissimilarities between science and history. In the field of history itself thinkers reflected on the principles that might underlie historical development, on the existence or lack of pattern in history, on chance and necessity, the role of Providence and great individuals, and the role of the state in Russian history. Almost invariably Russian thinkers were also – perhaps above all – preoccupied with the problem of the historical destiny of individual nations, the relationships between nations and in particular the relationship of 'Russia' to 'the West' (though these two concepts, it should be noted, reached beyond geopolitical entities and were no less broad and abstract than the concept of the *narod*).

However, the categories under which the preoccupations of Russian thinkers can be listed constantly overlap. It would be hard to classify most of the major Russian thinkers of the mid-nineteenth century – Belinskii, Chaadaev, Chernyshevskii, Granovskii, Herzen, Kavelin, Khomiakov, Ivan

Kireevskii – as primarily sociologists or political economists or political commentators or theologians or moral or political philosophers, let alone metaphysicians (though clearly literary criticism was the main vehicle for Belinskii's ideas and history for Granovskii's). For on the whole these thinkers tend to resist confinement within specific intellectual disciplines and the consequent fragmentation of knowledge. Their endeavours in the many fields of 'science' (the Russian term, *nauka*, has a broad scope) are generally held together by the centripetal force of moral zeal, faith or conviction in some system, ideal or idea. This force lends their thought a fierce engagement or 'commitment', to use Isaiah Berlin's term.[9] Russian thinkers, like Marx, tend to want not only to understand the world but also to change it: they aspire to translate utopian dream into reality, and desire – at their most millenarian – to realise the kingdom of heaven on earth. Their striving for integrity or wholeness and purpose is partly defensive, a response to the fear that the centre cannot hold, an attempt to create a bulwark against the social fragmentation and ontological disintegration threatened by rapid economic and social change and the influx of Western values. But in a more positive sense this striving is to be conceived as a reassertion of a spiritual quest for a synthesis of reason and faith or – in the case of radical thinkers who had lost faith – a replacement of the Orthodox Christian vision with a new, equally coherent, all-embracing, all-explaining set of values.

The minority cultivating intellectual life in the conditions and of the sort described manifested immense ambition. This intelligentsia wished to transcend the limits that seemed to many Russian thinkers from the mid-nineteenth century to inform Western life as a whole. It was the peculiar destiny of the Russians, Herzen claimed, 'to see further than their neighbours, to see in darker colours and to express their opinions boldly'.[10] Characteristic of the Russian spirit, at least as most nineteenth-century Russian thinkers conceived of it, is a restless expansiveness compatible with the immensity of the Russian landscape, a yearning to be free of constraint like the Cossacks who roamed at the limits of the Muscovite state. A people with a spirit of this sort was likely to chafe at the restrictions – temporal laws, rules, conventions, proprieties – imposed by the well-ordered, economically effective society in which industrious and thrifty citizens aspired to enjoy the fruits of their labour and legal protection of their persons and property. It would despise materialism, which it associated with the bourgeois world whose triumph was confirmed by the suppression of republican insurrection in France in the 'June Days' of 1848. Against this world successive Russian thinkers at both ends of the political spectrum, Romantic conservatives like the Slavophiles (and Dostoevskii himself) and socialists like Herzen, Chernyshevskii and the Populists, railed repeatedly. Any thinker who rued a perceived lack of a sense of limits in the Russian character, such as Chicherin, tended to be regarded as dry, formalistic and even alien – in fact like tsarism's officials, many of them of Germanic origin, whose position disqualified them from inclusion in the ranks of the intelligentsia.

The Dostoevskian novel is on one level a quintessential expression of the life and thought of the Russian intelligentsia as it has been described here. This statement is valid in the sense that many of Dostoevskii's characters represent artistic embodiments of the ideas, values, attitudes, concerns and moods of the intelligentsia. As Martin Malia observes in his essay on the intelligentsia: 'in his various Raskolnikovs, Verkhovenskys and Kiril[l]ovs' Dostoevskii 'has given perhaps the most unforgettable, if highly caricatured, portraits' of the new rootless intellectual, the 'insulted and the injured' emerging from the underground, 'from all the human degradation of sub-gentry Russia' into 'the light of "consciousness", "humanity", "individuality", and "critical thought"' (Malia, 'What is the intelligentsia?', p. 11). But the statement also holds good in the sense that Dostoevskii himself was an *intelligent*, both inasmuch as he made a livelihood by intellectual activity and – more importantly for us here – in that it was his vocation, or perhaps mission is a more apt word, to help to construct a broad, humane culture characterised by passionate engagement with ideas, moral commitment, a quest for the integration of reason and faith, and great, even millenarian, expectations. As evidence of the scope and consciousness of this mission we may point to the fact that Dostoevskii, more than any of the other major classical novelists, participated in another medium which flourished alongside, or rather developed hand in hand with, imaginative literature as a vehicle for the expression of the intelligentsia's ideas and aspirations, namely what was known as 'publicism' (*publitsistika*). (The term 'publicism' is as unfamiliar in English as the intellectual group to whose life it gives voice and may therefore be more naturally – though also more cumbersomely – rendered as 'social and political journalism' or 'writings on current affairs'.)[11] It was in publicism, through his own contribution to the polemics of the early 1860s, that Dostoevskii organised the coherent view of the world that informs the novels for which he is chiefly remembered. We shall therefore examine his journalism of 1861 and early 1862[12] and then look more closely at one work in particular, his *Winter Notes on Summer Impressions* (1863), a memoir of his journey to the West in the summer of 1862, which encapsulates the qualities we are associating with the intelligentsia and links his early publicism to his major fiction.

Intellectual life in Russia after the Crimean War (1853–6) was characterised by an increasing fragmentation of the intelligentsia into factions, the sharper definition of the factions, and the politicisation of their outlooks. That part of the intelligentsia which described itself as Westernist split more clearly in the late 1850s into two groups, the embryos of which were apparent in the previous decade. A moderate faction, associated with the 'men of the 40s' and labelled 'liberal', advocated gradual, limited, peaceful change through reform carried out by the existing state. A radical faction, dominated by younger men and influenced by utopian socialism, dreamed of more far-reaching social change and – if it was necessary to achieve such change – political revolution. At the same time the Slavophiles – that is to say that section of the intelligentsia which in the 1840s had opposed the Westernisers – became more active after the so-called 'seven dismal years' of reaction (1848–55) with which the reign of Nicholas I (ruled 1825–55) had ended. Alongside Slavophilism there emerged a further expression of Romantic nationalism in the form of 'native-soil conservatism' (*pochvennichestvo*) formulated by Grigorev, Strakhov and Dostoevskii himself.[13]

One sign of the reinvigoration of intellectual life and the crystallisation of factions in the intelligentsia was the increase in journalistic activity and the clarification of journals' individual ideological positions. Certain journals that had been established in the reign of Nicholas were revived (for example, *Notes of the Fatherland* [*Otechestvennye zapiski*] and *The Contemporary* [*Sovremennik*], both of which adopted a more or less radical stance, and *Library for Reading* [*Biblioteka dlia chteniia*], which under the editorship of Druzhinin espoused the cause of art for art's sake, a cause that in Russian conditions was by no means apolitical). At the same time entirely new journals were now created (for example, *Russian Herald* [*Russkii vestnik*], which represented the renascent 'liberalism', *Day* [*Den'*], an organ for Slavophilism, and *Russian Word* [*Russkoe slovo*], which in due course became a mouthpiece for nihilism). Dostoevskii himself was *de facto* editor of two journals which sprang up in this period, *Time* (*Vremia*, 1861–3) and *Epoch* (*Epokha*, 1864–5), both of them formally managed by his elder brother Mikhail.

Time fully conformed to the norms of the publicism through which the intelligentsia expressed itself. The conjunction of cultural and political roles that has already been noted is explicitly accepted, for the journal is described on its title page as 'literary and political'. It engaged in topical debate on a multiplicity of subjects. The subjects of Dostoevskii's own contributions to it ranged from the development of literacy among the masses and the emancipation of women to aesthetics, literary criticism, literary history, Russian history in the Muscovite and Petrine periods, and ultimately the question of Russia's relation to Europe. The polemical nature of Dostoevskii's journalism – which incidentally already displays the lively dialogic form characteristic of the major fiction – is evident from the very titles of some of his pieces: 'A Reply to *Russkii vestnik*', 'A Necessary Literary Explanation', 'Two Camps of Theoreticians' or – in the *Epoch* period – 'Mr Shchedrin, or the Schism among the Nihilists'. We might add that these articles also suffer from what might now seem flaws that are inseparable from the publicism of the age, such as irritability, personal animus, discursiveness, repetitiousness, the interpolation of long quotations from other works and fondness for the seemingly interminable paragraph. (Not all of these flaws remain flaws, however, when transported into Dostoevskii's fiction and embodied in fictional characters.)

Dostoevskii helped to define his outlook by means of polemical offensives on several fronts. The Slavophile Ivan Aksakov, in spite of the fundamentally sympathetic attitude of the *pochvenniki* towards Slavophilism, was castigated for the theoretical nature of his views, an allegedly aloof attitude towards contemporary Russian literature, intolerance, and lack of capacity for reconciliation (XIX, 58–63; see also XX, 6, 8–13). Nor did Dostoevskii idealise pre-Petrine Muscovy or take such a wholly negative view of Peter the Great as did the Slavophiles, since he recognised that Peter was right to carry out his reforms, even if the form which those reforms took was 'wrong' (XIX, 18; XX, 12, 14–15). Within the Westernist camp advocates of art for art's sake were chastised for supposedly running the risk of fettering the artist by altogether prohibiting 'accusatory' literature (XVIII, 79). The moderate journal *Russian Herald* was attacked for its denial of national character (*narodnost'*) (XIX, 18, 173), for its bookish distance from real life (XIX, 108, 123), for its Anglophile stance (XIX, 139, 177), and for its assumption of a policing role in literature (XIX, 116). Together with *Notes of the Fatherland* and *The Contemporary*, *Russian Herald* was also taken to task for its comments on Pushkin, whom Dostoevskii already regarded as a true voice of the Russian people, taken as a whole (XIX, 112, 114–15, 132–8). However, it was Westernism in the extreme radical form it began to take in the latter half of the 1850s, through exponents such as Chernyshevskii (up until his arrest in 1862) and Dobroliubov (up until his death in 1861), that evidently seemed to Dostoevskii most objectionable and – because it was in the ascendant – most threatening, and it was perhaps this body of thought that served as Dostoevskii's most useful polemical target.

Dostoevskii holds it against the radical view of the world – and more broadly against the Western intellectual tradition from which that view stems – that it relies exclusively on the findings of human reason and disregards the higher understanding to which spiritual insight may lead. In particular he rejects the claims made by his radical contemporaries on behalf of that crowning achievement of rational enquiry, the natural sciences, which were making great advances in Dostoevskii's lifetime. Radical thinkers in general and Chernyshevskii in particular ingenuously believed that by applying scientific method – by which they understood observation, experimentation, measurement and formulation of 'laws' – one could fully know, describe and predict every aspect of the world, including human behaviour, the art that humans had created, and the societies in which they lived. The triumph of reason, manifested in scientific discovery, seemed to assure the further march of the technological progress generated by the industrial revolution and the perfection of human institutions and societies. For Dostoevskii this position was highly abstract, simplistic and 'theoretical': it did not take account of the complexity of disorderly reality which will not always fit into neat intellectual schemes and may not accord with the needs of human nature. One could not calculate and precisely foresee 'every future step of all mankind'. There were things – *The Iliad* is an example to which Dostoevskii alludes in one article of this period, 'Mr —bov and the Question of Art' – whose usefulness could not be measured 'in pounds, *puds*, *arshins*, kilometres, degrees and so on and so forth' (XVIII, 95).[14]

A second source of conflict was the radical view of the function of art and its importance in human life. In his famous – or to his opponents, infamous – dissertation on aesthetics, 'The Aesthetic Relations of Art to Reality', Chernyshevskii had rejected the essentially Platonic notion that there exists beyond everyday reality a higher plane of perfect forms whose beauty writers, painters and musicians strive to capture in their art. He asserted instead that the material world, the mundane here and now, is all there is and that art is a more or less mechanical reproduction of it. The success of a work of art, Chernyshevskii believed, should be judged against some educative or civic criterion. Dostoevskii vigorously challenged this utilitarian view of art, which stemmed in part from an exclusively rational and scientific approach to human creativity. For Dostoevskii art answers man's eternal craving for beauty, a craving which is normal, healthy and at least as vital in his life as those physical appetites which seemed to the radical camp to be of preeminent importance. Moreover, aesthetic beauty had for Dostoevskii a moral and spiritual dimension which it could not in Chernyshevskii's view possess: the beauty embodied by great art Dostoevskii equates with harmony, tranquillity, spiritual perfection. As for utility, the true work of art could not help but be 'modern and real', whereas when art was pressed into the service of some topical cause and thus deprived of freedom of inspiration it lacked 'artistry' (*khudozhestvennost'*) and lost its capacity to exercise an influence (XVIII, 70–103, esp. 93–4, 98, 101–2; XIX, 181–2).

A third area of disagreement with the radical thinkers concerned the philosophical materialism they espoused. Chernyshevskii is an atheist who follows

Feuerbach in holding that God is a creation of human consciousness rather than a supreme being with an objective existence. After the fashion of crude materialists such as Büchner, Moleschott and Vogt, he contends that people are the product of their physiological composition and environment, that their actions can be described as reactions to various stimuli, that they have no spiritual dimension or independent will, and that they are therefore not morally responsible for their actions. From this determinism there flows a view of crime as a consequence of material hardship, social inequality or institutional failings. In this event individual responsibility for 'bad actions' – as Chernyshevskii coyly calls crime – is diminished and moral judgements of the wrongdoer tend to lose force. To Dostoevskii, on the other hand, those who reduced the world to an exclusively material dimension and denied the existence of free will lost sight of an inalienable part of human nature and tried to confine mankind in a prison (*ostrog*) more fearsome than the Siberian jail in which Dostoevskii had himself been incarcerated.

A fourth objection to Chernyshevskii concerned his utilitarian ethical system, which denied the existence of altruism and conceived all actions as driven by man's selfish desire to seek pleasure and avoid pain. The goodness of an action, according to this ethical system, is not intrinsic but relative to the degree to which the action furthers an end that is perceived as good or bad. The greatest good is the good of the greatest number. Chernyshevskii reconciles this ethic with socialism by means of a 'rational egoism' according to which humans, although driven by selfishness, may also be persuaded, since they are rational beings, that it is in their own interests, as members of society, to derive their selfish pleasure from performing acts of general utility. For Dostoevskii Chernyshevskii's rational egoism takes no more account of human nature than do his aesthetic doctrine or his materialism. For humans have an innate love of their neighbours, a capacity for compassion and for personal fulfilment through self-sacrifice, and an ability sometimes even to derive pleasure from pain (IV, 56, 67–8; XIX, 131–2).

Beyond all these differences lay fundamental disagreements as to whether human nature was everywhere the same, what future Western civilisation had, and how useful the West was as a model for Russian development. The radical thinkers were cosmopolitan, in that they assumed that humans in all places functioned in the same way. Dostoevskii, on the other hand, insisted on the importance of one's own climate, upbringing and 'soil' (XIX, 148). He castigated those who sought to create a universal ideal character for mankind, 'some highly impersonal thing' that was invariable in spite of climatic and historical circumstances (XX, 6–7). Repeatedly he likened those who would with equanimity erase national differences to worn coins which one could see were of a certain metal but whose nationality and year of coinage had been obliterated (XIX, 29, 149; XX, 6). It was not just that Russia was socially different from the West in that it had nothing like the English lords or the French bourgeoisie and would not in future have that bane of Western life, a proletariat (XIX, 19). More importantly, the Russian people had a character of their own. They possessed an innate moral rightness, depth and breadth (XIX, 185) and were free of the 'national egoism' of the English, French and Germans (XX, 21). Their most distinctive characteristic, paradoxical as it might seem, lay in their universality, as attested by their capacity to receive as their own the culture of the West (XVIII, 99).

Nor, finally, did Dostoevskii share Chernyshevskii's belief that the Western peoples, far from being decrepit, were only just beginning to live their historical life and that their thought provided a key to the solution of Russia's problems. On the contrary, it was precisely the fracture produced by Westernisation between 'society', which was 'civilised "in the European manner"', and 'the people', that is to say the *narod* (XIX, 6; XX, 15–17), that the Russian intelligentsia now had to try to heal. Dostoevskii argued that the government, by means of the emancipation of the serfs in February 1861, had begun the task of filling in the moat that separated the two Russias; now 'society' must complete the task by earning the trust of the people, loving them, suffering, absorbing the 'popular element', transfiguring itself (the biblical allusion is implicit in the verb *preobrazit'sia*) (XIX, 7–8). As to the feasibility of this task, Dostoevskii is full of optimism. Members of the educated class had not ceased to be Russian as a result of Westernisation; national character (*narodnost'*) continued to exist. Having passed through an age of 'civilisation', during which Russia had come close to 'Europe', educated Russians now sensed the need to turn to their native soil. There, armed with the awareness of their universality gained as a result of their metaphorical journey to the West, they would find their true identity through coalescence (*slitie*) with the people (XIX, 6–8, 18–20, 113–14).

Many of the main ideas and conclusions put forward in Dostoevskii's publicism in 1861 find equally vigorous, adversarial, multifaceted, but more succinct, coherent, powerful and ambitious expression in his travelogue, *Winter Notes on Summer Impressions*. Here he again addresses questions of literary history and ethics and discourses on human nature, the relation of culture and society to ethnic character and the relationship of Russia to the West. In the process he challenges the assumptions of the Westernist intelligentsia about the continuation of its civilising role, seeks to undermine both the liberalism and the socialism espoused by that intelligentsia, and begins to outline an alternative utopian model based implicitly on Orthodox spirituality.

Russian literature possesses a large corpus of accounts of travels in foreign lands, from examples from the age of Catherine such as Fonvizin's *Letters from France* (1777–8) and Karamzin's *Letters of a Russian Traveller* (1791–2) to works by the Westernisers of the age of Nicholas I such as Annenkov's *Letters from Abroad* (1841–3) and *Parisian Letters* (1847–8), Botkin's *Letters from Spain* (1847–9, republished in book form in 1857), and Herzen's *Letters from France and Italy* (1847–52). Grigorev, while abroad in 1857, wrote a book *To Friends from Afar*, which was never published but evidently contained much that prefigured Dostoevskian themes and imagery.[15] The journal *Time* printed travel sketches by other less well-known writers. At the radical end of the spectrum stand Mikhailov's *Paris Letters* and *London Notes* (1858–9), and Shelgunov's essay 'The Workers' Proletariat in England and France' (1861), all of which were published in *The Contemporary*. In the summer of 1862 Herzen was embarking on a further cycle of letters, *Ends and Beginnings*, which while not exactly of the genre of the travelogue were close to it. In these letters Herzen – whom Dostoevskii met in London in July of that year – reiterates theses from his cycle *From the Other Shore*, namely that contemporary bourgeois civilisation was a 'despotism of property', a consummation of the mediocre and the vulgar, which worshipped Baal and in which individual characteristics were lost. This world had reached the limit of its development, and its centres, Paris and London, were 'closing a volume of world history' (Herzen, *My Past and Thoughts*, pp. 1680–749). Thus Dostoevskii's *Winter Notes on Summer Impressions*, which purport to be an account of his first trip abroad in the period June to September 1862, belong to an established tradition. Indeed it is clear that the *Winter Notes* are conceived as a distinctive contribution to this tradition. For in the first chapter, when he belatedly appreciates the beauty of Cologne Cathedral, Dostoevskii compares himself to Karamzin, who had wanted to fall on his knees before a Rhine waterfall in atonement for not having done justice to it the first time he had seen it (v, 48). The second chapter Dostoevskii begins by quoting an aphorism from Fonvizin's *Letters from France* (v, 50), on which he comments at length in Chapter 3 (v, 53).

The genre of the travelogue, like the genre of the novel to which Dostoevskii was shortly to progress, offers considerable opportunities to the Russian *intelligent* as he has been depicted here, with his wide-ranging cultural, moral, social and political interests, his quest for comprehensive, nationally or universally valid explanations of things, and his large horizons, both geographical and spiritual. It allows enormous freedom to describe, report or discourse on whatever he will: a building, a town or natural scenery, the thoughts and emotions excited by them, the people he has met and the conversations he has had with them, the plays he has seen and the galleries and museums he has visited, the history, politics, literature and manners of the country to which he has been. The travelogue may be both concrete and abstract, objective and subjective, descriptive and reflective, cerebral and emotional. Most importantly, it afforded unlimited potential for comparison of the Russian world and the world beyond Russia. The Russian examples of the genre do of course tell us something about life in the foreign lands – mainly England, France, Germany, Italy, Spain and Switzerland – visited by the Russian travellers. And yet they were also essays in a form of Russian cartography: they represented explicit or implicit attempts to define the social, cultural, moral and spiritual topography of Russia herself at a time when it was becoming urgent for Russians – or at least for the Russian intelligentsia – to find a plausible and distinctive definition of their nation's identity.

It soon becomes clear in the *Winter Notes* that Dostoevskii is more concerned with cultural and spiritual space than with geographical territory. For the traveller – whom there is no need to see as a narrator independent of Dostoevskii himself – treats geographical space in cavalier fashion. We are told at the outset that in the course of two and a half months he has visited, among other places, Berlin, Dresden, Wiesbaden, Baden-Baden, Cologne, Paris, London, Lucerne, Geneva, Genoa, Florence, Milan, Venice and Vienna (v, 46; Ch. 1). However, any hope the reader may have of an orderly account of this itinerary is immediately dashed. There is no material at all on three of the countries that Dostoevskii says he has visited, Switzerland, Italy and Austria, and none on Germany beyond the introductory chapter. It is only after he has showered the reader with impressions of Berlin, Dresden and Cologne (and the impressions of Cologne are based partly on his second visit to the city, on his way home from Paris) that Dostoevskii describes his departure from St Petersburg en route for the Russian border with Prussia. Although the traveller arrives in Paris before he visits London, he chooses to describe London before Paris. Moreover, the longest chapter in the work, Chapter 3, does not relate directly to the physical journey at all but describes a mental excursion supposedly undertaken while Dostoevskii is on the train conveying him to Paris. Indeed the heading of the chapter describes it – aptly, if the fiction that it is the physical journey that is in the foreground is to be maintained – as 'completely superfluous'. And so carried away is the traveller by his thoughts in Chapter 3 that he seems to forget where he is and thinks he is nearing the Russian border with Prussia when in fact it is France that he is approaching (v, 63).

The real purpose of the *Winter Notes*, then, is not to give an account of a breathless touristic journey along the itinerary which the traveller misleadingly advertises on the first page of the work but to conduct the reader on an odyssey, spanning almost a hundred years, through carefully mapped cultural and spiritual territory. The land through which we first pass on this odyssey, after the fleeting, flippant, provocatively superficial preliminary impressions of German cities, is 'Russian Europe' (v, 63–4; Ch. 3), that is to say the world of the Westernised Russian educated class since the age of Catherine, to which Chapters 2 and 3 of the *Winter Notes* are dedicated. 'Russian Europe' is conceived as a sort of colony of 'Europe' or 'the West', which is itself a 'land of holy miracles', a 'promised land' (v, 47; Ch. 1), the source of almost every worthwhile Russian development in science, art, citizenship and humanity (*chelovechnost'*) (v, 51; Ch. 2). Russians have been bewitched by 'Europe' and have found it impossible to withstand her influence (v, 51; Ch. 2). With its uncritical worship of Western fashions and practices and their habitual rejection of native ones as barbaric (v, 61; Ch. 3), the Russian educated class in general is implicitly likened to those Russian tourists who, once they cross the Russian border, remind Dostoevskii of little dogs running around in search of their masters (v, 63; Ch. 3). This state of thraldom, whose development Dostoevskii charts in the works of Fonvizin and Griboedov, began in the age of Catherine, but its consequences were not at first so far-reaching or serious as they have subsequently become. In the eighteenth century Russians harboured a naive faith in the efficacy of things European and a misapprehension that when the nobleman had donned silk stockings, wigs and a sword he was a 'European' (v, 56–7; Ch. 3); and yet *mores* remained patriarchal, noblemen still took bribes, brawled and thieved (*brali, drali, krali*) and life was more straightforward as a result, so that even the Russian peasant, the *muzhik*, knew where he stood. In due course, though, this masquerade, the 'phantasmagoria' of French fashions, settled very well in Russia, particularly in St Petersburg, 'the most fantastic city with the most fantastic history of all the cities on Earth' (v, 57; Ch. 3), and ultimately Westernisation threatened to obliterate national personality, as Dostoevskii, in his publicism, had feared it would. There emerged a self-satisfied educated class, a 'privileged and approved handful' divorced from the mass of 'simple Russians' fifty million strong (v, 51, 59; Chs. 2, 3). These 'Europeans', convinced of their civilising vocation, decided questions from on high, believing that

> there is no soil, there is no people, nationality is just a given taxation system, the soul is *tabula rasa*, a little piece of wax out of which one can in an instant mould a real person, a universal everyman (*obshchechelovek*), a homunculus [the artificial man whom medieval alchemists dreamed of creating] – all one has to do is apply the fruits of European civilisation and read two or three little books. (v, 59; Ch. 3)

The urgent need for Russia to liberate herself from this thraldom is pointed up by a comparison of the traveller's own position with the national destiny.

For the fate of the Russians in general, who live without a business or cause of their own, is compared to that of the passenger who passes the time with idle thoughts in the train. It can be tedious and even distressing to be transported, cared for and cosseted, to sit and wait. One is tempted to jump out of the coach and run alongside the train: it might be perilous and tiring to do so, and yet one would have found a purpose, one would be doing something oneself and one would not be locked inside if the train were to crash (v, 52; Ch. 2).

Having alerted his readership to the dangers of continued cultural thraldom Dostoevskii then presses home the case for national emancipation by recording his impressions of the hearts of darkness of 'European Europe', that is to say London and Paris, to which Chapters 4–8 of the *Winter Notes* are devoted. Any reader of Westernist sympathies who might argue the case for Western superiority over Russia on the grounds that the Russian state is oppressive is immediately disarmed by Chapter 4, in which Dostoevskii is concerned to establish the pervasiveness of espionage (*shpionstvo*) in French life. This phenomenon Dostoevskii first experiences in the form of police surveillance of foreigners on the train taking him into France and then encounters again as his Parisian landlady and landlord labour over a report on their tenant for the police (v, 64–8). There follows in Chapters 5–8 a devastating denunciation of British and especially French *mores* that is reminiscent of Fonvizin's condemnation in the 1770s and has a similar purpose: to challenge the sense of adulation of the foreign model which, after a period of Russian intoxication with German cultural influences in the 1820s and 1830s, is again regnant. At the same time, in Dostoevskii's treatment of the bourgeoisie, as in other respects, the *Winter Notes* represent a continuation of a debate precipitated in the Russian intelligentsia in the 1840s by Herzen's scathing attack on the class in his *Letters from the Avenue Marigny*.

Dostoevskii deplores the numerous vices of the French bourgeoisie. The class – and indeed the French more generally – allegedly exhibits not only an extraordinary proclivity to *shpionstvo*, but also a lackey's nature, a gift for flattery, a conceited conviction that Paris is the centre of the universe, a taste for oratory and an infatuation with eloquence, which the traveller finds everywhere from the law courts to the Pantheon (v, 82–90; Ch. 7). It is prone to sentimental hypocrisy and has a craving for 'the elevated', for 'inexpressible nobility', which is manifested in the melodrama. (Dostoevskii emulates Herzen in examining the bourgeoisie's preferred art forms as a key to its morality.) It loves stability and propriety, which are maintained – not least by means of the material reward of virtue – in all the variants of melodramatic plots that Dostoevskii rehearses at the end of his work (v, 95–8; Ch. 8). There is a deceit and falsehood in bourgeois *mores* that are embodied by Parisian woman as Dostoevskii describes her in his closing satire on the virtue of bourgeois matrimony. Game, intrigue and pretence are everything for this affected, unnatural, unintelligent but modish and superficially attractive coquette. She is adept at feigning feeling and is less concerned that love should be true than that the display of it should be convincing (v, 92–3; Ch. 8).

The most deep-rooted flaw in the bourgeois nature, it seems, is materialism. The desire to make a fortune and accumulate as many material possessions as possible has become more than ever before the 'main code of morality, the catechism of the Parisian', the only key to respect and self-respect, despite his tendency to flirt with nobler ideas and to parade a love of virtue in the theatre. So powerful is the mercenary instinct that stealing in order to make a fortune is condoned, whereas stealing for a motive such as procuring food to stay alive is considered unforgivable (v, 76–8; Ch. 6). The bourgeois preoccupation with money and possessions is evident in the institution of marriage, a 'matrimony of capital', as Dostoevskii puts it. Marriages are contracted on the basis not of love but self-interest: conclusion of the contract is preceded by financial calculation designed to reassure both sides that there is 'equality of pockets'. This mercenary way of life, Dostoevskii maintains, is 'on its soil' in France, autochthonous, national (v, 91–2; Ch. 8). Not that one should assume that such mercenariness is exclusive to the French bourgeoisie. The French workers too are highly acquisitive, which is why the bourgeois, in spite of his complete triumph in 1848 and his security under Napoleon III (ruled 1852–70), is so afraid of them (v, 78; Ch. 6). As for the French agriculturalists, they are 'arch-proprietors', 'the best and fullest ideal of the proprietor that one could imagine' (v, 78; Ch. 6). Nor is the evil confined to France: what one finds there is the 'source and embryo of that bourgeois social form which now reigns throughout the world in the shape of eternal imitation of the great nation' (v, 92; Ch. 8).

London, on a superficial level, is very different from Paris. Here Dostoevskii is disoriented by the noise, bustle and congestion of city life, the railways above ground and under it (the first length of underground line was then being built), and the boldness of the spirit of enterprise. He is shocked by the extremes of rags and riches: 'terrible corners' like Whitechapel, with its half-naked, wild and hungry people and the social problems of pauperism, drunkenness and prostitution, stand in stark contrast to magnificent parks and squares. And yet the descriptions of London and Paris in the *Winter Notes* merge seamlessly into one another (v, 68–9, 74; Ch. 5) and the principles at the heart of the two cities are not fundamentally dissimilar. The worship of acquisition and profit may be more blatant, less hypocritical, in London, where the spirit of Baal reigns. Nevertheless the 'personal principle', which is engaged there in a stubborn struggle to the death with the need of humans somehow to live together in a community, an anthill, without devouring one another, is 'pan-occidental' (*vseobshchezapadnoe*) (v, 69; Ch. 5).

It is indicative of the general distaste in the Russian intelligentsia for capitalism and liberal politics that there are substantial points of contact between Dostoevskii's critique of the bourgeoisie and Chernyshevskii's. Both writers contend that abstract freedoms are meaningless for the majority under the material conditions of the bourgeois order. Chernyshevskii, for example, argued in an article on French politics of the period of the Bourbon Restoration that legal rights had value only when one had the material where-withal to take advantage of them.[16] Similarly, Dostoevskii maintains that although in theory *liberté*, one of the great slogans of the French Revolution, is the freedom of all to do what they like within the law, in reality one may only do what one likes when one has a million, and a person without a million is one with whom others do as they wish (v, 78; Ch. 6). Like Chernyshevskii again, Dostoevskii also disparages eloquence as a flatulent liberal virtue: reporting on the practice of allowing liberal deputies repre-sentation in the French legislative assembly under Napoleon III, he dismisses their fine speeches as empty rhetoric, words which lead to no disturbance of the good order of the city (v, 86–7; Ch. 7).

Nevertheless the polemical energy of the *Winter Notes* is directed as much at the contemporary radical camp and socialism as at the bourgeois or-der and liberalism. Even on the stylistic level the *Winter Notes* run counter to Chernyshevskii's writings. For one thing Dostoevskii's traveller seems to parody Chernyshevskii's informal, at times infantile, dialogue with his read-ers and his frequent parenthetical explanations. For another he cultivates an apparent disorderliness and unreliability which fly in the face of the care-ful, honest exposition that scientific method demands, apologising for stray-ing from the subject and even confessing to a tendency to lie (v, 47, 49, 74, 93; Chs. 1, 5, 8). On a more substantial level, Dostoevskii recoils at Chernyshevskii's reverence for the achievements of Western technology and challenges his assumption that scientific progress represents an unqualified good for mankind. Thus whereas Chernyshevskii admires suspension bridges as feats of Western engineering,[17] Dostoevskii is wounded by this evidence of Western superiority and consequently harbours a silent malice towards the man collecting tolls from visitors to the recently completed bridge at Cologne (v, 48–9; Ch. 1). The Crystal Palace (for Chernyshevskii a sym-bol of the radiant utopia of the future) is presented by Dostoevskii as an awesome, overpowering temple to a false god, which seems to demand to be worshipped by the silent hordes of visitors and before which individual humans are humbled and submissive (v, 69–70; Ch. 5).

Most importantly Dostoevskii takes issue with Chernyshevskii's rational egoism and tries to demonstrate the impossibility of building a socialist utopia on such a foundation. He mocks the unsuccessful attempts of early French socialists such as Cabet and Considérant to put their utopian schemes into practice. Such schemes, he believes, were bound to founder on the requirement to sacrifice an element of personal freedom in exchange for guarantees of food and employment. For people prefer complete freedom (*volia*) to constraint (invoked by the recurring image of prison [*ostrog*]), even though when they are at liberty they may be beaten and unemployed and threatened with starvation. No matter that the socialist will call them idiots for not understanding where their interest lies and say that even the ant is more intelligent because in the anthill – an image used by Chernyshevskii in a positive sense[18] – everything is neatly arranged and everybody is full and happy and knows his job. In any case the Western socialist, Dostoevskii argues, seeks to create a brotherhood where, given the isolation of the individual person, who demands rights with a sword in his hand, none can actually exist. Nor was there any hope that the flawed Western personality, driven by its heightened sense of self as an 'autonomous, separate principle absolutely equal and of equal value to everything that exists apart from it', would change. For regeneration takes thousands of years, and can only take place at all when such ideas as true brotherhood have entered 'the flesh and blood' (v, 79–81; Ch. 6). Thus the view of societies as being founded on certain moral principles deeply rooted in the nature of a people – in this case the French – enabled Dostoevskii to tar socialists with the same brush as the bourgeoisie, difficult as the feat might seem at first sight.

In contrast to the soul-destroying socialist dystopia emanating from France Dostoevskii offers his own utopian alternative rooted in what he perceives as Russian reality. In Dostoevskii's utopia the rebellious and demanding personality (*lichnost'*) of Western society is replaced by one which offers itself up completely and unconditionally to the collective, so that brotherhood may flourish. Society, for its part, acknowledges that such sacrifice is too much to ask, and in its concern for the welfare of all its members, offers whatever it can give, including constant protection and concern. Such willing, conscious and unforced self-sacrifice for the benefit of all, the laying down of one's life for others on the cross or at the stake, by no means amounts to an obliteration of the personality, a reduction of the individual to impersonality (*bezlichnost'*). On the contrary, Dostoevskii sees it as an expression of the highest development of the personality, a supreme exercise of free will. Indeed self-sacrifice, free from any consideration of self-interest, is what a normal person inclines to, a 'law of nature', Dostoevskii remarks, challenging Chernyshevskian axioms. However, realisation of a utopia based not on rational egoism but on altruism is contingent upon the existence of the loving, harmonious, communal principle at a deep, subconscious level in the nature of the tribe. Dostoevskii reassures his readers – lest they fear that the nation's historical experience has brutalised the Russian *narod* – that this principle may survive despite the suffering, ignorance, servitude and foreign invasions that a people has endured (v, 79–80; Ch. 6). Evidently it is primarily the common people, about whom Dostoevskii apparently spoke with naive enthusiasm when he met Herzen in London in July 1862, rather than Westernised educated society, who have preserved this principle in Russia and give Dostoevskii hope that utopia may be realised there. The people's powerful spirit is briefly glimpsed in the *Winter Notes* in the unassuming person of Pushkin's nurse Arina Rodionovna, without whom, Dostoevskii surmises, there might have been no Pushkin, the prophet and harbinger who was so closely linked to his native soil (v, 51–2; Ch. 2).

Thus in the final analysis Dostoevskii offers alternative conceptions of personality, which flow from the instinctive Western and Russian natures respectively, and correspondingly antithetical social visions. One type of personality is dynamic, to be sure, but also selfish, materialistic, destructive of community and therefore ultimately unfulfilled. Despite its intellectual strivings and its promotion of the concept *fraternité*, it will achieve only the dystopia which Dostoevskii claims to have seen at first hand in 'Europe'. The other type of personality is loving, yielding, finds fulfilment in communion with the larger flock, and is capable of realising true brotherhood, *bratstvo*. In Russia, where this type of personality supposedly prevails, it will be possible, as the bubble of the bourgeoisie bursts (v, 78; Ch. 6) and the old world dies, to construct a utopia based on nature and feeling rather than reason.

It has been argued here that our understanding of Dostoevskii's fiction is enriched if we remember that the author vigorously participated in the life of the Russian intelligentsia in the early 1860s as the ideological fissures within it widened and as the political positions of the emergent factions hardened. To be sure, Dostoevskii was concerned to save literature from those who demanded journalism of it, and by embodying polemical ideas in characters who live out their potentialities he rises, as a novelist, above partisanship. Nevertheless his fiction is itself saturated with the themes with which journalism was preoccupied. Engaged as nineteenth-century Russian novelists in general are with topical issues, in none is the link between publicism and fiction quite so close and indissoluble. Concerns of lasting universal validity that are explored in Dostoevskii's novels – for example, the catastrophic loss of the individual's moral bearings in a world in which religious faith is being undermined by reverence for rational knowledge, and the attendant threat of ontological crisis, social disintegration and political revolution – grow out of the local polemical ferment among the group which sustained an independent culture and social and political thought in the period of reform after the Crimean War.

The *Winter Notes*, with their sweeping glance at Russian and Western culture and *mores* and their over-arching interest in human nature and the moral identity of peoples, illustrate the link between publicism and fiction more clearly than any other work of Dostoevskii's. For they look both back to the polemical articles of 1861, whose conclusions they distil, and forward to the thematically related but more overtly fictional *Notes from Underground* (which, however, Dostoevskii still conceived in the first instance as an 'article' for *Epoch*, in other words a further essay in publicism, in which he would review Chernyshevskii's novel *What is to be Done?*). In particular the *Winter Notes* address the question of national self-identity which above all others had preoccupied the intelligentsia at least since 1836, the date of publication of the 'Philosophical Letter' in which Chaadaev (from whom Dostoevskii distances himself in the *Winter Notes* [v, 50; Ch. 2]) had dismissed the Russians as a people living outside history and occupying no mappable moral or spiritual territory. With their critique of the morals and social and political values of 'Europe' and of 'Russian Europe' the *Winter Notes* throw down a challenge to the Westernised intelligentsia. At the same time they contribute, with an ambition and polemical tone typical of that intelligentsia, to its fevered speculation about the prospects for regeneration in a country which is not yet completely conquered by Europe's rationalist intellectual tradition or corrupted by its bourgeois ways.

Notes

1 See, for example, Michael Confino, 'On intellectuals and intellectual traditions in eighteenth- and nineteenth-century Russia', *Daedalus* 101 (1972), no. 2, pp. 117–49, and Martin Malia, 'What is the intelligentsia?' in Richard Pipes (ed.), *The Russian Intelligentsia* (New York: Columbia University Press, 1961), pp. 1–18.

2 See Sigurd Shmidt, 'Otkuda vzialas' "intelligentsiia"?' (Where does 'intelligentsia' come from?), *Literaturnaia gazeta*, 1996, no. 23 (5 June).

3 *Oxford English Dictionary*, 2nd edn, 20 vols. (Oxford: Clarendon Press, 1989), vol. 7, p. 1070.

4 Ibid.

5 *Grand Larousse de la langue française*, 7 vols. (Paris: Librairie Larousse, 1971–8), vol. 4, p. 2744; see also *Le Grand Robert de la langue française*, 2nd edn, 9 vols. (Paris: Le Robert, 1985), vol. 5, p. 659.

6 See Shmidt, 'Otkuda vzialas' "intelligentsiia"?' The italics are mine.

7 A. I. Herzen, *Ends and Beginnings*; see *My Past and Thoughts: The Memoirs of Alexander Herzen*, trans. Constance Garnett, revised by Humphrey Higgens (London: Chatto and Windus, 1968), vol. 4, p. 1720.

8 Andrei Sinyavsky, *The Russian Intelligentsia*, trans. Lynn Visson (New York: Columbia University Press, 1997), p. 2.

9 Isaiah Berlin, 'Artistic commitment: a Russian legacy' in Henry Hardy (ed.), *The Sense of Reality: Studies in Ideas and Their History* (London: Chatto and Windus, 1996), pp. 194–231.

10 See Herzen's introduction to his *From the Other Shore*, trans. Moura Budberg (London: Weidenfeld and Nicolson, 1956), p. 6.

11 These are the translations offered in *The Oxford Russian–English Dictionary* by Marcus Wheeler, 2nd edn (Oxford: Clarendon Press, 1984), p. 650.

12 See especially the following articles: 'Gospodin – bov i vopros ob iskusstve' (Mr —bov and the question of art) (XVIII, 70–103); 'Knizhnost' i gramotnost'' (Love of books and literacy) (XIX, 5–20 and 21–57); 'Poslednie literaturnye iavleniia: gazeta "Den"'' (The latest literary events) (XIX, 57–66); 'Obraztsy chistoserdechiia' (Models of candour) (XIX, 91–104); ' "Svistok" i "Russkii vestnik"' ('The Whistle' and 'Russian Herald') (XIX, 105–16); 'Otvet "Russkomu vestniku"' (A reply to 'Russian Herald') (XIX, 119–39); 'Po povodu elegicheskoi zametki "Russkogo vestnika"' (A propos of 'Russian Herald's' elegiac notice) (XIX, 169–77); 'Rasskazy N. V. Uspenskogo' (The stories of Uspenskii) (XIX, 178–86); 'Dva lageria teoretikov' (Two camps of theoreticians) (XX, 5–22); and the invitations to readers to subscribe to the journal *Vremia* for 1861 (XVIII, 35–40) and for 1862 (XIX, 147–50).

13 On native-soil conservatism and its representatives see Wayne Dowler, *Dostoevsky, Grigor'ev, and Native-Soil Conservatism* (Toronto: University of Toronto Press, 1982); idem, *An Unnecessary Man: The Life of Apollon Grigor'ev* (Toronto: University of Toronto Press, 1995); Linda Gerstein, *Nikolai Strakhov* (Cambridge, Mass.: Harvard University Press, 1971); Joseph Frank, *Dostoevsky: The Stir of Liberation, 1860–1865* (Princeton University Press, 1986), especially Chapter 4.

14 *Puds* and *arshins* are Russian pre-revolutionary units of measurement of weight and length respectively.

15 Dowler, *An Unnecessary Man*, pp. 111–15.

16 Chernyshevskii, 'Bor'ba partii vo Frantsii pri Liudovike XVIII i Karle X' (The struggle of parties in France) in *Polnoe sobranie sochinenii* (hereafter *PSS*), 16 vols. (Moscow: Gosudarstvennoe izdatel'stvo 'Khudozhestvennaia literatura', 1939–53), vol. 5, p. 217.

17 Idem, 'O prichinakh padeniia Rima' (On the causes of the fall of Rome), *PSS*, vol. VII, pp. 662–3.

18 Idem, 'Lessing, ego vremia, ego zhizn' i deiatel'nost'' (Lessing: his life, times and activity), *PSS*, vol. 4, p. 210.

7

ROBERT L. BELKNAP

Dostoevskii and psychology

Dostoevskii's background in psychology

In Dostoevskii's time, the boundary between science and philosophy was as indistinct as it had been before Socrates, and the study of the psyche merged inseparably with that of religion, politics and all of nature. As a man of his times, Dostoevskii knew a number of psychological systems: some entered his imagery and his cultural awareness; some shaped the way he described his characters; and the struggle between two of these systems interacted with his most basic social ideas. He knew the Renaissance theory of the four humours, for example, which ascribed human character, behaviour and state of mind to the balance or imbalance of four fluids in the body: choler, phlegm, bile and black bile, which made humans choleric, phlegmatic, bilious or atrabilious, and may directly or indirectly explain why the hero's liver is referred to as diseased at the start of *Notes from Underground* (V, 99; Pt 1, Sec. 1). Dostoevskii had also encountered the ancient science of physiognomy, which discovered character in facial features, and Franz Joseph Gall's (1758–1828) popular theory of phrenology, which traced our character to the anatomy of the brain as reflected in protruding or sunken regions of the skull. He knew the Pythagorean and Asian theory of transmigrating souls, and Plato's theory of the tripartite soul, with reason, passion and appetite competing for control. But like most of his contemporaries, he drew his central psychological doctrines from two great traditions, both thousands of years old, but both growing directly out of eighteenth-century thinking: the tradition of the neurologists, and that of the alienists.

Philosophically, the neurologists were materialists, like Leucippus, Democritus and the ancient Epicureans, but these ancients had carried materialism much further than their more modern counterparts and believed perceptions and ideas themselves were actually made of atoms flying off objects in the world and retaining their arrangement until they hit our eye, whereas an eighteenth-century *philosophe* like Diderot believed that perception and consciousness resided in our nerves or their activities. In his famous *Discourse with D'Alembert*, Diderot compares the associative powers of the mind to the harmonic resonances that make certain instrument strings and not others vibrate when a given string has been struck. The nineteenth-century positivists were more naive and tried to realise this metaphor, as their microscopes traced the nerve axons around the body and their electric charges made muscles twitch. Philosophers admitted that they had not yet seen nerves vibrate, but believed that science soon would reduce the whole human mind to a collection of observable vibrations. Claude Bernard (1813–78), who conducted the most famous experiments on frogs and other animals, also wrote the most eloquent exposition of the scientific method as it had been codified in positivist thought. The most influential Russian exponent of this neurological approach to the workings of the mind never existed: Turgenev's Bazarov may have been fictional, but the 'nihilism' he propounded shaped the understanding and the attitudes of the generation that followed the appearance of *Fathers and Sons* in 1862. Among real scientists, Ivan Sechenov (1829–1905) was the most prominent in Dostoevskii's generation, and his follower Ivan Pavlov (1849–1936) set the scene for the whole behaviourist movement in more recent psychology.

Philosophically, Dostoevskii rejected this neurological psychology, along with the varieties of nihilism, rationalism, positivism, scientism, atheism, socialism, internationalism and feminism that the materialists of the time also tended to favour, although his curiosity about his own epilepsy and about the theories of his ideological foes kept him alert to medical developments in the neurological area.[1] In *The Brothers Karamazov*, Dmitrii's heavy-handed sarcasm vents some of his creator's impatience at the simplistic complacency of the positivist psychology he has heard from Rakitin, the nasty little seminarian on the make:

> 'I feel sorry for God.'
> 'How can you be sorry for God?'
> 'Just imagine: It's in the nerves there, in the head, that is, there in the brain these nerves (oh, to Hell with them!)... there are these sort of tailicues – the nerves have these tailicues, and, oh, as soon as they wiggle there... that is, you see, I look at something with my eyes, like this, and they wiggle, these tailicues... and that's why I perceive, and then I think it's because these tailicues are there, and not all because I have a soul or because I'm any sort of Image and Likeness. That's all stupidity.'   (xv, 28; Bk 11, Sec. 4)

Dostoevskii felt much closer to the work of the practical healers of psychic ailments, often called alienists in the nineteenth century. Their tradition also had its closest roots in the eighteenth century, but not altogether respectable ones. The idea of 'Animal Magnetism' had been popularised all over Europe by Friedrich Anton Mesmer (1733–1815), who was either a conscious fraud or a self-advertising enthusiast. He claimed to have techniques for controlling a magnetic fluid which resembled that which made magnets work, according to the physics of that time, but Mesmer's fluid worked on plants and animals instead. He held seances where he hypnotised people and sometimes produced certifiable cures. In the nineteenth century, his successors, working in Scotland, Belgium and elsewhere, rejected the idea of a magnetic fluid but explored the phenomenon of hypnotic sleep, often called somnambulism at that time. In the 1830s doctors described amputating a leg under hypnotic anaesthesia and then waking the patient, who asked when they were going to operate. Hypnotists explored dreams, hallucinations, latent memories, aberrant actions, and used the concept of the unconscious to explain diseases and strange behaviour. When Sofia Kovalevskaia accused Dostoevskii of deriving Alesha Karamazov from the hero of her sister Anna Korvin-Krukovskaia's story 'Mikhail', which he had published in his journal *Epoch*, he struck his forehead and said, 'You're right, but it was completely unconscious.'[2] The Russian periodicals often contained articles on the scientific progress of this branch of psychology, but Dostoevskii hardly needed to read the scientists; his favourite authors already had caught the spooky sensationalism of the subject. E. T. A. Hoffmann, Dumas, Dickens, Edgar Allan Poe and the English Gothic novelists all used the hypnotic tradition to shape their plots, their imagery and the relationships among their characters. The terrifying gaze of Murin in Dostoevskii's *The Landlady*, or of Rogozhin in *The Idiot*, or of Stavrogin in *The Devils* thus need not come directly from the gaze described or practised by any hypnotist; it was in the literary air that Dostoevskii breathed. *The Double* is Dostoevskii's first elaborated picture of a man disintegrating into madness, and of a doctor trying to treat him, but the whole series of Petersburg stories he wrote in the late 1840s deals with characters who seem to need psychological help, each with a different set of symptoms, as if Dostoevskii were exploring the world of psychopathology in a scientific manner. In *The Double* and these other early stories, but also in Dostoevskii's mature work, much of the psychopathology follows the traditional symptomatology of his own day: the inability to see the whole, the focus on a star, a button, a single concept; the attribution of will to inanimate things; the acting out of theoretical positions; the generation of and interaction with a non-existent character, often embodying some components of the sick person's identity; the obscuring of the line between fantasy and reality; and finally, the complete loss of contact with reality.

Near the end of his career, when Dostoevskii set out to describe Ivan Karamazov's feverish hallucination of the devil, he tried his text out on an

alienist, a doctor who did not so much oppose as ignore the doctrines of
the neurologists, just as, on the other side, Bazarov ignored the intellectual
background of healers like his father. Dostoevskii had grown up in a charity
hospital and shared lodgings later on with a doctor, and his sympathies lay
far closer to the healers than to the scientistic researchers who were remaking
psychology in his own lifetime. But unlike Bazarov or the alienists, he did
not ignore either of these two competing schools of psychology. His lists
of intended readings would often include the names of Carl Gustav Carus
(1789–1869), George Henry Lewes (1817–78) and other explorers of the
psyche. Dostoevskii was more like his contemporary, Jean-Martin Charcot
(1825–93), who used both hypnotism and neurology at the Salpêtrière in
Paris to produce the great synthesis of these two psychological schools. When
Charcot's student, Freud, went on to generate one of the chief psychological
systems of the twentieth century, he expressed his indebtedness not only
to his medical mentors, but also to the insights of Dostoevskii, probably
without realising that they had the same intellectual underpinnings.

The psychological novel

Dostoevskii's intellect operated novelistically far better than it did system-
atically. On psychological issues, as on political, religious, educational and
other issues, his journalistic writings have contributed to our thinking primarily as notebooks or footnotes to his fiction, not as the exposition of a
coherent body of understanding. The psychological novel has a rich past
in the seventeenth- and eighteenth-century works of Mme de Lafayette, the
Abbé Prévost, Samuel Richardson, Jean-Jacques Rousseau and many others, but it goes on being disinvented by ideologues and reinvented by their
opponents, because the subtleties of psychology defy most ideologies. In
the early 1860s Chernyshevskii's *What is to be Done?* held the public eye.
Dostoevskii reacted against the utopian and utilitarian politics of this novel,
but he also reacted against it novelistically. Let us consider the scene where
Chernyshevskii's narrator asks what sort of a person his hero Lopakhin is,
and answers that he is the kind of person who, impoverished and dressed in
rags, refuses to give way to a domineering and self-satisfied officer whom he
meets striding down the street. Instead, Lopakhin picked the man up, cast
him into a muddy ditch and threatened to drag him through it, then pulled
him up, behaved as if the man had had an accident, and sent him on his way.
Novelistically, Dostoevskii reacted angrily against the fact that Lopakhin
fulfilled the needs of Chernyshevskii's egalitarian politics and theories of
universal human dignity, but had no psyche or inner motivation. He wondered what kind of a human being in modern times would bother to defend

his right of way on the pavement or be much concerned with his costume while doing so. Robin Hood in Merrie England, or Tybalt in fair Verona, might care about such things, but a nineteenth-century Russian who worried that much in that way about his dignity must be very strange. So Dostoevskii invented a psychology for Chernyshevskii's hero: a man so insignificant that he tended to be ignored, and so insecure about existing at all that he constantly, offensively demanded attention. The Underground Man challenges Chernyshevskii's doctrines in many ways, but the childishness of the former's psychology challenges the whole idea of writing a novel made up of exemplary characters and exemplary actions, but of nothing Dostoevskii would consider to be an inward life. For the Underground Man, giving way on the street acquires an enormity whose morbidity draws attention to Lopakhin's lack of any psychology at all.

Chernyshevskii might ignore the psyche and isolate the social motives of his heroes, but Dostoevskii could not ignore the social; he had to realise that most of our actions emerge from the interplay between our social and our psychological identities, but as a novelist he discovered several ways of exploring the psyche in isolation from the social. The Underground Man theorised about determinism and its implication that our actions were entirely external in origin, that we only react like piano keys, as predictably as logarithms, but he countered with the assertion that in reality we often act contrary to our external interests, or ignore them completely. This assertion of the gratuitous opens an area where a novelist can explore the psyche in pure action, undiluted by reaction. In the language of Emile Zola's later essay 'Le roman expérimental' (1880), the gratuitous act allows a novelist to conduct this part of his experiment with pure chemicals and reveal the true nature of a given character's psyche. Dostoevskii uses the probe of the gratuitous to explore the identity of his unreasonable characters. Goliadkin sometimes responds to the words or actions of his colleagues in the office, or of his doctor, but we learn most about him when he simply surveys his nose, charters a carriage, walks into a store and buys nothing, or ruinously crashes a party. These actions are uncaused, and thus outline the extraordinary concern with his appearance that enables the illusion, the reality or the practical joke of a double to destroy him. For other characters, the gratuitous acts may be rare, but they reveal the psyche with the same clarity. Fedor Karamazov usually behaves as a cunning and successful, if self-indulgent, businessman, but when he disrupts an important meeting with a series of disreputable stories, he reveals the high comic creativity of his depraved imagination. In the same way, Raskolnikov's murder is over-determined; we know his reaction to his sister's engagement to Luzhin, his superstitious reaction to a chance encounter with the idea of such a murder, his longing to be one of the élite who are eligible for crime, etc., but we really learn about the Raskolnikov who emerges at the end of the novel from his gratuitous gifts to the Marmeladovs, his helping a stranger on the street, his running into a burning building to rescue children he does not know, or his own engagement to a dying girl.

These gratuitous acts reveal Raskolnikov more clearly than the caused ones. They also reveal an interesting difference between Dostoevskii and Freud. For Freud, the subconscious lacks the ability to analyse and moralise. In *Crime and Punishment*, the subconscious is deeply moral; Raskolnikov's dreams and impulsive actions struggle against his rational mind's rejection of moral values. There is nothing original in Dostoevskii's use of the gratu-itous for the exploration of unusual psychologies. Poe, Laclos, Balzac and countless others had used it before him, but he made it a major instrument for investigating one of the key elements of psychology, which Poe had called the perverse, and Dostoevskii called the paradoxical.

A second way of exploring a psyche outside the realm of caused actions and reactions is to place a character in a position of total helplessness where nothing he does will make any difference. What one does at such a moment expresses one's pure identity. Marmeladov places himself in such a position, and tells Raskolnikov, 'You know perfectly well in advance that this per-son, this excellently intentioned and supremely useful citizen, will no way give you any money. [. . .] And then, knowing in advance that he won't give it, you set out anyway' (VI, 14; Pt 1, Sec. 2). The gentle creature from the story of that name marries the horrible pawnbroker when the alternative is apparently equally horrible. The child Stavrogin rapes, or the abused children Ivan Karamazov describes, all experience this total helplessness which en-ables them to express suicidal despair, faith in a child's God, or whatever else constitutes the centre of the identity Dostoevskii has created for them. A major character like Dmitrii Karamazov reveals his particular pattern of dependency and childlike credulity when he visits Kuzma Samsonov and Mme Khokhlakova at a moment when there is absolutely no chance that they or anybody else will offer him the money to save what is left of his honour. Such situations are cruel, and many readers have ascribed a morbid fascination with cruelty to Dostoevskii. Maksim Gorkii said that sadism was a central feature in his novels and his motive for writing them, and that he was 'our evil genius'.[3]

Dostoevskii's own psychology

In general, Dostoevskii's readers have had a great deal to say about his own psychology. Often they derive their observations from the behaviour or the speeches of his characters – a great mistake, because Dostoevskii's fiction is a made thing, not an emanation of his spirit. When Gorkii calls Dostoevskii a sadist, he is not reacting to any biographical information. Dostoevskii could be nasty on occasion, but there is no evidence that he enjoyed inflicting pain or derived the slightest sensual pleasure from the pain he saw so often in his life. Other readers assert that Dostoevskii believed that suffering was good for the psyche, and therefore made his characters suffer. In most of his writings, however, the pain enters his novels for novelistic reasons. It can be argued, in fact, that characters who suffer in Dostoevskii novels are morally and spiritually worse after suffering than before. Certainly Varvara in *Poor Folk* was heroically generous in her love for the dying Pokrovskii, and after suffering became far more practical in the ways she handled the adoration of Devushkin and of Bykov. And Marmeladov's wife in *Crime and Punishment* was an ordinary, silly provincial girl who married Marmeladov out of pity, suffered, and afterwards became a screaming monster who put on pretentious airs, exacerbated her husband's retreat into alcohol, drove her stepdaughter into prostitution, and spent her desperately needed money on a ridiculous funeral feast. Many Dostoevskii characters speak in favour of suffering, but Mikhail Bakhtin's criticisms have made it clear that we can never say 'Dostoevskii says' and complete the sentence with a quotation from one of his characters. Dostoevskii does not use *raisonneurs*, or spokesmen for his own views, although some remarks are closer to his own views than others. His meaning must emerge from the interplay of many characters' statements and actions. Only one set of his novelistic characters gives credibility to the beneficial value of suffering in the overall shape of their careers: the murderers. Raskolnikov suffers and is saved. Svidrigailov does not, and destroys himself horribly. Dmitrii Karamazov wants to suffer in a prison camp, but Alesha urges him not to because he is not a murderer.

A simpler explanation for much of the cruelty in Dostoevskii's fiction lies in the psychology of his readers and of his characters. The victims of cruelty become psychologically transparent in their helplessness, and we understand their unmotivated actions as pure expressions of their psyche. In addition, the injustice of their predicament, coupled with our natural sympathy for certain kinds of victim, involves us as readers in the action of the text more violently than more easily acceptable situations. The novelistic explanation for these passages seems more persuasive than any biographical explanation that lacks biographical confirmation.

Sigmund Freud believed that all of a human being's actions, passions and productions are part of a whole, and that if we know enough, we can guess at the interconnections among them. In his article on Dostoevskii and parricide, he used the fiction he had read and the pieces of biographical lore he could acquire (much of it from Jolan Neufeld, a psychiatrist in Russia, and some from his famous patient, the Wolf Man, who was a Russian) to form a picture of Dostoevskii.[4] On the biographical side, he concentrated on Dostoevskii's epilepsy, his pathological gambling, and on the murder of Dostoevskii's father; on the fictional side, he used *The Brothers Karamazov* and other materials relating to parricide. He felt that Dostoevskii's epilepsy was psychological in origin and was in some sense a way of punishing himself for having desired the death of his father, which then occurred. James Rice argues tellingly that Freud did not know of Dostoevskii's epileptic symptoms before his father died and did not understand that hysterical epileptics never have seizures in their sleep or injure themselves in a seizure, or feel terrible after a seizure, all of which Dostoevskii did, and in general that Freud was speculating unnecessarily on matters that were knowable. Other scholars have cast doubt even on the murder of Dostoevskii's father, although evidence for or against a cover-up in a corrupt bureaucracy that collapsed more than eighty years ago tends to be tenuous. In any case, from the psychological point of view, Dostoevskii's belief about how his father died matters more than what happened, and he does not discuss it. Dostoevskii's insights certainly helped Freud to formulate the idea that a normal upbringing leads a boy to want to kill his father. Some of those insights come from Dostoevskii's reading, some from his observation, and some from the depths of his psyche, but Freud's article should caution us all against undertaking to read Dostoevskii's fiction as autobiographical.

The psychology of crime

In the early twentieth century, many articles appeared on Dostoevskii's psychology of crime, especially in French psychological and criminological journals. Dostoevskii had known more criminals than most authors, having spent half a decade in a prison camp, and his *Notes from the House of the Dead* offers many insights into the criminal mind. One of the most telling cases presents a man who murdered a stranger to steal something insignificant, and then ran back to abuse the corpse because the act of killing had aroused so much anger. For several centuries, Russia has exiled many of its most articulate people, and a huge memoir literature records their experiences; but Dostoevskii wrote one of the few accounts of prison life that went inside the minds of the prisoners and offered serious material for the study of crime. But in his other writings, he brought his direct understanding of criminal psychology into contact with that of the great masters of the European novel from whom he learned his profession: Hugo, Dickens and Balzac. Dostoevskii's own journal had published the first Russian translations of Edgar Allan Poe, who is often considered the inventor of the modern detective story, and Porfirii Petrovich in *Crime and Punishment* ranks among the finest of the early detectives. Porfirii has read the theory Raskolnikov drew from Napoleon III's *Life of Julius Caesar*, that crime is the prerogative of a small élite whose value to mankind puts them above punishment or guilt. But Porfirii's own theory about major crime confronts Raskolnikov's theory provocatively: criminal behaviour is the result of a disease which has two symptoms, the need to commit a crime and the need to get caught. Criminals therefore boast of their crimes, revisit the scene of the crime, flaunt their wealth, tease the police, or, if all else fails, confess. If they do not, they kill themselves. Porfirii is completely convinced of this theory. Upon parting with Raskolnikov after his last interrogation session, Porfirii tells him that he will almost certainly confess, but that if he does not, he should do Porfirii a great favour: leave a note. Dostoevskii also seems to believe this theory; at least, he elegantly confirms it by having Raskolnikov, after several rehearsals, confess, and Svidrigailov, the 'control' murderer, commit suicide.

Dostoevskii's thinking about the psychology of crime did not stop with *Crime and Punishment*. As a journalist, he attended sensational court trials, such as that of a woman who had slashed her sleeping rival with a knife, or of one who had thrown her baby out of a fourth-story window (it was unhurt). He wrote about these cases and used elements from them in his fiction. Gradually, the question of guilt came to occupy the centre of his thinking. He had always rejected the idea that the milieu can explain and even justify crime. His sense of human beings as paradoxically free agents in a world of deep determinism made that modish idea repugnant to him. In *The Devils*, he explored a political crime which was designed to use shared guilt to guarantee the loyalty of the co-conspirators. The psychological pathologies of the political criminals continue the pattern Dostoevskii had used in *Notes from Underground*, where the man's thirst for reassurance as to his own existence leads to his terror at doctrines of determinism and human subordination to nature. The conspirators in *The Devils* have morbid ideologies and morbid psyches, each in some sense a dramatisation of the other. Kirillov's suicide constitutes the *reductio ad absurdum* of pre-Nietzschean assertions of the will, carrying the Underground Man's existential insecurities to their logical conclusion, but he is a psychological as well as a philosophical suicide, a character who has lost most of the skills for living and let his obsessions break down his contacts with reality. He is a madman with a mad theory. But madness enables us to dismiss some of the conundrums posed in a work of literature, and Dostoevskii did not want to make the experience of *The Devils* easy for his readers. At the very end of the novel, a doctor examines Stavrogin's brain and declares that no madness is present.

Today no doctor could do that, but the neurologists of the nineteenth century and their journalistic followers like Dobroliubov asserted confidently that every case of madness was associated with an observable lesion in the brain. In Stavrogin, Dostoevskii is continuing his investigation of an aberration short of madness, the mind of a spoiled aristocrat who seeks to break every taboo, in pursuit not of pleasure but perhaps of guilt itself, a modification of one of Raskolnikov's motives, the idea of a crime to demonstrate one's exceptionality.

Dostoevskii's study of the psychology of crime culminates in *The Brothers Karamazov* with an elaboration of the psychology of guilt. Ivan argues for the excommunication of criminals as the strongest sanction against crime, but Zosima encounters a woman who apparently murdered her husband and assures her that God's mercy extends to every crime if there is true repentance. He also encounters a mysterious visitor crushed by his guilt for a murder and hovering between public confession and the murder of Zosima to conceal his trial confession to him. This figure carries Raskolnikov's predicament a further step, with half-confessed guilt leading not to suicide but to further crime. But Zosima himself teaches guilt as a universal experience that unifies mankind. Ivan asks why God permits innocent suffering, and Zosima describes a world in which every good or evil deed has effects that have effects that have effects that eventually influence the ends of the world, so that God's responsibility for crime is shifted to every one of us who has ever hurt anybody or failed to do good. This universal guilt becomes the central moral experience of mankind, and expands the psychology of crime to include us all.

The psychology of art, creation and perception

Dostoevskii wrote about the psychology of creation in his letters, his journalism and his fiction. In his letters, his attitudes vary with his correspondent. With his wife or his brother Mikhail, he discusses creation as a practical professional matter, considering his royalties, his schedules, etc. With Pobedonostsev, the Procurator of the Holy Synod, he asks for prayers to help him answer the arguments of the Grand Inquisitor. With the poet Apollon Maikov, he describes the moment when a writer (he often uses the word 'poet' regardless of genre) comes upon a 'diamond' that will form the heart of a work of literature. This discovery is uncaused and unpredictable, but it is only the beginning of the creative process, which then demands polishing and perfecting. In his correspondence with his wife, he discusses the importance of the 'idea' of a work or art, and she urges him not to hurry ahead until it is properly formed, reminding him of a time he had to scrap a hundred pages because he had started prematurely. This sense of the un-programmable and probably unconscious moment in the creative process as the key to the excellence of the whole underlies Dostoevskii's most significant journalistic study of the psychology of creation, the article entitled 'Mr —bov and the Question of Art'. This article attacks Dobroliubov for praising the stories of a radical Ukrainian writer, Marko Vovchok, as badly written but politically correct. Dostoevskii concedes that all art has to be socially activist unless it is written by a madman, but argues that it will be ineffective unless it is well written. He goes on to say that it will never be well written if it is constrained by censorship or ideology. This tight link between freedom and the central creative moment underlies the thinking about creation in Dostoevskii's fiction as well.

Two of Dostoevskii's novels can be read as aesthetic manifestos: *Poor Folk* and *The Idiot*. In *Poor Folk* Makar, the exploited copyist, is a writer in the literal sense, and aspires to be one in the creative sense. The purity of heart with which he reacts to the greatest authors of his time, Pushkin and Gogol, belongs in the world of total unsophistication, but after all, he does create half of one of the most socially and emotionally moving novels of the nineteenth century. He believes that art is a wonderful thing and sets out to acquire an imitative style, but his own mix of styles, bureaucratic, literarily pretentious, simply narrative and deeply personal, becomes the voice of a character whose feelings grow in response to literature as he relives the life of Gogol's poor clerk or Pushkin's stationmaster and makes us experience what it must have felt like for them to live out their careers as victims. *Poor Folk* investigates the psychology of artistic reception as a generator of human identity. *The Idiot* carries this reception psychology much further, but also explores the psychology of creation. Prince Myshkin imitates the calligraphers of the past, and Aglaia and her sisters turn to Myshkin for the generating 'diamond' upon which they would have the skills to elaborate a work of art. General Ivolgin also draws on the newspapers and other sources for the germ of the tall stories he tells, and Lebedev displays a more original, but still derivative, creative mind. The central exploration of the psychology of art in this novel, however, involves not creation, but what art or beauty do to the psyche. When Myshkin or Rogozhin or Gania or Totskii look at Nastasia Filippovna or even a picture of her, their life history changes. Myshkin has almost mystical visions when he sees a spectacular landscape, or when he sees a man about to be hanged, but Rogozhin and Gania are philistines and Totskii is a spoiled sensualist, and they all react with the same desire for the possession of beauty. When such people see the Holbein Deposition, they react with equal power. The work of art has the capacity to destroy one's faith, operating directly on the psyche, much as

Ippolit's vision of pure ugliness reflects his ideas as well as his psychological state. Dostoevskii's understanding of the creative process was essentially
romantic, and his understanding of the psychology of perception belonged
somewhat more to the realistic school of thought; but in this area, as in his
criminal psychology, his contribution to our understanding lay more in his
clarity and integrity of impact than in new insights into the psychology of
art and beauty.

Love and violence

Psychology in Dostoevskii is often linked with that special quality the
Russians call *dostoevshchina*. It involves gloom, paradox, suffering, self-
will, self-pity, hysteria and other exaggerated and sometimes pathological
emotions which often appear in Dostoevskii's fiction. Curiously these elements are among the least unique in Dostoevskii's repertory. They are the
stock in trade for the most popular prose writers of the nineteenth century,
Hoffmann, Dickens, Hugo, Sue, and all the Gothic and sensationalist novelists of that period. Certain patterns, however, are genuinely peculiar to
Dostoevskii and deserve more psychological attention than they have received. Let us consider violence, for example. There is no shortage of it. In
Crime and Punishment alone, Aliona and Lizaveta have their skulls bashed
in; a landlady is seriously beaten in one dream, and a horse beaten to death in
another; Marmeladov's wife hales him about by his hair and slams his head
against the floor; an angry coachman catches Raskolnikov with his whip;
Razumikhin knocks a watchman off his feet; a prostitute, an abused child and
Svidrigailov attempt suicide, the last two successfully; and in Raskolnikov's
final dream, the entire world is engulfed in lucidly self-righteous violence.
Curiously, however, all this violence does not include a single good fight.
With the exception of the completely abstract slaughter in the final dream,
every one of these attacks is a beating. The nearest thing to a fight in *Crime
and Punishment* is the scrap between the two painters after a day's work
together: 'I grabbed Mitka by the hair and knocked him down and started
tearing at him, and Mitka grabbed me by the hair, from under me, and
started tearing at me, and we did this not in anger, but in all affection, in
play' (VI, 108; Pt 2, Sec. 4). Lizaveta does not even raise her hand to deflect
the axe, and Marmeladov, who 'himself assisted [his wife's] efforts', looks up
from the floor and tells Raskolnikov that this beating brings him 'enjoyment'
(*naslazhdenie* – VI, 24; Pt 1, Sec. 2).

Plainly, however, this one-sidedness in violence does not come from any
inherent inability of the Dostoevskian characters to resist aggression, or any
universal masochism. As his journalistic career shows, Dostoevskii was good

at mutual hostility. The number of two-sided contests at the verbal level in his works is at least equal to the number of beatings on the physical level. Raskolnikov insults Razumikhin, Porfirii and the explosive lieutenant at the police station, and all of them give as good as they get. Luzhin and Svidrigailov respond to his insults with greater restraint or irony, but certainly could never be called compliant like Lizaveta or Marmeladov. In this novel, and in general in Dostoevskii, if violence is reciprocal, it is not physical; if it is physical, it is not reciprocal. The reverse of these statements does not hold true. If an assault is not physical, it may or may not be reciprocated: Razumikhin does not always answer Raskolnikov's verbal assaults, and Sonia never does. If an assault is not reciprocated, it may or may not be physical: Marmeladov welcomes verbal as well as physical assaults.

Readers often remark how few happily married husbands and wives there are in Dostoevskii, although he himself was a devoted and loving family man. Rima Shore has pointed out that in *Crime and Punishment* the two unhappy couples, the Marmeladovs and the Svidrigailovs, are all dead by the end of the novel, and that Raskolnikov confesses to the only surviving father, the explosive lieutenant, rather than to the emphatically unmarried Porfirii, as one might otherwise expect (unpublished Columbia dissertation). This absence of happy marriages might be ascribed to a novelistic tradition which marries characters off only at the end of the book after a series of impediments and travails that constitute the plot of the novel. In Dostoevskii, however, there is virtually no good clean sex outside of marriage either, and the novelistic tradition of his day certainly accepted that. The absence of happy marriages and healthy extra-marital sex might be ascribed to prudery, but that explanation will not work either, because in many of Dostoevskii's novels there is no shortage of depraved sex, which is subject to stricter taboos. In *Crime and Punishment*, Svidrigailov rapes a little girl, and someone like him misuses the girl Raskolnikov tries to rescue on the street; Sonia and the prostitutes near Raskolnikov's apartment earn their living through the loveless and eventually fatal selling of their bodies to satisfy desire.

This limitation of sexual encounters to depraved ones persists in all of Dostoevskii's stories and novels. It is hard to find happy marriages or mutually fulfilling sex in any of his works. But this limitation does not come from any Dostoevskian hostility to marriage or love. Razumikhin and Dunia are two of the liveliest and loveliest lovers in all of literature, and Raskolnikov and Sonia save each other through their love, but these loves go unconsummated through the entire novel, as tends to happen with the happy love in all Dostoevskii's other works.

There are many definitions of depravity, but for the purposes of this study, I should like to define it as consummated but unreciprocated desire. This definition leads to a puzzle that demands attention. Like aggression, desire in Dostoevskii's works, if physically consummated, is not reciprocated, and if reciprocated, is not consummated. As with violence, this pattern does not work backwards; unreciprocated desire may be either consummated, like that of Sonia's customers, or unconsummated, like Luzhin's, while un-consummated desire may be reciprocated, like Razumikhin's for Dunia, or unreciprocated, like Luzhin's. In short, in two apparently unrelated regions of Dostoevskii's oeuvre, desire and violence, if it becomes physical, it is not reciprocal, and if it's reciprocal, it's not physical.

This pattern has at least four possible explanations. Socially, in a society like Russia's, where some people owned others, the consummation of un-reciprocated desire becomes a part of inter-class rather than inter-personal relations and may radiate from that centre throughout the society. And in a society where the gentry dreaded the corporal powers of the tsarist bu-reaucracy, as Irina Reyfman has pointed out, single combat became a defin-ing prerogative of the gentry, who go practically unrepresented in *Crime and Punishment* and under-represented in most of Dostoevskii's works. This pair of explanations might play a small part in explaining the number of beatings and depraved sexual encounters, but it is of little use in explain-ing the absence of fights or sexual mutuality, which transcend all social limitations.

Psychologically, Dostoevskii may well have believed that in sex one partner was always stronger, more sophisticated, and in a position to exploit the more innocent and weaker. His sense that his sister Varvara was victimised by her older, richer husband fused with much of his reading in George Sand, De Quincey, the Gothic novelists and all the heirs of Richardson to generate a pervasive picture of exploitative physical love – sometimes reciprocated at a comparable level, as Samsonov's practical affection for Grushenka seems to be in *The Brothers Karamazov*, but often depraved, like Bykov's for Varvara in *Poor Folk*. Dostoevskii's psychological vision certainly paid due attention to the phenomenon of dominance by the strong, and submissiveness by those who must submit. His psychology of desire may have simply amplified this awareness into a universal pattern. With violence, however, this pattern does not work at all. In fact, the weaker often assault the stronger, who do not reciprocate. Marmeladov, Fedor Karamazov, Maksimov and others are not weaklings, but are physically beaten by their wives. Here Dostoevskii is exploring some sort of moral dominance which does not fall within the traditional range of psychological enquiry.

If a psychological or a social explanation both seem inadequate for this mutual exclusion of the physical and the reciprocal, a literary explana-tion remains worth exploring. The novelistic tradition emerges from earlier traditions of unrequited or unfulfilled love. Greek romance left its heroes physically victimised and their love unconsummated until an epilogic moment, and medieval romance tended to do the same, as did later novels which Bakhtin characterises as ordeal novels. Moreover, a beating or a one-sided assault can produce a moral sense of wrong done, while a fair fight stimulates very different emotions. The assaults in Dostoevskii, and the consummation of depraved desire, both can appeal to our moral indignation in ways that a fair fight or happy love cannot. This is the spirit not of the ordeal, but of melodrama, in which the goodness of the victim involves the readership in the story. At every step of a literary plot, it is helpful to have a wrong that needs to be righted. The reader desires justice, and whether the author ultimately satisfies that desire or not, the reader continues to turn the pages in the hope of satisfaction. This explanation works for much of the violence and the depraved love in Dostoevskii, but not all of it. Raskolnikov's encounters with the abused girl or the prostitutes on the street have marks of closure which make them too episodic to produce any reader expectations at all. The majority of the assaults on Fedor Karamazov seem eminently satisfying, and Marmeladov certainly deserves the treatment his wife gives him, although it may not work as negative reinforcement.

To seek a solution to this puzzle about the parallel structures of desire and violence in Dostoevskii, let us turn to one of the many moments when these two elements share the stage: Dunia's visit to Svidrigailov in his apartment. Svidrigailov in the past has been the victim and the beneficiary of Marfa Petrovna's unreciprocated desire, selling himself much as Sonia does professionally and as Dunia has tried to do as the victim and beneficiary of Luzhin's unreciprocated desire. In the past, Svidrigailov has tried to exploit his lordly provincial power over Dunia, but her spiritedness has, as he puts it, 'done more harm to me than I to you, even in the country' (VI, 375; Pt 6, Sec. 5). Now, he has the new power of blackmail over her, threatening to denounce her brother as a murderer, and in addition, as he points out, he is twice as strong as she is (VI, 380; Pt 6, Sec. 5) and in a completely isolated apartment, the standard location for melodramatic victimisation. Svidrigailov is not Luzhin; for him, power is an instrument of lust, not an object of it, but he is prepared to use it ruthlessly until Dunia pulls a revolver on him, to which he responds, 'Well, that altogether changes the course of events.' Certainly, a revolver does alter the power relationships. Rape might at first seem to be the place where desire and violence meet most clearly, but rape seems to be motivated by power more often than by desire. The assault on Dunia that Svidrigailov contemplates may be exceptional in using violence for the sake of desire and not of power. He continues, however, 'You are simplifying the matter extraordinarily, Avdotia Romanovna.' 'The matter' is probably not Svidrigailov's anticipated suicide; the decision on that is not final until after Dunia rejects him definitively. Rather, he is stating that his newly acquired weakness gives him some power over Dunia, just as her powerlessness in the provinces coupled with a little bit of luck gave her the power to reject him. Indeed, with a little bit of luck and the power of helplessness, he turns her unreciprocated assault with a gun into a complete defeat when she casts the revolver aside, returning herself to helplessness. At this point she regains that same power she had possessed in the provinces. He puts his arm around her waist and she beseechingly says, 'Let me go!' He trembles and asks, 'So you don't love me?' She shakes her head, and he whispers, in despair, 'And... You can't, ever?' When she answers, 'Never', he lets her go. Here, we have desire which may at some point have been reciprocated; the text offers no hard evidence to support either Dunia's angry denial or Svidrigailov's insinu-ating assertion. Since his wife's death, in any case, his desire has been entirely unreciprocated, and only power can lead to its physical consummation. But power in this scene works backwards, as it tends to work in Svidrigailov's life. He kills the wife who holds power over him, and the people he kills all haunt him, as Lizaveta and the old pawnbroker haunt Raskolnikov, from the total powerlessness of death.

If power forms the link that explains the parallel mechanisms of violence and desire in Dostoevskii, it is paradoxical power more often than not. The beaten and the sexually exploited inherit the earth. In both these cases the power of weakness becomes central. I would suggest that the unifying element that explains the incompatibility of the reciprocal and the physical may well be this paradox of power in these two areas, desire and aggression. For Dostoevskii, the victims turn into victors. If tragedy is about the weakness of the strong, novels, or at least this kind of novel, are about the power of the weak.

This insight was not original with Dostoevskii; Jesus, for example, had had it earlier, and Dostoevskii was deeply Christian. But Dostoevskii's con-tribution to the history of psychology does not lie in the originality of his discoveries. It lies in the way he brought the insights of his time before the kind of reader who passionately intellectualises a fictional world. He made the psychological novel a philosophical instrument by exploring the relation between characters' ideas and their drives and personalities.

And because his novelistic, his religious, his social and his psychological imperatives each reinforced all the others, he could control all the elements in his fiction to achieve the integrity of impact that made his vision of humanity particularly contagious. He makes us feel psychology as part of a novelistic whole.

Notes

1 James L. Rice, *Dostoevsky and the Healing Art: An Essay in Literary and Medical History* (Ann Arbor: Ardis, 1985).
2 S. V. Kovalevskaia, *Vospominaniia i pis'ma* (Reminiscences and Letters) (Moscow: Nauka, 1961), p. 96.
3 Maksim Gorkii, 'O Karamazovshchine' (On Karamazovism) in A. A. Belkin (ed.), *F. M. Dostoevskii v russkoi kritike* (Dostoevskii in Russian Criticism) (Moscow: Goslitizdat, 1956), p. 391.
4 'Dostoevskii and Parricide' in Sigmund Freud, *Complete Psychological Works* (London: Hogarth Press, 1961), vol. 21, pp. 177–94.

8

MALCOLM V. JONES

Dostoevskii and religion

I

Dostoevskii was a Christian novelist. Some readers will regard this as a simple statement of an obvious truth, while others may regard it as a denial of all that is modern and of enduring importance in his work. On one thing both camps will agree, however. Dostoevskii, and his novels, take the claims of religion seriously on its own terms: religion does not occupy the peripheral place that it does in most notable English novels of the period. Moreover, Christianity, both in his life and his work, was engaged in pitched battle with the most desolate atheism. In Dostoevskii, neither is of that untroubled, optimistic variety which is often held to be characteristic of the Victorian age. Only towards the end of his life, while writing *The Brothers Karamazov*, was he able to comment in his notebook with some semblance of tranquillity that he had reached faith ('moia osanna') through a furnace of doubt ('gornilo somnenii') (XXVII, 86). Awaiting his own execution on the Semenovskii Square in 1849, he had murmured the words: 'Nous serons avec le Christ' (We shall be with Christ). His companion, the atheist Speshnev, had rejoined dryly: 'un peu de poussière' (specks of dust).[1] Whatever thoughts on life and death had passed through Dostoevskii's mind before this moment, the burden of Speshnev's words, in one form or another, refused thereafter to go away.

Most disagreements about the nature of Dostoevskii's presentation of religion consequently pivot on the ratio of faith to unbelief in his fiction. Some readers see his life and writing as a triumph of the Christian spirit (a 'podvig') in which an ultimately unshakeable faith in the image of Christ sustained him from the cradle to the grave and preserved him from succumbing to the many radical challenges which he encountered in his own tormented life and in the intellectual climate of his time, all reflected so graphically and so passionately in his fiction. His ambition, in the years of his maturity after his return from Siberia, to use his novels as vehicles for a religious debate in which the Christian world-view would ultimately be victorious is reflected in the structure and content of his major literary works, which in turn cannot be fully appreciated unless they are read against this background.[2]

Other readers, while granting that in times of desolation he found personal comfort in a traditional religious piety, particularly on the scaffold, in his travails in Siberia and again towards the end of his life, see his greatness in his ability to transcend such comforting illusions and to present, through his characters and narrators, those unresolved and irresolvable conflicts of the spirit which he called the 'accursed questions' ('prokliatye voprosy'). Such readers may doubt whether his restless mind ever reached any final resolution, or, if it did, whether this is in the least bit relevant to our reading of his novels, which are essentially about conflict and irresolvability. Indeed, it has been observed, Dostoevskii presents the case for atheism so persuasively, and so variously, that many readers, among them such eminent literary figures as D. H. Lawrence, Albert Camus and V. Rozanov, have been forced to conclude that this is what, in his heart, he really believed. Such readers stress the strength and persistence of his religious doubts, amounting almost to atheistic convictions, and his undiminished ability to express them in their most ardent and compelling form to the very end of his life, notably in *The Brothers Karamazov*. By contrast, many such modern readers find his depiction of religious characters and arguments far from compelling. He was, as he says elsewhere, 'a child of his age' (XXVIII/1, 176; letter of end January – 20 February 1854), and this was an age in which a radical intelligentsia which had finally rejected religion was energetically propounding various forms of scientific atheism; an age, like our own, in which Christianity, at least among the educated classes, was liable to go by default, to be seen as a curious survival of pre-scientific folklore or as evidence of mental derangement.

A less fundamental, but no less passionate, debate hinges on the character of Dostoevskii's Christianity. Is it to be read uniquely in the spirit of that Slavophilism which he professed with increasing urgency towards the end of his life – an Orthodoxy infused with Russian nationalism? This is a view which has won favour among some Orthodox readers and which is currently being rediscovered by Dostoevskii scholars in post-Soviet Russia. Or is the Christianity of his novels essentially of a non-sectarian and even heretical brand, still bearing traces of the Christian socialism of his youth, a religion in which there is little sign of God, of theology, of dogma, of the Orthodox liturgy, or indeed of church-going? Does it even prefigure radical developments in Christian spirituality and theology in the latter part of our own century? However we approach it, Dostoevskii's Christianity contributes significantly to the intellectual engagement that his novels demand of the reader.

II

If Christianity usually went by default in educated Russian families in Dostoevskii's day (as it did, for example, in the Tolstoi and Turgenev families), this was certainly not the case with the Dostoevskiis.[3] In his *Diary of a Writer* for 1873 Dostoevskii recalled that he came from a pious Russian family and knew the gospels from earliest childhood (XXI, 134; Sec. 16). Both factors – the earliest memories and the pious family environment – were vitally important to him. As a child he would be called upon to recite prayers in the presence of guests. His brother Andrei recalled that they would unfailingly attend mass every Sunday and also on Saints' Days, with vespers the previous night, in the church attached to the Moscow hospital where his father worked as a doctor.[4] His parents were not just conventional observers of religious practice. Andrei says that they were both deeply religious, especially their mother. Every significant event in the life of the family would be marked by the appropriate observance, and Dostoevskii received religious instruction from the deacon at the hospital. In his *Diary of a Writer* for August 1877 he describes how before he even learned to read, his imagination was fired by events from the lives of the saints (XXV, 215), providing models of asceticism, compassion, suffering, humility and self-sacrifice, based on the example of Christ. These impressions were reinforced by the family's annual pilgrimage to the St Sergius Trinity Monastery about sixty miles outside Moscow. These major family events continued until Dostoevskii was ten. In a letter to A. N. Maikov of 25 March 1870, he claims expertise on monasteries on the grounds that he has been acquainted with them since childhood (XXIX/1, 118). Dostoevskii's biographers also never fail to mention that his mother taught him to read from a Russian translation of a well-known German eighteenth-century religious primer by Johannes Hübner, entitled *One Hundred and Four Sacred Stories from the Old and New Testaments Selected for Children,*[5] which was also the childhood reading of the Elder Zosima in Dostoevskii's last novel (XIV, 264; Bk 6, Sec. 2). The significant thing about this book, which was supposed to be learned by heart, is that it contained so many of the Bible stories which were later to play a key role in Dostoevskii's own major novels, including the stories of the Fall in the Garden of Eden, of Job, and of the Raising of Lazarus. Probably the story of Job's unmerited sufferings and his rebellion against God (which he also associates with Zosima and which is the implied response to Ivan Karamazov's rebellion) made the deepest impression on Dostoevskii. He had read it for himself by the age of eight and he read it again in his mid-fifties, when he was working on *A Raw Youth* and *The Brothers Karamazov* (XXIX/2, 43; letter of 10 June 1875).

It was also in childhood that he learnt to associate the Russian people with a deep spirituality. The story of the peasant Marei, who rescued the young Fedor when he thought he was being pursued by a wolf, is well known. The man's surprising tenderness as he made the sign of the cross over the comforted child remained in Dostoevskii's memory all his life. He told the story in his *Diary of a Writer* for February 1876 (XXII, 46–50). Childhood memories were very important for Dostoevskii, as is emphasised in some of his character portrayals. Alesha Karamazov, for example, says at the end of the novel that people talk a lot about education, but the best education of all is perhaps some beautiful, sacred memory, preserved from childhood (XV, 195; Epilogue, Sec. 3).

From 1838 to 1843, Dostoevskii studied at the Military Engineering Academy in St Petersburg, where he was known for his hermit-like habits, and for spending all his free time reading. A. I. Savelev, who was an officer at the Academy at the time, noted that Dostoevskii was very religious and scrupulously observed all the obligations of the Orthodox church. He possessed copies of the gospels and of Heinrich Zschokke's *Die Stunden der Andacht* (Hours of Devotion). After Father Poluektov's lectures on religion, Dostoevskii would stay behind and engage in long conversations with him. The other students called him 'the monk Fotii' (Dolinin, *F. M. Dostoevskii v vospominaniiakh sovremennikov*, vol. 1, p. 97). An interesting feature of Zschokke's book, according to Dostoevskii's biographer Joseph Frank, was that it 'preached a sentimental version of Christianity entirely free from dogmatic content and with a strong emphasis on giving Christian love a social application' (Frank, *The Seeds of Revolt*, p. 78), a creed which Dostoevskii tried actively to put into practice in the Academy and which won the respect of his fellow students. There is therefore reason to believe that his tendency towards a Christian socialism with Western European sources began at this time. While it did not apparently involve any lessening of his Orthodox observance, it nevertheless harmonised with his romantic enthusiasm for those Western novelists, poets and playwrights whose work he began to devour with such unbridled enthusiasm. Some of them, such as Schiller, Hugo and George Sand, he saw as great Christian writers, and it is worthy of note that this was not for reasons which were unique to the Orthodox faith. On the occasion of George Sand's death, Dostoevskii wrote in his *Diary of a Writer* for June 1876 that although she could not bring herself to subscribe consciously to the idea that 'in the whole universe there is no name other than His through which one may be saved' – the central idea of Orthodoxy – she concurred in thought and feeling with one of the basic thoughts of Christianity, namely the acknowledgement of the human personality and its freedom and responsibility. Dying a deist, with a firm faith in

God and immortality, she was possibly the most Christian woman of her age (XXIII, 37).

There is little doubt that these words combine the views both of the young and of the mature Dostoevskii, a Dostoevskii capable of seeing Western European Christian socialism not simply as a step on the baleful, downward path from Catholicism to atheistic socialism, as he was later to insist so stridently, but also as a bright reflection of the central idea of Orthodoxy. For Dostoevskii was able to appreciate the central ideas of Orthodoxy wherever he found them, even in Western Europe, even when entirely shorn of their Orthodox context and colouring. At the Engineering Academy, his infatuation with the works of Schiller, Sand and the cohorts of Romantic writers whose work enshrined all that was pure and noble in the human spirit was stimulated and reinforced by his intense friendships with Berezhetskii and Shidlovskii. At the same time he was also reading those other Romantic writers who celebrated the supernatural, the dark side of the human soul, the individual's Faustian pact with the devil, and the sacrilegious attempt to usurp God's place in the universe: works by such writers as Hoffmann, Balzac, Eugène Sue and Goethe himself.[6]

In 1844 Dostoevskii resigned from the army for the precarious life of a professional writer, and not long afterwards the manuscript of his first novel, *Poor Folk*, received a rapturous welcome from the doyen of the Natural School, Vissarion Belinskii. It was inevitable that Dostoevskii, like everyone else who met him, should fall under Belinskii's spell. For a while he was fêted in the literary circles of St Petersburg. Many years later he recalled Belinskii's passionate socialism, which in many ways accorded with values to which he was already attracted. For example, Belinskii acknowledged the moral basis of true socialism and appreciated the dangers of the ants'-nest society. Yet, recalls Dostoevskii, unlike the utopian socialists, he felt impelled to destroy Christianity: Belinskii's socialism was atheistic. Writing in the *Diary of a Writer* for 1873, Dostoevskii remembered an occasion when in the middle of a tirade against Christ, Belinskii pointed at Dostoevskii and turned to a friend with the words: 'Every time I mention Christ the expression on his face changes; he looks just as if he's going to burst into tears.' Belinskii, says Dostoevskii, went even further than Renan (who saw Christ as the ideal of human beauty) seeing him either as the most ordinary man or at best as a possible recruit to socialism. Dostoevskii remembers George Sand, Cabet, Pierre Leroux, Proudhon and Feuerbach as Belinskii's particular heroes at this time, Fourier having already fallen out of fashion (XXI, 8–12; Sec. 2). Quite likely Belinskii also introduced him to the works of Strauss and Stirner. In the same article of 1873, Dostoevskii gives the impression that he had been entirely won over to Belinskii's position, which must have included his atheism, and later in the year he even reflected that he might have been capable of becoming a follower of the unprincipled Nechaev (XXI, 129; Sec. 16). But there is other evidence, for example, that of Dr S. D. Ianovskii (Dolinin, *F. M. Dostoevskii v vospominaniiakh sovremennikov*, vol. 1, p. 169), who saw him frequently in the mid to late 1840s, which directly contradicts this, and most scholars nowadays believe that in this respect Dostoevskii retrospectively exaggerated his capitulation to Belinskii. Joseph Frank has argued persuasively that he found support for his own progressive, moral-religious views in the Beketov Circle, and in his friendship with Valerian Maikov (Frank, *The Seeds of Revolt*, pp. 195, 201, 210).

It seems very likely that Dostoevskii wavered in both his religious views and his religious observance, finding himself caught between two irresistible imperatives: his commitment to Orthodoxy and the image of Christ, and his rage at the oppression of the lower social classes. Both sometimes led him to excess and the resulting pressures must have caused him great anguish. When he was eventually arrested in 1849 for his part in the Petrashevskii political conspiracy, the principal charge against him was that he had read Belinskii's letter to Gogol in public. In this letter, Belinskii upbraids Gogol for mixing up Christ, who brought freedom, equality and brotherhood to humanity, with the Orthodox church, the servant of despotism and superstition.[7] No doubt Dostoevskii went along with this. However far he strayed into the utopian socialist camp under the influence of Belinskii, and later, in his fateful association with the Petrashevskii Circle, he always drew the line when it came to attacks on the image of Christ, which never ceased to move him deeply.

Notwithstanding his commitment to the image of Christ, Dostoevskii continued to expose himself to philosophies which incorporated and gave expression to radical atheistic ideas, and to be drawn into their orbit. His regular visits to meetings of the Petrashevskii Circle began in the autumn of 1848, and this provided a forum in which he encountered the ideas of the leading European socialist and materialist thinkers of the day. A. Boyce Gibson is right in saying that Feuerbach's *The Essence of Christianity* is a work always to be reckoned with in the study of Dostoevskii; whether he read it or not is beside the point, because all around him were talking about it. According to Feuerbach, religious experience is not to be discounted, but it is to be seen as a projection of the human mind.[8] And the degree to which the most radical questioning of religious claims becomes the ideological cornerstone of Dostoevskii's major novels likewise testifies to the deep and permanent impression which thinkers like Belinskii, Petrashevskii and the even more extreme Speshnev made on his creative consciousness during this formative period in his life.

There is plenty of evidence that during the period of his association with the Petrashevskii Circle and its offshoots Dostoevskii was moved to indignation by violence against the oppressed and the underprivileged, but none that he looked to revolution from below as a solution, like Petrashevskii and Speshnev. Nevertheless he was arrested on 23 April 1849. There followed incarceration in the Peter and Paul Fortress, and the gruelling investigation. When conditions were alleviated, he managed to read and even to write. He read anything available, but seems to have been particularly interested in two accounts of pilgrimages to the Holy Places, and the works of St Dmitrii of Rostov (XXVIII/I, 157; letter of 18 July 1849), which included plays on religious themes in the medieval tradition. He asked his brother for the Bible (both Testaments), in both the French and Slavonic versions (XXVIII/I, 158–9; letter of 27 August 1849). However, there is no suggestion that he abandoned worldly thoughts in order to immerse himself exclusively in religion, for he also urgently requested copies of *Notes of the Fatherland* and Shakespeare. His writing also testifies to this: it was here that he wrote *A Little Hero*, which has no more religious significance than the rest of his early work. Nevertheless, as Frank speculates,[9] this period may mark the beginning of that process of close reading of the Scriptures which reached its zenith during the four years he was to spend in the Fortress at Omsk, with the New Testament as his only reading matter.

In spite of Dostoevskii's words to Speshnev at the scaffold ('Nous serons avec le Christ'), his spirit was far from tranquil at that moment. The unexpected death sentence followed by the unexpected last-minute reprieve would have put the faith of the most devout saint to the test. Dostoevskii seems to have continued to hope for something after his physical death and to have been terrified by the unknown as much as by the imminent prospect of extinction. At all events it would be inappropriate to draw any general conclusions about his religious views from his feelings at such a moment. Some years later he was to put the experiences of a condemned man on the way to execution into fictional form in Prince Myshkin's anecdote to the Epanchin family in *The Idiot* (VIII, 51–2; Pt I, Sec. 5). Whether or not they faithfully reflect his own experience in every detail, he was undoubtedly able to write from first hand. From that moment he knew that matters of faith were not peripheral to living and dying, but vitally relevant to every minute of his experience.

III

The years in the Fortress at Omsk made an indelible impression. At Tobolsk each of the Petrashevskii convicts was given a copy of the New Testament in modern Russian. This was the only book they were allowed in prison and therefore the only book Dostoevskii read for the next four years. His copy has survived, complete with markings made with his fingernail at the time and later underlinings and annotations in his hand. It has been carefully scrutinised by scholars, especially by Geir Kjetsaa, for clues as to what was most important to Dostoevskii,[10] and these findings are reflected in what follows.

His outlook on life, and with it his spiritual life, could not fail to undergo lasting change as a result of the eight years of exile, especially the four years in the Fortress. He encountered evil at first hand and the Schillerian utopianism of his youth suffered a fatal blow. At the same time he got to know the Russian people in its deepest degradation and to believe in its spiritual worth. In the *Diary of a Writer* for August 1880, in response to Gradovskii's objections to his Pushkin speech, he recalled his experiences in Omsk and defied his critic to say that he did not know the people, adding that it was from them that he had again received into his soul that Christ whom he knew first in his parents' home as a child and whom he had nearly lost when, in his turn, he transformed himself into a European liberal (XXVI, 152). For all the alleged shortcomings of the Orthodox church, he insisted, it had kept the people faithful to the truth of Christ through their long centuries of suffering by its hymns and prayers, notably the prayer of Saint Ephraim the Syrian, beginning 'God and Lord of my life', which contained 'the whole essence of Christianity' (XXVI, 151). Dostoevskii was impressed by the devout prayers of the prisoners, in whom the spark of the divine had never been extinguished.

On his release from the Fortress in January 1854, he wrote his now-famous and much-quoted letter to Natalia Fonvizina, from whose hands he had received his copy of the New Testament:

> I have heard from many sources that you are very religious, Natalia Dmitrievna, but it is not because you are religious, but because of what I have experienced and felt myself, that I tell you that there are moments when one thirsts for faith like 'parched grass', and finds it, for the very reason that truth shines more clearly in affliction. As for myself, I confess that I am a child of my age, a child of unbelief and doubt up to this very moment and (I am certain of it) to the grave. What terrible torments this thirst to believe has cost me and continues to cost me, burning more strongly in my soul the more contrary arguments there are. Nevertheless God sometimes sends me moments of complete tranquillity. In such moments I love and find that I am loved by others, and in such moments I have nurtured in myself a symbol of truth, in which everything is clear and holy for me. This symbol is very simple: it is the belief that there is nothing finer, profounder, more attractive, more reasonable, more courageous and more perfect than Christ, and not only is there not, but I tell myself with jealous

love that there cannot be. Even if someone were to prove to me that the truth lay outside Christ, I should prefer to remain with Christ than with the truth. (XXVIII/I, 176; end January – 20 February 1854)

The significance of this passage for the later Dostoevskii has been much debated, especially his prediction that he would remain a child of unbelief and doubt to the grave. Certainly the Dostoevskii of the late 1870s wrote nothing to confirm this. Yet the ability to identify imaginatively with the extremes of doubt and unbelief never left him, and this is something which those who wish to stress the depth of his faith in his later years sometimes gloss over. At the same time the letter testifies to three important, positive facts: the first is that Dostoevskii sometimes experiences moments of great spiritual tranquillity; the second is that atheistic arguments, far from undermining his faith, seem to provoke an intense thirst for it; the third is the immense power over him of the image of Christ as ideal, a power which would withstand, as one of his characters in *The Devils* later puts it, even mathematical refutation (X, 198; Pt 2, Ch. 1).

On his release and transfer to Semipalatinsk, Dostoevskii certainly did not become a wholly conventional Orthodox believer. Wrangel recalls how in Semipalatinsk their favourite occupation was to lie on the grass on a warm evening gazing at the millions of stars twinkling in the sky. In these moments an awareness of the greatness of the Creator, of an omniscient, omnipotent divine power, softened their hearts, while the consciousness of their own insignificance quietened their spirits. Wrangel observes that in Semipalatinsk Dostoevskii 'was rather pious, but did not often go to church, and disliked priests, especially Siberian ones. But he spoke about Christ ecstatically' (Dolinin, *F. M. Dostoevskii v vospominaniiakh sovremennikov*, vol. 1, p. 254). There is some evidence too that he was keen to explore the philosophical and psychological aspects of spiritual life, and even study Islam. Writing to his brother in February 1854, he entreats him to send copies of the Koran, Kant's *Critique of Pure Reason* and Hegel's *Philosophy of History* (XXVIII/I, 173). At about the same time Wrangel reports that they were planning to translate together Hegel's philosophy and Carus's *Psyche* (Dolinin, *F. M. Dostoevskii v vospominaniiakh sovremennikov*, vol. 1, p. 250). Such evidence, combined with what we know of Dostoevskii's intellectual interests after his return to metropolitan Russia, suggests that he was keen to place Christianity in a wider context and to explore ways in which modern idealist philosophy had enabled his contemporaries to re-evaluate the religious tradition without entirely abandoning it. A further dimension to Dostoevskii's religious experience at this time is provided in an anecdote told by S. V. Kovalevskaia, according to which Dostoevskii related to her the experience of an epileptic fit one Easter in Siberia, during which he was convinced that, like Mohammed, he had really visited Paradise and apprehended God (ibid., pp. 346–7). Such experiences are reflected in those of Prince Myshkin in *The Idiot* (VIII, 188; Pt 2, Sec. 5). 'For several moments,' Dostoevskii told Strakhov, 'I experience a happiness that is impossible under ordinary circumstances, and of which most people have no comprehension. I feel a complete harmony within myself and in the whole world, and this feeling is so strong and affords so much pleasure that one could give up ten years of one's life for several seconds of that ecstasy, perhaps one's whole life' (Dolinin, *F. M. Dostoevskii v vospominaniiakh sovremennikov*, vol. 1, p. 281). Although they varied in frequency and intensity, Dostoevskii's epileptic fits continued until the end of his life (Catteau, *Dostoyevsky and the Process of Literary Creation*, pp. 90–134).

In spite of the occasional moments of tranquillity, and the ecstatic commitment to the image of Christ, the picture we have of Dostoevskii as he returns to Russia at the close of the 1850s is that of a troubled, questing spirit, open to intense momentary mystical experiences, who becomes progressively convinced of the spiritual treasures in the soul of the ordinary Russian people and of the damage done to the Russian spirit by Westernisation and the divorce of Russian youth (including, for a time, himself) from its native soil.

On his return to European Russia these views were reinforced in Dostoevskii's mind in a variety of ways. His travels in Europe, his experience of the revolutionary movement after the Emancipation, his discussions with Herzen in London and Italy, and with Grigorev and Strakhov on the two journals *Time* (*Vremia*) and *The Epoch* (*Epokha*) which he edited with his brother Mikhail until Mikhail died in 1864, all led him to formulate, with his colleagues, a doctrine which they called 'pochvennichestvo', a term which is easy to understand, but difficult to translate. Some call it 'native soil conservatism' and its object was to bridge the gulf between Westerners and Slavophiles in post-Reform Russia. In later years Dostoevskii moved further into the orbit of the Slavophiles. While accepting the need to take the best of Western civilisation on board, he called for a return to Russian values, which he increasingly saw as the key to universal salvation, not only to that of Russia. Like the Slavophiles, he preached that Europe had long ago sold its soul to the principles of abstract rationalism, legalism and individualism, which the Catholic church had inherited from Rome and passed on to Protestantism and thence to socialism, which inevitably became atheistic. Russia, on the other hand, with its ideals of universality and reconciliation, and its ability to understand other peoples and unite them in a grand synthesis, had preserved its sense of organic community in the Orthodox conception of 'sobornost'' (spiritual oneness). These values are reflected in his

Winter Notes on Summer Impressions (an account of his visits to Europe in 1862 and 1863), in the editorial policies of the two journals, in the articles published in his *Diary of a Writer* (from 1873 to 1880), and from time to time through the mouths of characters in his novels. Such ideas underlay his sensationally successful Pushkin Speech in 1880. It is this outlook which Dostoevskii was referring to when he wrote in his *Diary of a Writer* for 1873 of the 'regeneration of his convictions' (XXI, 134; Sec. 16). The source of the values underlying it was to be found in the tradition of the Russian Orthodox church as interpreted by the leading Slavophiles, and there is no doubt that the development of a coherent world-view along these lines did much to stabilise Dostoevskii's intellectual and emotional life, and to restore his respectability in Russian high society. In later years he became close to Konstantin Pobedonostsev, the Procurator of the Holy Synod, and to the Imperial Family. There was to be no more flirting with liberal or revolutionary ideas, though, as we have seen, Dostoevskii retained fond memories of the Romantic European writers whose works he had devoured in his youth.

It has to be admitted that most non-academic admirers of Dostoevskii have not found his 'pochvennik'/Slavophile ideas very interesting, and there are good reasons why this is so. In the first place there is their strident, didactic, nationalistic tone, at times tinged by anti-semitism; in the second, they display no intellectual originality and, some would say, lack intellectual integrity. Not least, as Geir Kjetsaa puts it, one is irritated by his tireless assertion of Russia's excellence, and by his bitter complaints that this excellence cannot be understood by Western Europeans (Kjetsaa, *Fyodor Dostoyevsky*, p. 285). But, most importantly, they seem to cast little light on what is original and insightful in Dostoevskii's major fiction and to have little in common with those qualities which have established him as a world-ranking author. Not a single character in the great novels, and that includes the narrators, subscribes to Dostoevskii's personal philosophy as a whole. Even Shatov in *The Devils*, who shares his views about many things (Russia as a God-bearing people; the importance of the aesthetic principle; the prospect that the Second Coming of Christ will take place in Russia), cannot yet bring himself to confess belief in the existence of God.

In fact, it is not the ideology of the later Dostoevskii but the struggles of the earlier Dostoevskii which give us the most valuable clues to the reading of his novels. And this should not surprise us. After all Dostoevskii reminds his readers more than once that it is the voyage that matters, not the arrival at one's destination. As Ippolit says, in *The Idiot*:

> You can be certain that Columbus was happy not when he actually discovered America, but during the process of discovering it. You can be certain that the

moment when he was happiest of all was perhaps exactly three days before he
discovered the New World, when his mutinous crew almost turned the ship
back to Europe in despair [. . .] It is life that matters, life alone – the continuous
and everlasting process of discovery, and not the discovery itself. (VIII, 327;
Pt 3, Sec. 5)

Similar sentiments are expressed in Dostoevskii's article of 1861 'Mr —bov
and the Question of Art' (XVIII, 97) and by the hero of *Notes from Underground* (V, 118; Pt 1, Sec. 9). What one observes in Dostoevskii's novels is a
reflection of the process of discovery – or rediscovery – of the Christian tradition, in the face of its most deadly (one might say 'mutinous') opponents.
It is a process of rethinking Christianity in dialogue, a process which reached
no final conclusion in his novels, whatever may have been the case with his
own spiritual pilgrimage. Indeed, when Dostoevskii committed his thoughts
to paper in his notebooks for 1864 on the occasion of the death of his first
wife, Maria Dmitrievna, he made this very argument the cornerstone of his
belief in immortality. Reflecting that to love another person as oneself according to Christ's commandment is impossible, because a man's ego holds
him back, Dostoevskii affirms that Christ alone was able to do this and he
is the perpetual ideal towards which the individual strives and must strive
in accordance with a law of nature. Since the appearance of Christ in the
flesh it has become evident that he represents the ultimate development of
the human personality. The highest use the individual can make of his ego is
therefore to annihilate that ego, to give it totally and unselfishly to everyone.
At this point the law of the ego and the law of humanism both annihilate
themselves and fuse. But if this was the final goal of humanity, there would
be no more point in living once it had been achieved. Therefore on earth
the individual is in development, unfinished, transitional: 'It is completely
senseless to attain such a great goal, in my view, if on attaining it everything
is snuffed out and disappears, that is if there is no more life for the individual on the attainment of this goal. Therefore there is a future, heavenly life'
(XX, 172–3; entry dated 16 April). As we shall see, belief in immortality is the
one article of traditional Christian doctrine which Dostoevskii consistently
affirms, and it is predicated on the belief that here on earth the individual's
spiritual business is necessarily unfinished.

By the mid-1860s, therefore, Dostoevskii's religious consciousness had
many strands. Publicly, he had succeeded in knitting them together in the
ideology of 'pochvennichestvo', but the uncritical passion with which he
sometimes preached its tenets, especially in later years, is perhaps a measure
of the fragility of the edifice that he had created. At all events, when it
came to writing novels, he adopted a quite different mind-set, a mind-set

which has still perhaps not been satisfactorily described in the voluminous critical literature, but which has something in common with his metaphor of Columbus and his mutinous crew on the verge of discovering America. When Dostoevskii says that affliction (which includes spiritual despair) prompts faith, that points to something very striking about the ideological composition of his fiction. It is as if all his major works revolve around some radical contemporary challenge to Christianity, some expression of unbelief, to which in the course of writing, or planning, Dostoevskii tries to work out the appropriate Christian response.

IV

We come to the major works. Although religious motifs are difficult to find in *Notes from Underground*, it is typical in taking as its central character an intellectual obsessed – as Dostoevskii was – with ultimate philosophical questions. Ostensibly the hero is in rebellion against the dominant progressive ideas of the 1860s, above all the idea that human beings are rational creatures who have only to be shown their true rational interests in order to follow them, and the idea that human beings are part of a natural world which has been shown by science to be subject to iron laws of cause and effect, with the result that belief in freedom of the will is deluded, and all notion of moral responsibility illusory. Against these ideas the hero protests that reason accounts for only a fraction of human faculties and rarely if ever determines actions; moreover, whatever science may say about freedom being illusory, people will simply refuse to accept it. In fact, if ever a perfect rational society were created, people would conspire to bring it tumbling down. The hero also has deeper philosophical problems which are more rarely commented on, such as the impossibility of finding any stable basis at all for philosophical certainty. Ostensibly, again, the hero's answer is frantically to assert the claims of the individual will, a stance which has caused Dostoevskii to be seen as a proto-existentialist. However, there are both textual and extra-textual reasons for rejecting this protest as the hero's final word. The appalling consequences of the unfettered play of the individual will are depicted in Raskolnikov's Siberian dream in *Crime and Punishment* and again in 'The Grand Inquisitor' in *The Brothers Karamazov*, and we know that Dostoevskii had originally intended to provide a Christian solution to the Underground Man's problems. He wrote the words on the death of his wife just as he had completed Part 1 of his story, so perhaps they give a clue to what this might have consisted of. We are left however only with hints in the text, the most important of which is the hero's intuition that there is a better solution than the one he has inscribed in his notes, and that this perhaps has something to do with 'living life' ('zhivaia zhizn'') (v, 121, 178; Pt 1, Sec. 11, Pt 2, Sec. 10). This is a vitally important point to note in respect of Dostoevskii's treatment of religion. It recalls Christ's 'I am the way, the truth and the life' (John 14:6; Kjetsaa, *Dostoevskii and his New Testament*, p. 39) and reminds us that Christianity for Dostoevskii was less a set of prescribed beliefs and more what Stewart Sutherland, taking his cue from Wittgenstein, has called a 'form of life',[11] a form of life which takes all human faculties, including the thirst for the holy, fully into account. As Dostoevskii said in one of his notebooks: 'The gospels foresee that the laws of self-preservation and scientific experiment will discover nothing and will never satisfy people, that people are satisfied not by progress and necessity, but by a moral acceptance of a higher beauty.'[12] *Notes from Underground* seems to pose the question 'What happens to an intellectual of our time who has lost his sense of the holy and his grasp of living life, and finds himself in the thrall of fashionable progressive ideas?' The Man from Underground is Dostoevskii's answer. In this way he sets out to counter some strong and insistent challenges to religion: rationalism; deterministic physics; historical optimism; utilitarian ethics; nihilistic amoralism; the inadequacy of human language to reach certain truth. But he does so here by a negative route, by displaying the dreadful consequences for the individual and for society of such ideas taken to their logical conclusion, and just hinting that there is another way.

In *Crime and Punishment* the main challenge to religion again comes from an intellectual of the 1860s, who hubristically takes on himself the role of God (the Man-God as Dostoevskii was later to call him), believing that he has the right to determine the life or death of others, to sit in judgement on other people and even to divert the course of history, if he is in truth a great man with a new word for humanity. Raskolnikov persuades himself that he is such a person (though this is a gross over-simplification of his psychology), and he commits two murders. The rest of the novel is taken up with events which accompany a process of self-questioning and eventual surrender to the authorities. Dostoevskii saw this intellectual hubris exemplified in the young nihilists of the 1860s, inspired not just by utilitarianism debased by a form of Social Darwinism, but also by the cult of the great man, typified by the achievements of the first Napoleon and the aspirations of the third. Together with an emphasis on the individual will, the novel shows that Raskolnikov feels that fate is playing a hand in his life.

It is in planning his murder that Raskolnikov accidentally hears of the young prostitute Sonia Marmeladova and resolves eventually to make his confession to her. Sonia is the first of Dostoevskii's major saintly characters: characters, that is, whose life is based on acceptance of life, rather than on taking up arms against it, characters who echo the tradition of the 'iurodivyi' or 'holy fool' and whose personalities express a simple faith characterised by humility ('smirenie'), compassion ('sostradanie'), insight ('prozorlivost'') and spiritual tenderness ('umilenie'). Perhaps it is this last which is the least accessible to the Western mind. V. N. Zakharov has shown how the idea plays a key role in Dostoevskii's poetics, from the sentimental *Poor Folk* onwards. A Western reader may mistake 'umilenie' for sentimentality. But there are further dimensions to the Russian idea: it is a softening of the heart, an arousal of tender emotions which combines the richness of Christian love with veneration and piety expressive of the grace of God.[13] Sonia is by no means a tranquil person. Her faith is easily disturbed. But she is the agent of Raskolnikov's spiritual rebirth, which she sets in motion when she reads to him the story of the Raising of Lazarus from St John's Gospel (John 11). The story expresses the idea of death and resurrection, the Easter motif, and looked at from the Christian point of view it is this myth that structures Raskolnikov's destiny in the novel, from his spiritual suicide when he commits murder to the beginnings of his spiritual renewal in Siberia. It can be argued, as Roger Cox does, that in fact it structures the whole novel,[14] cutting across the counter-structure of pride and retribution into which the reader is lured by the novel's title, with the result that most secular readers seem to find the religious alternative implausible. Cox also argued, long before the fact was rediscovered by specialists working in Russia, for the special place of the Johannine scriptures in Dostoevskii (that is, John's Gospel, the Letters of John and the Book of Revelation), in particular John's insistence on the priority of Grace over Law, an emphasis which, of course, he shares with Paul. It is an idea associated with the Russian acceptance of the criminal as an 'unfortunate' rather than as an outcast, an idea which pervades the whole of *Crime and Punishment*. Geir Kjetsaa has noted that a study of the underlinings in Dostoevskii's copy of the New Testament confirms the significance of the Johannine scriptures, with their emphasis on the commandment to love and definition of sin as a rejection of Jesus (Kjetsaa, *Fyodor Dostoyevsky*, p. 222).

However, neither traditional Orthodox theology nor the church plays a significant role in the novel and, as a consequence, nor does the notion of 'sobornost'' (the church as fellowship under God) which was later to be so important to Dostoevskii. Raskolnikov's 'resurrection' is made possible by his Christian upbringing (Gibson, *The Religion of Dostoevsky*, pp. 92–3), for like Dostoevskii, he has warm childhood memories which seem to have been revived by the arrival of his mother and sister. Neither Sonia nor any other character seeks to mount counter-arguments against Raskolnikov's atheism. She is no intellectual, nor is she a traditional Orthodox saint. And if she echoes the type of the Holy Fool, it is only distantly. She has not chosen a life of renunciation, feigning foolishness in order to vanquish her spiritual pride, but has been forced into prostitution to support her family. Her literary ancestry includes representatives of the 'pure prostitute' from the European Romantic tradition. She presents an alternative form of life, but Dostoevskii does not simply juxtapose the alternatives. He causes his characters with their philosophies to interact. And as we shall see, there is no certainty as to which will emerge victorious within the framework of any given fiction.[15]

The figure of Prince Myshkin in *The Idiot* has produced much heated discussion. If we did not know that Dostoevskii had conceived him (very late in the day, within two months of completing Part 1) as a 'positively beautiful man', had referred to literary models such as Dickens's Mr Pickwick, Cervantes's Don Quixote and Hugo's Jean Valjean (xxviii/2, 251; letter of 1 January 1868), and left notes in which 'The Prince' is juxtaposed with the name of Christ, there might be less to dispute. But it is certainly the case that, especially in the first part of the novel, Myshkin is associated with numberless Christian motifs, deriving from both the New Testament and the Russian religious tradition. In his long stories to the Epanchin women, Myshkin evokes the gospels, not least in his own childlikeness and his liking for children, his fondness for the donkey, the story of Marie, and the very fact that he is prone to contribute to conversation by means of parables. L. Miuller stresses that Myshkin displays all the qualities emphasised in the beatitudes in the Sermon on the Mount: he is 'poor of spirit', meek, merciful, pure of heart, a peacemaker. Likewise he displays those virtues commended by St Paul (1 Corinthians 13:4–7): he is patient, kind, envies no one, is never boastful, nor conceited, nor rude; he is never selfish nor quick to take offence, keeps no score of wrongs, does not gloat over other men's sins, delights in the truth, believes that there is nothing love cannot face, and that there is no limit to faith, hope and endurance based on love.[16] In addition, Myshkin's religious experience incorporates a spiritual dimension unique in Dostoevskii's fiction, based on his own epileptic aura, a blinding inner light which momentarily floods his soul and conveys a deep calm, full of serene and harmonious joy and hope, full of understanding of the last cause, the very synthesis of beauty and prayer, the highest synthesis of life (VIII, 195; Pt 2, Sec. 5).

At first sight *The Idiot* seems an exception to the rule that Dostoevskii's novels focus on the mutinous crew rather than on the captain inspired by faith in what lies over the horizon. Yet although it begins by introducing a saintly hero in the person of Prince Myshkin, it is evident (both on textual grounds and from what we know of its complex creative history) that the author/narrator becomes increasingly uncomfortable with this arrangement. Something odd happens at the end of Part 1. It is as if some magnetic force draws Dostoevskii, and his fiction, back into the usual configuration. By the time he is writing the third part of the novel, his notes contain a marginal reminder to write concisely and powerfully about Ippolit, and to focus the whole plot on him (IX, 280). Shortly before he noted: 'Ippolit is the main axis of the whole novel. He even has a hold on the Prince, though in essence he realises that he can never possess him' (IX, 277). This is an extraordinary move with respect to a character who in other respects seems minor and peripheral, and who is essentially an afterthought in the author's scheme of things.[17] Yet it is foreshadowed as early as Part 2, where a quite different, and devastatingly negative, image of Christ is introduced, by means of Rogozhin's copy of Holbein's picture of Christ taken from the Cross. Rogozhin likes looking at the picture. Myshkin is horrified, remarking that it could cause a person to lose his faith. Much later in the novel, as he confronts his own imminent death, Ippolit gives an extended comment:

> Here one cannot help being struck by a question: if death is so horrible and the laws of nature so powerful then how can they be overcome? How can they be overcome when they were not even conquered by the one who during his lifetime conquered nature and whom nature obeyed . . . ? When one looks at that picture, nature appears in the form of some huge, implacable and dumb beast, or to be more exact (much more exact, however strange it may seem) in the form of some huge machine of the latest design which has senselessly seized, cut to pieces and swallowed up, impassively and unfeelingly, that great and priceless being, a being alone worth the whole of nature and all its laws, the whole earth, which was possibly created solely for the appearance of that being.
> (VIII, 339; Pt 3, Sec. 6)

There is no doubt that the mutinous crew comes into its own as the novel progresses – embodying cupidity, pride, humiliation and the demand for rights – and if Myshkin for a time learns to cope with it, it is at the expense of his saintliness. The transition is marked by a shift from motifs reminiscent of the gospels to apocalyptic motifs recalling the book of Revelation. One of the characters, Lebedev, even sets up as an interpreter of the Apocalypse and the narrative takes on a dizzy momentum which Myshkin is powerless to stop. The key to life always remains for him beyond the horizon, as it does for Nastasia Filippovna – who also presents an image of Christ, this time accompanied by a child, his gaze fixed on a distant point on the horizon, a great thought, as great as the universe, in his eyes (VIII, 380; Pt 3, Sec. 10). It is worth noting that the positive image of Christ contained in the novel is presented not by Myshkin but by Nastasia Filippovna. At the end of the day Myshkin is not the Russian Christ, as some readers have wished to see him – he succeeds in 'resurrecting' no one – and he is scarcely a traditional saint. Although he embodies to an unusual degree those features which Dostoevskii associates with the Christian personality (compassion, insight, humility, sensitivity to beauty, tenderness of heart, forgiveness) and shares Dostoevskii's own glimpse of paradise through the aura of an epileptic fit, this glimpse is followed by a sense of utter desolation, and is associated more with the Prophet Mohammed than with Christ. Moreover, he is unable to remember his Russian roots, bringing with him into the novel only mixed memories of Protestant Switzerland. Nor does he seem to be a practising Christian in the conventional sense: he does not attend Orthodox church services or observe the Orthodox church year, and General Ivolgin's seems to be the first Orthodox funeral he has ever attended. The other characters perceive him in a wide variety of ways, ranging from idiot, holy fool, democrat and manipulative rogue to Pushkin's Poor Knight and Cervantes's Don Quixote, but not as an Orthodox saint. Those who persist in seeing in him an image of Orthodox saintliness should ask themselves whether he is in the end the sort of person the Russian Orthodox church would be likely to canonise. Yet he succeeds in holding up to other characters an image of the best in themselves and a hint of a higher reality in which time shall be no more (VIII, 189; Pt 2, Sec. 5). Although the conception and characterisation of Myshkin is an artistic triumph, and almost certainly the most memorable portrait of Christian saintliness in the realistic novel, his performance as an embodiment of Christian virtues, a 'positively beautiful man', remains controversial. Among those who lament his failure, there are some who ascribe it to his Christianity, and others for whom he is not Christian enough (Gibson, *The Religion of Dostoevsky*, pp. 112–13). Both positions are defensible. Dostoevskii himself felt that he had not achieved his aim, that the novel did not express a tenth of what he had intended (XXIX/I, 10; letter of 25 January 1869); yet he had poured his most intense spiritual experiences into it, raising the discussion from the level of historical processes in his previous novel to that of the nature of the universe.

V

Dostoevskii spent the years 1867–71 in Europe with his second wife, Anna Grigorevna. As Gibson remarks (*The Religion of Dostoevsky*, p. 38), so far as we can tell Dostoevskii was in 1869 full of religious sentiment and less suspicious of the church than formerly, but still in trouble on the intellectual front. He did not seem to have advanced much beyond the Myshkin who, convinced that 'compassion is the chief law of human existence' (VIII, 192; Pt 2, Sec. 5), tried to persuade himself that 'the atheist is always talking about something else' (VIII, 184; Pt 2, Sec. 4). Yet by the time he returned to Russia his friend Nikolai Strakhov could testify (and Anna Grigorevna confirms what Strakhov says) that it was while abroad that the revelation of the Christian spirit which had always dwelt in him came to fruition. He continually steered the conversation on to religious themes. Moreover, his conduct changed, acquiring a great gentleness expressive of the highest Christian feelings.[18] Of course Dostoevskii was not always like this, as other witnesses testify,[19] but his years of exile in Europe do seem to have strengthened the Slavophile Christianity of his last decade. There is another significant change, as the following extract from his notes for *The Devils* makes clear. Christ appears in his thoughts not as an ideal of perfection, unattainable here on earth, but as the ideal in human form, in other words the Word incarnate of St John's Gospel:

> Many think that it is enough to believe in the moral teaching of Christ to be a Christian. It is not Christ's moral teaching, not Christ's doctrine, that will save the world, but faith that the Word has become flesh [. . .] Only in this faith can we achieve divinisation, that ecstasy which binds us most closely to him and has the power of preventing us from straying from the true path.
>
> (XI, 187–8)

The Devils, Dostoevskii's next major novel, based in part upon his unrealised plan for 'The Life of a Great Sinner', contains many religious motifs, some notable dialogues on religious topics, hallucinations of the devil, a holy fool and a 'Bible woman', but does not make a major contribution to his religious evolution. There is no doubt that the mutinous crew is in command here and it is therefore not surprising that many of the religious motifs are apocalyptic, as in the later parts of *The Idiot*. Dostoevskii reverts to his preferred structure, in which the central character expresses, or provokes others to express, forms of desolate atheism and amoralism. Although the novel was inspired by the Nechaev episode, and Nechaev is represented in the novel by Petr Verkhovenskii, the central character is Nikolai Stavrogin. In a note reminiscent of the one on Ippolit, Dostoevskii wrote in his notebooks: 'Everything is contained in the character of Stavrogin. Stavrogin is ALL' (XI, 207).

Indeed, as the novel shows, Stavrogin has inspired the ideas not only of Verkhovenskii, but also of Shatov and Kirillov. As for himself, he has never found a task worthy of his strength, or even capable of commanding his attention for any length of time. In the censored chapter 'At Tikhon's' in which he presents his confession to Bishop Tikhon in a local monastery, he asks Tikhon to recite a passage from Revelation in which the 'lukewarm' are condemned (Revelation 3:14–16). That is Stavrogin himself. Tikhon declares that a complete atheist stands on the next to top rung of the ladder of perfect faith, but Stavrogin cannot manage even that. His short-lived enthusiasms have produced passionate disciples, however. From the point of view of Dostoevskii's presentation of religion, Shatov and Kirillov are the most important of these. Shatov, who displays some of the personal characteristics of Dostoevskii's saintly types, also, as we have already noted, subscribes to some of the main points of his Slavophile creed; in particular he proclaims his belief that the aesthetic principle in human affairs is much more important than science and reason, that Russia is a God-bearing people, that the Second Coming of Christ will take place in Russia – and, significantly, he expresses in his own words Dostoevskii's idea that humanity is driven by a force which is the source of 'an unquenchable desire to continue to the end and at the same time to deny an end' (x, 198; Pt 2, Ch. 1). But although Shatov believes in these things, he can affirm only that he *will* believe in God. As a representative of Dostoevskii's Slavophile creed, Shatov seems to fall at the vital hurdle. Gibson is surely right in saying that the Shatov–Stavrogin dialogue shows us Dostoevskii ruthlessly probing into his own religious advances, and finding them hollow (*The Religion of Dostoevsky*, p. 142). Kirillov, confused though he seems to be, does fatally assert his atheism. His picture of a universe without God is as bleak as Ippolit's, and seems to echo Dostoevskii's own exchange with Speshnev at the scaffold. In it Christ – without whom the whole planet is utter madness, founded on lies, 'a vaudeville of the devil' – is himself the victim of an illusion, for there is no paradise or resurrection (x, 471; Pt 3, Ch. 6). Kirillov shares Myshkin's epileptic aura. He too momentarily feels eternal harmony in all its fullness, and has a joyful sensation of the whole of nature and truth for which he would give his whole life; but it is an experience alien to a physical life in which people are tormented by pain and fear, and Kirillov sees it as his quasi-messianic mission to sacrifice himself in order to demonstrate that if God does not exist then everything is a matter of the self-will of the individual who can conquer pain and fear in the most significant way possible, by taking his own life (x, 470; Pt 3, Ch. 6).

If Shatov's and Kirillov's religious views have fatal flaws, the same may be said for Stepan Verkhovenskii, father of the young nihilist and mentor of Stavrogin. At the close of his life, he too stumbles upon and is enthused by the key passage from Revelation (3:14–16), together with the passage from Luke about the Gadarene swine, which Dostoevskii's narrator uses as his epigraph (Luke 8:32–7). But, unlike Stavrogin, of whom it is said that 'when he believes he does not believe that he believes, and when he does not believe he does not believe that he does not believe' (x, 469; Pt 3, Ch. 6), Verkhovenskii senior discovers that his main trouble is that he believes himself even when he is lying (x, 497; Pt 3, Ch. 7). It hardly needs to be said that such thoughts put a huge question mark against the reliability of all belief systems. It may be asked why Dostoevskii should have devoted so much space to various forms of eccentric religious belief in a novel which was ostensibly based on political events with no evident religious content. The answer is not that Dostoevskii hypothesised that the political events and the accompanying moral and spiritual confusion were the inevitable by-product of a society which had lost its 'binding idea' and faith in the image of Christ, though this is the case. It is because he was still wrestling with the accursed questions himself, and his novels inescapably reflect that process. This is true even of *A Raw Youth*, his penultimate major novel. Although space precludes its treatment here, not only does this novel, as Gibson reminds us, contain interesting religious discussions, but the characters quote Scripture as they never did, for example, in *The Idiot* (*The Religion of Dostoevsky*, p. 153). Moreover the narrator's stepfather (Makar) and his natural mother (Sofia) embody a positive conception of peasant religion unparalleled elsewhere in Dostoevskii's fiction, in which *umilenie* has a prominent place. The novel also takes up a curious theme which found its first expression in Stavrogin's Confession (XI, 21–2) and which subsequently emerges in two forms in *A Raw Youth* (XIII, 290, 374–9; Pt 3, Ch. 1, Ch. 7), then in the story 'The Dream of a Ridiculous Man' (XXV, 104–19), and finally in Ivan Karamazov's poem on 'The Geological Upheaval' (XV, 83; Bk 11, Sec. 9). The theme is that of the 'Golden Age' on earth. In three of its manifestations it is based on Dostoevskii's interpretation of Claude Lorrain's painting *Acis and Galatea*, which he saw in the Dresden Art Gallery. What they have in common is a depiction of an idyllic, pastoral life in the distant past in a mythical Greece, a paradise on earth in which human beings live in joy, peace, harmony and plenty. Gibson compares and contrasts all these passages (*The Religion of Dostoevsky*, pp. 154–68). In 'The Dream of a Ridiculous Man' paradise is destroyed by the introduction of the lie. It is a reworking, using classical rather than Hebrew motifs, of the myth of the Fall as told in the book of Genesis. And the consequences of the Fall from innocence, as retold here, are that human language ceases to be a reliable vehicle of truth. Makar Dolgorukii (*A Raw Youth*), in extolling God's creation in the present, represents a step forward from Myshkin in this respect. The latter typically feels alienated from Nature, while the former believes that everything is a mystery, the greatest mystery of all being what awaits us after death (XIII, 290; Pt 3, Ch. 1). The word most often associated with Makar is *blagoobrazie* (beautiful form); what he has to offer is not an abstract philosophy of life, nor reflections on the atheistic desolation of an Ippolit or a Kirillov, but an alternative 'form of life' in which a foretaste of eternal life is to be experienced here and now.

Dostoevskii's last novel is unique in many important ways. But we have it on his own repeated testimony that he wished *The Brothers Karamazov* to serve as a vehicle for the vindication of the Orthodox faith. There is no doubt that he went to great lengths, in both his reading and his field research, to give an authentic rendering of the life of the Orthodox monastery. His visit with the young Vladimir Solovev to the monastery at Optina Pustyn in the summer of 1877 played a part and was supplemented by his extensive reading of religious texts. It is impossible to do full justice to the richness of the religious texture of this novel in this short chapter. It contains many of the motifs we have noted in the earlier novels, including apocalyptic motifs. The association of the Christian life with tender spiritual feelings – compassion, humility, beauty, childlikeness, non-judgementalism, love for one's neighbour – are all present, together with allusions to transfiguration and *sobornost'*. Zosima's address to the company as he brings his duel to an end (XIV, 272; Bk 6, Sec. 2) seems to echo Makar in its paean to God's creation. It is arguable that the Easter motif (echoed in the epigraph taken from John 12:24) structures the whole novel. The powerful anti-religious polemic contained in the chapters entitled 'Rebellion' and 'The Grand Inquisitor' has alone inspired a multitude of articles and even books; it has attracted the attention of leading Catholic, Protestant and Orthodox theologians and philosophers of religion. To a lesser extent the same is true of the figure of Zosima and his 'Testament', designed, according to Dostoevskii's plan, to refute the views of the Grand Inquisitor. Nor, of course, is the religious significance of the novel limited to these chapters. All three brothers, Ivan, Alesha and Dmitrii, make their own contributions to the dialogue, as, in semi-caricature, do Fedor Karamazov, Miusov, Smerdiakov, Rakitin and the monks in the local monastery.

In brief, the heart of the religious polemic is again the mutinous crew, whose chief representative is the young intellectual Ivan Karamazov. Echoing Belinskii's famous rejection of Hegel in his letter to Botkin, he tells his brother, the novice Alesha, a whole series of heart-rending anecdotes about inhuman atrocities committed against children, which he has collected from the newspapers, and concludes that he reserves judgement about the existence of God; but if He exists, and this suffering is the price we are required to pay for future entry into paradise, then the cost is too high and he 'respectfully returns the ticket'. He continues by recounting his own idea for a narrative poem, full of allusions to religious texts, set in Seville in the sixteenth century, in which an aged Grand Inquisitor is supervising the burning of heretics. Into this scene steps the figure of Christ who, having performed a number of acts which echo the gospel narrative, finds himself in the Inquisitor's cell where the latter, far from acknowledging the incongruity of burning one's fellow humans in the name of a doctrine of love, proceeds to justify his procedure, and that of the Catholic Church, at very great length. This he does by allusion to the gospel story of Christ's temptation by the devil in the wilderness (Luke 4:1–13), concluding that the devil was right and Christ was mistaken. Christ offered people freedom, but the burden of freedom and knowledge of the truth that there is no God is too much for all but a small élite to bear. What people really crave are the three principles (which the Inquisitor derives from the devil's temptations) of 'mystery', 'miracle' and 'authority', or in more concrete terms, something to worship, the satisfaction of their daily material needs, and the political and moral authority of the church. This is what the church offers, having corrected Christ's teaching. Christ has no right to come back and interfere. In Ivan's poem, Christ makes no answer, but kisses the old man and is allowed to leave. The significance of that act has been much debated by readers of Dostoevskii's novel – as indeed has the significance of the poem as a whole, some seeing it as a brilliant anticipation of the totalitarian orders of the twentieth century, not least in Dostoevskii's homeland. One of the best discussions of 'The Grand Inquisitor' is by Roger Cox, who acutely points out that what the Inquisitor is really offering is not 'mystery, miracle and authority' but 'magic, mystification and tyranny' (Cox, *Between Earth and Heaven*, p. 210). However this may be, these two chapters have been widely seen as containing powerful and irrefutable arguments against the Christian faith: the first, that a God who permits such suffering is unworthy of worship; the second, that Christ fundamentally over-estimated the spiritual resources of members of the human race and their ability to act as morally free agents. Dostoevskii was aware of the strength of these arguments and anxious lest he fail to refute them effectively in the rest of the novel. Refutation was to be achieved not by logical argument, however, but indirectly by the juxtaposition and interaction of alternative forms of life. The chief exponents of the Christian form of life are Ivan's brother Alesha and his Elder in the local monastery, Zosima.

To Ivan's hatred of the order of creation and his assertion that if there is no immortality and God does not exist then everything is permitted, Zosima juxtaposes a belief in the efficacy of a life of active love and the conviction that each person is responsible for everything and for all (xiv, 270; Bk 6, Sec. 2), a view which the whole novel demonstrates in relation to the murder of Fedor Karamazov and the conviction of his son Dmitrii. Zosima believes that the source of such a life of active love lies beyond the natural world. It certainly has nothing to do with the atheist's abstract love for humanity. If you actively love everything you will perceive the divine mystery in things and you will begin to comprehend it more every day (xiv, 289; Bk 6, Sec. 3):

For on earth we seem in truth to be wanderers, and, without the precious image of Christ before us, we should have perished and lost our way altogether, like the human race before the flood. Many things on earth are hidden from us, but in exchange for that we have been given a mysterious, precious sense of our living bond with another world, with a higher, heavenly world, and the roots of our thoughts and feelings are not here but in other worlds. That is why philosophers say that it is impossible to fathom the essential nature of things on earth.   (XIV, 290–1; Bk 6, Sec. 3)

The precious image of Christ, preserved in the Russian monasteries, is our sole reliable compass in life. Without it humanity would have destroyed itself. To Ivan's complaint about innocent suffering, Zosima juxtaposes the magnificence of the book of Job, whose hero praises God in spite of his undeserved suffering (XIV, 264–5; Bk 6, Sec. 2) – a suffering which may be necessary as a condition of happiness.

The young Alesha has a mystical experience himself after falling asleep at the reading of the story of the Wedding at Cana in Galilee (John 2:1–11) over Zosima's coffin: he experiences something glowing in his heart, something that fills it until it aches with tears of ecstasy welling up from his soul. Outside he throws himself on the ground and kisses the earth, drenching it with his tears. In this mystical experience Alesha senses the threads of all God's innumerable worlds meeting in his soul; something as firm as the firmament itself enters it. He has the sensation of someone visiting his soul, of an idea gaining ascendancy over his mind that will last for the rest of his life. The silence of the earth seems to merge with the silence of heaven; the mystery of the earth with the mystery of the stars (XIV, 328; Bk 7, Sec. 4). Three days later, following his Elder's command, Alesha leaves the monastery to live in the world. This emphasis on the silence of heaven has been associated by some with the apophatic strain in Orthodox theology, according to which the essence of God is unknowable and a sense of the presence of God is to be attained only through spiritual tranquillity and inner silence, for which all mental images are obstacles. At all events it harmonises with Dostoevskii's view that human language is incompetent to express the deepest truths (XXIX/2, 102; letter of 16 July 1876).

In letters to his editor N. A. Liubimov (XXX/1, 63–5; 10 May 1879) and to Pobedonostsev (XXX/1, 120–2; 24 August 1879), Dostoevskii affirms both his intention of vindicating Christianity and his anxiety lest he should fail. But to read the novel exclusively from this point of view is highly problematic, for both structural and biographical reasons. In the first place many readers find such a reading counter-intuitive. They sense, correctly, that Dostoevskii's point of departure is not 'A Saint's Life' but 'The Life of a Great Sinner'; they are also aware that Dostoevskii's novels are so constructed that they do not privilege one point of view over another. The novel can equally well be read from Ivan's point of view and, more profitably still, as what Bakhtin has called a 'polyphonic novel', in which all voices carry equal weight, including that of the author/narrator. Whatever the 'real author' may have protested, the 'implied author' of the text confronts us with a world in which such questions are ultimately unresolved and irresolvable; in which we are travelling, but never quite reach the promised land.[20]

While the religion of *The Brothers Karamazov* bears a strong family resemblance to Orthodoxy in its general ethos, there are also significant departures which have been widely discussed. It is often justly remarked that Zosima's doctrine that each person is responsible for everything and for all is an expression of the Orthodox notion of *sobornost'*, but in this case it is extremely odd that the traditional corporate life of the church, with its liturgy, its dogma, its regular observance of its rituals and sacraments, plays such a slight role. As Gibson says, Dostoevskii revered Christ but sat loose to all theology (*The Religion of Dostoevsky*, p. 14). Moreover, as Hackel, Linnér and others have shown, the images of Zosima and Alesha owe at least as much to European fictional models (for example, Victor Hugo and George Sand) as to those of Orthodox sainthood. Gibson has pointed out, and Hackel agrees, that in the last analysis the novel is evasive even about God, preferring to describe the profoundest religious ecstasies in terms which at best seem cosmetic from a Christian point of view. This is not to say, of course, that the religious text of the novel may not be illuminated and energised by reference to the Orthodox intertext. It is to say simply that Dostoevskii's text as we have it presents us with something significantly different. It is this 'something different', the shoots of a new religious perception growing in an Orthodox soil and fertilised with an admixture of European images, which has sometimes caught the imagination of religious thinkers wrestling with the problems of the twentieth century.

And what of Dostoevskii's biography? Whatever other sources may be available, his fiction is itself the best testimony to what was actually going on in Dostoevskii's mind. While we may indeed hope that he ended his troubled life in a haven of spiritual serenity, Dostoevskii himself always insisted that the important thing was not the achievement of the goal but the process of striving to reach it. And in his case this process was very far from tranquil. His declaration that he achieved faith through a furnace of doubt is usually seen as an affirmation of triumphant faith. It is no less a statement about the intensity of the experience of doubt. Right up to the end, in the person of Ivan Karamazov, we hear the authentic voice of a soul in torment. No one could write like this unless his own soul shared that torment, at least during the process of literary creation itself. No one could bring himself to write like this, if these issues were not intellectually and emotionally compelling for him, himself, at that moment. Yet, as Dostoevskii had said in his letter to Fonvizina so many years before, it was in such moments of affliction that the image of Christ burned strongest. And perhaps after all this is the true measure of Dostoevskii's legacy. What we cannot doubt, in reading Dostoevskii, is that we are in the presence of a genius wrestling with the problems of rethinking Christianity in the modern age.

Notes

1 Quoted in F. N. L'vov, 'Zapiska o dele petrashevtsev' (A note on the Petrashevskii affair), *Literaturnoe nasledstvo*, vol. 63 (Moscow: ANSSSR, 1956), p. 188.

2 See Donald Nicholl, *Triumphs of the Spirit in Russia* (London: Barton, Longman and Todd, 1997), pp. 119–76.

3 See Joseph Frank, *Dostoevsky: The Seeds of Revolt, 1821–1849* (Princeton University Press, 1976), pp. 42–53; Geir Kjetsaa, *Fyodor Dostoyevsky: A Writer's Life* (London: Macmillan, 1987), pp. 1–18.

4 A. S. Dolinin (ed.), *F. M. Dostoevskii v vospominaniiakh sovremennikov* (Dostoevskii in the Recollections of his Contemporaries), 2 vols. (Moscow: Khudozhestvennaia literatura, 1964), vol. 1, p. 61.

5 Leonid Grossman, *Seminarii po Dostoevskomu* (Seminar on Dostoevskii) (Moscow and Petrograd: GIZ, 1922), p. 68.

6 A detailed account of Dostoevskii's reading may be found in Jacques Catteau, *Dostoyevsky and the Process of Literary Creation* (Cambridge University Press, 1989), pp. 33–62.

7 V. G. Belinskii, *Sobranie sochinenii v trekh tomakh* (Collected Works), 3 vols. (Moscow: OGIZ, 1948), vol. 3, p. 709.

8 A. Boyce Gibson, *The Religion of Dostoevsky* (London: SCM Press, 1973), p. 10.

9 Joseph Frank, *Dostoevsky: The Years of Ordeal, 1850–1859* (Princeton University Press, 1983), p. 23.

10 Geir Kjetsaa, *Dostoevsky and His New Testament* (Atlantic Highlands, N.J.: Humanities Press, 1984).

11 Stewart R. Sutherland, *Atheism and the Rejection of God: Contemporary Philosophy and 'The Brothers Karamazov'* (Oxford: Blackwell, 1977), pp. 85–98.

12 'Neizdannyi Dostoevskii' (The unpublished Dostoevskii), *Literaturnoe nasledstvo*, vol. 83 (Moscow: ANSSSR, 1971), p. 675.

13 V. N. Zakharov, 'Umilenie kak kategoriia poetiki Dostoevskogo' (Spiritual tenderness as a category in Dostoevskii's poetics) in Knut Andreas Grimstad and Ingunn Lunde (eds.), *Celebrating Creativity* (Bergen: University of Bergen, 1997), pp. 237–55.

14 See Roger L. Cox, *Between Earth and Heaven: Shakespeare, Dostoevsky and the Meaning of Christian Tragedy* (New York: Holt, Rinehart and Winston, 1969), pp. 140ff.

15 For an account of the psychological strategies underlying this interaction, see Malcolm V. Jones, *Dostoyevsky after Bakhtin* (Cambridge University Press, 1990), pp. 77–95.

16 L. Miuller, 'Obraz Khrista v romane Dostoevskogo *Idiot*' (The image of Christ in Dostoevskii's *The Idiot*), in V. N. Zakharov (ed.), *Evangel'skii tekst v russkoi literature XVIII–XX vekov* (The Evangelical Text in Russian Literature), vol. 2 (Petrozavodsk: Izdatel'stvo Petrozavodskogo universiteta, 1998), pp. 374–84.

17 See Gary Saul Morson, 'Tempics and *The Idiot*' in Grimstad and Lunde (eds.), *Celebrating Creativity*, pp. 108–34.

18 A. G. Dostoevskaia, *Vospominaniia* (Memoirs) (Moscow: Khudozhestvennaia literatura, 1971), p. 201.

19 Compare, for example, V. V. Timofeeva's account of Dostoevskii's ranting in 1873–4 about the coming of the Antichrist (Dolinin, *F. M. Dostoevskii v vospominaniiakh sovremennikov*, vol. 2, p. 170) or Leskov's account of his sullen, ill-tempered, stubborn defence of Orthodoxy against Protestantism (N. S. Leskov, *Sobranie sochinenii* [Collected Works], 11 vols., Moscow: Khudozhestvennaia literatura, 1956–8, vol. 11, pp. 134–56).

20 Space precludes a full discussion of alternative modes of reading the religious dimension of the novel, which I have attempted elsewhere. See Malcolm V. Jones, 'The death and resurrection of Orthodoxy in the works of Dostoevskii' in Jostein Børtnes and Ingunn Lunde (eds.), *Cultural Discontinuity and Reconstruction: The Byzanto-Slav Heritage and the Creation of a Russian National Literature in the Nineteenth Century* (Oslo: Solum Forlag, 1997), pp. 143–67. See also George Pattison and Diane Oenning Thompson (eds.), *Dostoevsky and the Christian Tradition* (Cambridge University Press, 2001).

9

SUSANNE FUSSO

Dostoevskii and the family

At the heart of Russian literary thought about the family in the 1860s and 1870s – in particular Dostoevskii's thought – stands Ivan Turgenev's 1862 novel *Fathers and Sons*. Although that work is ostensibly about chaos and destruction, as embodied in the 'nihilist' Bazarov, both the family structures depicted in it and the structure of the novel itself are remarkably harmonious and stable. Not only does Bazarov's callow friend Arkadii have a loving and devoted father and uncle, but Bazarov himself has salt-of-the-earth parents who worship the ground he walks on. The novel is built on the classic structure of comedy: by the end, the disruptive character who calls the social order into question (Bazarov) has been neutralised (by typhus), and an idyllic family group, which has incorporated the peasant mistress and her illegitimate son as lady of the manor and young master, gathers to celebrate a new patriarchal order presided over by the just-married son Arkadii.

Dostoevskii's creative efforts in the last years of his life were dominated by his desire to produce his own 'Fathers and Sons'. His last three novels, *The Devils*, *A Raw Youth*, and *The Brothers Karamazov*, can be seen as in part motivated by this quest to rewrite Turgenev. Dostoevskii's vision of the late-nineteenth-century Russian family is the polar opposite of Turgenev's comedic idyll. As the former famously wrote in the drafts to *A Raw Youth*: 'In everything is the idea of decomposition, because everyone is separate and there are no bonds remaining not only in the Russian family, but even simply among people' (XVI, 16).[1] The question of the historical and sociological accuracy of Dostoevskii's view of the family is beyond the scope of this essay, but I suspect that he greatly exaggerated the magnitude of the changes in the Russian family from the 1840s to the 1870s. His views can be seen perhaps most vividly in the 1876 sketches to which he gave the heading 'Fathers and Sons'. In the space of less than two printed pages of the Academy edition of his works, Dostoevskii presents a grim kaleidoscope of family disintegration: a boy sits in a juvenile penal colony and dreams of being rescued by his relatives (whom he imagines as princes and counts); a man kills his wife in front of his nine-year-old son, who helps him hide the body under the floor; a father, who has learned after his wife's death that their son is not biologically his, abandons the boy on the street in the freezing cold; children run away from their father (XVII, 6–7). There is also an allusion to the recently reported Kroneberg child-abuse case, in which a father was charged with the torture by beating of his seven-year-old illegitimate daughter (of which more later), and to homosexual seduction in a public bath. This unrealised 'Fathers and Sons' was to depict a familial nihilism far beyond the imaginings of Turgenev.

We know from the essay portions of the *Diary of a Writer* that Dostoevskii saw the depiction of the Russian family's dissolution as a civic duty. In his view, only by first recognising and describing the chaos could one even begin to dream of a new form of order. Dostoevskii writes in the *Diary of a Writer* for January 1877:

> There are the features of some kind of new reality, completely different from the reality of the becalmed and long-established Moscow landowning family of the mid–upper circles, whose *historian* for us was Count Lev Tolstoi. [...] And if even an artist of Shakespearean dimensions would not be able to search out a normative law and governing thread in this chaos in which for a long time, but especially now, our social life has abided, then who at least will illuminate even a part of that chaos, without even hoping to find the governing thread? [...] We indisputably have a decomposing life and consequently a decomposing family. But there must also be a newly forming life, based on new principles. Who will notice them, and who will indicate them? Who can even begin to define and express the laws both of that chaos and of the new creation?   (XXV, 35)

Throughout the *Diary of a Writer* Dostoevskii repeatedly casts Russia's social dilemma in terms of 'fathers and sons':

> The 'accidental' quality of the contemporary Russian family, in my opinion, consists in the loss by contemporary fathers of any universal idea in relation to their families, universal for all fathers, binding them all together, an idea in which they themselves would believe and would teach their children to believe, would convey to them this faith in life.   (XXV, 178; July–August 1877)

> You are the fathers, they are your children, you are contemporary Russia, they are the future Russia; what will happen to Russia if Russian fathers evade their civic duty and begin to seek solitude or more precisely isolation, a lazy and cynical isolation from society, their nation, and their most important obligations to that society and nation?   (XXV, 192; July–August 1877)

Dostoevskii's last three novels are devoted to exploring the ways in which the fathers of Russia have failed in their obligations to the sons, and therefore to the nation's future. In the process Dostoevskii questions accepted definitions, both radical and conservative, of the family itself.

The decomposition of the Russian family is, in Dostoevskii's view, at least in part the result of experimenting with new forms of family life by radical intellectuals from Aleksandr Herzen to Nikolai Chernyshevskii and beyond. In both life and literature, these thinkers sought ways to disrupt the bourgeois patriarchal order, usually through the toleration of adultery. Irina Paperno, who has thoroughly analysed the experiments of Herzen and Chernyshevskii, highlights the positive significance of the new family arrangements:

> In accordance with a cultural tradition that associated stability in marriage with the stability of society at large, Chernyshevsky proposed to make the rearrangement of family life into the basis for the rearrangement of society. [. . .] But contrary to the opinion of Chernyshevsky's critics, the form of adultery advocated in the novel was not intended to undermine or destroy society. What appeared as a form of adultery [. . .] was for Chernyshevsky the foundation for emotional and social harmony and equilibrium.[2]

What seems to be lacking in the theories and practice of these intellectuals, and what Dostoevskii was to emphasise in his critical and literary responses, is any serious thinking through of what happens to the children produced by non-traditional sexual arrangements. In his highly influential novel *Who Is to Blame?* (1845–6), Herzen, himself illegitimate, depicts illegitimacy as one of the evil products of the stable patriarchal family. This is presented most pointedly in a scene in which the tyrannical landowner Negrov orders his valet to marry the peasant woman who has borne Negrov's daughter. In anticipation of the order, the valet says: 'Whom can we oblige if not Your Excellency; you are our father, we are your children [vy nashi ottsy, my vashi deti].'[3] In contrast, Dostoevskii is preoccupied with the illegitimate and/or abandoned children sired not by old-fashioned patriarchs but by intellectuals under the ideological influence of George Sand, Aleksandr Druzhinin, Herzen and Chernyshevskii. Druzhinin's Sand-inspired novella 'Polinka Saks' (1847), in which a civil servant nobly steps aside so that his wife can be united with her lover, thus earning her undying admiration and devotion, was of particular interest to Dostoevskii. Arkadii Dolgorukii, the narrator of *A Raw Youth*, clearly attributes his own illegitimate origins to the fact that his father, the nobleman Versilov, had read the novella just before visiting his estate, where he began an affair with a married serf woman, Arkadii's mother. Arkadii sarcastically refers to Druzhinin's story as a literary piece 'that had a boundless civilising influence on the generation that was then coming of age in Russia' (XIII, 10; Pt 1, Ch. 1). In *The Devils* (where 'Polinka Saks' is also mentioned – see x, 409–10; Pt 3, Ch. 3), the liberal Stepan Verkhovenskii is discovered by his radical son Petr reading Chernyshevskii's novel *What Is to Be Done?* (1863), in which a *ménage à trois* on rational principles figures prominently. Stepan has claimed that the novel represents 'our idea' (x, 238; Pt 2, Ch. 4). Almost immediately afterwards, Petr reminds Stepan that he had questioned Petr's parentage in conversations with Petr himself during his adolescence.

In the *Diary of a Writer*, Dostoevskii's most striking case in point of what happens to the children of radical experiments with the family is the suicide of Herzen's own daughter Liza. Liza was the product of Herzen's affair with Natalia Tuchkova-Ogareva, the wife of his friend Nikolai Ogarev.[4] She killed herself in Florence in December 1875 at the age of seventeen (almost six years after Herzen's death). Dostoevskii wrote about her suicide and especially her suicide note (which he embellished with a couple of telling details) in the *Diary of a Writer* for October and December 1876. In the essays Dostoevskii does not mention her name but identifies her rather unmistakably for his readership by calling her 'the daughter of a too-famous Russian émigré' (xxiii, 145). Liza's suicide appears to have been prompted by an unhappy love for an older married man, but Dostoevskii traces it – or rather the malicious tone of it as reflected in her suicide note – to her irregular upbringing and in particular to the role of theory in family relations: 'I expressed the supposition that she died from anguish [*toska*] (a too early anguish) and the aimlessness of life – only as a result of her upbringing, *perverted by theory*, in her father's home, an upbringing with a mistaken conception of the higher significance and aims of life, with the intentional destruction in her soul of all faith in her own immortality' (xxiv, 54; emphasis mine). Earlier, in the *Diary of a Writer* for March 1876, Dostoevskii had seen a glimmer of hope in the possibility that the children of the liberal and radical experimenters with the family would revolt against their parents not by means of suicide but by finding a new path:

> What could the children of that time see in their fathers, what memories could they have preserved about them from their childhood and boyhood? Cynicism, desecration, merciless attacks on their children's first tender holy beliefs; and quite often the open debauchery of their fathers and mothers, with the assurance and the *teaching* that this is how it should be, that these are the true 'sober' relationships. [...] But since youth is pure, bright and magnanimous, it may of course happen that some of these youths would not want to take after such fathers and would reject their 'sober' instructions. [...] And it is perhaps those very youths and adolescents who are now seeking new paths and who begin directly by repulsing that hateful cycle of ideas that they encountered in their childhood, in their pitiful natal nests. (xxii, 102)

In his novels Dostoevskii presents a range of possibilities for the children of what he calls (in *A Raw Youth*) 'accidental families', from suicide to the Christ-like behaviour of Alesha Karamazov, itself a kind of radicalism in the opposite direction from that of Herzen.

Dostoevskii's last three novels focus on sons of the new, 'decomposed' Russian family who encounter their fathers for the first time only after reaching maturity. In *The Devils* and *A Raw Youth*, the contribution of radical ideology to the family's disintegration is pronounced; by the time of *The Brothers Karamazov* one has a sense of a more pervasive and deeply rooted evil undermining the foundations of the Russian family and society. The hero of *The Devils*, Stepan Trofimovich Verkhovenskii, is a liberal of the Herzen generation who has seen his son Petr only once since his infancy. The child's mother died in Paris when he was five years old and he was sent to Russia, 'where he was raised by some kind of distant aunts somewhere in the backwoods' (x, 11; Pt 1, Ch. 1). When the twenty-seven-year-old man appears in Mrs Stavrogina's salon near the beginning of the novel, it takes his father several minutes to recognise him, even though his arrival has been expected (x, 143–4; Pt 1, Ch. 5). Arkadii Dolgorukii, the illegitimate hero-narrator of *A Raw Youth*, was raised 'v chuzhikh liudiakh' (by strangers; XIII, 14; Pt 1, Ch. 1) almost from birth and comes to know his father and mother only at the age of nineteen. Arkadii has a vivid memory of meeting and 'falling in love with' his father on one occasion as a child, after which he was packed off to a boarding school where he was mercilessly taunted about his parentage. His life since then has been given up to dreaming of his father Versilov: 'I wanted all of Versilov, give me a father . . . that's what I demanded' (XIII, 100; Pt 1, Ch. 6). Fedor Karamazov, of course, abandons not one but three (possibly four) sons after the deaths of their mothers, as described by Diane Oenning Thompson in a chapter effectively entitled 'Forgetting'. Thompson eloquently summarises the failings of most of the adults in *The Brothers Karamazov*:

> What should be remembered, children, neighbours, family, serfs who have legitimate claims on the attention of those responsible for their welfare, have been ignored, neglected, obliterated from memory. [. . .] Forgetting, here in the form of social and parental neglect, functions as a critical index of morality, personal, familial, societal and national.[5]

In *The Brothers Karamazov*, as in *The Devils* and *A Raw Youth*, the action proper of the novel begins as the sons make the acquaintance of the fathers who 'missed' their childhood, boyhood and youth.

In all three novels, fathers and sons separated physically have created mental images of each other – have 'invented' each other. Stepan Verkhovenskii writes letters about his intimate affairs to a son in Paris who, far from being the sympathetic confidant Stepan imagines, turns out to be a vile intriguer who blurts out Stepan's indiscreet complaints and fears in the middle of Mrs Stavrogina's crowded drawing room:

> 'You wouldn't believe it, right next to the happiest lines he writes the most despairing ones. In the first place, he asks my forgiveness; just imagine, the man has only laid eyes on me twice in his life, and that was by accident, and all of a sudden now, when he's about to get married for the third time, he imagines that by doing so he's transgressing some kind of parental obligations and begs me at a distance of a thousand versts [a 'verst' (*versta*) is approximately equal to one kilometre] to forgive him and give him my permission!'
>
> (x, 161; Pt 1, Ch. 5)

The narrator tells us that Stepan's disappointment in his son is 'a deep and *real* sorrow' (x, 163; Pt 1, Ch. 5). In *A Raw Youth*, Arkadii Dolgorukii similarly has to cope with a reality that fails to live up to the dream: 'It turns out that this man is just my dream, a dream from my childhood. It's me who invented him this way, but in reality he turned out to be someone else, falling far short of my fantasy' (XIII, 62; Pt 1, Ch. 4). And Dmitrii Karamazov reveals his own fantasy at the meeting in Father Zosima's cell: '"I thought . . . I thought," he said somehow quietly and with restraint, "that I would come to my native town with the angel of my soul, my fiancée, in order to cherish him in his old age, but I see only a debauched sensualist and a base comedian!"' (XIV, 68–9; Bk 2, Sec. 6). In each case the fantasy is based on almost nothing, but it takes on reality as an obstacle to the already difficult process of a father's getting to know his adult son.

The orphaned children in these novels cope with their abandonment in two major ways: by finding surrogate fathers who provide the love and moral guidance their biological fathers have deprived them of, and by seeking closeness and solidarity with their siblings. Arkadii's surrogate father is, ironically, his legal father, the peasant Makar Dolgorukii, who offers Arkadii a model of ascetic pilgrimage and the quest for *blagoobrazie* (blessed form), in stark contrast to the Herzenesque godless theorising of Versilov. An artistically more successful version of a similar relationship is embodied in Alesha Karamazov's devotion to the elder Zosima. Dmitrii's connection to his serf 'father' Grigorii is more elemental and earthy, based on the very mundane tasks Grigorii performed for the abandoned boy: 'This old man – after all, he carried me in his arms, gentlemen, he bathed me in a trough when everyone had abandoned me, a three-year-old child, he was my own father [otets rodnoi]!' (XIV, 414; Bk 9, Sec. 3).

God is of course the ultimate 'surrogate father', but one who is also capable of abandonment, as dramatised most vividly in *The Brothers Karamazov*.

It is not surprising that Ivan Karamazov is drawn to a medieval Orthodox tale about the Virgin's journey to hell in which it is said of some sinners in a burning lake that 'God is already forgetting about them' (XIV, 225; Bk 5, Sec. 5). Versilov depicts a world without God as a world in which humans would discover a new brotherly love: 'Orphaned people would immediately begin to press more closely and lovingly to each other; they would seize each other by the hand, understanding that now they alone were all in all for each other. [...] They would become tender to each other and would not be ashamed of it as they are now, but would caress each other like children' (XIII, 378–9; Pt 3, Ch. 7). Arkadii and his sister Liza find, if only briefly, this kind of tenderness and consolation in each other in the midst of their 'accidental family' (XIII, 161–2; Pt 1, Ch. 10). Throughout *The Brothers Karamazov* Alesha strives to provide for his brothers the love and caring their father has denied them, and often succeeds. As well as such love, sibling hostility also surfaces in both novels. In a brilliant set piece Arkadii's half-brother, Versilov's legitimate aristocratic son, treats him like a footman (XIII, 397–401; Pt 3, Ch. 9). Ivan and Dmitrii Karamazov are locked in rivalry over a woman, and Smerdiakov – who may or may not be the Karamazovs' brother but who certainly thinks he is – hates Ivan, Dmitrii and Alesha. The ancient history of brotherly hostility is evoked in *The Brothers Karamazov* through references to the biblical stories of Cain (XIV, 206, 211; Bk 5, Sec. 2, Sec. 3) and Joseph (XIV, 266; Bk 6, Sec. 2).

In contrast to Arkadii and the Karamazovs, Petr Verkhovenskii has neither surrogate father nor siblings, and this may account for the fact of his almost unalloyed evil. Instead of seeking a surrogate father, he sets himself up as a despotic father-figure to his cell of five conspirators: 'What is needed is a single magnificent, idol-like, despotic will, which rests on something that is not contingent and that has its own independent existence' (X, 404; Pt 3, Ch. 3). Instead of a true sibling he has a parodic double in the form of Fedka the Convict, a serf whose life of crime is blamed on the fact that Stepan 'lost him at cards', i.e. sold him into the army in order to pay his gambling debts (X, 181, 204; Pt 2, Chs. 1–2). Stepan is confronted with his responsibility for Fedka in the middle of his appearance at the literary festival sponsored by the Governor's wife. A provocateur in the audience interrupts Stepan's incoherent speech:

> Stepan Trofimovich! [...] Here in town and in the outskirts Fedka the Convict, an escaped prisoner, is now prowling around. He has been committing robberies and not long ago he committed a new murder. Allow me to pose the question: if fifteen years ago you had not given him up to conscription in order to pay your gambling debts, that is if you hadn't simply lost him at the card table, tell me, would he have ended up in a Siberian prison? Would he be cutting people's

throats, as he is now, in the struggle for existence? What do you have to say,
Mr Aesthetician?   (x, 373; Pt 3, Ch. 1)

The question, parodic as it is, resonates as a question about Stepan's
responsibility for his own abandoned son, who like Fedka is 'prowling about
the town', perpetrating atrocities and murder, including ultimately the murder of his 'sibling' Fedka.

Responsibility is the key question when considering the Russian family, as
the title of Herzen's novel, *Who Is to Blame?*, reminds us. In Dostoevskii's
novels, Russian fathers do not prove to be very good at accepting responsibility for what has become of their sons. Stepan claims rather unconvincingly
to have suffered throughout his absentee parenthood:

[Petr says] I gave him neither food nor drink, I sent him off from Berlin to ***
Province, a babe in arms, in the mail, and so on and so forth, I'll admit
it [...] 'You,' he says, 'gave me no drink and sent me off in the mail, and
then you robbed me.' But, you unfortunate man, I cry to him, you know I
suffered in my heart for you all my life, even if I did send you off in the mail!
(x, 171; Pt 2, Ch. 1)

Versilov too refuses to accept full responsibility for his 'accidental family', yawning openly in response to Arkadii's tales of his forlorn childhood
(XIII, 98, 101–2, 103, 110; Pt 1, Chs. 6–7). And of course Fedor Karamazov's
sense of guilt over the abandonment of his sons is virtually non-existent.
At the meeting in the monk's cell he manages to shift the focus of blame
to Dmitrii, the 'parricide' (XIV, 69; Bk 2, Sec. 6). Fedor's evocation of the
ultimate crime of parricide is subliminally bolstered by two of his references.
He twice alludes to Schiller's play *The Robbers* (*Die Räuber*, 1782), which
includes the speech: 'The laws of God and Man are set at naught, the bond of
nature is severed, the primal struggle is back, the son has killed his father.'[6]
In addition, Fedor's repeated mention of the murder of von Sohn, whose
name can be translated as 'by [the] son', increases the weight of the premonition that Dmitrii is to kill his father. In all three novels, the centre of
attention becomes the sins of the sons, not the fathers: Petr's incitement of
riot, chaos and murder; Arkadii's plan to blackmail an older woman into
a sexual relationship; and, of course, the long-drawn-out scene of Dmitrii's
trial for murder, in which the words 'ottsa ubil' (he killed his father) become
an insistent refrain.

The speech at the trial by the defence attorney Fetiukovich poses the
problem of the family in the starkest terms. Fetiukovich, a deconstruction-
ist *avant la lettre*, calls into question the existence of all the elements of
the alleged crime. The centrepiece of his summation is his reduction of the

terrifying taboo word *ottseubiistvo* (parricide) to the status of *predrassudok* (lit. 'prejudice,' but with the connotation of 'superstition'). Fetiukovich asserts that blood relationship is not sufficient to make one worthy of the name of 'father':

> Yes, it's a terrible thing to shed the blood of one's father – the blood of the one who conceived me, the blood of the one who loved me, the blood of the one who did not spare his own life for me, who ailed along with me in all my illnesses since my childhood, who suffered for my happiness all my life and who lived only through my joys and my success! Oh, to kill such a father – but it's impossible even to think of such a thing! [. . .] [But] my client grew up with only God's protection, in other words like a wild beast. [. . .] We will prove [. . .] that the progress of recent years has reached even Russia in its development and we will say straight out: the one who conceives a child is not a father; a father is the one who both conceives and is worthy of the name of father.   (xv, 168, 170; Bk 12, Sec. 13)

If Fedor has not earned the title of 'father', the logical conclusion is that Dmitrii's alleged murder of him is not parricide: 'No, the murder of such a father cannot be called parricide. Such a murder can be accounted a parricide only through superstition [*predrassudok*]!' (xv, 172; Bk 12, Sec. 13). Fedor seems to have had a premonition of the defence attorney's argument when he says to Alesha: 'In today's fashionable world it's become the thing to consider fathers and mothers a superstition' (xiv, 158; Bk 4, Sec. 2).

The use of the word *predrassudok* in relation to the family marks Fetiukovich as a person conversant with radical ideology, despite his constant references to the gospel. In *The Devils*, the town radicals at a secret gathering begin a discussion of the *predrassudok* of the family:

> 'We know, for example, that the superstition about God originated in thunder and lightning,' the female student suddenly burst in again, almost jumping at Stavrogin with her eyes. 'It's very well established that primitive humanity, frightened of thunder and lightning, deified their unknown enemy, sensing their own weakness in relation to it. But where did the superstition about the family (*predrassudok o semeistve*) originate? Where could the family itself come from?'
>
> 'I think that the answer to such a question would be indecent,' Stavrogin answered.   (x, 306; Pt 2, Ch. 7)

Stavrogin's answer points to a fact that Fetiukovich also stresses: the family originates in the act of sex. This fact is used by Fetiukovich to undermine the supposed holiness of family ties:

The sight of an unworthy father, especially as compared with other fathers, worthy ones, of the other children his age, inevitably suggests painful questions to the youth. His questions are answered pro forma: 'He conceived you, and you are his blood, and therefore you must love him.' The youth involuntarily falls to thinking: 'But did he love me when he was conceiving me?' he asks, becoming more and more amazed, 'did he really conceive me for my sake? He didn't know me or even what sex I was at that moment, the moment of passion, perhaps inflamed by drink, and maybe he passed on to me his inclination to drunkenness – that's the extent of his benevolence... Why do I have to love him, just because he conceived me, and then failed to love me my whole life?'   (xv, 171; Bk 12, Sec. 13)

The defence attorney's speech evokes two reactions in his audience. The sophisticated townspeople, including 'fathers and mothers', applaud the idea that sons have a right to demand that their fathers explain why they should love them (xv, 171; Bk 12, Sec. 13). As a conversation between two of the onlookers goes: ' "If I had been in the defence attorney's place I would have said straight out: he killed him, but he's not guilty, and the hell with you!" "But that's just what he did, only he didn't say 'the hell with you' " ' (xv, 177; Bk 12, Sec. 14). The other reaction, borne out in the guilty verdict by the *muzhichki* (peasants) on the jury, is expressed by another member of the audience: 'Yes, gentlemen, he's eloquent. But after all, we can't allow people to bash in their fathers' heads with steelyards. Otherwise where will we end up?' (xv, 177; Bk 12, Sec. 14).

Is the family a sacred institution or is it a superstition? Does the name of 'father' have to be earned by one's actions? Dostoevskii had tackled the same questions in the *Diary of a Writer* for February 1876, and had come to conclusions that are superficially similar to those of Fetiukovich, even as he did rhetorical battle with an attorney, Vladimir Spasovich, who later served as a prototype for the sophistic defence attorney in *The Brothers Karamazov* (xv, 347). The second part of the *Diary of a Writer* for February 1876 deals with the Kroneberg child-beating case (actually Kronenberg but I will use Dostoevskii's spelling), referred to earlier. The child in this case had been raised by Swiss peasants and then by a pastor in Geneva until the age of seven, when Kroneberg took her with him to Russia. Dostoevskii quotes the defence attorney's speech, which defends Kroneberg's rights as a father to punish his own child: 'I think that to persecute a father because he punished his child painfully but *justly* does a disservice to the family, a disservice to the state, because the state is only strong when it is founded on a strong family' (xxii, 68). Dostoevskii argues, however, that a father's rights must be earned, and that a father who missed his child's infancy, who doesn't really know his child, has a long way to go before he has any claim to sacred rights:

These creatures [children] only enter into our souls and become attached to our hearts when, after giving birth to them, we follow their development from childhood, without being separated from them, from their first smile, and then we continue to become close to them in soul every day, every hour over the course of our whole life. That is a family, that is something sacred [*sviatynia*]! After all, families are also *created*, not given ready-made. [...] The family is created by the untiring labour of love (*neustannym trudom liubvi*). (XXII, 69–70)

Dostoevskii refuses to admit an *a priori* sacredness for the family: 'We love the sacred thing that is the family when it is in fact sacred, and not just because the state is firmly founded on it' (XXII, 72).

Why is it that in his essays on the Kroneberg case Dostoevskii seems to agree with Fetiukovich that a father has to earn his parental rights by 'the untiring labour of love', while in *The Brothers Karamazov* that position is lampooned? The difference is one of context and purpose. Fetiukovich presumes that Dmitrii actually did kill his father, and is trying to help him evade responsibility by arguing that that father was not really a father at all. He is trying to get a guilty man off the hook. In the *Diary of a Writer*, Dostoevskii is trying to put the father Kroneberg back on the hook. Kroneberg has no more right to be absolved because 'the family is a sacred thing' than Dmitrii, had he actually killed his father, would have a right to be absolved because 'families are created through the untiring labour of love'. Dmitrii is no longer a child. Just because his father failed in his responsibilities to him, Dmitrii is not excused from the requirement to engage in 'the labour of love', no matter how unworthy the object, from his own position as adult son.

Dostoevskii offers an answer to the radical student's question, 'Where does the family come from?' in the drafts to *The Brothers Karamazov*. Father Zosima was to have said, 'Bog dal rodnykh, chtob uchit'sia na nikh *liubvi*. Obshchecheloveki nenavidiat lits v chastnosti' (God gave us relatives so that we could learn through them *how to love*. Lovers of humanity hate persons in particular; XV, 205). It is somewhat strange that this statement did not make it into the novel, linked as it is to Ivan's struggle with his inability to 'love his neighbour', his repulsion from the sight of a 'litso v chastnosti' ('person [lit. face] in particular'). The family situation presents this dilemma in its most concentrated form: in the family we are bound by nature to people whom it is our duty to love, but whose personalities, moral character, even physical appearance, we may in fact dislike or hate. Thus, as Zosima in this draft indicates, loving our families can be excellent practice for loving all our fellow human beings. Such love is truly labour (*trud*), but it is also the only way to have any sort of claim to familial rights, as Dostoevskii points out in the *Diary of a Writer* for July–August 1877: 'Only with love can we buy the hearts of our children, and not merely with our natural rights over them' (XXV, 193).

The most beautiful family love in Dostoevskii's world is that which is given freely, not in exchange for good behaviour. Arkadii Dolgorukii's mother in her Christian naïveté expresses this idea with inadvertent humour in a dialogue with Arkadii: '"Family love is immoral, mama, precisely because it is not earned. Love must be earned." "Well, you'll earn it some day, but meanwhile we love you for no reason at all." Everyone burst out laughing' (XIII, 212; Pt 2, Ch. 5). A similar idea is expressed in *The Brothers Karamazov* by Snegirev and approved heartily by Alesha:

> 'Allow me to complete my introductions: my family, my two daughters and my son – my brood, sir. If I die, who's going to love them? And while I'm alive, who besides them is going to love nasty old me? This is a magnificent arrangement the Lord has set up for every person of my type, sir. For it is necessary that even a person of my type be loved by at least someone, sir.'
> 'Oh, that's so very true!' exclaimed Alesha.   (XIV, 183; Bk 4, Sec. 6)

'The family is created by the untiring labour of love', but before offering that love one cannot first demand proof of it from the other. The most meaningful examples of family love in Dostoevskii's last three novels are those in which nothing is offered in return: Arkadii's love for Versilov, Alesha's love for Fedor and Stepan Verkhovenskii's love for his son Petr, which is lost in the face of the grown son's evil but recovered at the brink of death. Petr has been absent from Stepan's thoughts during his final pilgrimage, but he surfaces, named by an affectionate diminutive, in Stepan's last words before lapsing into unconsciousness:

> Long live the Great Idea! The eternal, boundless Idea! Every person, no matter who, has a need to bow before the Great Idea. Even the most foolish man has a need for something great. *Petrusha* ... Oh, how I want to see them all again! They don't know, they don't know that even in them the very same Great Idea is contained!   (X, 506; Pt 3, Ch. 7 – emphasis mine)

Stepan's remembrance of 'Petrusha', the son he lost through his failure to perform the untiring labour of love, is all the more poignant for having come far too late.

One aspect of the father–son relationships in Dostoevskii's last novels that I have not yet discussed relates to the role of women. In both *A Raw Youth* and *The Brothers Karamazov*, a major component of the plot is a sexual rivalry between father and son. Both Arkadii and Versilov are obsessed with Katerina Nikolaevna Akhmakova; Dmitrii and Fedor are locked in a fierce struggle over Grushenka. (In both cases the son 'gets the girl' in the end, as the father has been neutralised by madness [Versilov] or murder [Fedor].) Such relationships are often called 'Oedipal', with the Freudian sense of the term in mind. It could be argued that Dostoevskii's version of the father–son rivalry is closer to the original myth of Oedipus (and its treatment in the tragedy by Sophocles) than to Freud's version. Freud's Oedipus theory arose in the context of the intact bourgeois family, in which children are lodged close enough to their parents to observe 'primal scenes', and mothers are on hand to notice childish masturbatory play and threaten castration. But Oedipus, like Arkadii and Dmitrii, was an abandoned child, left 'on Cithaeron's slopes / in the twisting thickets' because of the prophecy that he was to kill his father and marry his mother.[7] In both *Oedipus the King* and Dostoevskii's novels, the father, encountered for the first time in adulthood, is perceived not as a father but as just another man. Although both Arkadii and Dmitrii express horror at the thought that they are competing sexually with their own fathers, one does not have the sense that the horror goes very deep (certainly not deep enough to stop the competition). The explanation for this surely lies in the fact that these sons have not known their fathers as fathers on an everyday basis, from childhood on. They meet their fathers on equal ground, man to man, as Oedipus met Laius at the crossroads. For Freud the emotional weight and significance of the story lie in the fact that the son eliminates his father and has sex with his mother. But when read from the vantage point of Dostoevskii's preoccupations of the 1870s, it becomes a story of abandonment. It is Laius' abandonment of Oedipus that makes psychologically possible the realisation of the prophecy he fears. Oedipus kills a father who is not really a father (and marries a mother who is not really a mother) in Fetiukovich's sense, and in the definition offered by Dostoevskii in the Kroneberg essays.

In his novel *The Unbearable Lightness of Being* (1984), Milan Kundera returns to the Oedipus of Sophocles, ostentatiously omitting any mention of Freud. His hero Tomas offers a metaphorisation of the Oedipus tragedy that has nothing to do with sex and everything to do with guilt and responsibility, specifically the responsibility of those who led the countries of Central Europe into communism:

> Oedipus did not know he was sleeping with his own mother, yet when he realised what had happened, he did not feel innocent. Unable to stand the sight of the misfortunes he had wrought by 'not knowing', he put out his eyes and wandered blind away from Thebes.
>
> When Tomas heard Communists shouting in defence of their inner purity, he said to himself, As a result of your 'not knowing', this country has lost its freedom, lost it for centuries, perhaps, and you shout that you feel no

guilt? How can you stand the sight of what you've done? How is it you aren't horrified? Have you no eyes to see? If you had eyes, you would have to put them out and wander away from Thebes![8]

This is the dimension of the story that is also closest to Dostoevskii – and even to Freud, if we look beyond the 'scandalous' sexual content of his theory to its moral core. As the historian of psychoanalysis John E. Toews has recently written: 'recognising ourselves in Oedipus is something of an ethical achievement, an assumption of guilt and responsibility in the creation of human suffering, including our own'.[9]

The question 'Who is to blame?', fathers or children, emerges in an interesting way in the historical development of Freud's theory. Freud began with the 'seduction theory', which posited that adult neuroses stemmed from actual sexual abuse by parents of their children. This theory 'blamed the sufferings of the younger generation on the secret sexual perversions of their hypocritical elders, on those who held power over their fate and who had betrayed their trust. It traced the source of human suffering to the acts of the powerful and absolved the victims of complicity in their fate' (Toews, 'Having and being', p. 69). The development of the Oedipus theory shifted responsibility from parents to children: 'After 1897 Freud's focus shifted to the agency of the child as a sexual subject, to the originating role of infantile psychosexual "desire" in the formation of the human subject and its inner conflicts' (ibid., p. 71). Frederick Crews offers a much less sympathetic description of this shift: 'Psychoanalysis came into existence when Freud reinterpreted the very same clinical data to indicate that it must have been his patients themselves, when scarcely out of the cradle, who had predisposed themselves to neurosis by harbouring and then repressing incestuous designs of their own.'[10] Crews discusses the development in the 1980s of 'recovered memory therapy', in which patients are guided to 'remember' childhood sexual abuse by their parents (abuse which the patients had somehow completely repressed until therapy 'recovered' the memory of it). Crews sees this development as another swing in the pendulum of blame from one generation to the other: 'If early events are to be regarded as causes of later neurosis, it is easier to picture them as physical assaults on the child than as mere imaginings about penisectomy at the hand of a father who, the toddler supposedly reasons, must adopt that means of keeping him from realising his goal of fornicating with his mother' (Crews, *The Memory Wars*, p. 22).

The artistic complexity of Dostoevskii's world makes such extreme vacillations impossible, just as it makes impossible the explanation of all psychic disturbances by a single factor such as sexual abuse. In Dostoevskii's vision, guilt is not passed back and forth between fathers and sons. The defence attorney in *The Brothers Karamazov* tries to pin blame and responsibility on the fathers by selectively quoting the New Testament, Colossians 3:21: 'Ottsy, ne ogorchaite detei svoikh' (Fathers, do not provoke your children – xv, 169, 601n; Bk 12, Sec. 13). He leaves out the two phrases that bracket this command in the Bible and that, when restored, are a microcosm of the Dostoevskian view of the family. The phrase quoted by Fetiukovich is preceded by a paraphrase of the Fifth Commandment: 'Children, obey your parents in everything, for this is your acceptable duty in the Lord' (Colossians 3:20).[11] Children are responsible too, and their responsibility is mentioned first. Even more significant for Dostoevskii's universe is the phrase that follows the attorney's quotation: 'Fathers, do not provoke your children, *or they may lose heart*' (Colossians 3:21; emphasis mine). The father's duty not to provoke his children is not for the purpose of avoiding being murdered by them, but of preserving their spiritual strength.

In the last analysis what is most important for Dostoevskii is not one's generational position. Neither father nor son is categorically guilty or innocent. As a result, one cannot, like Spasovich, absolve Kroneberg by virtue of his being a father, or, like Fetiukovich, absolve Dmitrii by virtue of his being a son. The key moment is the individual's own acceptance of responsibility, as Dostoevskii illustrates vividly in the *Diary of a Writer* for July–August 1877, in an imaginary speech by a presiding judge to a real-life couple who had abused their children:

> The main thing is that there is much to forgive on both sides. They [the children] must forgive you for the bitter, difficult impressions on their childish hearts, for the hardening of their spirits, for their vices. And you must forgive them for your egoism, your neglect of them, the perversion of your feelings for them, your cruelty, and the fact that you had to sit here and be tried because of them. I say this because you will not accuse yourselves for all this when you leave the court, but them, I'm sure of it! So as you begin the difficult labour of raising your children, ask yourselves: can you blame all these crimes and misdemeanours not on them but on yourselves? If you can, oh, then you will succeed in your labour! (xxv, 191)

One must not be misled into thinking that this remarkable speech is directed only at the fathers; it could just as easily be directed at sons like Dmitrii, Arkadii and Petr. The 'untiring labour of love' that creates the family must be carried out by everyone.

Dostoevskii's definition of the family – the family that can truly be called a sacred thing – conforms neither to the conservative's blind worship of the name of 'father' nor to the radical's attempt to 'make the rearrangement of family life into the basis for the rearrangement of society' (Paperno,

Chernyshevsky and the Age of Realism, p. 157). For Dostoevskii, the traditional relationship of father and child must be preserved, but must be based on the difficult, day-to-day labour of love – not merely on biological connection and the title of 'father', a title which fathers like Stepan Verkhovenskii, Versilov and Fedor Karamazov assume only when it is convenient for them. If a conservative (or a liberal masquerading as a conservative, like Spasovich) claims to value the family because it is the foundation of the state, Dostoevskii, in both his artistic and journalistic works, values the family because it is at least potentially the foundation of the spiritually healthy individual. Like Freud he seeks the origins of spiritual disease in childhood, but he does not fall prey to determinism. The best proof of this is the three (or four) Karamazov brothers – all abandoned and abused, but each with his own spiritual and moral path.

Notes

I would like to thank Robert T. Conn and Duffield White for their comments on this essay.

1 See the admirably succinct discussion of Dostoevskii's view of the Russian family in W. J. Leatherbarrow, *Fyodor Dostoyevsky: The Brothers Karamazov* (Cambridge University Press, 1992), pp. 21–30.

2 Irina Paperno, *Chernyshevsky and the Age of Realism: A Study in the Semiotics of Behavior* (Stanford University Press, 1988), p. 157.

3 A. I. Gertsen [Herzen], *Povesti i rasskazy* (Stories and Tales) (Moscow: Khudozhestvennaia literatura, 1967), p. 106.

4 See the excellent discussion of Liza Herzen's suicide in Irina Paperno, *Suicide as a Cultural Institution in Dostoevsky's Russia* (Ithaca: Cornell University Press, 1997), pp. 178–82.

5 Diane Oenning Thompson, *'The Brothers Karamazov' and the Poetics of Memory* (Cambridge University Press, 1991), p. 165.

6 Schiller, *Five Plays*, trans. Robert David MacDonald (London: Absolute Classics, 1998), p. 167.

7 Sophocles, *Oedipus the King*, in *Greek Tragedies*, ed. David Grene and Richmond Lattimore, vol. 1 (Chicago: University of Chicago Press, 1960), p. 154. Fedor's accusations of Dmitrii in the elder's cell are an echo of the prophecy that haunted Oedipus' father Laius: 'the thing he feared, / death at his son's hands' (p. 142).

8 Milan Kundera, *The Unbearable Lightness of Being*, trans. Michael Henry Heim (New York: Harper and Row, 1984), p. 177.

9 John E. Toews, 'Having and being: the evolution of Freud's Oedipus theory as a moral fable' in Michael S. Roth (ed.), *Freud: Conflict and Culture* (New York: Knopf, 1998), p. 67.

10 Frederick Crews, *The Memory Wars: Freud's Legacy in Dispute* (New York: New York Review of Books, 1995), p. 57.

11 The Fifth Commandment reads: 'Honour your father and your mother, so that your days may be long in the land that the Lord your God is giving you' (Exodus 20:12).

10

DIANE OENNING THOMPSON

Dostoevskii and science

People who say *two times two is not four* do not at all intend to say exactly
that, but, without doubt, mean and want to express something else.

F. M. Dostoevskii[1]

In the summer of 1862, Dostoevskii made his first trip to Western Europe.
In his account of this journey, *Winter Notes on Summer Impressions* (1863),
he first broaches the problem of science in connection with his visit to the
World Exhibition in London. The Exhibition was devoted to celebrating the
achievements of science and technology and was sited in the Crystal Palace,
an enormous glass and iron structure, itself a feat of engineering. Victorian
Britain was the world centre of industrial development and technological
invention. This was the period of heroic materialism, the heyday of faith
in material progress and human improvement driven by scientific discovery.
The age-old dream of conquering Nature and perfecting human nature and
society would now, thanks to science, be achievable on earth. Dostoevskii
found the Exhibition 'staggering'; there was nothing remotely like it in backward Russia. But it also aroused in him a profound disquiet:

> You feel a terrifying force which has joined here all these numberless people
> who have come from all over the world into the one fold; you're aware of
> a gigantic thought, you feel that something here has already been achieved,
> that here is a victory, a triumph. You even, as it were, begin to be afraid of
> something. However independent you may be, for some reason you become
> frightened. Is not this really the achieved ideal? [. . .] Is not the end here? Is
> not this in fact the 'one fold'? Won't you really have to accept this for the
> complete truth and fall silent once and for all? It's all so triumphant, victorious
> and proud [. . .] It's a kind of biblical picture, something like Babylon, some
> kind of prophecy from the Apocalypse being fulfilled before your eyes. You
> feel you'll need a great deal of perpetual spiritual resistance and denial not to
> give in, not to submit to the impression, not to bow to the fact, not to idolise
> Baal, that is, not to accept what exists as your ideal.   (v, 69–70; Ch. 5)

The apprehension about science expressed here was to remain with Dostoevskii to the end. Characteristic of his eschatological imagination are the apocalyptic imagery and biblical allusion to Christ's prophecy (John 10:16); and so is his determination to resist taking the new scientific, technological future as his ideal. Two visions of an ideal future collide in this passage: the new apocalypse of science, which looks as if it is already 'fulfilled' and the biblical apocalypse to come, when all will be gathered together into 'one fold', united in universal love and led by Christ. The Exhibition epitomised the nineteenth-century belief that science was going to solve the world's problems 'once and for all', which is to say that the 'complete truth' of science is a finite truth. For Dostoevskii, though, truth is infinite, to be sought only in Christ, and the search for the truth in Him was a lifelong dialogic quest. Hence, to 'fall silent once and for all' is to be absolutely dead as a human being. Thus, the worship of science and progress, which the Exhibition so stunningly embodied, was, for him, tantamount to idolatry (Baal), for it was threatening to turn people away from the 'one fold'. Given that Russia looked to the West as a model to be emulated, Dostoevskii could only fear that what he saw here was a prophetic image of Russia's future, an anxiety that was exacerbated by the sudden, rapid arrival of science in his homeland.

The scientific revolution came to Russia later than to Western Europe, but its impact was no less profound. The way for its acceptance had been prepared by the successive waves of Western influence on Russian society, beginning with the reforms of Peter the Great in the early eighteenth century. The steady Westernisation and modernisation of Russia had led by the mid-nineteenth century to the gradual secularisation of Russian culture and society. Science took this process much further. For science is not merely an accumulation of facts but a whole new way of looking at the world.[2] Scientific ideas and methods spread into areas of thought where they had hitherto been absent: into biblical scholarship, history, philosophy and social and political theory. With the rise of science, the old debate between faith and reason progressively shifted in favour of reason. Science gave new, powerful legitimisation to philosophical materialism and thus encouraged determinist and positivist ideas. The claims of religion to absolute truth were being steadily undermined by science to the extent that the very notion of truth changed: science and truth came to be synonymous, and religion was relegated to the sphere of myth and superstition. Dostoevskii was well informed of all these new trends.

Up to the mid-nineteenth century, science had made little impression on Russian literature. In Dostoevskii's pre-Siberian works references to the natural sciences are virtually non-existent. But towards the second half of the nineteenth century, news of scientific ideas and discoveries began to sweep into Russia from the West so that by 1860, when Dostoevskii returned from Siberia, he was confronted with quite a different intellectual landscape from the one he had left. Science had captured the allegiance of the young radical intelligentsia who were atheists and politically on the left. They were convinced that the unprecedented and powerful tools of prediction, calculation and validation that the natural sciences offered to humanity could be applied to the solution of social and political problems.

Turgenev was the first of Russia's great writers to depict a representative of the new scientific world-view in his hero, Bazarov, the nihilist medical scientist in *Fathers and Sons* (1862). However, Turgenev, unlike Dostoevskii, was not preoccupied with the challenge science presented to faith. Of all the great nineteenth-century writers, it was Dostoevskii who most acutely saw science as a major religious, philosophical and social problem, fraught with immense implications for the notion of truth, the conception of the human being and the future organisation of society. A detailed knowledge of Dostoevskii's biography and his historical and cultural context is essential for a full understanding of his attitudes to science. The focus here is on a poetic interpretation of scientific allusions in Dostoevskii's literary works, and on the meanings which emerge from them and point beyond them. In literature, and especially in Dostoevskii's art, we are concerned not with the validity of scientific ideas or facts, but with how they impinge on the consciousnesses of his heroes and their worlds, and what their responses tell us about the human condition. As Bakhtin has shown, for Dostoevskii there are no ideas in themselves; an idea is always *somebody's* idea. Thus, references to scientific facts become utterances, that is, charged with a person's intentions, questions, aspirations and anticipations of the other's response. Primary attention will be devoted to the two works that deal most fully with the problem of science: *Notes from Underground*, the first major work of Dostoevskii's post-Siberian period, and his last, *The Brothers Karamazov*.

Notes from Underground

It is in Part 1 of *Notes from Underground* (1865) that Dostoevskii engages head on with the scientific world-view in his depiction of his first fully fledged ideological hero, or 'anti-hero', an unnamed Russian intellectual who conducts an impassioned polemic with contemporary ideas. *Notes from Underground* is an intellectual drama which enacts in one head the conflict between free will and necessity. In the light of this philosophical agenda, it is particularly significant that the Underground Man's word is replete with references to science, from medicine, physiology, logic, mathematics, statistics, biology, economics and psychology to evolution. However, it is not science itself which most concentrates his attention, but those recent social and philosophical theories from the West that aimed to model human society and behaviour on scientific paradigms as their proponents understood or misunderstood them. Common to all these nineteenth-century theories – positivism, evolution, utopian socialism, utilitarianism, empiricism, rational egoism, social Darwinism – is a philosophical grounding in materialism and determinism, underpinned by scientific thought and methodology.

Part 1 is set in what the Underground Man calls 'our negative age' (v, 110; Pt 1, Sec. 6), that is, in the 1860s, that crucial decade for Russian thought when many of the young intelligentsia were rejecting the religious, social and aesthetic values of their predecessors. Alone, self-imprisoned in his no-home of the underground, obsessed with abstract ideas, he resides in St Petersburg, the 'most abstract and premeditated city in the entire globe' (v, 101; Pt 1, Sec. 2). His internal dialogue is divided into two voices, his own and that of various imaginary interlocutors whom he constructs as defenders of the new scientific thinking, trying to reason with an exasperating man who persists in being irrational.

The hero begins his *Notes* complaining that he is ill and mocking medicine. His liver aches but he won't go to a doctor 'from spite' (v, 99; Pt 1, Sec. 1). But whom is he spiting? One cannot spite medicine, only a person. Since the Underground Man lives in self-imposed isolation, there is no one to be spiteful towards; consequently, he spites himself, he mentally beats himself. It turns out that he is not suffering from a physical illness, but from an unrelenting 'hyper-consciousness': to be 'overly conscious', he maintains, is 'an illness' (v, 101; Pt 1, Sec. 2). But consciousness of what? Of the fact that he, being a clever, educated man, is acutely aware that his mind is constantly running up against a 'stone wall', his metaphor for 'the laws of Nature, the deductions of the natural sciences, mathematics' (v, 105; Pt 1, Sec. 3). The Underground Man feels insulted, hurt and humiliated by the laws of Nature and the reasons for his grievance against them are the main subject of his discourse. Precisely the *laws* of Nature, for the advent of science compelled a change in the way Nature was viewed. Nature was no longer a manifestation of God's creation, but of its own immanent laws; and these laws, which were interpreted in a strictly positivist sense, had become the object of scientific study. Nature became thoroughly rationalised, and depersonalised.

The Underground Man's consciousness of the laws of Nature is constantly taking him along an endless mental route from 'the most inevitable logical combinations to the most repulsive conclusions' (v, 106; Pt 1, Sec. 3). His self-torture is an ineluctable symptom of his spiritual dead end, of his desperate though admittedly perverted attempt to assert his human feelings against the grain of intellectually persuasive ideas, to make himself feel something in a world drained of feeling by compulsive abstract reasoning. All his feelings, even spite, undergo 'chemical dissolution' owing to these 'damn' laws' (v, 108; Pt 1, Sec. 5). Perhaps he would be glad of a slap but, should he feel magnanimous and wish to forgive his offender, it would be utterly useless, since his offender might have hit him 'because of the laws of Nature, and one cannot forgive a law of Nature' (v, 103; Pt 1, Sec. 2). Yet he cannot forget the slap, nor see it as other than an insult. 'I'm guilty without guilt', he complains, because of the laws of Nature (v, 103; Pt 1, Sec. 2). One can only be guilty before a person: that is, conscience presupposes a person to whom one is accountable; one cannot be accountable to a voiceless, personless law of Nature. Since there is no one to feel guilty before, he can only be hyper-conscious of his guilt, but can never expiate it or repent. Nor can he regenerate or transcend himself from his self-consciousness alone. Thus, two key Christian tenets, the action of conscience and the imperative to forgive, are rendered meaningless. The result is a transfer of responsibility from the subject (the old morality) on to an impersonal agent (a law of Nature), which by definition cannot be held responsible. Hitherto one could blame other persons, or personified beings such as the gods, God or the devil, or – in case of one's own sins – oneself. But now no one is responsible and so there is no one to blame. Thus, 'it turns out that there is no one even to be angry with; that an object does not exist, and perhaps, will never be found' (v, 106; Pt 1, Sec. 3). Seeking a responding subject, he encounters only an eternal stone wall.

Psychology has also contributed to a reductive view of the person with its axiom of man's innate selfishness: 'If they prove to you that one drop of your own fat must be more precious to you than one hundred thousand of your fellow men, and that all the so-called virtues and obligations are just ravings and prejudices, then accept it, there's nothing to be done because twice two is mathematics. Just try to object' (v, 105; Pt 1, Sec. 3). The result is the nullification of the central Christian virtue of self-sacrifice. The theory of evolution, of which the Underground Man is already aware, has fundamentally altered the modern conception of the human being: 'Once they prove to you that you're descended from a monkey, there's no point in frowning about it; accept it as it is' (v, 105; Pt 1, Sec. 3). If we are evolved animals, more complex, more developed animals, to be sure, but animals nonetheless, then we cannot have been created in the 'image and likeness' of God. What we see here is the relentless stripping away of the traditional Christian virtues and humane values owing to a radical redefinition of the human being as a species of animal conditioned and determined by the laws of Nature. Apparently, though, the idea of human descent from the apes did not unduly trouble Dostoevskii. In a letter of 1876, he says:

Christ directly announces that in man, besides the animal world, there is a spiritual one. Well, and so what – let man originate from anywhere you like (in the Bible it's not at all explained how God fashioned him from clay, took him from the earth), but it is said that God *breathed into him the breath of life* (though sometimes man in his sins can turn into a beast again).

(XXIX/2, 85; letter of 7 June 1876)

The concept of the person: I. the scientific view of the future person

Science is above all oriented towards the future. According to the scientific outlook, all the laws of human nature are already given, they need only to be detected. In other words, man is a finite entity susceptible to being completely understood, and hence finalised. The project of the radical utopian socialists was nothing less than the remaking of human nature along rational, scientific lines. Science legitimated the case for viewing the human being as a material object, as solely a product of Nature whose mind and behaviour would eventually be brought under total rational control. This new way of defining man gave impetus to the tendency to move in the direction of reification and away from personality, from the conception of the person as a developing, creating human being full of unpredictable potentials. The Underground Man takes this tendency to its ultimate, logical conclusion: the radical de-personalisation of the person. Insistently running through the *Notes* are the questions: who are we, who (or what) are we becoming, and where are we going?

The Underground Man's opponents are convinced they have the answer. The 'human being of the future', they maintain, won't go against reason, or his own best interests: 'that's mathematics' (V, 115; Pt 1, Sec. 8). Human will 'will coincide with the laws of natural science and arithmetic' (V, 117; Pt 1, Sec. 8). Science, having 'anatomised' the person, has demonstrated 'that wanting and so-called free will' are illusions (V, 114; Pt 1, Sec. 8).

Science itself will teach man [. . .] that he really has neither free will nor caprice and never did, and that he himself is nothing more than a kind of piano key or organ peg [. . .] everything he does, he does not at all according to his wanting, but according to the laws of Nature. Consequently, one only has to discover these laws of Nature and then man will not answer for his acts [. . .] All human actions, of course, will then be calculated by these laws, mathematically, like a table of logarithms, up to 108,000 and entered into a calendar.

(V, 112–13; Pt 1, Sec. 7)

But the statisticians, he counters, have taken into their register of human benefits only the statistical mean drawn 'from statistical figures and scientific-economic formulae'; they always leave out that 'most beneficial benefit' which evades any 'classification', namely, one's own 'independent', 'voluntary and free wanting' (v, 110; Pt 1, Sec. 7). However:

> I was just about to shout that wanting, the devil knows on what it depends and thank God, perhaps, for that, but then I remembered science and . . . lost my confidence [. . .] if they really find some day a formula for all our wanting and caprices, that is, what they depend on, by precisely what laws they occur, precisely how they spread [. . .] that is, a real mathematical formula – then man will, perhaps, immediately stop wanting [. . .] Well, who wants to want according to a little table? Moreover, he will immediately turn from a man into an organ peg.　　　　　　　　　　　　　　　　　　　(v, 114; Pt 1, Sec. 8)

What makes the Underground Man falter here is his anxiety that the champions of science may be right. He already likens himself to a laboratory instrument, remarking that he (like all those afflicted with hyper-consciousness) has not been 'born from Nature, but from a retort' – he is, he says, a 'retort man' (*retortnyi chelovek*) (v, 104; Pt 1, Sec. 3). For if all human responses are automatic, if they are all determined and can be mathematically calculated and predicted, then we no longer have a person but a thing, an organ peg. This is the logic, and in fact it is quite tight.

This has the most fundamental moral consequences: if man is a puppet ruled by the laws of Nature, then he cannot 'answer for his acts'. Science in itself offers no ground for morality. Scientific explanations of human behaviour are by and large contrary, or inimical, to the idea of the person as a free moral agent. Moral decisions depend on free choice, and if, according to science, there is no free will, then there can be no morality. Dostoevskii was to be preoccupied with this problem of moral responsibility for the rest of his life. Ivan Karamazov's idea of 'all is permitted' is a consequence of there being no one to be answerable to if there is no God.

'Thing and personality', remarks Bakhtin, are 'the two limits' in the spectrum of relating to others.[3] The human personality is infinite in its meaning and 'immortal' in its 'creative nucleus' (hence his idea of the non-coincidence of a person with himself).[4] The closer one moves towards personality, the less applicable are generalisations, abstractions. As Bakhtin observes: 'into the subject matter' of science 'the speaker and his word do not enter'; 'the mathematical and natural sciences' are 'directed towards mastery over *mute objects, brute things*, that do not reveal themselves in words, that do not *comment on themselves*'.[5] Science is thus by necessity 'monologic'. 'Science, in objectifying the subject, turns it into a voiceless thing. Any object of knowledge (including man) can be perceived and cognised as a thing. But a subject [. . .] cannot be perceived and studied as a thing' because 'it cannot become voiceless and consequently, the cognition of it can only be dialogic'.[6]

Science is a collection of statements, rationally argued; literature, a body of utterances artistically organised. You cannot address scientific statements, nor anticipate their responses, nor can they answer you. Consequently the whole dialogic structure, built on utterance, anticipation and response, so distinctive of Dostoevskii's poetics, has no place in science. Science treats everything it investigates as objects, units, aggregates, whereas Dostoevskii's characters are pre-eminently subjects, personalities. The scientific word is no one's word, or anyone's word; it does not have an author whose response inheres in it, it does not normally evoke the image of a person; it is face-less, or anyone's face, its speakers are completely interchangeable. It does not represent someone's semantic position, it cannot assuage the heart, it cannot offer a word of love or hate. Which is to say, it tends to the extreme of de-personification.

The natural sciences and mathematics are context-free object systems, devoid of subjects, of human reference; they are not bound by history, by specific times and places. The Pythagorean theorem is true no matter where, when or who states it; its meaning exists only as an object of pure abstract cognition. The Underground Man's famous attack on the arithmetical formula 'two times two equals four' has become symbolic of human rebellion against the whole rationalist world-view: 'twice two is four is no longer life, gentlemen, but the beginning of death [...] two times two is four is a most unbearable thing. Two times two is four – this is, in my opinion, just impudence. Two times two is four is a cocky-looking fop, who stands in your way, arms akimbo, and spits' (v, 118–19; Pt 1, Sec. 9).

Here Dostoevskii's profoundly personalist poetics and vision of the world emerge with striking clarity. From an abstract arithmetical formula the image of a person assumes bodily form and human qualities: a person who taunts and insults the hero and blocks his way to any further word, to any further seeking in life. 'After two times two, of course, there will no longer be anything not only to do, but even to find out' (v, 119; Pt 1, Sec. 9). Twice two thus robs the person of potentials and reduces him to finitude; it is the end of dialogue – for Dostoevskii, the end of life. In the face of such insolence, the Underground Man can only hurl back his challenge of 'two times two is five is a nice little thing too'. Dostoevskii was always personifying, giving voice, trying to elicit a response; in every significant phenomenon, he sought a word. The Underground Man's objection that 'twice two will be four without my will' succinctly expresses the fact that science, its truths and judgements, are indifferent, impervious to our reactions (v, 117; Pt 1, Sec. 8). As his imaginary critics tell him: 'Nature doesn't ask you; it doesn't care about your wishes, whether you like its laws or not' (v, 105; Pt 1, Sec. 3).

And yet, twice two is four is irrefutable; it is a final word or idea. You can have a view about it, but it will change nothing. The hyper-developed consciousness of a clever man sees there is no way out. The result is paralysis. Unable to act, but possessing a hyperactive mind, full of *idées fixes*, voice-ideas obsessively spinning around in his head, he says, in effect: 'I think, therefore I do nothing.' His helpless rage against the choking-off of his word and feelings by the implacable laws of Nature induces crippling inertia. He cannot break through to a potentially convinced word. His mind comes up against brute facts, mute objects which he personifies either directly, or by introducing imaginary hostile interlocutors who smugly believe in the new ideas, whom he cannot rationally defeat, but whom at the same time he despises. He feels predetermined by impervious manipulators of the laws of Nature who view him as an object, who reduce him to a thing.[7] All he can do is rebel, 'stick out one's tongue', send 'all these logarithms to the devil!' (v, 113; Pt 1, Sec. 7).

The Underground Man is the most isolated of all Dostoevskii's ideological heroes. He has an animated relationship with quasi-personified ideas, but no communion with real, living persons. In his youth (in the 1840s) he felt: '*I am alone and they are everyone else*', a remark that is one of the most profoundly formulated expressions of the solipsistic consciousness in Dostoevskii's fiction (v, 125; Pt 2, Sec. 1). As Bakhtin observes, everyone is 'other' for him, he 'reduces all people to a single common denominator'.[8] In the 1840s, though, he, a Westernised Russian, saw himself as a Romantic hero, above the run of ordinary people, whereas in the 1860s, with the rise of science, this fantasy seems ridiculous, totally unsustainable. The young radicals of the 1860s, armed with science, are a hard-headed version of the Westernised Russian who scorns the Romantic aesthetic and humanitarian values of the 1840s. Now the Underground Man finds himself consigned to the reductive category of a retrograde, irrelevant 'other', despite his efforts to accept their views.

The Underground Man maintains that he, like any clever, hyper-conscious man of 'our unfortunate nineteenth century', must be 'without character' and self-respect (v, 100; Pt 1, Sec. 2). This is because he has been trying to live by those rational, positivist certitudes that subvert the very basis of character and deny the reality of any transcendent ideals. Focussed on abstractions and not on persons, he has 'not succeeded in becoming anything', or anyone, and he never will (v, 100; Pt 1, Sec. 2). 'I cannot be other than I am for there is nothing to remake myself into!' (v, 102; Pt 1, Sec. 2). Thus in Part 1, Dostoevskii, with consummate artistic precision, represents him as a nameless, disembodied voice. To be nameless means to be without personal identity, to sink to the status of a thing. Consequently, he is adrift, without roots: 'Where are the primary foundations', he asks, 'on which I can rest?' (V, 108; Pt 1, Sec. 5). He strives to assert himself as a person, but cannot become a person in a world he has de-personalised and which now de-personalises him. He cannot 'respect' himself because he fears that he may be just a product of natural forces, a predetermined being without a spiritual, moral dimension, without free will and hence without dignity. Yet he cannot expunge the sense of himself as a person from his soul. Bereft of any higher model, human or divine, with which to construct his identity, he issues his challenging appeal: 'give me another ideal [. . .] show me something better, and I will follow you' (V, 120). He knows full well that 'the underground is not at all better, but something different, completely different, which I long for but will in no way find!' (V, 121; Pt 1, Sec. 11).

The Underground Man opposes the reductive rationalist view of the person with a rhetoric of parts versus the whole. 'Life', he counters, 'is not just the extraction of square roots' (V, 115; Pt 1, Sec. 8). 'Consciousness is infinitely higher than twice two', because it embraces the whole person with all his or her desires (V, 119; Pt 1, Sec. 9). Rational operations satisfy only our rational capacities. Man is much more than that. The reach of imagination, of consciousness, is infinite. Feelings make life meaningful. The Underground Man's rebellion is evidence that his heart, though in a state of terminal atrophy, is not dead yet, nor is his conscience. He inveighs against the reduction of the person to things, to inanimate abstractions that can be manipulated by impersonal agents. He rails against the Crystal Palace, the utopian dwelling of the new rational people of the future envisaged in Chernyshevskii's novel *What Is to Be Done?*. The Crystal Palace is no one's home; there is no structure more 'abstract and premeditated' than the Crystal Palace. These are metaphors for all those views that deny the 'most important and most precious thing', a person's 'individuality', his or her unique 'personality' (*lichnost'*) (V, 115; Pt 1, Sec. 8). This insistence on the primacy of 'personality', 'caprice', 'independent wanting' and free will is not a plea for unbridled licence. Rather his objection to the finite, deterministic view of human beings goes to the heart of a fundamental ideal: the absolute, irreducible value of a person.

The concept of the person: II. the theological view

A person is a relational concept. Every person is a unique, unrepeatable centre of human relationships; one cannot be a self except among other selves. One becomes a person in interaction, in communion with others. Dostoevskii's conception of the human being rests on the biblical definition according to which God created man in His 'image and likeness' (Genesis 1:26). With the

Incarnation, this expression received a human form and historical content which offered humanity a model which all may aspire to realise in their lives. It also inspired the theological idea of personhood. The concept of the person derives from the Greek Fathers who, in their meditations on the Triune God, held that God is a person, moreover, that He exists in the person of the Father Who 'begat' the Son and brought forth the Holy Spirit out of His love. God is love and His mode of existence is an act of continual trinitarian communion in which all can freely participate. A relationship with God, then, is a personal relationship, loving and unending. And because God freely willed man to be, freedom became an inalienable constituent of human dignity. It was this understanding of the person's free, inviolable, sacred core that was being relentlessly undermined by science and the atheist social theories it generated or supported. In the words of the Orthodox theologian John Zizioulas: 'It is atheistic humanism which has detached the concept of the person from theology' – and science, we may add, has been its strongest ally.[9] In the Orthodox tradition, to which Dostoevskii belonged, the person's uniqueness is absolute; it resists being 'regarded as an arithmetical concept', 'combined with other objects, or used as a means, even for the most sacred goal [. . .] The goal is the person itself: personhood is the total fulfilment of being.'[10] For Dostoevskii, truth resides not in concepts, but in a person, in Christ, the uniquely perfect Person, the model of personhood. If truth inheres in science, and not in Christ, then science can and will dispense with Christ. Confronted with this bleak eventuality, Dostoevskii, as is well known, chose to 'remain with Christ' (XXVIII, 1, 176: undated letter of January–February 1854 to N. D. Fonvizina).

Christ is not present in *Notes from Underground*. Dostoevskii originally included a passage in Chapter 10 which 'deduced the need for faith and Christ', but it was excised by the censors (XXVIII/2, 73; letter of 26 March 1864). He never restored the cuts. Aesthetically and rhetorically he was right to leave the content of his ideal implicit in his hero's existential malaise. For had the Underground Man already realised that he needed 'faith and Christ', he would have glimpsed a prospect towards heaven and thus would have ceased to be 'underground'. In that case, the image of a Russian intellectual unhinged by Western rationalism would have been considerably weakened since, in Dostoevskii, this realisation alone begins to be transformational.

Notes from Underground is the most concentrated and sustained exploration in Dostoevskii's œuvre of the problems science posed for the individual person, and by implication, for society. The Underground Man, as Frank argues, is conceived as 'a satirical parody' who exemplifies the dire consequences of taking to the limit the radically determinist ideas of the 1860s, and, we may add, without having anything to replace or transcend them.[11] He is also a cautionary figure of universal significance who, despite his cynical wit, suffers from genuine existential dilemmas, a man of intense feelings who protests against being regarded as an object, against being reified in the name of science. Dostoevskii's depiction of an acutely self-conscious man registering his awareness of the far-reaching implications of science on his thoughts and feelings is what makes this work seem so astonishingly modern, and so relevant to present dilemmas. The problems it raises about science reappear in Dostoevskii's subsequent major fiction in dialogues between embodied persons, where they become entangled with real-life dramas, with crimes, which acutely pose the question of 'the need for faith and Christ'.

In *Crime and Punishment*, one short episode brings into clear relief how the new scientific thinking underpinning social theories can affect behaviour in pressing, practical situations. In Part 1 (before the murders) Raskolnikov, while walking along the street, notices a young girl of 'about fifteen or sixteen' staggering ahead of him. She has obviously been drugged with drink, sexually abused and abandoned, and is being pursued by a predatory 'dandy'. Like the biblical prototype of the Good Samaritan, Raskolnikov takes energetic measures to help her. Full of indignation towards the man and compassion for the girl, completely heedless of any danger to himself, he rushes at the 'dandy' with clenched fists. A policeman intervenes, Raskolnikov explains the situation and gives him all his coins to call a cab for the girl. However, 'something' suddenly 'stings him', prompting a cynical volte-face: 'Leave off', he tells the policeman, 'What's it to you? Let him amuse himself' (VI, 42; Pt 1, Sec. 4). Left to himself, Raskolnikov surmises that the policeman will accept a bribe from the man to leave him alone with the girl. 'Let them swallow each other alive! – what's it to me?', a sentiment that will be echoed by Ivan Karamazov when, apropos his detested father and brother, he exclaims: 'One reptile will eat another reptile, and serve them both right!' (XIV, 129; Bk 3, Sec. 9). Both utterances betray the influence of social Darwinism, of the 'survival of the fittest', and both, significantly, are expressed shortly before their authors murder, or let a murder take place. After these 'strange words', Raskolnikov suddenly feels 'very depressed'. 'Poor girl!', he says, noticing the 'deserted corner of the bench' on which the girl had been sitting. Her absence sets him to musing. He imagines a short and terrible future for her in which she will end as a diseased, broken prostitute by the age of 'eighteen or nineteen'. He continues:

> Such a percentage, they say, go every year this way . . . somewhere . . . to the devil. They say, that's how it has to be in order that the rest be refreshed and not bothered. A percentage! They really have these splendid little words: they are so soothing, scientific. Once you say 'percentage', then there's nothing to

worry about. And if they used a different word, well then . . . it would, perhaps, be more disturbing . . . But what if Dunechka [his beloved sister] fell into this percentage? And if not in this one, then in another one?

(VI, 43; Pt 1, Sec. 4)

Once human beings and their tragedies can be converted into numerical aggregates, into ciphers in a deterministic table of statistics, they can be erased from conscience. The calculations of sociological utilitarianism overwhelm Raskolnikov with a sense of the futility of even attempting to perform a good act and induce an attitude of moral nihilism. And this chimes in with Marmeladov's earlier remark about 'a follower of the new [utilitarian] ideas', who explained to him 'that compassion in our time is even forbidden by science' (VI, 14; Pt 1, Sec. 2). Raskolnikov falls back into the grip of his idea, and under the influence of the same type of calculations, of a particularly lethal combination of Romantic, utilitarian and nihilistic ideas, he suppresses his moral sensibilities, and goes on 'mechanically' to murder two women. Nevertheless, at least one 'statistic' was briefly endowed with flesh and blood, thanks to the hero's ability to 'linger intently' over another person's life in un-self-interested detail. Raskolnikov's sympathetic imagination, his ability to forget himself and go spontaneously to the aid of others, are qualities which guarantee his eventual 'resurrection'. But then the affirmation of Christ's raising of Lazarus organises the whole novel; hence resurrection is affirmed as a real possibility for all those who accept Him. In Dostoevskii's next novel divine, and consequently human, resurrection is put under severe doubt by the 'laws of nature'.

In *The Idiot* Ippolit, the dying young man, describes his reaction to Holbein's painting of the dead Christ Who is depicted totally alone, in a cramped tomb, His wounds rendered in uncompromisingly naturalistic detail, and without any marks of His divinity:

here is only Nature [. . .] Christ did not suffer figuratively, but really and His body was fully and completely subject to the law of Nature [. . .] would His disciples [. . .] looking at such a corpse, believe that this martyr would arise? [. . .] if death is so terrible and the laws of Nature so powerful, then how can they be overcome [. . .] when even He, Who conquered Nature in His lifetime, did not conquer them now? He Whom Nature obeyed, Who said 'Talitha kumi' and the girl arose? [. . .] Looking at this picture, Nature appears [. . .] in the shape of some huge machine of the most recent construction which senselessly seized, smashed and swallowed into itself a great and precious Being, such a Being worth all of Nature and all its laws [. . .] The idea of a dark, insolent and senselessly eternal force, to which everything is subjected, is expressed by this picture and conveyed to you.

(VIII, 339; Pt 3, Sec. 6)

The latest 'machine' may stand as a metaphor for the technological age, for blind mechanical necessity, for the crushing triumph of a brute man-made thing over the only Person free from causality and the laws of Nature. Holbein's Christ is only a corpse, a person reduced to a thing. As Jostein Børtnes has pointed out, the dead Christ 'is the central symbol of *The Idiot*', but one that 'has been emptied of its divine content'; therefore His sacrifice, and consequently the whole Christian tradition, 'has lost its meaning'.[12] No consolations are offered. The failure of Myshkin to save anyone is a reflection of the absence of the divine Christ in the world of *The Idiot*. Dostoevskii was never again to put his ideal to such unsparing scrutiny. Only a troubled awareness of the scientific basis of the laws of Nature, in which miracles have no place, could have generated such a conception.

In *The Devils*, the socialist theorist Shigalev asserts that all previous creators of ideal social systems went hopelessly astray because they 'understood absolutely nothing about natural science and that strange animal called man' (x, 311; Pt 2, Ch. 7). He bases his 'system' for solving the social problem and organising a future society on 'scientific data' and a programme of eugenics. The human 'herd', which will comprise nine-tenths of humanity, will be deprived of their 'personality' and 'entire generations' will undergo 're-education', resulting in a number of 'rebirths' until they achieve a state of 'primeval innocence' (x, 132; Pt 1, Ch. 5). This will regrettably entail 'unlimited despotism' by the élite, but there is no other way to attain the 'earthly paradise'. What was adumbrated in *Notes from Underground* is spelled out in 'Shigalevism', where science underpins and legitimates the loss of personality and freedom in the name of establishing a perfect society.

Hitherto Dostoevskii has been primarily concerned with the misapplication of scientific thought and practice to the problematics of society and the person. From the mid-1870s he begins to incorporate recent mathematical and cosmological concepts of infinity into his characters' dialogues on ultimate questions, whereby biblical morality and eschatology come into conflict with the modern scientific view of the cosmos. The impact of contemporary astronomical theories prompts Arkadii Dolgorukii, the hero of *A Raw Youth*, to nihilistic reflections on faith and morality which anticipate Ivan Karamazov's dilemmas:

> Why should I love my neighbour or your future mankind, which I'll never see, which will not know about me and which [...] will be reduced to dust, without any trace or memory [...] when the Earth will [...] turn into an icy rock and will fly in vacuous space along with an infinite number of the same kind of ice rocks [...]? One cannot imagine anything more senseless.
>
> (XIII, 48–9; Pt 1, Ch. 3)

Here Dostoevskii uses a current astronomical speculation about the earth's future in order to formulate one of his most disturbing moral questions. If this is the ultimate future of humanity, what will keep us on the path of virtue, or, as Arkadii asks, why should we be 'noble'?

These questions return with enhanced poetic and philosophical depth in Dostoevskii's last novel, *The Brothers Karamazov*, where he introduces his first hero-scientist, Ivan Karamazov, who had completed a 'course in natural sciences' and was reputed to be an atheist. Ivan is a dreamer and theoretician on a cosmological scale. For Dostoevskii, to seek the truth is to transcend the limits of this world in a quest to divine the Word of Christ. Ivan too seeks the truth beyond the limits of this world, but chooses the direction offered by a scientific view of the cosmos. Science and mathematics also deal with concepts of infinity; but they do not locate the infinite in the human soul or a transcendent God, but in the relationships between matter, in the great abstractions of space, time and number. These ideas Ivan finds intellectually compelling, but they do not satisfy the deepest longings of his 'higher heart'.

During his conversation with Alesha on the incompatibility of the existence of God with an unjust world, Ivan introduces the recent discovery of non-Euclidean geometry, one of the great breakthroughs in mathematics. Euclid's geometry, which had long been taken as universal truth, postulated that parallel lines can never meet. However, Euclid did not have the notion of infinity; his laws applied only to finite planes. Non-Euclidean geometry demonstrated that there exist parallel lines that meet at infinity. It thus opened up another reality beyond our finite, three-dimensional world, but it also had a destabilising effect on old certainties. The demotion of Euclid's geometry from its pinnacle of immutable truth was correlated with the contemporary failure of revealed religion to explain various natural phenomena. Ivan makes a somewhat similar correlation, drawing a parallel between the incomprehensibility of non-Euclidean geometry and the senseless suffering on earth. The human mind, he says, being created with a conception of only three dimensions, can no more grasp such notions as infinity, which are 'not of this world', than the ways of God which are manifestly unconcerned with the concrete, unjust suffering of this world. Ivan then uses this mathematical discovery to construct an accusation against 'God's world' and to tempt Alesha into joining him in his rebellious despair. For Ivan, non-Euclidean geometry is a metaphor for God's absence from this world, for the *Deus absconditus*. Since God cannot be watching over this world, 'all is permitted'. It is this idea which precipitates the tragedy of the murder of Fedor Pavlovich.

Ivan's brother Mitia (Dmitrii) has his views on science, though in quite a different key. Visiting Mitia in prison on the eve of his trial for the murder of their father, Alesha finds him distraught, confused and despondent. However, it is not his impending trial that is 'killing' him, but 'various philosophies': 'Well, Aleksei, now my head's lost, not my head, but what was in my head is lost [. . .] Ideas, ideas, that's what! Ethics. What is ethics? [. . .] some kind of science? [. . .] Claude Bernard? What is it? Chemistry or something? [. . .] Ugh, these Bernards! A lot of them are breeding! Why am I lost? Hmm. In essence . . . on the whole – I'm sorry for God, that's why!' (xv, 28; Bk 11, Sec. 4). One would be hard put to find such a sentiment, such an inversion of the relationship between man and God, before the age of science. It emerges that Rakitin (a shallow progressive careerist) has been giving Mitia lessons in material determinism, with explanations of the vasomotor system which had been recently discovered by Claude Bernard, the French positivist physiologist. Says Mitia:

> in the brain are these nerves [. . .] they have little tails [. . .] as soon as they begin to quiver, an image appears [. . .] this is why I visualise, and then think . . . because of these little tails, and not at all because I have a soul and am a kind of image and likeness . . . It's splendid, this science, Alesha! A new man will come, this I understand . . . But all the same, I'm sorry for God [. . .] Chemistry, brother, chemistry! Nothing can be done about it – move over a little, Your Reverence, chemistry is coming!   (xv, 28–9; Bk 11, Sec. 4)

Science is redefining man and God has to 'move over' to make way for the 'new man', who is a material object without a soul, who can be cognised and broken down into his physiological components. Mitia echoes the Underground Man's sense of helplessness before the triumphant advance of the 'new men'. In Mitia's sorrowful tones sounds the pathos of the great historical drama of the eclipse of Christianity by the emergent scientific world-view.

Precisely when Ivan can no longer hide from himself his complicity in his father's murder, his ideas, now repugnant to him, come to haunt him in the guise of the devil. The devil is an ancient transcendent figure of cosmic significance, laden with evil associations, who roams the cosmos at will. In Dostoevskii's novel, he has taken up residence as a voice in Ivan from which the latter now vainly struggles to dissociate himself. The result is a split in Ivan's consciousness which precipitates his descent into mental breakdown. It is his devil who quotes Ivan's scientific ideas back to him, only in tones of mockery. And it is his devil, evidently the first in European literature, who invokes a host of scientific ideas as instruments of torment. Reminding Ivan that they share the 'same philosophy', the devil continues: 'Really, I myself, just like you, suffer from the fantastic, and that's why I love your earthly realism. Here you have everything defined, here is the formula, here is geometry, but all we have are indeterminate equations' (xv, 73; Bk 11, Sec. 9).

As the reader knows, Ivan does not love 'earthly realism' or its 'Euclidean nonsense' (XIV, 222; Bk 5, Sec. 4). He rejects this world while secretly hoping for a better one beyond; but having no factual evidence of it, he despairs of its existence. But the devil demolishes Ivan's tenuous hope when he defines his realm in terms of total mathematical indeterminacy, and implies there is nothing else. For the devil has no fixed spatial, temporal location, but comes from the infinite reaches where 'non-Euclidean geometry' and 'indeterminate equations' are the norm, where there are no defined outlines and thus no stable images, where there is no up or down, high or low, right or wrong. His frequent motifs of Nature turned upside down serve the same purpose of tormenting Ivan with the idea of an absurd, utterly meaningless universe.

Referring to recent advances in earthly science, the devil says:

> 'all of us there are agitated now, and it's all because of your sciences. While there were still just atoms, five senses, four elements, well then everything somehow held together. They had atoms in the ancient world too. But when we found out that you had discovered your 'chemical molecule', and 'protoplasm', and the devil knows what else [. . .] real confusion set in.'
>
> (XV, 78; Bk 11, Sec. 9)

The science of classical Greece not only co-existed with Christianity, but was accepted by the church as immutable truth. This religious and scientific stasis 'held together' for many centuries. But the growth of modern science is sowing confusion in the devil's realm, for if it is a threat to faith it is also a threat to the devil, since an atheist neither worships the one nor fears the other. Not surprisingly, then, Ivan, the 'atheist' who wishes to believe, 'strangely, suddenly' says to the devil: 'I, however, would like to believe in you!'

Complaining about his baffling role of negation in the universe, the devil returns to his metaphor of mathematical indeterminacy: 'I suffer, but still I don't live. I am the x in an indeterminate equation.' X is the symbol used when something, such as a person's name, is unknown, or is to be left undetermined, and this accords with the devil's having 'forgotten' what to call himself. But now the devil takes the metaphor much further: he is that critical element which converts determinacy into indeterminacy, faith into doubt. 'I am the x' is a maximally abstract version of Christ's self-defining metaphors of the type A is B ('I am the light of the world', 'I am the door') where the concrete metaphors are aimed at showing the listener the way to reach the light, to approach God. The devil's 'x' leads to anything, or nothing.

The same type of metaphor is embedded in the devil's subsequent mathematical reference where he depicts himself as a long-suffering victim who has been assigned the onerous task of leading people into temptation. Why this should be so is a mystery to him: 'I know, after all, there is a secret here, but they do not want for any price to reveal the secret to me, because then, having guessed what it's about, I might shout "hosanna" and then the necessary minus would immediately disappear and in the whole world reasonableness would set in' (xv, 82; Bk 11, Sec. 9). Another non-self-definition involving a mathematical symbol yields the metaphor 'I am the necessary minus.' 'Necessary' implies a plan. If the devil is 'necessary', it can only be a divine plan. Now 'minus' is equivalent not to non-existence but to a negative quantity or quality. In other words, if we have $-x$ we still have a notion of x. Even the devil is not equal to that 'absolute zero' Ivan gave in reply to Fedor's query whether there exists 'just a tiny little bit' of God and immortality (xiv, 123; Bk 3, Sec. 8). The devil uses figures of mathematical indeterminacy in order to torture Ivan on his sorest point, his wish to know once and for all 'Does God exist or not?' But from the devil he gets only indeterminate answers: 'My dear fellow, honest to God, I don't know' (xv, 77; Bk 11, Sec. 9).

Continuing his torment of Ivan, the devil advances a vision of cosmic palingenesis drawn from recent geological and astronomical findings:

> Really, the present earth may have repeated itself a billion times; it died out, iced over, cracked, crumbled, disintegrated into its constituent elements, again the waters which were above the firmament, then again a comet, again the sun, again from the sun the earth – really, this development may have been repeated an infinite number of times, and always in the very same form, to the smallest detail. A most indecent bore. (xv, 79; Bk 11, Sec. 9)

All the verbs the devil intones to depict the terrestrial cycles are intransitive, conveying self-repeating processes of disintegration, annihilation and colossal movements of massive inanimate matter. Significantly, the devil quotes only a fragment of Genesis 1:7: 'And God made the firmament, and divided the waters under the firmament from the waters above the firmament; and it was so.' Omitting the biblical subject, God, and the transitive verbs signifying His cosmic creative acts, the devil banishes God the Creator from the universe, and replaces Him with a positivist, self-existent, self-acting and self-perpetuating cosmogony. If for Ivan God is absent from this world, the devil insinuates that He is absent from the universe, that He is not even at that place where parallel lines meet. Annexing the idea of an infinitely repeating series, the devil converts terrestrial and solar evolution from a linear one, in which change is possible, into a cosmogony of the vicious circle, of doomed repetition. Implicit in his scheme is the idea that human beings are helplessly trapped, condemned perpetually to re-experience their earthly misery 'to the smallest detail'. Forever spinning around with insentient inorganic masses in an immutable cycle, humanity approximates the attributes of brute matter. No one can ever ascend to a higher level of spiritual being; there is no redemption, salvation or divine love and mercy. This means that innocent suffering can never be atoned; worse, it has been and ever will be eternally repeated 'to the smallest detail'. Thus, the devil insidiously extends Ivan's accusations against God on the grounds of innocent, unatoned suffering. The sombre implication is that the Crucifixion will be infinitely repeated, and thus Christ's coming achieved nothing, and never will. It would be hard to imagine a more hellish vision.

The infinity Ivan's devil presents to him is an evil infinity which opens out into nothing, into a void where man is in free fall. Father Zosima's vision of infinity is one where 'the roots of our thoughts and feelings are in other worlds', and everything lives thanks to this 'feeling of contact with mysterious other worlds' (xiv, 290; Bk 6, Sec. 3). For Zosima, the universe is presided over by 'our Sun', a loving Person, Who is 'infinitely merciful', and ceaselessly inviting us to Him 'forever and ever' (xiv, 327; Bk 7, Sec. 4).

Nearing the end of their conversation, the devil sums up Ivan's recent composition on a future utopian society. To create the new society, the 'new people' do not need to destroy anything, averred Ivan, except 'the idea of God':

> Once humankind to a person renounces God (and I believe that this [. . .] will come to pass), then the whole former world-view will fall away of itself, without anthropophagy, and – the main thing – so will the whole former morality, and then everything new will come. People will join together to take from life everything that it can give, but absolutely for happiness and joy only in this world. Man will be exalted with a divine spirit, a titanic pride, and the man-god will appear. Every hour conquering Nature, now without limits, with his will and science, man every hour will feel a delight so lofty that it will take the place for him of all the former hopes of heavenly delight.
>
> (xv, 83; Bk 11, Sec. 9)

This is the ultimate secularisation and destruction of Christianity, and science is the indispensable instrument of its demise. God must not only 'move over' but be permanently expelled from every head. The new men of science will take over the Orthodox ideal of theosis and turn it into self-deification. They will appropriate the Christian hope of immortality and turn it into prolonging life on earth, into an ideology of prolongevism, perfectibilism and hedonism. Man will become omnipotent over matter, over Nature. What Mitia sorrowfully intuited about the 'new men of chemistry', Ivan openly promoted in adopting the serpent's temptational promise: 'Ye shall be as gods'

(Genesis 1:35). The 'terrifying force' Dostoevskii anxiously apprehended at the Great Exhibition is here given poetic expression in a young Russian scientist's prophetic fantasy of a future technological golden age which he had viewed as the 'final' stage of human development, its final achieved ideal.

Afterword

Since the nineteenth century Christianity has been finding itself increasingly on the defensive, while science has gone its own way and has now become virtually identified with truth. Science, says Bakhtin, knows only 'its own immanent law' and because it evades the question of its purposes, it 'may serve evil rather than good'. Dostoevskii did not deny the benefits of science, but he was more concerned to emphasise the dangers. He knew very well that, as Bakhtin says, a scientific advance that is initially rationally defensible can develop into a 'terrifying, deadly' and 'irresponsibly destructive force' when divorced from life.[13] The famous twentieth-century dystopias of Evgenii Zamiatin (*We*), Aldous Huxley (*Brave New World*) and George Orwell (*1984*) project totalitarian world orders which use advanced science and technology as instruments of total control over human beings, and, in so doing, take the reification and de-personalisation of humans beings to their limits. We now live in what is already called a post-Christian society. Though some warn against the dangers of scientism, science has now become unstoppable. Says the Underground Man: 'If we really are rushing towards [...] the retort, what can we do, we'll have to accept the retort! Or else, it will get accepted of itself, without you' (v, 115; Pt 1, Sec. 8). It is not Zosima's vision, as Dostoevskii hoped, but Ivan Karamazov's utopian ideas which are being fulfilled before our eyes. Indeed, some of Dostoevskii's worst fears have already been realised in those scientific trends and discoveries of today which aim to make man omnipotent over his own organism, trends such as behaviourism, cloning – including the 'therapeutic cloning' of human embryos for spare parts – the human genome project (which is not very far from the Underground Man's 'calendar' of 108,000 human actions), robotics, cryonics, genetic engineering, 'virtual reality' people, designer babies, artificial intelligence, and on the social level, hedonism, the breakdown of community and a sense of pervasive anonymity. 'We have long ceased to be born from living fathers. Soon we shall contrive to be born somehow from an idea', says the Underground Man at the end of his *Notes* (v, 179; Pt 2, Sec. 10). Whether we and our descendants will like such a world remains an open question. As early as the 1860s Dostoevskii foresaw the dilemmas with unparalleled depth and prescience.

Notes

Capitalisation of personal and possessive pronouns relating to God and Christ, intended by Dostoevskii but excised from Soviet editions of his works, has been restored in quotations in this article.

1 Quoted by N. N. Strakhov in *F. M. Dostoevskii: Novye materialy i issledovaniia* (New Materials and Studies), *Literaturnoe nasledstvo* 86 (Moscow: Nauka, 1973), p. 560.
2 The Russian *nauka* means both 'science' and 'scholarship'. The context determines which sense is meant. By Dostoevskii's time it had come increasingly to be used for the natural sciences, mathematics, statistics and economics.
3 M. M. Bakhtin, *Speech Genres and Other Late Essays*, trans. Vern W. McGee, ed. Caryl Emerson and Michael Holquist (Austin: University of Texas Press, 1986), pp. 138–9 and 164–5.
4 Ibid., p. 168.
5 M. M. Bakhtin, *The Dialogic Imagination*, trans. Caryl Emerson and Michael Holquist, ed. Michael Holquist (Austin: University of Texas Press, 1981), p. 351.
6 Bakhtin, *Speech Genres*, p. 161.
7 M. M. Bakhtin, *Problems of Dostoevsky's Poetics*, ed. and trans. Caryl Emerson (Manchester University Press, 1984), p. 236.
8 As Bakhtin puts it: 'In everything he senses above all *someone else's will* predetermining him' (ibid., p. 253).
9 John D. Zizioulas, *Being as Communion* (London: St Vladimir's Seminary Press, 1985), p. 27.
10 Ibid., p. 47. Some humanist atheists invoke the sacredness of the person as an ethical principle, but in their case 'sacred' is an empty concept since they have nothing transcendent to attach it to. Their appeal to 'sacred' is but a fading echo of a once living idea.
11 Joseph Frank, *Dostoevsky: The Stir of Liberation, 1860–1865* (Princeton University Press, 1986), p. 314.
12 Jostein Børtnes, 'Dostoevskij's *Idiot* or the poetics of emptiness', *Scando-Slavica* 40 (1994), p. 13. I thank Jostein Børtnes for kindly reading an earlier version of the present chapter.
13 M. M. Bakhtin, *Toward a Philosophy of the Act*, trans. Vadim Liapunov, ed. Vadim Liapunov and Michael Holquist (Austin: University of Texas Press, 1993), pp. 7–8.

II

GARY SAUL MORSON

Conclusion: reading Dostoevskii

You had to be there

'At the very moment when our professor was insisting that life is thoroughly unpredictable and unplannable, and I was wondering "then why are his lectures so perfectly structured?", this person came in from the hallway and shouted rudely that the professor was lecturing too loudly and he couldn't study next door. I wondered if *that* was part of the lecture, too, but the professor was so surprised it clearly wasn't. Well, you had to be there.'

'Yes, well something similar happened to me. Our philosophy professor told us grandly that the most important thing to remember in reading Nietzsche is that *God is dead!* – and just at that minute . . .'

'Don't tell me. There was a giant thunderclap.'

'Well, you had to be there.'

(Overheard)

You had to be there: when do we say this? It is usually when we narrate an incident that is just like a story even though there was no author. It really happened! If the professor had planned the rude student's interruption, he would not have created the same experience of life actually turning out like a story. Such events are striking because events happen as if already narrated and so evoke the eerie suspicion that we are like fictional characters.

In *Through the Looking Glass*, when Alice contemplates the sleeping king, Tweedledum and Tweedledee tell her that she is 'only a sort of thing in his dream' and that if he were to awake 'you'd go out – bang! – just like a candle!' When she cries at this suggestion, and then observes that if she were not real, she could not cry, Tweedledum asks rhetorically: 'I hope you don't suppose those are *real* tears?' This passage is usually taken as an allusion to the idea that we exist only in the mind of God, but it might equally well serve to illustrate what it would be like to imagine oneself as a mere character in an already-written story. What happens to us when the author takes a break from writing? If he abandons the story altogether, do we go out like a candle or do we remain forever in an unmoving present? We cannot persuade the author to let us go on living, for he exists in a time totally inaccessible to us: when Alice tells the pair of Tweedles not to shout, lest they wake the king, Tweedledum replies, 'Well, it's no use *your* talking of waking him when you're only one of the things in his dream.' But we cannot believe any of this, because we *sense* our existence, sense above all that we can *do something* unexpected and unscripted by someone else: but then, maybe Raskolnikov did, too, and he was a character, after all.[1]

When life resembles a story, it feels distinctly strange. In *War and Peace*, Tolstoi evokes such a moment when the genuine moans of the wounded soldiers somehow sound feigned to the young Rostov. One expects real experiences to be unlike stories, and these cries seem artificial precisely because they are too much like the way he has heard them described. On the other hand, do we maybe moan the way we do because we have been taught to do so by stories – something like the Underground Man's description of the man with a toothache who moans with 'trills and flourishes' – in which case our very expressions of pain are both real and artificial, spontaneous and cited?

Tolstoi is always raising questions like these. *War and Peace* constantly contrasts the neatness of narrative accounts with the messiness of lived events. The only times when events resemble narratives take place when people who have read too much history try to behave 'historically', by which they mean 'as is written in histories'. Then their behaviour becomes both absurd and ineffective. The Tsar and Napoleon, who repeatedly act out striking moments for future narratives, thus become comic figures, and even the Austrian Emperor Franz, who can only ask what time something happened, at least seems more serious and more rooted in the present. In this context, the passage about feigned moans seems to go to the heart of Tolstoi's method and evokes sceptical thoughts even about *War and Peace* itself.

Dostoevskii was keenly aware of Tolstoi's contrast between narrative and life. This theme partially explains his love for *Don Quixote* and why he had Nastasia Filippovna read *Madame Bovary*. It appears in his works from *Poor Folk* and *White Nights* to *Notes from Underground* and *The Gambler*; in *The Brothers Karamazov*, it surfaces repeatedly in the descriptions of Kolia and of Dmitrii's trial. Indeed, one reason the gambler loves roulette is that the moment of winning, and the thrill of anticipation, have not been already determined and written down in advance. They are utterly, and he believes metaphysically, unpredictable: pure chance. Unlike a story, the outcome of roulette is not predetermined, but really depends on the movements of that little ball around the wheel, which no one can foresee in any particular case. The money he might win does not interest him: when he does win, he immediately squanders it. No, what he loves is the metaphysical jolt, the intensity of *presentness*, which is stronger even than in his erotic encounters. Play conquers all. If only God would play dice with the universe!

The Hundred Years War

'You had to be there': this comment evokes the inadequacy of any *account* of an event. We always say these words with a gesture or tone of frustration at not being able to convey the sense of gratuitous appropriateness that made the incident so memorable. Upon reflection, we see just why such an event must be extremely difficult, if not impossible, to convey adequately. The very fact that we are narrating it, have made a story or anecdote out of it, already promises in advance that something narrative-worthy has taken place, and yet the whole point of the story is that just when we had no reason to expect life to resemble a story it did. The listener cannot be surprised as we were because he cannot help anticipating a story. You might as well try to catch time by the tail.

Some thinkers and movements have had a profound belief in the storiness of the world. I do not want to evaluate the cliché that, with the Hebrew prophets, the West invented a linear, storyline time as opposed to a cyclical one, but it is worth mentioning that linear time confers more value on present events than its rival does. For if the cycles repeat, then nothing has a unique determining influence. To be sure, cyclical time mitigates remorse, but by the same token it weakens the sense that what we do now really matters. The devil mocks Ivan Karamazov with precisely this devaluing aspect of eternal recurrence.

But for thinkers who believe in the supreme value of present action, even narrative time does not place enough emphasis on it. You had to have been there: for in narrative, the event is already *over*. As a child, I once read an encyclopaedia account of the Hundred Years War and cheered for the English. I won't elaborate on the discomfort that Joan of Arc caused my younger self. I delighted in Crécy, Poitiers and Agincourt, adored that thug the Black Prince, and was profoundly disappointed when, at last, my team lost. And then I reflected: how could I have read a historical account and *hoped* for an outcome, when the outcome was long since determined (not that it would matter if it were only just determined). I thought of the joke about the boy who asks God that Toronto should be the capital of Canada because that is what he answered on his geography test. There are circumstances in which hope is out of place.

Yet the experience of reading a novel depends on our intermittent forgetting of this fact. Insofar as we identify with a character, we place ourselves in the character's time, and so vicariously share hopes and fears. On the other hand, we also step back, and, observing the emergent structure of the whole story, anticipate the outcome already written down. Any successful reading does both. We hope that the Underground Man will marry Liza, but we also know that the structure precludes it. What we hope for would not please us if we got it, because it would violate that structure and make the work a bad one.

This divergence between the desire of identification and the desire for aesthetic coherence testifies to the radical disjunction between presentness and structure. Literary works demand both, but life affords only presentness. And so with our hunger for narrative we embrace prophets, from Moses to Marx. We know that prophets limit our freedom, that if the future is already given as surely as the end of a novel is already written, our actions matter less. No matter what we do, we are doomed to victory. We want to be free (or feel we are free) but also, as the Grand Inquisitor insists, have the future decided for us. The burden of genuine uncertainty is too great and so we embrace unfreedom that calls itself the reverse. And we read novels.

God in time

If there ever was a writer who believed in human freedom, it was Dostoevskii. Laws of Nature and history do not provide an exhaustive account of what people do: they choose, and might choose otherwise. If that were not so, there would be no morality and life would have no meaning: we would be nothing but sentient puppets. Of course, such a view put Dostoevskii at odds with the materialism and scientism of his age, with its 'moral Newtonianism', as Elie Halévy famously called the dream of a social science.[2] Less obviously, it also put him at odds with the dominant Christian theological tradition, which, from Augustine to Leibniz and beyond, insisted upon divine omniscient knowledge of the future. In the famous thirteenth chapter of the *Discourse on Metaphysics*, Leibniz contends that every last thing we are to do is already contained in our 'concept', which God knows from eternity. To say that the future could be more than one thing would be to assume either that God could be mistaken or that he could change his mind. In either case, he would then be a being *in* history, not outside it – a being in time who could be affected by events. God does not suffer through a succession of wills, is not determined by events, but has one perfect will from eternity to eternity. He is not like Zeus – or, we might add, the God actually depicted in the Hebrew Bible, who does frequently get angry, express surprise and disappointment, and change his mind. The theologians typically explained such passages away as metaphorical concessions to the limited capacities of a vulgar people from an ancient tribe. Materialist determinism essentially posits the same position as Leibniz: everything is given in advance by the laws of Nature and society. In fact, we may refer to moral Newtonianism as a God substitute.

Peter Damian drew the logical conclusion that, since God is outside history, he must possess as much power to change the past as to change the future, and if he did not do one – that is, admit a mistake – he would not do the other. From this position, it is difficult to understand why we pray, let alone hope, regret, condemn and praise. In much the same way, we know, when half-way through reading a published novel, that the author will not alter the ending we are approaching any more than he will change the beginning we have encountered. Woody Allen notwithstanding, that's not what we mean when we say that the novel is different every time we read it. Raskolnikov kills the old lady every time, and no hope or fear on our part will persuade Anna to avoid railway.

If the future is given, how can we be free, as both Augustine and Leibniz, as well as most of their God-substituting materialist followers, insist we are? The most common answer, in both its theological and secular form, is to *re-define* freedom so that it means absence of external compulsion. God knows, and the laws of nature ensure, what we will freely choose. Milton's formu-lation of this idea is perhaps the most memorable. In Book III of *Paradise Lost*, God explains:

> So will fall
> Hee and his faithless Progeny: whose fault?
> Whose but his own? Ingrate, he had of mee
> All he could have; I made him just and right,
> Sufficient to have stood, though free to fall.
> [...]
> They therefore as to right belong'd,
> So were created, nor can justly accuse
> Thir maker, or thir making, or thir Fate;
> As if Predestination over-rul'd
> Thir will, disposed by absolute Decree
> Or high foreknowledge; they themselves decreed
> Thir own revolt, not I: if I foreknew,
> Foreknowledge had no influence on their fault,
> Which had no less prov'd certain unforeknown.
> So without the least impulse or shadow of Fate,
> Or aught by me immutably foreseen,
> They trespass, Authors to themselves in all ...[3]

I find it intriguing that in this very passage the God outside of time intervenes in the ongoing seventeenth-century theological debates that so engaged – shall we say, His creator? In Milton's theology, people are like characters in a novel who freely choose what the pattern demands. The literary equivalent of 'Fate' in these lines would be a gratuitous *deus ex machina*, a sort of miracle resolving the story by means other than its own unfolding pattern, that would be sensed as a flaw. But in a well-structured novel, the author's foreknowledge has no influence on the characters' fault. Though immutably foreseen, the characters' actions are decreed by the characters themselves.

The author of *Notes from Underground*, *The Gambler* and *The Idiot* found both this world-view and its literary analogue entirely unacceptable. Everyone knows that Dostoevskii fought the materialists of his time and insisted on free choice. The theological dimensions of Dostoevskii's position are less widely appreciated, but they have no less significant consequences for his narrative practice. The God who foreknows all – God the Father – has little, and grudging, place in Dostoevskii's Christianity. Rather, he stresses the Son, who participated in history and suffered with us, and, in *The Brothers Karamazov*, the Holy Spirit, which does indeed intervene in the world. Dostoevskii's is a strange heresy, which to my knowledge never developed a name: stressing both the second and third persons of the Trinity at the expense of the first. God willing, there is no God, only his Only Begotten Son born of a virgin, and the Holy Ghost.

Suspense

To understand Dostoevskii's most remarkable innovations in narrative, we must appreciate his conviction that at any moment of time more than one thing (though not everything) is possible. And if there are just two possibilities – not thousands, just two – at even a single moment, then determinism and Leibnizianism fall to the ground. In fact, multiple possibilities characterise most, if not all, moments. Novels must not therefore be written with a structure that tacitly affirms closed time by tying events together so closely and making the ending seem so inevitable that any alternative would be absurd. Here, then, is the central problem of Dostoevskii's thought and quest for form: how to conceive and represent people as genuinely free in this sense?

I would like to discuss four methods Dostoevskii derived. The first may be discussed briefly, because it is relatively obvious and because Mikhail Bakhtin explored it so brilliantly: the intensification of the present moment of choice. We are placed so deeply in the character's moment that we experience the agonies of his indecision: and, from such a perspective, the idea that somehow the decision has already been made for all eternity seems palpably absurd.

When Dmitrii Karamazov, obscured in the shadow and with pestle in pocket, stands beside the window out of which his father has stuck his loathsome face, we are given such an inside perspective on his thoughts and feelings. He lives an extraordinarily intensified present, a moment in which he must decide once and for all whether to kill his father:

> Mitia [Dmitrii] looked at him from the side without stirring. The old man's profile that he loathed so, his pendant Adam's apple, his hooked nose, his lips that smiled in greedy expectation, were all brightly lighted up by the slanting lamplight falling on the left from the room. A horrible fury of hatred suddenly surged up in Mitia's heart, 'There he was, his rival, the man who had tormented him, had ruined his life!' It was a rush of that sudden, furious, revengeful anger of which he had spoken, as though foreseeing it, to Alesha four days ago in the arbour, when, in answer to Alesha's question, 'How can you say you'll kill our father?': 'I don't know, I don't know,' he had said then. 'Perhaps I shall not kill him, perhaps I shall. I'm afraid he'll suddenly be so loathsome to me at that moment. I hate his double chin, his nose, his eyes, his shameless grin. I feel a personal repulsion. That's what I'm afraid of, that's what may be too much for me . . .' This personal repulsion was growing unendurable. Mitia was beside himself. He suddenly pulled the brass pestle out of his pocket.
>
> (XIV, 354–5; Bk 8, Sec. 4)

Perhaps I shall not kill him, perhaps I shall: what we are given here is the intensity of a choice, entirely unpredetermined, that must be taken *now*, one way or the other. *Now* is not already given, and *now* happens only once: if not me, who? and if not now, when? This passage takes us deeper and deeper into Dmitrii's consciousness, beginning in third-person language expressing Dmitrii's own thought – the sort of language Bakhtin analysed so well – and then merging entirely into inner quotation. We see here a reason for Dostoevskii's compulsive use of 'suddenlys' as they further intensify the sense of a moment outside of time, a singularity of pure choice, a pure now. Bakhtin is not quite correct when he observes that such moments in Dostoevskii totally obliterate the past because awareness of a past would detract from the intensity of the present. Dmitrii remembers his conversation with Alesha. The past does play a role here, but it is one of redoubling the present. In this moment Dmitrii remembers (and we do, too) what he said to Alesha about such a moment should it ever come: and this means that he is both experiencing the intense division he has described and remembering the description at the same time. For this reason, the moment of choice is even more intense than he anticipated because he did not anticipate remembering the anticipation.

The intensity, the repulsion and the attempted restraint, are growing 'unendurable'. The intolerability of a moment so intense is, of course, a common theme in Dostoevskii. In *The Idiot* Myshkin's epileptic fits, for instance, include such an instant in which he suddenly understands the extraordinary saying from the Apocalypse that there shall be time no longer. He lives the moment when there was not time enough for a drop of water to fall from Mohammed's pitcher while 'the epileptic prophet had time to gaze on all the habitations of Allah' (VIII, 189; Pt 2, Sec. 5). At executions, the sheer intensity of the horrible expectation provokes the victim to wish he could be *shot more quickly*: surely a Dostoevskian thought if ever there was one. And in a scene in *Crime and Punishment* that looks forward to Dmitrii's choice, Raskolnikov – agonisingly aware that Koch is outside the door latched from inside, knowing that Koch suspects that a perpetrator of foul play is just on the other side of the keyhole, and watching in blank terror as Koch shakes the door so hard it could tear the latch right out of the wall – thinks several times that he should 'end it all at once and shout to them through the door. Now and then he was tempted to swear at them, to jeer at them, while they could not open the door' (VI, 68; Pt 1, Sec. 7). Here and later, he longs to be found out more quickly!

What is Dmitrii to do? Whatever he does will be a free choice, and yet once done, irrevocable. The intensity of the experience, along with the use of the internal perspective, makes us share his anticipation: and then the text breaks. For a second – how long is an instant? – we are left in our own agony of doubt and anticipation. Dostoevskii uses breaks in the text frequently, but this one, which places the reader in the character's position, is doubtless his most effective.

Thus *suspense*, exaggerated as only Dostoevskii knew how, becomes one way to make us feel the reality of choice – phenomenologically, so to speak. It almost overcomes 'you had to be there', almost puts us there. Having felt that way, can we believe in determinism?

The cloud of possibilities

Dostoevskii's second narrative method demonstrates the untenability of determinism in a way apparently opposite to the first. Since I have described it in detail elsewhere,[4] let me here just offer one example. In *The Devils*, the young and wealthy reprobates of the town visit the mad 'prophet' Semen Iakovlevich. Just as they are leaving, Liza Nikolaevna and Stavrogin appear to jostle each other in the doorway, and the chronicler goes on:

> I fancied they both stood still for an instant and looked, as it were, strangely at one another, but I may not have seen rightly in the crowd. It is asserted, on the contrary, and quite seriously, that Liza, glancing at Nikolai Vsevolodovich [Stavrogin], quickly raised her hand to the level of his face, and would certainly

have struck him if he had not drawn back in time. Perhaps she was displeased with the expression of his face, or the way he smiled, particularly just after such an episode with [her fiancé] Mavrikii Nikolaevich. I must admit I saw nothing myself, but all the others declared they had, though they certainly could not all have seen it in such a crush, though perhaps some may have. I remember, however, that Nikolai Vsevolodovich was rather pale all the way home. (x, 260–1; Pt 2, Ch. 5)

'Perhaps', 'on the contrary', 'I may not have seen rightly', 'I fancied': language like this is irritatingly common in Dostoevskii's narrative. Something may or may not have happened; and if it did (which is by no means certain, though perhaps it could have happened, though many doubt it, but then they are unreliable, though not always mistaken . . .) – if it did happen, it might be part of many sequences, each of which may suggest an endless series of ramifications. In any case, the action that may or may not have happened was itself a non-action, a slap that *could* have been given, but was not. The narrator tries to decide whether Liza meant to slap Stavrogin but did not or, on the contrary, simply did not slap him.

As in so many of such descriptions in Dostoevskii, the point is not what did happen: it is that any of the suggested events *could* have happened. Sometimes Dostoevskii suggests a haze of rumours, each suggesting a possibility that, whether or not it is true, could be. We gradually learn to see time not as a line of single points but as a *field of possibilities*. If the tape were played over again, a different possibility might be realised. Contrary to the determinists or Leibnizians, we live in a world where more than one thing is possible at any moment. Possibilities exceed actualities. Whatever happens, something else might have, and to understand a moment is to grasp that 'something else.' By the same token, each of us is capable of living more lives than one, and to understand a person is to intuit what *else* he or she might have been or done. Dmitrii *might* have been a murderer, and Alesha, we are told, might easily have been a revolutionary.

Such suggestions are also made at the global level. Consider: in *The Devils* we never learn whether Petr Stepanovich killed Fedka; whether the workers rebel; whether this town's group of five is or is not the only one in Russia; whether Petr Stepanovich is in fact a police agent; and, oddly enough, whether he is Stepan Trofimovich's son (he points out that his mother had taken up with a Pole at the time, which Stepan Trofimovich almost confirms). The political significance of the novel obviously depends on several of these suggestions, and the very nature of what has happened depends on all of them. The suggestion of 'another father' threatens the entire fathers-and-sons theme; which is also the case in *The Brothers Karamazov*, when we are offered the tantalising possibility, unlikely but never refuted, that not Fedor

Pavlovich but an escaped convict named Karp might just be Smerdiakov's father. No, time is not linear, we can do many different things, and the world could easily have been different.

Processual intentionality

But is it really possible that, if the tape were played over, we might behave differently, even with the very same influences working on us? Could the same set of causes produce varying results? If it could, determinism would be refuted, and the whole idea of a social 'science' – whether of the mind, of history or of morals – would go down the drain.

To prove this contention, so contrary to the main tradition of European philosophy from Leibniz on, Dostoevskii turns to his strong suit, psychology. He examines the nature of intention, so intimately related to that of free choice. In the May 1876 *Diary of a Writer*, Dostoevskii reports on the trial of a woman, Kairova, accused of attempted murder. Attempted murder, like an attempted slap, concerns what *might* have happened. Is it one and only one thing? Kairova discovered that her lover was asleep with his wife, Velikanova, in Kairova's own bed, procured a razor, and attacked the wife; but the couple awoke and prevented the attack from going further. If the couple had not awoken, would she have killed Velikanova? Was that 'her purpose' in slashing her, as the prosecution contends? For Dostoevskii, the question presumes that an action necessarily depends on a prior, fully formed intention: then, if no obstacle intervenes, the intention is carried out. That, by the way, was John Locke's description: we may change our will many times, but our actions follow from the 'last determination' of the will. In some cases, that is true, Dostoevskii argues, but in others it is sheer, linear nonsense.

Kairova may not have formed an intention at the outset. She was angry, murderously angry, and purchased a razor, but with what precise purpose she had not determined – just as, in *The Brothers Karamazov*, Dmitrii seizes a pestle without yet knowing what he will do with it, if anything:

> Most likely she hadn't the slightest idea of this even when sitting on the steps with the razor in her hand, while just behind her, on her own bed, lay her lover and her rival. No one, no one in the world could have the slightest idea of this. Moreover, even though it may seem absurd, I can state that even when she had begun slashing her rival, she might *still not have known* whether she wanted to kill her or not and whether *this was her purpose* in slashing her.   (XXIII, 9)

The jury has been asked to decide whether 'this' – that is, murder – 'was her purpose', her intention; but according to Dostoevskii she had no formed intention. Her intention was not a thing, but a process: evolving moment by moment, always entertaining several possibilities and looking for others, changing in response to things outside and to its own development, and always capable of moving in different directions. Nor can it be said that Kairova was acting unconsciously: no, she was in fact intensely aware of what she was doing at each moment. But she was never sure what she would do the next moment. Unlike the intentionality assumed by the prosecutor, and defended by Locke, this kind of intention exists in open time. It is not already *over* and merely being carried out. The actions Kairova takes are part of the process, not just the result of it.

If Kairova had not been restrained, she might have done many things. Perhaps she would have simply passed the razor over Velikanova's throat 'and then cried out, shuddered, and run off as fast as she could'. Or she might have turned the razor on herself. Or – this is Dostoevskii we are reading – she might have become enraged 'and not only murdered Velikanova but even begun to abuse the body, cutting off the head, the nose, the lips; and only later, suddenly, when someone took that head away from her, realised what she had done' (XXIII, 10).

Dostoevskii's 'perhaps' and his list of possibilities express not our lack of knowledge of what *would* have happened – as if only a single thing could and we simply must guess what it is – as the prosecutor assumed. No, this 'perhaps' is genuine: any of these very different things 'could have happened and been done by the very same woman and sprung from the very same soul, in the very same mood and under the very same circumstances'. Play the tape over, get a different ending. Identical situations leading to different outcomes: this is precisely what the determinist world-view denies and the belief in open time affirms. Human intention need not be linear.

Narratology is theology

If human intentions are not linear, if time is open, and if the possibilities for each moment are more than one, then the traditional forms of narrative must be regarded as seriously wanting. For, with very few exceptions, they create a sense of time in which one and only one thing is possible at any given moment. In determinism, the only thing possible is the actual; but in a world of open time, there is always (as Bakhtin might have said) *a surplus of possibilities*. Structure tacitly favours the determinists; we derive a pleasing sense of inevitability, a fatalism of form. (This is what I understand Bakhtin to mean when he speaks of 'aesthetic necessity'.)

The 'rightness' of an ending depends on our sense that, yes, it had to happen in just that way. As the author paraphrases the hero of *The Double* in its concluding line, 'Alas! For a long while he had been haunted by a presentiment of this' (I, 229). And for all the Underground Man's attempt to prove his freedom, the very structure of the whole indicates that the dynamics of this very attempt are governed by laws. The fatalism of form is isomorphic with the determinism of action. Thus, the words of the 'editor', voicing the implications of the form, carry a heavy irony: 'The author of these "Notes" and the notes themselves are of course imaginary. Nevertheless, such persons as the writer of these notes not only may, but positively must, exist in our society, considering those circumstances under which society was in general formed' (v, 99; Pt I, Sec. I). It would seem that the hero's very revolt against determinism was inevitable; and we are left to imagine his sense of insult should he read this commentary.

Why should structure create a sense of inevitability? Why is there, so to speak, a 'bias of the artefact' towards inevitability and closed time? The answer, I think, lies in the very idea of structure, as it has governed most theory and practice at least since Aristotle. Behind Aristotle's idea that action must be a unity, and that episodic plots are therefore the worst, lies the belief that in a well-constructed story actions should all tend to a single result, which we feel to be the inevitable outcome of what came before. No ending but what happens was ever possible; events that seem to tend elsewhere ironically contribute to the ending that does take place. Otherwise, the work would lack a satisfying sense of what we have come to call closure. Closure and structure are twin concepts, and where one is weak, so is the other.

Consider how, in approaching the end of a novel, we mentally pair off all the unmarried young males and females and guess how things will work out. In life, we do not assume that there is a moment at which all pairings will take place, but in novels and plays double or triple weddings, and simultaneous resolutions of conflicts, are surprisingly common. Or rather, unsurprisingly common, because we know that there is a structure, which is producing this result. Our confidence in such prediction is dependent on our awareness that a skilled author will have designed a satisfying structure in just this way. It is based primarily not on events in the depicted world but on the structuring activity that has made it.

Structure in literature makes time symmetrical, as it is not in life. In life, events are caused by prior events, but in novels, they are caused both by prior and by subsequent ones – by the end to which they are tending. Every reader knows to look for tacit or explicit foreshadowing – the backward causation effected by the pre-given end. When the reader identifies solely with characters, he or she appreciates time as open and identifies with hope and fear: Oh, Oedipus, do not say that! But when a reader stands back to contemplate the whole, hope and fear diminish as he contemplates the perfect pattern. The moral concomitant of structure is stoicism. It is certainly no accident that religious consolation, and the comfort provided by prophetic theories of history, so often take the form of a divine or quasi-divine story, guided to a providential end. We are invited to contemplate the structure of time, the over-arching design that justifies all. In surrendering to such a view from outside, we anticipate the structure of time as a whole. In effect, we see the world not only as characters in it but also (we suppose) as readers outside it, readers of the historical novel that is life. Evil then becomes, like an Aristotelian peripety, a step that, ironically, leads to the predestined end it tries to thwart. The moment in Book III of *Paradise Lost*, when God describes the pattern of history and views Satan rushing off to de-rail a plan he is in fact fulfilling, joins both the theological and the narratological point. We view the author of the poem and the Author of All, together, describing not only what will happen, but what has really already happened, happened outside of time. And when Ivan Karamazov rejects all such theories on moral grounds, he insists both on the presentness of suffering that no larger story can justify and on the falsity of all narrative consolations. 'I want to stick to the fact', he repeats: the fact, not the story; the moment in its presentness not as part of a larger design. Narratology is theology.

Roulette

Narrative structure was therefore deeply disturbing to Dostoevskii, and he sought yet another way around it. He tried to find a literary form that would not implicitly endorse the wrong theology and the wrong view of life. In short, he needed to find an alternative to structure. He attempted several experiments at a work coherent enough to read but lacking an over-arching standpoint. He needed to dispense with a time outside of time and find a story in which there would be no equivalent to either Milton's God or Milton.

His idea was this: what if the author did not plan the work in advance, but instead created rich situations and let the work proceed as it would? – something I have referred to elsewhere as 'algorithmic' creation or as 'creation by potential'.[5] Would that not be closer to life? Would such a method not refuse both the consolation and the threat to freedom implicit in an over-arching design?

In that case, the intentionality responsible for the work would resemble Kairova's: it would be evolving, bit by bit. Like the God of the Hebrew Bible but not of the theologians, it would manifest a succession of wills. At every moment the author would know what he was doing, but not what he was going to do. He would be guided not by a single design but by an evolving set of possibilities, not by a drive towards closure but by an intense focus on the opportunities of the present moment. In such a work, there could never be an ending, if by an ending we mean a point at which all loose ends are tied up and the pattern governing the whole is revealed. For there *is* no pattern governing the whole, and while some conflicts might be resolved, others would remain: as in life. Recall, for instance, how much is left unresolved in *The Devils*. The first work in which Dostoevskii tried out his new method was *The Idiot*; but he developed the technique further in *The Devils* and, in most extreme form, in the *Diary of a Writer*. *The Brothers Karamazov* manages to combine structure and process in a unique and remarkably satisfying synthesis.

In creating his new processual form, Dostoevskii exploited a number of opportunities. To begin with, he discovered in his very frenetic and desperate style of working an opportunity. He made a virtue of circumstance. To recall the conditions of composition: Dostoevskii and his new wife went abroad in 1867 because he thought that the journey might ameliorate his epileptic seizures and to escape from his creditors. In dire poverty, the couple pawned their wedding rings, the presents he had given her, and (many times) clothing. Special poignancy characterises the letters in which he describes having sold their linen. The author suffered one of his seizures while his wife was in labour, and when the baby Sonia died, he blamed himself. He tried to win at roulette and, as always, lost. In these circumstances, he absolutely had to produce a novel, but insisted that he would not cheapen his work – 'worst of all I fear mediocrity'.[6] Yet had no time for careful planning.

He began writing the novel in August 1867 and produced several outlines and plans, which bear almost no relation to the work as we know it, except that a character resembling Nastasia Filippovna appears and the hero is both an expert in calligraphy and called 'the idiot'. He is not at all like Prince Myshkin. Dissatisfied with what he had achieved, and rushing to submit *something* for publication, Dostoevskii hit on a new approach, which he liked enough to send in an opening with no idea how the novel would develop. 'I turned things over in my mind from 4 December to 18 December', he wrote to his friend Maikov on 31 December. 'I would say that on the average I came up with six plans a day (at least that). My head was in a whirl. It's a wonder I did not go out of my mind. At last, on 18 December, I sat down and started writing a novel' (XXVIII/2, 240). The 'idea' of this novel, he explained further, 'used to flash through my mind in a somewhat artistic form, but only *somewhat*, not in the full-blown form that was needed. It was only the desperate situation in which I found myself that made me embark upon an idea that had not yet reached full maturity. I took a chance, as at roulette: "Maybe it will develop as I write it!" This is unforgivable' (XXVIII/2, 240–1). Writing like roulette: a great deal was at stake, and the outcome was left in great measure to chance, to what one could not predict. Could the necessity of writing that way be turned to advantage?

The other *Idiots*

Even the most cursory reading of the novel makes the lack of an overall plan apparent. It is filled with loose ends, inconsistencies, sudden eruptions of new ideas that have not been prepared for but which seem to have occurred on the spur of the moment – as, indeed, they usually did. *The Idiot* may stand as the opposite of *Bleak House*, with its amazingly complicated plotting in which the fates of many dozens of characters and incidents are resolved into an overall pattern. As Dickens is the greatest designer of plots in the history of the novel, Dostoevskii is the greatest improviser. If *Bleak House* cannot be read without being aware of an overall plan (for Dickens, the analogue of Providence), *The Idiot* cannot be read without sensing a succession of wills, an author tinkering with his material with no idea – or with many changing ideas – where he is going. He makes a lot of mistakes, of course, but that only makes the flashes of inspiration, at which readers are virtually present, all the more compelling. The heroic efforts of the best scholars to explain this effect away, to deny mistakes and discover structure, only testify to its pervading presence.[7]

There are notable inconsistencies. In Part 1, Myshkin appears childlike and he himself comments on this quality, but in Part 2, when Lebedev tries to deceive him, Myshkin remarks: 'You take me for a child, Lebedev' and, as with the young nihilists, shows some remarkable worldly wisdom. On the other hand, Part 1 gives no hint that Myshkin is an epileptic. So marked are these and other changes that Joseph Frank observes, with considerable justice, that Part 1 'perhaps may best be read as an independent novella' (Frank, *The Miraculous Years*, p. 325).

In Part 1 of the novel, Gania is a major character, and everything points to a major future conflict between him and Myshkin. No less than three times he calls the Prince ominously, and eponymously, 'an idiot'; and Gania swears that they will be either great friends or great enemies. They turn out to be neither. In Part 2 Gania has somehow become a sort of private secretary to the idiot, and thereafter he plays almost no role at all. Gania's is but one of many aborted plot lines, too many to list here. Some seem to be plants or, perhaps, what I like to call hats. They suggest a future complication or revelation, to which the author can turn whenever he has run out of ideas: they are hats out of which he can pull a needed rabbit. But many of these hats remain on the rack. Myshkin tells us that his father died in prison, and he would like to know why: but his father's imprisonment is never explained.

The reader senses that, had Dostoevskii needed some secret from the idiot's past, he would have invented a story to suit. In the same way, we learn that, in addition to Myshkin's guardian Pavlishchev, there is 'another Pavlishchev' – surely a plot nugget – but as Myshkin's father dies in a physical prison, this shadowy figure languishes in a narratological one, never to see the light of storytelling day. I picture a storytelling Bastille from which all such figures (and there are many) long to escape but never do. Yet the text records their existence, as if they had made their marks on the wall. The most noticeable 'hat' in this novel is the six-month hiatus between Parts 1 and 2, which turns out to have all sorts of incidents that come in handy to 'explain' some new plot line that has evidently just occurred to the author; a sort of *interim ex machina*. In *The Devils*, the characters' time in 'Switzerland' before the novel begins plays a similar role.

The novel's sensational ending, the murder of Nastasia Filippovna and Myshkin's insane night with Rogozhin by the corpse, has seemed to some readers as fully foreshadowed by earlier events. The opening is there because the conclusion is there. After all in the opening scene of the novel, Myshkin and Rogozhin meet on a train and the author observes: 'If they had both known what was remarkable in one another at that moment, they would have been surprised at the chance which had so strangely brought them together' (VIII, 5). Is this not a case of foreshadowing? To argue in this way is to commit what Tolstoi referred to as the 'fallacy of retrospection'.[8] After the fact, we look for, and inevitably discover, some tendency leading to the outcome that we know happened, and see in it the sign of the later event. And since there are always signs leading in every direction, it is not difficult to find one pointing in the desired direction. The method is well known to fortune-tellers, astrologers and economists.

The way to see whether there is genuine foreshadowing or only a 'retrospection' is to examine whether, if something else had happened, one could have found equally strong signs presaging that event. In this case, the answer is obvious: if the final conflict had been between Myshkin and Gania, whether over Nastasia Filippovna or Aglaia, surely Gania's threats in Part 1 would have been seen as an even more powerful case of 'foreshadowing'. What is really happening is that Dostoevskii, here as in *The Devils*, creates a sense of mystery whenever he has the chance. Then he can exploit the mystery or not as occasion dictates. These mysteries are as mysterious to the author as they are to the readers; that is, they are *real* mysteries, not a mere device.

If the test I have proposed fails to convince, consider the evidence of the notebooks. As scholars have repeatedly noted, the ending that the believers in structure find foreshadowed in the novel's opening scene did not even occur

GARY SAUL MORSON

to the author until he was writing Part 3 (of four). Even after that, right up through Part Four, Dostoevskii continued to explore other possibilities. He does not appear to have definitively chosen Nastasia Filippovna's murder any sooner than Rogozhin. Like Kairova's, Dostoevskii's intention was continually in process, and the notebook shows him repeatedly exploring multiple possible developments ('six plots a day').

As we read the notebooks for Parts 2 and 3, we may be amazed that, for the author, this plot was so open. In some versions Nastasia Filippovna commits suicide, in others dies a natural death. Aglaia either goes off with Rogozhin or marries Gania out of spite or murders Nastasia Filippovna or is saved by Myshkin. Myshkin falls in love with Adelaida, Nastasia Filippovna seduces Radomskii, and Ippolit kills someone. And so on. 'N.B. Should the novel end with a confession? Publish it openly'; 'Aglaia marries the Prince – or else the Prince dies'; 'Again orgies'.[9] To paraphrase the Kairova article, all these actions could have been taken by the very same people in the same initial circumstances. Time is radically open in *The Idiot*. There is no structure, there are only impulse, possibilities, experimentation – and process.

At some point in his writing, Dostoevskii evidently realised that time and process were in fact his central themes. The book, he discovered, was about the implications of how it was written. In Part 3, Ippolit, until then a minor character, delivers a forty-page confession that has just about no relevance to the plot. In any structuralist's abridgement, in any version of *The Idiot Rewritten by Henry James* (as Robert Graves 'improved' *David Copperfield*), this whole passage would have to be left out. And yet it is justly regarded as the novel's high point. It contains the lines that best express its self-referential theme of an open process:

> Oh, you may be sure that Columbus was happy not when he had discovered [*otkryl*] America but while he was discovering [*otkryval*] it. Take my word for it, the highest moment of his happiness was just three days before the discovery of the New World, when the mutinous crew were on the point of returning to Europe in despair. It wasn't the New World that mattered, even if it had fallen to pieces. [...] It's life that matters, nothing but life – the process of discovering, the everlasting and perpetual process, not the discovery itself at all. (VIII, 327; Pt 3, Sec. 5)

And we best appreciate *The Idiot* not when we have read it, but while we are reading it. *Otkryl, otkryval* – perfective, imperfective: *The Idiot* cultivates the aesthetics of the imperfective aspect.

In most works, knowledge of the ending allows us to contemplate the structure of the whole and so to understand the work most fully. In this

228

sense, such works are directed not so much at reading as at *re*reading, at the God's-eye view; and even a first reading often becomes an anticipated rereading, as we try to place details into a structure whose outlines we will know but which we now must limn. Or, to translate the point into politics and theology: in a first reading of a structured work, we are like Marxists or Leibnizians, guessing at the pattern of the whole, both experiencing a process and thinking it as a piece of structure. But *The Idiot* is not at all like that, and it tells us not to live like that either. We best understand this work when we are reading, not rereading; when we appreciate moments rich in possibilities and capable of multiple outcomes; and when we experience without thinking away an intense presentness. *The Idiot* is but one of many possible novels that could have arisen from the same material, and that is part of its point. It's life that matters, nothing but life, the everlasting and perpetual process, and not the outcome at all.

Serialisation and suspense

'On this narrow mountain pass in Norway, with sheer cliff rising on one side of me and falling into the fjord on the other, a truck suddenly came around a curve at top speed, occupying the whole road. There was no escape!'
'And did you survive?'

Dostoevskii therefore exploited the serialisation of his works to intensify the sense of presentness and open time. Serialisation is, of course, entirely compatible with structure, as we immediately see with Dickens and Trollope. But it is also understandable that Dostoevskii thought to exploit the dynamics of serialisation as a kind of processual form of publishing. He realised he could use it to signal that he knew no more of the characters' destiny than they did. Their fate was open or, rather, they had no fate. The work's sections were to be understood as tending to no predetermined result, not as the mere unfolding of a plan in several parts. We are not surprised to discover that Dickens's notebooks contain detailed outlines for *Bleak House*, but it would be amazing if anyone should discover such outlines for *The Idiot*. Quite the contrary: the novel's notebooks betray a drama of their own, as the author, no less than his characters, thrashes about to decide what he will do next.

Critics usually cite the real-world, recent crimes on which Dostoevskii drew for details of his novel, but they usually fail to appreciate that the novel responds to and is shaped by events in the press published *after* its opening sections appeared. And in case we miss the point, the characters themselves (Myshkin, Nastasia Filippovna, Kolia and Lebedev) quote from these articles! The repeated references to the Gorskii case, in Part 2 and

GARY SAUL MORSON

after, describe incidents Dostoevskii first encountered in *The Voice* in March 1868, months after the opening chapters were submitted and had appeared. Readers could not help being aware that the novel was responding to events that took place *between* instalments.

To describe the famous Mazurin and Gorskii cases as 'sources' of the novel, while true, misses the most important point. Characters in novels are usually unaware of their sources, and their resemblance to them does not result from conscious imitation. Otherwise every novelistic murderer would be a copycat killer. But Nastasia Filippovna reads about the Mazurin case, in which a man eerily like Rogozhin – both came from merchants' families, lived with their mother, and inherited two million rubles – commits a murder. She wonders if Rogozhin will do the same to her, and, perhaps aware of the story from Nastasia Filippovna herself, Rogozhin does kill her in the Mazurin way, covering her body with oilcloth and dispersing the smell of decay with 'Zhdanov's fluid'. The Gorskii case also inspires characters to react to its ongoing events. Original readers therefore knew that the incidents of this serialised novel cannot have been part of any original plan. The book *had* to be the product of a succession of wills, not a single design. For the author reacts to events beyond his control, much as the characters do.

Indeed, it could almost be said that the author – and I mean the real author, not the narrator or implied author – is another character *in* the novel. He is a chronicler in the real sense, recording events *as* they are happening, not after the fact. Presentness is not a mere literary device, but real – which makes it all the more effective as a device. Usually, suspense in a novel, however intense, is mitigated by our awareness of structure: the hero cannot die when three quarters of the novel remain. When we remember *the fact of artefact*, the sense of immediacy and presentness diminishes. But when the author himself literally does not know what is going to happen, when he must be guided by internal events as he has already written and published them and external ones he cannot control, then we have something more than the usual literary suspense. Unlike the God of Peter Damian, such an author can act only in the present, he cannot change the past to enable a future. We have genuine uncertainty of outcome. That, indeed, may be another secret for the intensity of suspense in Dostoevskii's works. Not just the character, but also the plot, indeed the novel itself, hangs in the balance.

Development itself

Dostoevskii exploited but did not invent many of these devices. His most obvious inspiration was *War and Peace*. Tolstoi's book was still being serialised when Dostoevskii was publishing *The Idiot*, which takes sly glances

230

at Tolstoi. Dostoevskii's previous novel, *Crime and Punishment*, was serialised in the same journal as the early sections of *War and Peace*; at one point, Porfirii Petrovich seems to quote from it. Life is fundamentally unpredictable, the detective explains to Raskolnikov: in thinking you could plan a perfect crime by pure reason, you resemble the unfortunate Austrian General Mack who (in Tolstoi's just-published account) thought he could plan a perfect battle (VI, 263; Pt 4, Sec. 5).

War and Peace was a processual work in the full sense. Like *The Idiot*, it was the product of a succession of wills, not a single will, and as a result lacks foreshadowing, closure and structure. It is deliberately replete with loose ends. Tolstoi made this technique explicit in his draft introductions to the book and in his published essay, 'Some Words about the Book *War and Peace*'. He insisted that his work 'can least of all be called a novel – with a plot that has growing complexity, and a happy or unhappy dénouement, with which interest in the narration ceases' (Tolstoi, *Polnoe sobranie sochinenii*, XIII, 54). What has come to be regarded as the greatest novel ever written denies being one – because a novel, in Tolstoi's view, has what we have come to call structure.

Far from having in mind a conclusion to which all events are tending, or designing an overall structure to which each successive instalment will contribute, Tolstoi insists that 'in printing the beginning of my proposed work I promise neither a continuation or a conclusion for it' (ibid.). Precisely because the work is written so as to lack structure, closure and dénouement, no matter how long it might turn out to be, the author may arbitrarily stop it at any point without damage to the whole. Contrast that with *Edwin Drood*, which lacks an ending only because Dickens did not live to write it: people have been guessing about its predetermined but unknown outcome ever since. Tolstoi stresses that his work could never *be* complete. It cannot *lack* an ending because it would not tolerate one. The work will of course have to be of *some* length, but in principle it could always be longer. Strictly speaking, *War and Peace* is not a very long book but a book of *indeterminate* length.

Tolstoi writes that he may – or may not – guide his characters through a series of 'epochs' (1805, 1807, 1812, 1825, 1856 – needless to say, he never came close to 1856) and watch what happens to them in each. 'I do not foresee the outcome of these [fictional] characters' relationships in even a single one of these epochs' (ibid., 55). He knows their future no more than they do. No part of the work looks forward to, or foreshadows, subsequent parts: 'I strove only so that each part of the work would have an independent interest.' Tolstoi then wrote and struck out the following remarkable words: '... which would consist not in the development of events, but in development [itself]' (ibid.). *War and Peace* not only discusses but also manifests *development itself*, not development toward something: presentness is neither pulled forward to a conclusion nor subservient to an overall structure.

As Dostoevskii extended Tolstoi's method, so Tolstoi evidently borrowed from a number of predecessors who had written works of process. Clearly, he relied on Pushkin's *Eugene Onegin*, which in turn was inspired by Byron's and Sterne's processual experiments, *Don Juan* and *Tristram Shandy*; and these were in turn indebted to some lesser-known precedents, such as Samuel Butler's seventeenth-century mock epic, *Hudibras*. This line of development, and its significance, are usually obscure to modern critics because we have no genuine poetics of process at our disposal, one that does not somehow impose some sort of structure 'by retrospection'.

Such a poetics is urgently needed. For not only do the processual works just mentioned include some of the greatest masterpieces of world literature, but there is also a strong processual element in a number of other works that manage to combine structure and process in a way we cannot even begin to understand without a better grasp of what process involves. A work may have a succession of wills because the author, either gradually or suddenly, alters his plan in response to external circumstances, as Dickens does in *Martin Chuzzlewit*; or he may, after the fact, decide to write a second volume, as with *Don Quixote*; and although it may fairly be said that each novel in Trollope's six-volume Palliser series is governed by a structure, an overall sense of process governs the whole. Indeed, it is easily possible to read the Hebrew Bible not as the rabbis did, as a simultaneous expression in which every part glosses every other, but as a composite work of process. That would have been much more to Dostoevskii's taste.

Freedom

'Development itself': Tolstoi posits the radical unpredictability of the world. No one can foresee the outcome of what Prince Andrei calls 'a hundred million diverse chances that will be decided on the spur of the moment' (*War and Peace*, p. 930). On the spur of the moment: since laws are all illusions, and the world is radically unpredictable, not science but an educated attentiveness pays off best, in battle and in the rest of life. That is why Kutuzov maintains that the best preparation for a battle is not a strategic plan but 'a good night's sleep'. Moreover, each moment possesses countless potential consequences for the next moment, and no one can foresee the consequences of consequences of consequences. There can be no social science, only social pseudo-science.

Tolstoi wavers between two reasons for this unpredictability of the world. Is human freedom one reason for our necessary uncertainty about the future? Sometimes Tolstoi endorses determinism. Unpredictability, he contends, has a quite different source. When Tolstoi argues in this way, he tries to break the traditional link between acceptance of determinism and belief that laws of society, analogous to those of planetary motion, can be discovered. Everything may be determined, but we are in principle forever ignorant of the determining laws, for many reasons. One example must suffice. Moral Newtonians assume that, in history as in the solar system, countless phenomena can be reduced to a few laws; but it is entirely possible – indeed, likely – that in history (which, after all, includes everything that happens) there are as many laws as there are phenomena. If so, then even if we could know the laws, our knowledge would do us no good. We may as well act as if there were no laws.

In other passages, Tolstoi does allow for human freedom: determinism, he writes, comes in degrees and binds the more strongly the higher one is in the chain of power and authority. Napoleon has no freedom, but Rostov does, and Lavrushka still more. In that case, there is a second reason for unpredictability. *War and Peace* alternates between these two positions in an unresolved dialogue. In either case, any narrative form that shows an overall structure will misrepresent reality.

Dostoevskii, by contrast, accepted both reasons for unpredictability. Ippolit enunciates the first reason when he explains: 'You know, it's a matter of a whole lifetime, an infinite multitude of ramifications hidden from us. The most skilful chess-player, the cleverest of them, can only look a few moves ahead [...] how can you tell what part you may have in the future determination of the destinies of humanity?' (VIII, 336; Pt 3, Sec. 6). In *The Brothers Karamazov*, Zosima echoes this view and makes it the basis of a prosaic theory of morality focussed on goodness in the present, not a foreseeable utilitarian outcome: cast a little bread upon the waters.

But Dostoevskii also believed in free will. Play the tape over, and something else might result. The future is unpredictable not only because of innumerable causal factors but also because the past does not wholly determine the present. It shapes, but does not make, our choices. That is why it was crucial to him not to close down time with structure, but to exploit the techniques of process literature to dramatise human freedom. Choice has weight, presentness matters, and to understand an event you must grasp the 'something else' that could have happened. You must not look back at the result and imagine that it was inevitable: you must immerse yourself in the moment in all its intensity. You have to be there.

Notes

Translations from Dostoevskii's novels are based on the Constance Garnett versions, tacitly amended by comparison with the Russian text. Translations from the *Diary of a Writer* are from Fyodor Dostoevsky, *A Writer's Diary: A Monthly Publication,* trans. Kenneth Lantz, Vol. 1 (Evanston: Northwestern University Press, 1993).

1 Lewis Carroll, *Through the Looking Glass and What Alice Found There* in *The Complete Works of Lewis Carroll* (New York: Modern Library, n.d.), pp. 189–90.
2 Elie Halévy, *The Growth of Philosophic Radicalism,* trans. Mary Morris (Boston: Beacon, 1955).
3 John Milton, *Paradise Lost* in Merritt Y. Hughes (ed.), *Complete Poems and Prose* (New York: Odyssey, 1957), pp. 260–1 (Book III, lines 95–122).
4 In Gary Saul Morson, *Narrative and Freedom: The Shadows of Time* (New Haven: Yale University Press, 1994), Chapter 4 ('Sideshadowing').
5 See Morson, *The Boundaries of Genre: Dostoevsky's 'Diary of a Writer' and the Traditions of Literary Utopia* (Austin: University of Texas Press, 1981); and *Hidden in Plain View: Narrative and Creative Potentials in 'War and Peace'* (Stanford University Press, 1987).
6 As cited in Joseph Frank, *Dostoevsky: The Miraculous Years, 1865–1871* (Princeton University Press, 1995), p. 245.
7 See, for example, Robin Feuer Miller, *Dostoevsky and 'The Idiot': Author, Narrator, and Reader* (Cambridge, Mass.: Harvard University Press, 1981).
8 Leo Tolstoy, *War and Peace,* trans. Ann Dunnigan (New York: Signet, 1968), p. 854. Translations from *War and Peace* are tacitly corrected by comparison with the Jubilee edition of his works: V. G. Chertkov *et al.* (eds.), *Polnoe sobranie sochinenii* (Moscow: Khudozhestvennaia literatura, 1929–58). Further references to *War and Peace* in the text are to this translation.
9 Edward Wasiolek (ed.), *Fyodor Dostoevsky: The Notebooks for 'The Idiot',* trans. Katherine Strelsky (Chicago: University of Chicago Press, 1968), pp. 170, 177, 208. See also Wasiolek's introductions to the volume and its specific sections.

GUIDE TO FURTHER READING

It is impossible to do justice to the richness of critical interpretation of Dostoevskii and his works in a bibliography of this size. Consequently the listing that follows confines itself to books, predominantly but not exclusively in English, which the Editor feels will permit the student to take further any interest stimulated by the present volume. For a more complete annotated bibliography, as well as a guide to other bibliographic sources, see W. J. Leatherbarrow, *Fedor Dostoevsky: A Reference Guide*, cited below.

Anderson, Roger B. *Dostoevsky: Myths of Duality*. Gainesville: University of Florida Press, 1986.

Bakhtin, M. M. *Problems of Dostoevsky's Poetics*, ed. and trans. Caryl Emerson. Manchester University Press, 1984.

Belknap, Robert. *The Genesis of 'The Brothers Karamazov': The Aesthetics, Ideology, and Psychology of Making a Text*. Evanston: Northwestern University Press, 1990.

   The Structure of 'The Brothers Karamazov'. The Hague: Mouton, 1967.

Bem, A. L. (ed.). *Dostoevskii: Psikhoanaliticheskie etiudy*. Berlin: Petropolis, 1938.

Berdyaev, Nicholas. *Dostoevsky*, trans. Donald Attwater. New York: New American Library, 1974.

Busch, R. L. *Humor in the Major Novels of Dostoevsky*. Columbus, Ohio: Slavica, 1987.

Catteau, Jacques. *Dostoyevsky and the Process of Literary Creation*, trans. Audrey Littlewood. Cambridge University Press, 1989.

Chapple, Richard A. *A Dostoevsky Dictionary*. Ann Arbor: Ardis, 1983.

Dalton, Elizabeth. *Unconscious Structure in 'The Idiot': A Study in Literature and Psychoanalysis*. Princeton University Press, 1979.

Dolinin, A. S. *Poslednie romany Dostoevskogo: Kak sozdavalis' 'Podrostok' i 'Brat'ia Karamazovy'* [Dostoevsky's Last Novels: How *A Raw Youth* and *The Brothers Karamazov* Were Created]. Moscow and Leningrad: Sovetskii pisatel', 1963.

Dolinin, A. S. (ed.). *F. M. Dostoevskii v vospominaniiakh sovremennikov* [F. M. Dostoevsky in the Recollections of His Contemporaries], 2 vols. Moscow: Khudozhestvennaia literatura, 1964.

Dostoevskaia, A. G. *Vospominaniia* [Memoirs]. Moscow: Khudozhestvennaia literatura, 1971.

Dowler, Wayne. *Dostoevsky, Grigor'ev, and Native-Soil Conservatism.* Toronto: University of Toronto Press, 1982.

Fanger, Donald. *Dostoevsky and Romantic Realism: A Study of Dostoevsky in Relation to Balzac, Dickens and Gogol.* Cambridge, Mass.: Harvard University Press, 1965.

Frank, Joseph. *Dostoevsky: The Seeds of Revolt, 1821–1849.* Princeton University Press, 1976.

Dostoevsky: The Years of Ordeal, 1850–1859. Princeton University Press, 1983.

Dostoevsky: The Stir of Liberation, 1860–1865. Princeton University Press, 1986.

Dostoevsky: The Miraculous Years, 1865–1871. Princeton University Press, 1995.

Gerigk, H. J. (ed.). *Die Brüder Karamasow.* Dresden University Press, 1997.

Gibson, A. Boyce. *The Religion of Dostoevsky.* London: SCM Press, 1973.

Grossman, Leonid. *Dostoevsky,* trans. Mary Mackler. London: Allen Lane, 1974.

Holquist, J. M. *Dostoevsky and the Novel.* Princeton University Press, 1977.

Ivanov, Vyacheslav. *Freedom and the Tragic Life: A Study in Dostoevsky,* trans. Norman Cameron. Wolfeboro, N.H.: Longwood Academic, 1989.

Jackson, Robert Louis. *The Art of Dostoevsky: Deliriums and Nocturnes.* Princeton University Press, 1981.

Dialogues with Dostoevsky: The Overwhelming Questions. Stanford University Press, 1993.

Dostoevsky's Quest for Form: A Study of His Philosophy of Art. Bloomington: Physsardt, 1978.

Jackson, Robert Louis (ed.). *Dostoevsky: New Perspectives.* Englewood Cliffs, N.J.: Prentice Hall, 1984.

Twentieth-Century Interpretations of 'Crime and Punishment': A Collection of Critical Essays. Englewood Cliffs, N.J.: Prentice Hall, 1974.

Jones, John. *Dostoevsky.* Oxford: Clarendon Press, 1983.

Jones, Malcolm V. *Dostoyevsky after Bakhtin: Readings in Dostoyevsky's Fantastic Realism.* Cambridge University Press, 1990.

Dostoyevsky: The Novel of Discord. London: Elek, 1976.

Jones, Malcolm V. and Terry, G. M. (eds.). *New Essays on Dostoyevsky.* Cambridge University Press, 1983.

de Jonge, A. *Dostoevsky and the Age of Intensity.* London: Secker & Warburg, 1975.

Kjetsaa, Geir. *Dostoevsky and His New Testament.* Atlantic Highlands, N.J.: Humanities Press, 1984.

Fyodor Dostoevsky: A Writer's Life. London: Macmillan, 1988.

Knapp, Liza. *The Annihilation of Inertia: Dostoevsky and Metaphysics.* Evanston: Northwestern University Press, 1996.

Kravchenko, Maria. *Dostoevsky and the Psychologists.* Amsterdam: Adolf M. Hekkert, 1978.

Leatherbarrow, W. J. *Dostoyevsky: The Brothers Karamazov.* Cambridge University Press, 1992.

Fedor Dostoevsky. Boston: Twayne, 1981.

Fedor Dostoevsky: A Reference Guide. Boston: G.K. Hall, 1990.

Leatherbarrow, W. J. (ed.). *Dostoevskii and Britain.* Oxford and Providence: Berg, 1995.

Dostoevsky's 'The Devils': A Critical Companion. Evanston: Northwestern University Press, 1999.

Linnér, Sven. *Dostoevskij on Realism*. Stockholm: Almqvist and Wiksell, 1962.
   Starets Zosima in 'The Brothers Karamazov': A Study in the Mimesis of Virtue. Stockholm: Almqvist and Wiksell, 1975.
Malia, Martin. 'What is the intelligentsia?' in Richard Pipes (ed.), *The Russian Intelligentsia*. New York: Columbia University Press, 1961, pp. 1–18.
Martinsen, Deborah A. (ed.). *Literary Journals in Imperial Russia*. Cambridge University Press, 1997.
Matlaw, Ralph. *'The Brothers Karamazov': Novelistic Technique*. The Hague: Mouton, 1967.
Meynieux, André. *La Littérature et le métier d'écrivain en Russie avant Pouchkine*. Paris: Librairie des cinq continents, 1966.
   Pouchkine homme de lettres et la littérature professionnelle en Russie. Paris: Librairie des cinq continents, 1966.
Mikhniukhevich, V. A. *Russkii fol'klor v khudozhestvennoi sisteme Dostoevskogo*. Cheliabinsk: Cheliabinsk State University Press, 1994.
Miller, Robin Feuer. *'The Brothers Karamazov': Worlds of the Novel*. Boston: Twayne, 1992.
   Dostoevsky and 'The Idiot'. Author, Narrator, and Reader. Cambridge, Mass.: Harvard University Press, 1981.
Mochulsky, Konstantin. *Dostoevsky: His Life and Work*, trans. M. Minihan. Princeton University Press, 1967.
Morson, Gary Saul. *The Boundaries of Genre: Dostoevsky's 'Diary of a Writer' and the Traditions of Literary Utopia*. Austin: University of Texas Press, 1981.
   Narrative and Freedom: The Shadows of Time. New Haven: Yale University Press, 1994.
Murav, Harriet. *Holy Foolishness: Dostoevsky's Novels and the Poetics of Cultural Critique*. Stanford University Press, 1992.
Nechaeva, V. S. *Zhurnal M. M. i F. M. Dostoevskikh 'Vremia' 1861–1863* [The Dostoevskii Brothers' Journal *Time* 1861–3]. Moscow: Nauka, 1972.
   Zhurnal M. M. i F. M. Dostoevskikh 'Epokha' 1864–1865 [The Dostoevskii Brothers' Journal *Epoch* 1864–5]. Moscow: Nauka, 1975.
Paperno, Irina. *Chernyshevsky and the Age of Realism: A Study in the Semiotics of Behavior*. Stanford University Press, 1988.
Pattison, George and Thompson, Diane Oenning (eds.), *Dostoevsky and the Christian Tradition*. Cambridge University Press, 2001.
Peace, Richard. *Dostoyevsky: An Examination of the Major Novels*. Cambridge University Press, 1971.
Perlina, Nina. *Varieties of Poetic Utterance: Quotation in 'The Brothers Karamazov'*. Lanham: University Press of America, 1985.
Pipes, Richard (ed.). *The Russian Intelligentsia*. New York: Columbia University Press, 1961.
Rice, James L. *Dostoevsky and the Healing Art: An Essay in Literary and Medical History*. Ann Arbor: Ardis, 1985.
Rosenshield, Gary. *'Crime and Punishment': Techniques of the Omniscient Author*. Lisse: Peter de Ridder, 1978.
Ruud, Charles A. *Fighting Words: Imperial Censorship and the Russian Press, 1804–1906*. Toronto: University of Toronto Press, 1982.

Sandoz, Ellis. *Political Apocalypse: A Study of Dostoevsky's Grand Inquisitor*. Baton Rouge: Louisiana State University Press, 1971.

Slattery, D. P. *'The Idiot': Dostoevsky's Fantastic Prince. A Phenomenological Approach*. Berne and New York: Lang, 1983.

Steiner, George. *Tolstoy or Dostoevsky? An Essay in the Old Criticism*. London: Faber, 1959.

Stites, Richard. *The Women's Liberation Movement in Russia: Feminism, Nihilism, and Bolshevism 1860–1930*. Princeton University Press, 1978.

Straus, Nina Pelikan. *Dostoevsky and the Woman Question: Rereadings at the End of a Century*. New York: St Martin's Press, 1994.

Sutherland, Stewart R. *Atheism and the Rejection of God: Contemporary Philosophy and 'The Brothers Karamazov'*. Oxford: Blackwell, 1977.

Terras, Victor. *The Idiot: An Interpretation*. Boston: Twayne, 1990.

  A Karamazov Companion: Commentary on the Genesis, Language and Style of Dostoevsky's Novel. Madison: University of Wisconsin Press, 1981.

  Reading Dostoevsky. Madison: University of Wisconsin Press, 1998.

  The Young Dostoevskij (1846–1849): A Critical Study. The Hague: Mouton, 1969.

Thompson, Diane Oenning. *'The Brothers Karamazov' and the Poetics of Memory*. Cambridge University Press, 1991.

Vetlovskaia, V. E. *Poetika romana 'Brat'ia Karamazovy'* [The Poetics of *The Brothers Karamazov*]. Leningrad: Nauka, 1977.

Vladiv, S. V. *Narrative Principles in Dostoevskij's 'Besy': A Structural Analysis*. Berne, Frankfurt and Las Vegas: Peter Lang, 1979.

Volgin, I. L. *Poslednii god Dostoevskogo* [Dostoevskii's Final Year]. Moscow: Sovetskii pisatel', 1986.

Ward, Bruce K. *Dostoyevsky's Critique of the West: The Quest for Earthly Paradise*. Waterloo, Ontario: Wilfried Laurier University Press, 1986.

Wasiolek, Edward. *Dostoevsky: The Major Fiction*. Cambridge, Mass.: MIT Press, 1964.

Wasiolek, Edward (ed.). *Fyodor Dostoevsky: The Notebooks for 'The Brothers Karamazov'*, trans. Victor Terras. Chicago University Press, 1971.

  Fyodor Dostoevsky: The Notebooks for 'Crime and Punishment', trans. Edward Wasiolek. Chicago University Press, 1967.

  Fyodor Dostoevsky: The Notebooks for 'The Idiot', trans. Katherine Strelsky. Chicago University Press, 1967.

  Fyodor Dostoevsky: The Notebooks for 'The Possessed', trans. Victor Terras. Chicago University Press, 1968.

  Fyodor Dostoevsky: The Notebooks for 'A Raw Youth', trans. Victor Terras. Chicago University Press, 1969.

INDEX

Note: Works are listed under author's name.

Aksakov, I. S., 117
Aleksandrov, M. A., 90
Alexis, Man of God (Orthodox saint), 31, 44
Annenkov, P. V., 78, 121
 Letters from Abroad, 121
 Parisian Letters, 121
Aristotle, 223–4
Augustine, St, 215–16

Bakhtin, M. M., 3, 40–1, 46, 137, 145,
 172, 193, 197, 199, 210, 211,
 217–18, 222
Balzac, H. de, 12, 13, 67, 71, 73, 136, 138,
 152
 Eugénie Grandet, 13, 67, 72
 Le Père Goriot, 71
Baring, M., 112
Batiushkov, K. N., 67, 76
Bayley, J., 60, 65
Belinskii, V. G., 3, 4, 48, 55, 58, 70, 71,
 73–4, 75, 76, 91, 113, 114, 152–3,
 169, 173
Belknap, R., 17, 80, 92
Berlin, I., 114, 130
Bernard, C., 132, 206
Bitov, A. G., 19
 Pushkin House, 19
Boborykin, P. D., 112
Børtnes, J., 204, 211
Botkin, V. P., 121, 169
 Letters from Spain, 121
Büchner, L., 119
Bulgarin, F. V., 67, 69, 78
Butler, S., 232
 Hudibras, 232
Byron, G. G. (Lord), 232

Cabet, E., 127
Camus, A., 1, 19, 149
carnival, 40–1
Carroll, L., 212–13, 234
Carus, C. G., 134, 156
Catteau, J., 110, 157, 173
censorship, 69, 141, 201
Cervantes, M., 163, 165, 213, 232
 Don Quixote, 163, 165, 213, 232
Chaadaev, P. Ia., 113, 129
Charcot, J.-M., 134
Chateaubriand, F.-R., Comte de, 47, 71
Chernyshevskii, N. G., 15, 17, 78, 79, 80,
 81, 113, 114, 117, 118–20, 126–8, 129,
 130, 134–5, 177, 200
 Aesthetic Relations of Art to Reality, The,
 118
 What Is to Be Done?, 81, 129, 134–5,
 178, 200
Chicherin, B. N., 115
Christa, B., 13, 18
Citizen, The (periodical), 16, 87, 88
Confino, M., 129
Considérant, V., 127
Constant, B., 71
Contemporary, The (periodical), 74, 75,
 76, 80, 116, 117, 121
Corneille, P., 12
Cox, R., 162, 170, 173
Crews, F., 188, 190

Darwin, C., 16, 161, 194, 195, 202
 Origin of Species, 16
Dawn (periodical), 86
Day (periodical), 116
Deed, The (periodical), 80

239

Hübner, J., 150
Hugo, V., 12, 71, 138, 142, 151, 163, 172
Huxley, A., 210
  Brave New World, 210

Ianovskii, S. D., 153
Ivanits, L., 33, 35, 36, 37, 45

Jones, J., 50, 51, 56, 65
Jones, M. V., 14–15, 20, 58, 65, 173, 174
Jonge, A. de, 1, 19
Joyce, J., 4

Kant, I., 156
Karamzin, N. M., 67, 69, 71, 121
  Letters of a Russian Traveller, 121
Katkov, M. N., 77, 81, 83–4, 85, 86,
  87, 90
Kavelin, K. D., 113
Kelly, C., 46
Khomiakov, A. S., 113
Kireevskii, I. V., 114
Kjetsaa, G., 155, 158, 161, 162, 173
Koreisha, I. Ia., 39
Korvin-Krukovskaia, A. V., 133
Kovalevskaia, S. V., 133, 147, 156
Kovalevskii, E. P., 78
Kraevskii, A. A., 75, 78, 83
Kundera, M., 187–8, 190
  Unbearable Lightness of Being, The,
  187–8
Kuznetsov, B., 20

Laclos, C. de, 54, 136
Lafayette, Mme de, 134
Lavrov, P. L., 112
Lawrence, D. H., 2, 20, 149
Leatherbarrow, W. J., 20, 35, 36, 44, 46, 190
Leibniz, G. W., 215–6, 221
Léonard, N. G., 49
Lermontov, M. Iu., 58, 67
Leskov, N. S., 174
Lewes, G. H., 134
Library for Reading (periodical), *see*
  Senkovskii, O. I.
Linnér, S., 172
literacy in Russia, 68–9, 83
Literary Fund, 78–9
Liubimov, N. A., 88–9, 90, 91, 171
Locke, J., 221–2
Lorrain, C., 168
Lotman, Iu. M., 46
Lotman, L. M., 46

Maikov, A. N., 5, 140, 150
Maikov, V. N., 153
Malia, M., 115, 129
Marlinskii, A. A. (Bestuzhev-Marlinskii), 26,
  49, 58
Martinsen, D., 89, 92
Marx, K., 16, 114
Melnikov, P. I. (Andrei Pecherskii), 87, 89
  In the Hills, 87
Meshcherskii, V. P., 88
Mesmer, F. A., 133
Mikhailov, M. L., 121
  London Notes, 121
  Paris Letters, 121
Miliukov, A. P., 85
Miller, R. F., 234
Milton, J., 216–17, 224, 234
  Paradise Lost, 216–17, 224, 234
Miuller, L., 163, 174
Mochulsky, K., 9, 56, 65
Moleschott, J., 119
Moore, G., 2, 20
Morson, G. S., 6, 7, 15, 19, 20, 174, 234
Moscow News (periodical), 84
Murav, H., 37, 38, 41, 42, 45, 46
Murry, J. M., 2, 20

Nabokov, V., 2, 19
'Natural School', 48–9, 55–6, 63, 74, 152
Nechaev, S., 153, 166
Nechaeva, V. S., 92
Nekrasov, N. A., 72–4, 76, 78, 88, 89
Neufeld, J., 138
Nicholl, D., 173
Nikitenko, A. V., 69, 78, 91
Notes of the Fatherland (periodical), 74,
  75, 76–7, 80, 87, 88, 89, 116,
  117, 154
Novikov, N. I., 67

Odoevskii, V. F., 50
Offord, D., 15–16, 20
Ogarev, N. P., 178
Old Believers (religious sect of), 29
Orwell, G., 210
  Nineteen Eighty Four, 210

Panaev, I. I., 76
Paperno, I., 19, 20, 32, 45, 46, 177,
  189–90
Pattison, G., 174
Pavlov, I., 132
Petrashevskii, M. V., 13–14, 153–4